North Eastern (LNER): the Raven 'Pacific' engine No 2400, at Kings Cross during the competitive trials of 1923 (the late W.J. Reynolds).

D1493451

LNW/LMS: the final development of the Crewe 8-coupled mineral engine—the LNWR 'G2' Class superheated with 175 lb per square inch pressure and classed '7F' by the LMS (British Railways).

BRITISH LOCOMOTIVES
OF THE 20th CENTURY
O.S.Nock

Volume 1 1900~1930

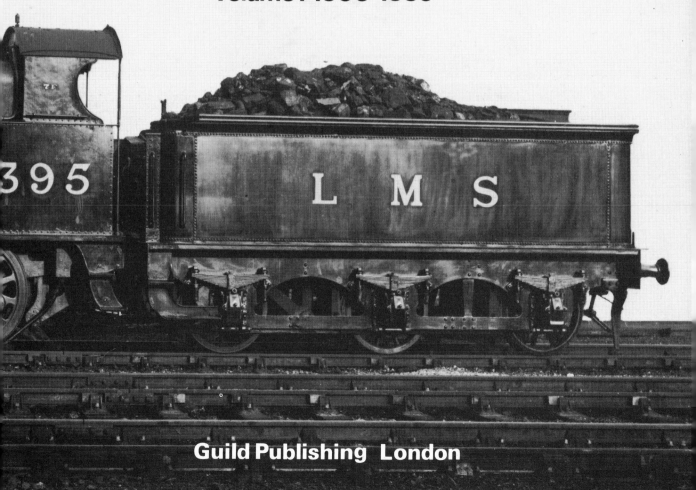

Guild Publishing London

This edition published 1983 by Book Club Associates
by arrangement with Patrick Stephens Limited.
Reprinted July 1984.
Reprinted March 1985

Photoset in 10 on 10 pt Baskerville
by Manuset Limited, Baldock, Herts.
Printed in Great Britain on 115 gsm Fineblade coated
cartridge by The Anchor Press, and bound by William
Brendon & Son, of Tiptree, Colchester, Essex.

Contents

Preface

To write the full history of the practice and development of British locomotives in the 20th century is indeed a challenge, because it involves such a diversity of subjects, not only in engineering science and the personalities immediately involved, but in national and international affairs, and a complete change in the world economic situation. Many locomotive histories of individual railways have been compiled and quite a few are my own; but to present the overall picture in the detail that is now required is another matter, particularly when it comes to the vexed question of railway amalgamation, and the transition from steam to other forms of motive power. It is difficult at times to prevent personal views from obtruding. The subject of locomotives in the 20th century must necessarily be taken in its broadest sense, and thus must include not only the new diesels and electrics, but also the form of power applied to multiple-unit and fixed formation passenger trains like the modern HST.

In taking up the story at the turn of the century I am very conscious of the work of earlier locomotive historians, notably E.L. Ahrons, who contributed the notable series of articles, 'Locomotive and Train Working in the latter part of the nineteenth century', in *The Railway Magazine*, a series that ran, with very few intermissions, from January 1915 to November 1926. The last few instalments, when the author was dealing with some of the Irish railways,

actually appeared after his untimely death, at the relatively early age of 60 years. Just prior to that he had completed the remarkable series of articles in *The Engineer*, in celebration of the Railway Centenary, in 1925, covering the development of the 'British Railway Steam Locomotive from 1825 to 1925'. The fact that these articles appeared serially in a weekly journal led to some compression of those dealing with the later period. In the concluding quarter-century, in particular, the subject matter would have been familiar to the majority of readers, so that in retrospect the final chapters of the work subsequently reprinted in book form are not so informative or comprehensive as his masterly coverage of the earlier period.

Equally in retrospect, the long series of articles in *The Railway Magazine* show some inconsistencies in treatment. Ahrons dealt first with the London and North Western Railway—in no more than four instalments. There was no mention of any freight locomotives and the express passenger engines, built since 1890, were dismissed in no more than a few lines. The Great Northern followed and received even briefer treatment. One can sense, however, that at their first launching there could have been some editorial hesitation as to how the series would go down, and that some restrictions in space were put upon Ahrons. By the end of 1915, however, its popularity was becoming evident and the Great Western instalments ran for over ten

months. In 1919-20 the Midland received even more space, despite post-war restrictions on paper; and taking a balanced view of the series as a whole, not even the most pervervid partisan could claim that the Midland justified an 11:4 advantage over the London and North Western!

In the more technical series of articles in *The Engineer*, Ahrons took the British locomotive in its broadest sense, including detailed reference to many notable locomotives built by British firms for service overseas; and, when I had the honour of continuing Ahrons' survey up to the end of steam locomotive building in 1965, I did the same. In the present instance, however, even with no more than the home railways to deal with, there is such a vast canvas on which to work that it has been thought better to exclude overseas developments, including those in Ireland, except where they have a direct bearing upon 'Home Rails'. To provide continuity, however, I have, in the earlier chapters, referred back to certain events in the last decade of the 19th century, particularly where they were covered no more than sketchily, if at all, by Ahrons.

At the end of the 19th century there were some 20,000 steam locomotives in service on the railways of Britain, and it would of course be manifestly impossible to refer to them all, even class by class. But at the outset it was determined that this book should be a continuous narrative, and no less a work of reference; and, as from many years of experience I have found that strings of dimensions and lists of engine numbers do not mix very well with ordinary reading matter, it has been decided to segregate the purely factual and numerical details into comprehensive tables, where particulars will be found of many more locomotives than could have been referred to in any detail in the text.

Although my own 'engine spotting' days date back to around 1907, I am immensely indebted to the back volumes of *The Locomotive, The Railway Magazine, The Engineer* and *Engineering* for authoritative information on events in my earlier life, while later, my professional work and membership of the Institutions of Civil, Mechanical, and Locomotive Engineers has brought me into personal contact and friendship with many men who have moulded the course of British locomotive practice. More particularly in the case of the second volume of this work, the list is indeed long of those to whom my gratitude is due.

So far as this one is concerned I must specially mention Messrs W. Barr, R.C. Bond, K.J. Cook, F.W. Hawksworth, H. Holcroft, H.G. Ivatt, R.A. Riddles, B. Spencer, and Sir William Stanier, most of whom have since passed on. But I am also most grateful to Mrs Violet Godfrey (daughter of Sir Nigel Gresley) and to surviving members of C.J. Bowen Cooke's family. I am equally much indebted to four former editors: A.R. Bell, of *The Locomotive*; J.A. Kay of *The Railway Gazette* and *The Railway Engineer*; Loughnan St. L. Pendred, of *The Engineer*, and W.A. Willox of *The Railway Magazine*.

O.S. Nock
Bath, April 1982

LNER: booster-fitted 3-cylinder 2-8-2 heavy freight engine, for Peterborough–London coal traffic (British Railways).

*The Caledonian 4-2-2, No 123, as pre-
served, hauling a train of two restored
Caledonian coaches near Auchterarder
(W.J.V. Anderson).*

1. The scene in 1900

The advent of a new century is essentially a time for taking stock: for reflection, for self-examination and, where railways are concerned, for taking a little modest pride in what has been achieved. Although the public railway, and all it had come to offer in the transport of passengers, goods and minerals was only three quarters of the way towards its own centenary in the year 1900, its effect upon the nations of the world had already been incalculable. And that turning point in the calendar was also in many ways a turning point in the development of the British locomotive. The advance in maximum speeds during the last two decades of the 19th century had been remarkable—perhaps a little too remarkable to be nice! After all the excitement of the races to the north in 1888 and 1895, and the alarming sequel to the latter at Preston in the following year, public opinion, and railway management too, felt that things had gone far enough for the time being. It was amid the reaction that set in afterwards that the history of the British locomotive began to take some very significant turns.

To appreciate something of the metamorphosis that was taking place before the new century was little more than 10 years old one must look at the railway scene in Great Britain in 1900, at any rate at the locomotives and the demands that were made upon them. Then—there are no other words to describe it!—the British locomotive was a world phenomenon. It was not so much in the finer points of its design, nor of its performance on the road, but in its decor and *finish*. Nowhere in the world, except perhaps on some of the British-owned lines in India, were locomotives so gorgeously arrayed and so marvellously kept as in Great Britain. It was not only the units allocated to the principal express trains that received such treatment. Everything—down to the little tank engines hauling the London commuter trains, to the obsolete near-museum pieces demoted to work on somnolent country branch lines—was groomed and polished fit to haul a Royal train. And then there were the colours! The National Railway Museum at York, magnificent as the displays round the two turntables are, can give no more than a glimpse of the splendour that was to be enjoyed from the station platforms not a quarter of an hour's walk from today's treasure house where, at the height of its diversity, the locomotives of no fewer than seven companies worked regularly.

It is fairly certain, however, that what would now be regarded as a breathtaking, day-long spectacle was then taken wholly for granted; and the railways of Britain generally were subjected to all the kicks and criticisms that prevail today—if not in the same detailed form, but building up to a similar monument of ill-informed and ill-humoured blather. Today we can rejoice that the National Railway Museum contains notable examples of all but one of the seven splendid liveries that were everyday sights on the station platforms of York 80 years ago; there are also examples from the three constituents of the Southern Railway, each in its gayest era. The only Great Western engine in the Museum, 2-8-0, No 2818, albeit a notable one from the performance viewpoint, is not unhappily representative of the sartorial style of the period in which it was built— 1905. When it was restored and prepared for exhibition, because it was a freight engine it was given the painting style adopted on the Great Western as an austerity measure for all locomotives during the First World War, and retained afterwards for all except the main line express passenger units. This would undoubtedly be the guise in which engine No 2818 would be familiar to an almost overwhelming majority of enthusiasts today; though actually, when first built, and for the first 10 years of its life, the engine was fully lined out in the passenger style, with copper capped chimney, and the coat of arms on the tender.

While there was justification for the use of the freight style on the 2-8-0 of 1905 vintage there is absolutely none for the iconoclastic treatment given to the ever-famous *City of Truro* when she was incarcerated in the Museum at Swindon. All Great Western enthusiasts rejoiced when the engine was brought out of the old railway museum at York in 1957 and put into full working order at Swindon— all the more so because the ornate livery in which she was decked at the time of the 1904 exploit was restored. And looking gorgeous she made many special excursion trips not only on former Great Western metals but in Scotland, on special trips in partnership with one or another of the preserved Scottish locomotives. When, however, the Great Western Railway Museum was established in 1962 someone who deserved to be hung, drawn and quartered decided to paint the engine in the plain war-time green of the 1915-1920 era devoid of any lining; and as such she remains today, representative of nothing!

In the splendid National Railway Museum at York one certainly misses the gay and distinctive liveries of the Scottish companies because, after a notable amount of running on special trains, all of them were enthroned in a special railway section of the Glasgow Museum of Transport. Curiously enough all except the little Glasgow and South Western 'pug' pose questions as to what the original liveries in use prior to 1900 really were. The celebrated Caledonian 'single', No 123, is in the livery that the great majority of enthusiasts would associate with that great railway, though actually it was not strictly the official colour. This was a very distinguished dark Prussian Blue; but in one works, where locomotives were being repaired, the painters found that they could make the blue go further by mixing white with it. White was 'free issue', but no one seemed to realise what was going on; and as the result was the beautiful 'sky blue' this latter became the recognised 'official' colour—'Caley Blue' as it is now generally termed.

The North British colour was also ringed with a slight uncertainty. One cannot take for absolute gospel the colour shown in contemporary reproductions. The early lithographed colour plates in *The Railway Magazine* were generally very accurate, and, while one has also the evidence of the famous series of coloured postcards issued by the Locomotive Publishing Company, the same could not be said of the results in this latter series, particularly the rendering of some of the greens which were well known to many connoisseurs. But *The Railway Magazine* lithographs and the LPC postcards were in close agreement that the North British locomotives were brown, a soft earthy colour, with a suggestion of green in it, but set off with such a profusion of red and yellow lining that the highlights seemed to partake of a reddish shade. Yet the beautifully restored *Glen Douglas*, which has built up such a notable mileage of excursion train running in Scotland, has a basic colour that is definitely bronze green.

The Great North of Scotland engine, the *Gordon Highlander*, is one of a batch introduced in 1920. As a war-time measure all engines on the line had been painted black, and the original green had not been restored when the new engines of Class 'F' were put into traffic. So the *Gordon Highlander* never carried the livery in which it has been preserved because, after the Grouping in 1923, the engines of the former GNSR were at first painted in the LNER apple-green style. Though not historically correct, so far as the individual engine was concerned, it was a happy thought to restore the original GNSR green livery when the *Gordon Highlander* was preserved, and put into working order for special train workings. How fortunate it was that the 'soulless person who debased the *City of Truro* had no influence in Scotland, otherwise the *Gordon Highlander* would assuredly have gone into black.

But the phenomenon among the preserved locomotives of Scotland is the 'Jones Goods' of the Highland, No 103, the first of the 4-6-0 type ever to run in Great Britain. When this engine was withdrawn for preservation in 1935, and repainted, *The Railway Magazine* not only commented upon the pity that the full Jones style had not been restored, but in its issue of January 1936 they presented a superb colour plate, from a painting by F. Secretan, showing how the engine was originally painted. I had occasion to call on the editor, W.A. Willox, soon afterwards on another matter, and found them in a state of the most utter confusion. Full of pride in the production of so beautiful a plate they had sent a copy to David Jones' surviving daughter, and received the startling reply: 'Very nice, but it's the wrong colour!' The old lady had the most vivid recollections of the first arrival of the great new engines, and she averred that they were painted yellow! This, entirely behind the closed doors of the *The Railway Magazine* offices it would seem, started no end of a witch-hunt, which was not satisfactorily resolved when war came, in 1939; but it had been taken up by that most erudite of locomotive historians, the late J.N. Maskelyne.

Below left *The pride of the LNWR in the 1890s was the Webb 3-cylinder compound No 2053,* Greater Britain. *These engines ran high mileages and were double-manned. The two regular crews are posed in front* (British Railways).

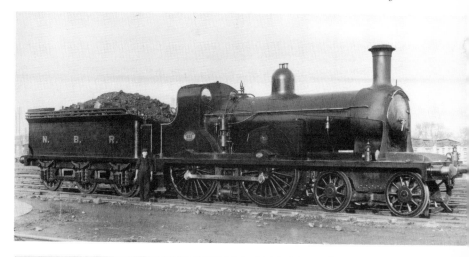

Above right *The North British express passenger 4-4-0 of the racing days of 1895 which was still the premier type of 1900. The handsome brown livery is not readily picked out by the photographic techniques of the day* (The Locomotive Publishing Company).

Right Gordon Highlander *of the Great North of Scotland Railway, splendidly restored and now preserved in the Glasgow Museum of Transport* (British Railways).

After the war, when the question came up of putting engine No 103 into full working order, sufficient research had been carried out to reveal that some at least of the Jones Goods 4-6-0s had been delivered to the Highland Railway from Sharp, Stewart's works in Glasgow in Stroudley's yellow livery, which went by the name of 'improved engine green'. This strikingly original and beautiful livery had been inaugurated on the Highland, before Stroudley went to Brighton, and retained for the first 15 years of the Jones regime, to 1885. Then the yellow had been replaced by a beautiful leaf green, with much the same style of lining out. Now the Jones Goods 4-6-0s of 1894 were the first engines Sharp, Stewart & Co had built for the Highland, and one just wonders if someone at Inverness sent them the earlier, rather than the later, painting specification. Be that as it may, when

No 103 was restored to full working order in the 1950s, to the delight of all enthusiasts she was decked in Stroudley's 'improved engine green'—in other words yellow ochre—and has remained so ever since.

One could continue gossiping about locomotive painting styles for whole chapters; but they formed such an essential part of the British railway scene in 1900 as to make reference to them essential. And one has not run the entire gamut of permutations in mentioning the styles that can now be seen at York, Glasgow or even at Swindon. Some of the minor railways sported liveries that promised to outshine some of the gayest of the major ones. There was that of the London Tilbury and Southend; of the Midland and Great Northern Joint, and of the North Staffordshire, while in South Wales the Barry and the Brecon and Merthyr had eye-

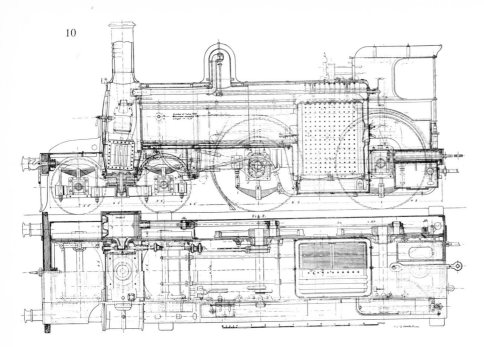

catching styles that were as finely maintained as any. Attractive painting may have been a hidden asset, so far as the company accountants were concerned, but everywhere it inspired a sense of pride in the job, particularly in those spacious days when, on so many of the British railways, each driver had his own engine.

Among those of the major countries of the world the British locomotives of 1900 were, collectively, rather small. Of the total of around 20,000 fully half were of the 4-4-0 and 0-6-0 types. These two constituted the typical British passenger and goods locomotive of the day. It was only the local railways in South Wales and a few smaller lines farther north that did not own some 4-4-0s, and on the leading trunk lines the work demanded of them, and regularly and efficiently performed, was a constant source of surprise to visitors from overseas.

There was a notable instance of this on February 2 1901. It was the day of Queen Victoria's funeral and the Royal Train conveying the late Queen's coffin and the principal mourners had to be worked from Gosport to Victoria, by the London Brighton and South Coast Railway from Fareham. For various reasons the train was 10 minutes late leaving Fareham, but because of King Edward's known dislike of unpunctuality the driver was urged to do his best to make up time. The train weighed about 190 tons behind the tender, and the engine was the Billinton 'B4' Class 4-4-0 No 54 *Empress*. The distance to be run, non-stop, was 87.6 miles, and if Victoria was to be reached on time it meant covering those miles in 112 minutes—not a very

spectacular average speed of 47 mph, but difficult enough over a route with many sharp gradients, and a tiresome succession of junctions where severe speed restrictions were enforced. King Edward was not kept waiting, for the Special arrived at Victoria two minutes early.

It was remarkable that Queen Victoria who, in her long reign, had always deplored any suggestion of speeding on railways, should have had her mortal remains hustled up to London in quite record style, because it was reported that on the level stretch between Havant and Ford the speed reached 80 mph. Some of the railway officials travelling on the train believed that a maximum of no less than 90 mph had been attained on the descent from the North Downs towards Dorking; but this was not definitely substantiated. The German Kaiser, grandson of the late Queen, was a passenger in the train, and was most impressed by the locomotive performance. On arrival at Victoria he sent an equerry to the footplate to convey his appreciation to the driver and fireman. It was not often that the 'All Highest' expressed any approval of anything British; but what seemed to have impressed him more than anything else was the small size of the engine compared to those currently in use in Germany. Actually the Billinton 'B4' Class were among the finest British passenger engines of the day.

On New Year's Day 1900, apart from the Jones '103' Class on the Highland, which were largely confined to freight service, there were only 26 10-wheeled passenger tender engines in the whole of Great Britain. Of these six could be considered still

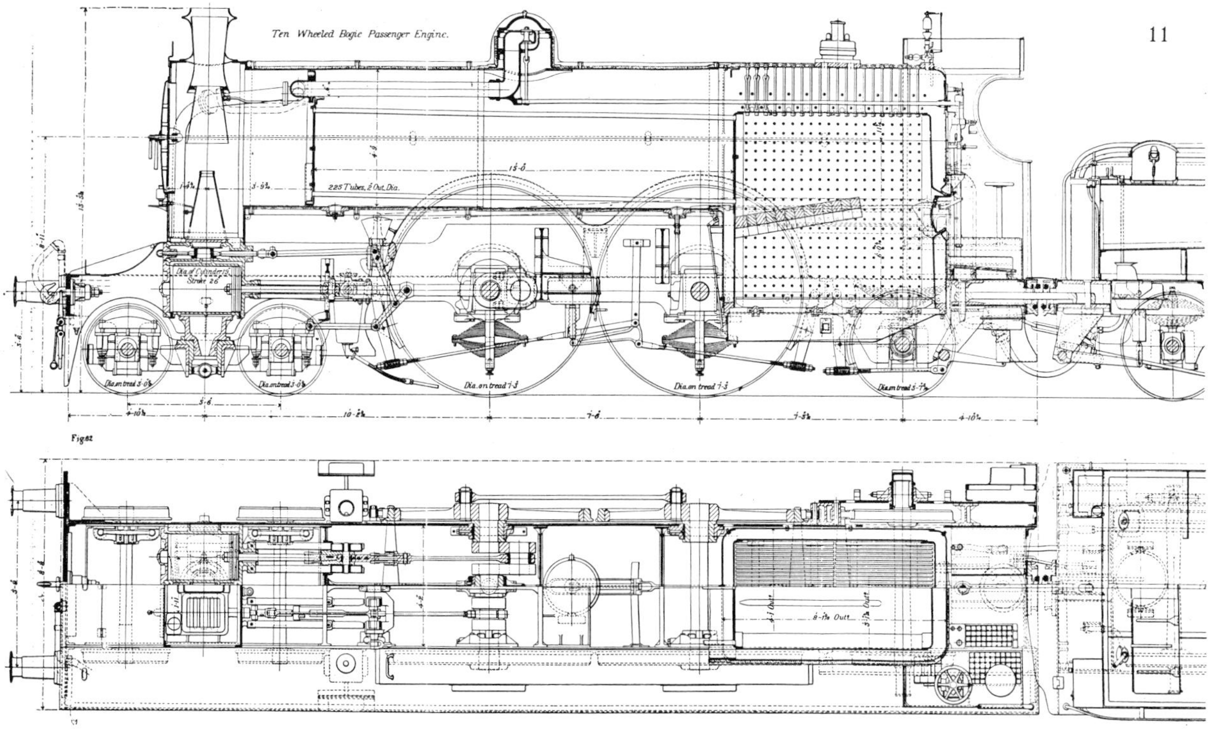

Ten Wheeled Bogie Passenger Engine.

Fig 2

as experimental. There was the one Ivatt 'Atlantic' on the Great Northern, dating from 1898, and Wilson Worsdell's 'S' Class 4-6-0s on the North Eastern which was quite early relegated to goods workings. It was only on the Lancashire and Yorkshire that anything in the way of a new standard *class* had appeared and there, in 1899, J.A.F. Aspinall had built a first batch of 20 of his impressive inside cylindered 'Atlantics'. Although the loads were not unduly heavy the L & YR was developing a highly competitive series of train services, and these fast and powerful engines proved an immediate success. It was a time when development in locomotives was, to the interested public, as much a topic of general conversation as the relative merits of cars and of aircraft are today.

Very soon some highly coloured stories of speed exploits by the Aspinall 'Highflyers' began to circulate, but none quite so fantastic as one 'splashed' in *The Locomotive Magazine*, of all journals, in its issue of August 1899. Were it not in cold print, before my eyes as I write, it would be almost beyond belief that such experienced engineer-editors as the brothers A.R. and W.J. Bell could have 'fallen' for such a story. It was headed: 'ONE-HUNDRED MILES PER HOUR', and it continued: 'On the 15th of July engine No 1392, one of the new large express engines on the Lancashire and Yorkshire Railway, is reported to have attained a speed of a hundred miles an hour whilst running between

Liverpool and Southport. The engine left Exchange Station, Liverpool, with five bogie cars at 2.51 pm, and passed the 17th mile post out at 3.3¾ pm (12¾ min) an average of 80 miles an hour. Allowing for getting-up speed, slows round curves, etc, this represents a remarkable performance, and the highest speed attained must have approximately been as stated'. Remarkable indeed on the Southport line, with all its curves and junctions! It would need good going by a modern HST set to cover the first 17 miles from a dead start in 12¾ minutes on a straight and level road. Feats of imagination apart, however, it was a venturesome thing to build a first batch of 20 of such a greatly enlarged design, particularly in respect of the boiler; other than a few minor teething troubles, however, these large engines were completely successful from the outset, and their prowess put Aspinall almost in a class apart from his contemporaries.

It was while Horwich Works was in full swing with the production of these engines, turning them out at the rate of two a week, that Aspinall, then aged 48, was invited to become General Manager of the L & YR. The 'Atlantics', of which a further batch of 20 was built in 1902, were not Aspinall's last locomotive design; because in 1899 the drawing office at Horwich was putting the finishing touches upon a big 0-8-0 heavy freight engine, with a boiler of the same size as that used on the 'Atlantics'. It took the road early in 1900, and between then and

January 1908 no fewer than 100 were built at Horwich. The Barry Railway had been the first to introduce the 0-8-0 type for heavy mineral working, in 1889, having then bought from Sharp, Stewart & Co, two outside cylindered engines built for a Scandinavian railway which could not pay for them! The London and North Western had followed in 1892, when F.W. Webb applied his rather freakish long boiler, with intermediate combustion chamber, to an 0-8-0 heavy mineral engine. This latter was a 2-cylinder simple, and in the next year a companion engine was built as a 3-cylinder compound. This latter engine had the same disposition of cylinders as in the various compound passenger engines, but all three cylinders drove on to the second coupled axle. Batch production of these engines had begun in November 1894, and by the turn of the century Crewe were turning them out at the rate of 10 a month, up to a total of 111 by the end of May 1900.

Although both in private conversation, or in public Webb made something of a show of avoiding publicity he was, in fact, a past master of the art; and when he was interviewed by the editor of *The Railway Magazine* in 1900 he was ready with a spectacular photograph of the first of the 3-cylinder compound 0-8-0s, carrying its original number, 50, (later 2525) with all the raw materials used in its construction selectively piled in front. It was a striking demonstration of the extent to which Crewe made everything from the basic materials. There was no question of buying finished proprietary fittings such as brake valves, injectors and such like from specialist manufacturers. Everything was 'home made' at Crewe, and to build the 49¼ ton 0-8-0 required nearly 139 tons of raw material, which included the coal, coke and limestone that were needed in the iron, steel, and non-ferrous foundries.

In the following year two other major companies began building 0-8-0 heavy mineral engines. The Great Northern variety, by H.A. Ivatt, was very similar to the Aspinall design on the Lancashire and

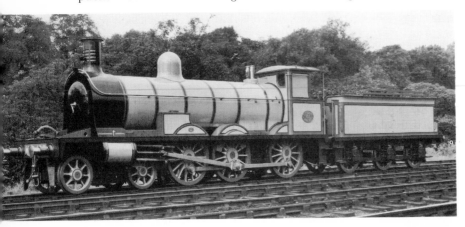

Left *Highland Railway: the 'Jones Goods' 4-6-0, No 103—the first of the type ever to run in Great Britain—restored to the celebrated 'yellow' livery. It made many special runs before entering the Glasgow Museum of Transport (British Railways).*

Left *The 'yellow' livery, taken by William Stroudley from the Highland Railway to that of the London Brighton and South Coast, does not show up so prominently in this contemporary photograph of one of the 'Grasshopper' Class (B2) 4-4-0s. This hauled the 'Sunny South Special' train (Liverpool and Manchester to Brighton and Eastbourne) and is seen here crossing Tooting Common in the early 1900s. The 'B4' was a development of this design.*

Above right *Lancashire and Yorkshire Railway: standard tender fitted with Aspinall water pick-up apparatus.*

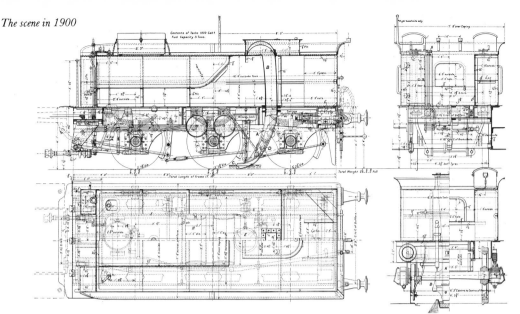

Yorkshire; but on the North Eastern, Wilson Worsdell was adopting outside cylinders for his 10-wheeled passenger engines, and his 0-8-0s of 1901, Class 'T', had outside cylinders driving on to the third pair of coupled wheels. The North Eastern had some very heavy freight-hauls, from Tyne Dock up to Consett, and from West Auckland over the Pennines to Tebay, with the iron ore and coke trains for Barrow-in-Furness. The Class 'T' 0-8-0s were some of the most beautifully adorned freight engines that have ever been built. They were decked in the passenger livery, fully lined out, with polished brass chimney caps, and safety valve covers, and in their early days always immaculately kept.

A very notable, and long-lived engine class of 1900, which, at the time, received less notice than it deserved, was the 'Castle' Class 4-6-0 of the Highland Railway. Its thunder had perhaps been to some extent stolen by the intense interest created six years earlier by the Jones Goods, as the first ever 4-6-0 in Great Britain; and the 'Castle' was set down as just a larger-wheeled version of the same design. Certainly David Jones had laid down its basic features before disability, following the personal accident on one of the big goods 4-6-0s, more or less compelled his resignation; but although Peter Drummond, as his distinguished successor, incorporated many of the family specialities in the finished engine, it remained in most of its essentials a Jones job, particularly in respect of the retention of the Allan straight link motion. The Highland 'Castles' were grand engines, as I was to experience many years later on the footplate. There is much to be told of them in later chapters of this book.

In 1900 the era of the express tank engine was only just beginning in Great Britain. The cult, if one may call it so, began on a relatively minor railway, the London Tilbury and Southend. Although that railway had been incorporated in 1862, for nearly 20 years the Great Eastern had provided the motive power; but by the end of the 1870s, with the growth of traffic, it was judged that the time had come for the 'Tilbury' to have its own locomotives and, in 1880, Sharp, Stewart & Co, delivered the first 12 4-4-2 tanks. Although by that time William Adams had transferred from the Great Eastern to the London and South Western it was generally understood that he had some part in the specification laid down for these engines, and he purchased some very similar ones for his new company from 1882 onwards. While there is some doubt as to the parentage of the original Tilbury 4-4-2 tanks, there is none about subsequent developments. With the first batch, from Sharp, Stewart's works in Manchester, there came a young engineer, Thomas Whitelegg, to act as locomotive foreman. He was a man of outstanding ability and quickly moulded his compact command on the Tilbury into a model of efficient railway operation. The so-called 'No 1 Class' of 4-4-2 tank engines, of which there were eventually 36, had coupled wheels of 6 foot 1 inch diameter; but in 1897, Whitelegg, having taken the measure of the growing needs of the railway, specified 6 foot 6 inch wheels for the enlarged engines purchased from Sharp, Stewart & Co, and in so doing he inaugurated the true 'express' tank engine that was developed to such effect in later years on several other railways as well.

On the Tilbury itself the new century was marked by the introduction of a larger version of the same design, one of the most handsomely proportioned engines in the evolving situation of the day. But while the proportions could be readily appreciated from a broadside photograph it was the colouring of these engines, and the way they were maintained, that led many of the connoisseurs of locomotive styling to consider they were perhaps the most beautiful of any on the railways of Great Britain. It was finely displayed in a colour-plate that formed the frontispiece to the January 1908 issue of the *Locomotive Magazine*. There was only one jarring note about the Tilbury engines. Whitelegg followed the precedent set by William Stroudley on the Brighton, of naming all except the goods engines after stations on the line. After all, Stroudley did have the whole of the Sussex countryside to draw upon, though one felt that he might have quietly skipped one station and missed out *Crawley*. It was such an appropriate name for so many of the 19th century Brighton trains! On the 'Tilbury' Whitelegg had used up all the best names on the 'No 1 Class', and he was getting down, if not to the dregs, then certainly to the incongruous when it got down to *Commercial Road, Mile End,* and *Black Horse Road.* Engine naming can always have its lighter moments, and on the Tilbury there was a good story

of an old lady who was seen rapturously admiring engine No 53 *Stepney Green,* and then remarking: 'Yes, it is a lovely colour!'

While in 1900 the portents of development in the new century could be discerned in 10-wheeled passenger engines both of the 'Atlantic' and the 4-6-0 type, by the growing introduction of eight coupled engines for heavy freight, and by the prowess of the 4-4-2 'express' tank engines on the Tilbury, an overwhelming proportion of the express passenger services of the country was being worked by 8-wheeled engines many of them of the 4-2-2 type. As late as July 1904 a survey of GWR expresses leaving Paddington on a busy Saturday showed that on 32 departures leaving between 9 am and 6.30 pm only 13 were hauled by 4-4-0s, whereas 18 were hauled by the beautiful Dean 7 foot 8 inch 4-2-2s. The remaining train was taken by one of the early Churchward 4-6-0s. On the Great Northern the preponderance in favour of 'singles' would have been even greater in 1900, because the Ivatt 4-4-0s were not built as replacements for the famous Stirling 'singles', but as a stop-gap measure while the 'Atlantic' design was being developed. The Midland was in a rather special position in that the portents of 1900 did not materialise, and the out-

Left *Great Northern Railway: one of H.A. Ivatt's small boilered 'Atlantics', the first of which, No 990, just preceded the Aspinall design on the Lancashire and Yorkshire Railway to be the first-ever British example of the 4-4-2 type* (The Locomotive Publishing Company).

Below *Lancashire and Yorkshire Railway: one of Aspinall's 'Highflyer' Atlantics of 1899 which caused something of a sensation from their great size and potential speed capabilities* (British Railways).

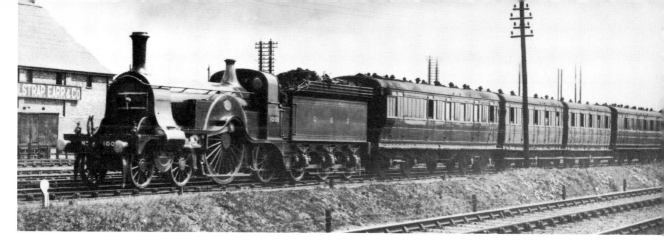

Above *On the GNR in 1900 single-wheelers were still doing most of the important mainline work. In this picture one of the very elegant Stirling 8 foot Class is hauling an express northbound from Peterborough (the late C. Laundy).*

Right *Ivatt himself introduced a new 4-2-2 Class in 1900, following a prototype built in 1898. Engine No 270 of this class, built at Doncaster in 1901, is nearing Peterborough with an express from Boston (the late C. Laundy).*

come will be discussed in some detail later.

The London and North Western had by far the heaviest traffic of any of the main line railways and, while at holiday times, as in the example of Paddington on a summer Saturday, there would be one or two trains pulling out with 11 bogie coaches, which would be reckoned as 'equal to 16½' on the North Western, many trains leaving Euston were made up to the maximum permitted by the traffic department, '20½', all the year round. The merits, or otherwise, of the Webb compound locomotives will be discussed in the next chapter; but so far as the motive power situation as a whole was concerned, a high proportion of the principal expresses needed two engines, and the retention in first class condition of the 245 6-wheelers (2-4-0) of the 'Precedent' and 'Whitworth' Classes, available to assist when necessary on the main line expresses, and also to work singly on many secondary passenger services, was justified. These little engines, weighing no more than 35½ to 36 tons, might have been considered obsolete and fit for nothing but the scrap-heap in an age that was developing large 'Atlantics' and 4-6-0s; but in 20th

century conditions, it was the Webb compounds and not these engines that came in for early replacement.

At the turn of the century considerable prestige value was attached to the making of long non-stop runs, and at that time, on each week-day, there were 107 runs of more than 100 miles made non-stop, of which the longest were those between Paddington and Exeter, 193¾ miles, then made via Bristol. But as might be expected, the London and North Western had the greatest number of such runs, 33; followed by the Great Northern with 23, and the Great Western, with 17. Those long runs were not always made non-stop, particularly on the North Western, because on double-headed trains a stop for water was sometimes necessary. An instance referred to in *The Railway Magazine* for June 1900 involved a stop by the 10.15 am Euston to Liverpool, at Nuneaton, towards the end of its Willesden-Stafford 'non-stop' run. The train was loaded 'equal to 20½', and was hauled by a 2-4-0 'Precedent' and a 3-cylinder compound of the 7 foot 'Teutonic' Class. In North Western reckoning at that time a six-wheeled coach counted as '1'; an 8-

wheeler '1½', and the big 12-wheeled dining and sleeping cars '2'. Actually, water troughs were so relatively frequent on the LNWR that when double-heading it was often the arrangement for the pilot and the train engine to take water at alternate troughs.

Although the North Western had been the world originators of water troughs, they retained, throughout the Webb regime, a most antiquated and inefficient arrangement for raising and lowering the scoops. Once in the trough it required the combined strength of driver and fireman to get it out again. In a chapter on the duties of enginemen, in his classic work, *British Locomotives*, C.J. Bowen Cooke wrote: ' . . . the moment the engine gets on to them [water troughs] the scoop must be let down by the fireman, and, as soon as the tank is full, the driver must assist in shooting back the scoop handle'. The need for the driver's participation was thus officially recognised. There were frequently times when the tank was full before the men could withdraw the scoop, and then the leading coach, or the second engine if there was one, would be smothered in spray. J.A.F. Aspinall, who had plenty of footplate experience during his early training at Crewe, patented a vacuum operating gear for raising and lowering water scoops on his Lancashire and Yorkshire engines, and Webb's successor on the North Western put on a greatly improved arrangement on all new engines built at Crewe from 1904 onwards.

One form of motive power that seemed more likely than any other to be affected by influences outside the railway world was that of the suburban or local train tank engine. In all towns of any size electric street cars were becoming well established, and in the larger conurbations the routes they followed were quite extensive. They had the convenience of being on the doorstep, as it were.

There was no need to go to a station, and look up a train in the timetable. In London particularly they were becoming serious rivals to the local trains. The streets were then relatively clear and progress was rapid. This is not to say that the railways had begun to feel the competition to the extent of losing traffic, but the suburban traffic problem from the operating point of view, was not getting easier. On lines like the Great Eastern, the South Eastern and Chatham, and the Brighton, the commuter trains, mostly composed of cramped little 'dog boxes' on four wheels, were trundled around by swarms of little six-wheeled tank engines, the design, finish, and upkeep of which was a phenomenon in itself.

In the National Railway Museum at York there is a gleaming Royal Blue 0-6-0 tank engine of the Great Eastern, decked in all the finery those little things sported when they bustled the teeming population of East London in and out of Liverpool Street. No mere period pieces either—for they were destined to play a predominant part in one of the most remarkable train service reorganisations ever carried out, as told in Chapter 10 of this book. Then there were the yellow Stroudleys of the Brighton, working in some of the smokiest and dingiest parts of London, and still kept immaculate. While if one went to Manchester, or Birmingham, or above all to Glasgow, where delightful little 0-4-4 tanks pounded their ways through the underground lines or round the Cathcart Circle in all the beauty of their Caledonian blue, the phenomenon of the British locomotive and its turn out was amply evident. But while there were many who rejoiced in the comings and goings of those little local train engines, and recorded them in notebooks and on film—unhappily before the days of colour—there were others who wondered for how long this state of affairs would last. Already there was much talk of electrification, and the price of coal was soaring.

Below left *London and North Western Railway, F.W. Webb's 4-cylinder compound express 4-4-0,* La France. *Its actual running number was 1926, but it was the 4,000th engine built at Crewe Works, and dated March 1900, and for a short time it ran with the number 4000, and was photographed as such* (British Railways).

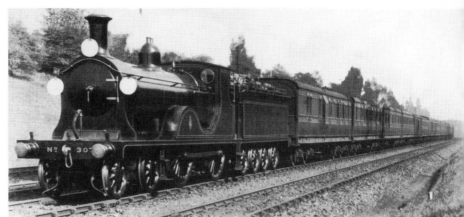

This page, top to bottom

Midland Railway: a celebrated engine of 1900. This railway did not make a practice of naming its locomotives, but this one, in company with the LNWR, La France, *was to be shown at the Paris Exhibition of that year and was named specially* Princess of Wales. *The lady in question, a year later, became Queen Alexandra.*

London and South Western: a Dugald Drummond classic design, the 'T9' 4-4-0, as yet devoid of her designer's later frills except the cross-watertubes in the firebox. One of the later examples of the class is here seen hauling a Bournemouth express.

On the Brighton line R.J. Billinton also made a brief trial of cross-watertubes, here seen on one of the powerful 'B4' Class 4-4-0s, No 45, Bessborough *(the late W.J. Reynolds).*

South Eastern Railway: a contemporary 4-4-0 to the LSWR 'T9' and the Brighton 'B4' was James Stirling's 'F' Class 4-4-0, of which no fewer than 88 were in service (The Locomotive Publishing Company).

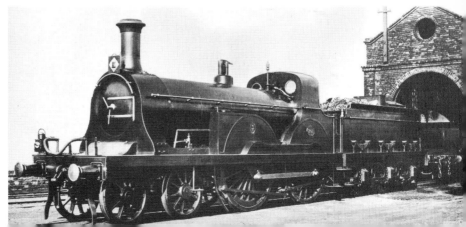

Highland Railway: Peter Drummond's celebrated 'Castle' Class 4-6-0, a passenger engine design developed from the very successful Jones Goods, here seen in the precincts of the Inverness roundhouse (The Locomotive Publishing Company).

North Eastern Railway: Wilson Worsdell's 'S' Class 4-6-0, built at Gateshead Works, 1899-1900. The engine illustrated was the first of a new series of the same design built at Darlington Works in 1906.

London Tilbury and Southend Railway: one of the handsomely proportioned '51' Class 4-4-2 express tank engines of Thomas Whitelegg, introduced in 1900, hauling the Ealing-Southend corridor train in Midland Railway days.

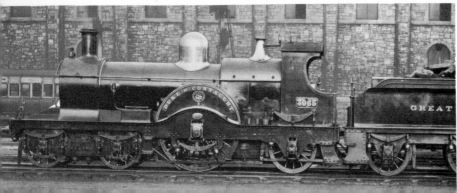

Great Western Railway: in 1900 the 4-2-2 was still the principal express locomotive type on the main lines radiating from London. Illustrated is the most famous of them all, No 3065, Duke of Connaught, which shared in the making of the record run of May 9 1904 with the Ocean Mail, from Bristol to Paddington (P.J.T. Reed).

2. Evolving practice in design

By the end of the 19th century British locomotive design had reached an enviable stage in compactness and simplicity. The most generally favoured forms of the 4-4-0 and 0-6-0 types had inside frames, inside cylinders, with the slide valves snugly ensconced between the cylinders and actuated by direct Stephenson link motion. But it was an arrangement that had virtually reached its limit. The distance between the frame plates could not be more than 4 feet 2 inches apart, and with 19-inch diameter cylinders, as on the famous 'Dunalastairs' of the Caledonian, it was becoming something of a tight squeeze. There was another factor also. As the power of locomotives increased, so it was necessary to provide increased bearing surfaces in the driving axle boxes. These could not be lengthened outwards, and inwards they tend to encroach along the length of the axle to the crank webs. To avoid this, and still provide adequate bearing surface, many types of locomotive were built with double frames having bearings both inside and outside the wheels. In 1900, apart from single-wheelers, this practice was confined to the Great Western Railway, so far as new construction was concerned, in such well known classes as the 'Atbaras', 'Cities' and 'Bulldog' 4-4-0s, and the 'Aberdare' 2-6-0.

The frames are not the most conspicuous, or glamorous part of the anatomy of a locomotive, but they are the very foundation that can govern the failure or success of a locomotive in traffic. This came to be borne out most poignantly as the wheel arrangement increased from 4-2-2 and 4-4-0, to 4-4-2 and 4-6-0. The frame structure could be expensive in first cost, and some engineers working on something of a shoe-string sought to reduce their budget estimates, if not actually by 'skimping', then certainly by working to rule of thumb methods in design. Not all railway managers in the early 1900s were convinced of the need for larger engines, and the high capital cost involved, not only in the actual materials required but in the patterns and other tooling needed for construction. Some British

engineers were reluctant to adopt outside cylinders, because it meant a departure from the neat and compact methods of mounting them inside. Attaching them outside was not always satisfactory, and more than one British railway had troubles with cylinders working loose. Then again, as the chassis lengthened, one could not run the risk of making it too stiff, because the longer the wheelbase the greater was there a need to have some flexibility to run smoothly round curves. This is all to suggest some reasons why not all the large 10-wheeled engines, introduced in the early years of the 20th century, were so successful as their eight wheeled predecessors, from the same drawing office and works.

On some of the leading railways of Great Britain the first introductions were taking place of piston valves to replace the traditional 'D' slide valve. In 1900 the foremost exponent of their use was Walter M. Smith, Chief Locomotive Draughtsman of the North Eastern Railway at Gateshead. After some early experiments his design of valve with segmental rings had been applied, in 1899, with success to the new 4-4-0 express passenger engines of the 'R' Class, having 19 inch by 26 inch cylinders, and 6 foot 10 inch coupled wheels. The accompanying drawings show details of the valve, and the method of mounting, beneath the cylinder, and the actuation, by the Stephenson's link motion. It must be appreciated that at that time the engines were using saturated steam and the design had to afford a free relief to any water trapped in the cylinders. In the Smith design the segmental form of the piston valve rings enabled them to collapse inwards, when excessive pressure due to trapped water occurred. With saturated steam there was always the risk of water in the cylinders due to condensation, though on the other hand saturated steam is a natural

The epoch marking 'Dunalastair' 4-4-0 of the Caledonian Railway which was introduced in 1896 and successively enlarged afterwards (The Locomotive Publishing Company).

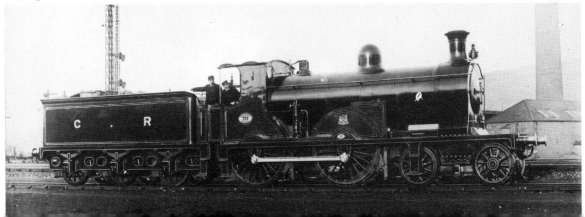

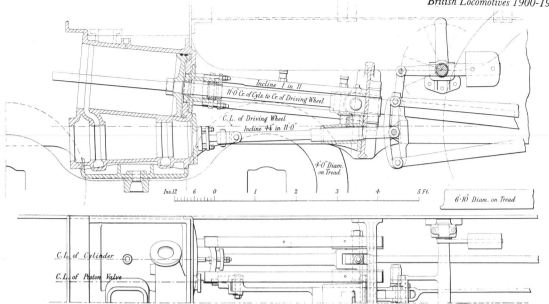

Incline 1 in 11
11'·0" Cr. of Cyls. to Cr. of Driving Wheel

C. L. of Driving Wheel
Incline 4½ in 11'·0"

4'·0" Diam.
on Tread

Ins.12   6   0   1   2   3   4   5 Ft.

6'·10" Diam. on Tread

C. L. of Cylinder

C. L. of Piston Valve

Above *North Eastern Railway: layout of cylinder, piston valve and motion, Class 'R' 4-4-0 express locomotive, by Wilson Worsdell.*

Below *North Eastern Railway: a 4-4-0 of the very successful 'R' Class, fitted with W.M. Smith's design of piston valves, with segmental rings* (Reverend T.B. Parley).

lubricant. In the later years of the steam locomotive, with which the great majority of readers will only be familiar, superheating was so general as to make the problems involved with non-superheated engines unfamiliar.

Before the days of superheating, steam was generated at a temperature corresponding to the boiler pressure. For example, at atmospheric pressure, as in a domestic kettle, steam is generated when the temperature of the water reaches 100 degrees C (or 212 degrees F), while in a boiler working at 150 lb per square inch, the temperature of steam formation is 181.3 degrees C. At a pressure of 225 lb per square inch it is 199.95 degrees C. The

advantages of heating the steam still further, before admitting it to the cylinders, superheating it, were only just being postulated in the first years of the 20th century, and the principle was taken up less readily in Great Britain than in many other countries. When the well-known editor of *The Railway Magazine*, J.F. Gairns, published his standard work, *Locomotive Compounding and Superheating*, in 1907, although in various parts of the world there were then some 500 superheater locomotives, mainly fitted with the apparatus designed by Herr Wilhelm Schmidt, apart from a few experimental instances on the Lancashire and Yorkshire Railway there was only one British locomotive so equipped, the Great Western two-cylinder 4-6-0 No 2901 *Lady Superior*, and that with the standard Schmidt type.

It was in his homeland, on the Prussian State Railways, that Schmidt had his earliest and most profound successes; but the attendant problems of superheating were such that British engineers were inclined to look askance at the principle. With

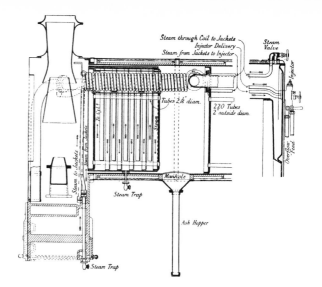

superheating there disappeared at once the natural lubricating quality of saturated steam, and the problems of lubrication in all parts of the steam circuit became immediate. In Great Britain the high and consistent quality of the fuel available made the need for improved thermal efficiency from other sources less urgent. Furthermore, there was an inborn reluctance to adopt foreign ideas on the part of many British locomotive engineers. Schmidt, in developing his superheater, accompanied his work by designs of piston valves, with special rings, and arrangements for mechanical lubrication, all of which were protected by a fully comprehensive and international series of patents. English managements of the day were not inclined to use apparatus that involved paying royalties to Germany. So, the use of saturated steam and slide valves remained the most general form of the British locomotive, for some years.

It was G.J. Churchward who opened a memorable paper to the Institution of Mechanical Engineers in 1906 with the sentence: 'The modern locomotive problem is principally a question of boiler'. That was when the development from the neat, traditional eight-wheeled passenger engine had scarcely begun. One can well appreciate how designers clung to the simplest of all boilers, as that which could be accommodated on a 4-4-0 locomotive of conventional style, with a deep narrow firebox set between the coupled axles. With all varieties of British coal it was incomparably the easiest to fire and, dumped in thick, steaming troubles were practically unheard of. Engines like the 'Dunalastair III' of the Caledonian, Billinton's 'B4' Class on the Brighton, the *Claud Hamilton,* of the Great Eastern, and the 'R' Class of the North Eastern were all the simplest design, with no fancy gadgets in the boiler or firebox, and all established a reputation for hard, reliable work on the road. It was only on the North Eastern 'R' that any departure from slide valves was seen, while in these the boiler

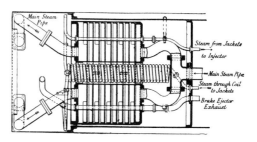

pressure was increased to 200 lb per square inch. When the 'Dunalastair III' Class was introduced a notice in the *Locomotive Magazine* stated that: '. . . the boiler is constructed of 9/16 inch plates for a working pressure of 200 lb per square inch . . .', and this gave rise to an assumption, in various publications, that this was the pressure actually used. This was not so. The pressure was 180 lb per square inch.

London Brighton & South Coast Railway: the Billinton 'B4' Class 4-4-0 express locomotive, No 70, Devonshire, *in the later chocolate brown livery (the late W.J. Reynolds).*

The North Eastern 'R' Class had the highest nominal tractive effort of any British locomotive with the conventional deep, narrow firebox, with a level grate—no less than 20,450 lb at 85 per cent boiler pressure; and in service these engines fully justified this claim. The accompanying drawing showing the general arrangement of the boiler is of interest as displaying the utmost that was achieved from this 19th century design; its life was to be greatly prolonged by superheating, indeed engines of the 'R' Class were still in passenger service in North-Eastern England as recently as 1952. Of those new designs of 1900-1, within the constraints of framing and wheel spacing, the boiler proportions were very similar; and all with 19 inch by 26 inch cylinders had closely corresponding tractive effort. A major breakaway from tradition in British 4-4-0 boiler design was to be seen in the first Midland compounds of 1902. To provide a much larger grate area, of no less than 27.14 square feet, the firebox had a sloping grate so as to clear the rear coupled axle, and this required considerably more skill in firing than the traditional deep, narrow box. Two other departures from the conventional, one no more than transient and the other leading to one of the most important developments of 20th century locomotive history, must be noticed before leaving the non-superheated 4-4-0 of 1900: the cross-watertubes of Dugald Drummond on the London and South Western, and the high raised Belpaire firebox and domeless boiler of G.J. Churchward on the Great Western.

The drawing above right shows a cross section of the firebox on a 'T9' 4-4-0 of the LSWR. In his celebrated lectures to his enginemen, Dugald Drummond claimed that the cross-water-tubes increased the heating surface in the firebox, where heating surface is most efficient, by anything up to 100 per cent; that they improved the general circulation in the boiler, particularly in the water

spaces, and that they also made a very efficient spark arrester. They were fitted on all Drummond's express passenger engines on the London and South Western from 1900 onwards though, whatever the theoretical claims made for them may have been, there were evidently practical disadvantages in maintenance. His successor, R.W. Urie, did not continue the use of them. On the Great Western, Churchward sought to minimise the undesirable phenomenon of priming, or the carrying over of water with the steam, from the boiler to the cylinders. This was caused by excessive foaming in the boiler, and certainly was not eliminated by having a large steam dome containing the regulator valve. By using a high raised firebox casing of the so-called wagon-top, or Belpaire type, with the liberal dimension of 2 feet between the top of the firebox itself and the inside of the casing, not only was the area on the water line in the hottest part of the boiler increased, but the steam space above the water line increased to such an extent as almost to eliminate foaming, and to obviate the need for a dome. In the first locomotive fitted with this arrangement the boiler barrel was parallel, and gave a rather ugly appearance; but the evolution of the tapered barrel at Swindon greatly improved this.

How the tapered barrel contributed to the later development of the British steam locomotive generally is discussed at some length in later chapters; but the gradual enlargement of boilers to suit the larger 10-wheeled engines being introduced in the early 1900s, as soon in retrospect, seems to indicate that the theory of boiler design had many side issues. In his paper of 1906 Churchward wrote: 'The ratio of diameter to length of the tube undoubtedly has a most important bearing upon the steaming qualities of the boiler and upon the efficiency of the heat absorption. This is more noticeable when the boilers are being worked to the limit of their capacity. If 2-inch tubes, say, are employed

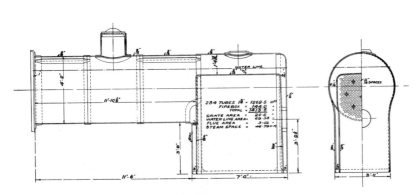

Left *NER: boiler of Class 'R' 4-4-0.*

Above right *London and South Western Railway: Dugald Drummond's arrangement of cross water-tubes in fireboxes.*

Right *Great Western Railway: one of the earliest 4-6-0s to have the taper boiler barrel. This was devised by G.J. Churchward, tapered only in the after portion and termed the half-cone boiler. This was the first GWR locomotive to have the high boiler pressure of 225 lb per square inch (British Railways).*

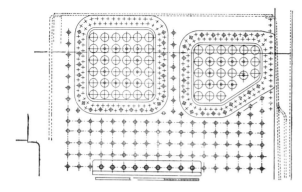

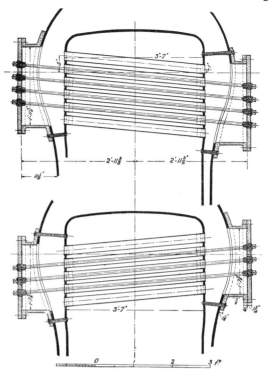

in barrels 11 to 12 feet long, when the boiler is being forced the length is not sufficient to absorb the heat from the amount of gases that a 2-inch tube will pass, and overheating and waste result'. The inside cylinder 4-4-0 engines previously discussed all had 1¾ inch tubes, for a barrel length of around 12 feet, while Churchward himself used 2 inch tubes in his standard No 1 boiler as used on the 4-6-0 and 2-8-0 engines, having a distance of 15 feet 2¼ inches between the tubeplates. The same diameter was used on the large 4-4-2 and 4-6-0 engines of the North Eastern Railway, while on the famous large-boilered 'Atlantics' of the Great Northern, with wide fireboxes, the tube diameter, for a 16 foot long barrel, was 2¼ inches, when those engines were non-superheated.

In 1900 compound propulsion was still very much in vogue in Great Britain. F.W. Webb was still in command at Crewe and, having changed from the 3-cylinder to the 4-cylinder type, naught but compounds were being built for heavy main line work on the London and North Western Railway. The trouble with these locomotives, and particularly the large 4-4-0s designed for the heaviest express passenger duties, was that they had Webb's arrangement for simultaneously linking up the valve gears of the high and low pressure cylinders. In practice this constituted a severe constriction through the low pressure side of the engine, and the choking effect was such as to restrict maximum speed severely. So that while the locomotives were very powerful in starting and accelerating heavy trains they could not make adequate speed on the faster stretches of the line. This characteristic was of no consequence on the heavy 0-8-0 mineral engines,

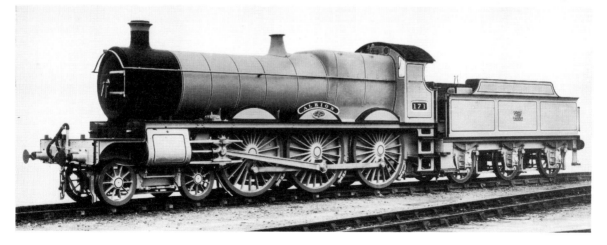

built from 1901 onwards, and many of these remained as compounds until after the First World War; but the same engine layout, applied to a series of 4-6-0 mixed traffic engines introduced in 1903, produced one of the least dependable of all Webb's compounds.

On the North Eastern Railway the Worsdell-Von Borries system of compounding, using two cylinders between the frames, had been abandoned, and the majority of engines so equipped had been rebuilt as 2-cylinder simples, with W.M. Smith's type of piston valves. To that very distinguished engineer, however, the British railway world was indebted for the introduction of a system of compounding that was eventually to have wide application. One of Wilson Worsdell's large 4-4-0s of Class 'M' that did such notable running in the Aberdeen 'Race' had been built as a 2-cylinder Worsdell-Von Borries compound and, when the time came for its conversion in 1898, it was rebuilt, not as a 2-cylinder simple but as a 3-cylinder compound in a form devised by Mr. Smith. This engine, No 1619, had one high pressure cylinder between the frames, with a piston valve immediately below, and two low pressure cylinders outside, with steam distribution from slide valves. Although this engine proved successful it remained the only one of its kind on the North Eastern, and it was on the Midland, under

S.W. Johnson, that the development of the Smith compound system began in earnest.

The two 4-4-0 engines, Nos 2631 and 2632, built at Derby in 1902, enlarged versions of the North Eastern No 1619, were indeed landmarks of British locomotive progress. They were originally confined to the Leeds-Carlisle road, over the 1,151 feet altitude of Aisgill summit, and with a specially selected individual crew to each engine, and no other. While independent reversing gears were provided for the high and low pressure cylinders, the mechanism was such that one handle would actuate both gears simultaneously if required. There was also a valve by which additional high pressure steam could be admitted to the low pressure steam chests for as long as necessary. The controls were indeed complicated, and called for intelligent and experienced handling by the driver. There was every reason for confining the manning of these two splendid engines to single crews, and they were soon doing some remarkable work with the Midland Scotch Expresses between Leeds and Carlisle. The cross-sectional drawing shows the neat arrangement of the front-end, with vertically mounted slide valves for the low pressure cylinders and a piston valve immediately below the high pressure cylinder. Three sets of Stephensons link motion were needed for the valve actuation but,

Left *London and North Western Railway: a 4-cylinder compound express engine on F.W. Webb's system, No 1941,* Alfred the Great *built at Crewe 1901* (British Railways).

Below left *North Eastern Railway: the 'M' Class 4-4-0 which made record running in the railway race of 1895. No 1621 of this class, in its modernised form, is preserved in the National Railway Museum at York* (The Locomotive Publishing Company).

Above right *Midland Railway: general arrangement drawing of the first Smith Johnson 3-cylinder compound 4-4-0.*

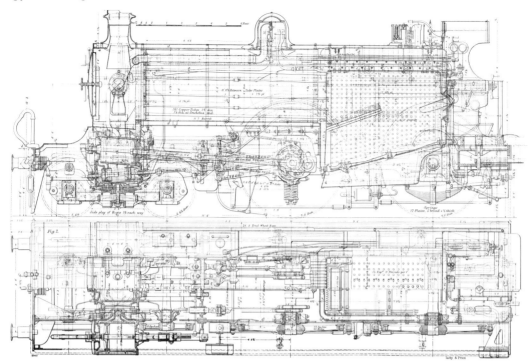

with only one inside cylinder, the attachments to the driving crank axle between the frames were not unduly crowded. It was only on the first two Midland compounds that independent control of the valve gears for the high and low pressure cylinders were provided. Three further engines built at Derby in 1903 had simultaneous control. These three went new to Kentish Town shed and worked north to Leicester, Nottingham and Derby.

While on the Midland in 1903 it was not clear that the compounds had come to stay, on the Great Western the trials of French built compound 4-4-2s of the 4-cylinder de Glehn type merely proved an important stepping stone to much better things with simple expansion. On the Great Northern, trials with compound 'Atlantics' proved inconclusive, and no developments followed. On the Lancashire and Yorkshire Railway, however, George Hughes, who had succeeded Hoy as Chief Mechanical Engineer in 1904, made an extended trial of compounding on a batch of 0-8-0 heavy freight engines, a 4-cylinder compound adaption of the standard Aspinall design. In addition to comparative tests with the dynamometer car a 24-month continuous observation period was conducted covering the 11 compound 0-8-0s and 11 2-cylinder simples. An aggregate of 600,000 miles of heavy freight haulage was involved; but, although the total coal consumption over this 2-year spell showed an advantage of

10 per cent in favour of the compounds, it would seem that the reduced fuel costs were outweighed by the higher maintenance charges of the more complicated 4-cylinder engines, and no further compounds were built by the LYR.

In the notable paper Hughes read to the Institution of Mechanical Engineers in 1910 he said at the outset: 'The author reasons that very little benefit will accrue from compounding express passenger engines. The value of compounding largely depends upon reduction of the range of temperatures in the cylinders. High piston speeds reduce this range in express work even with early cut-offs, and these conditions do not exist in slow running goods engines'. While there was a very distinguished audience for this paper, including Bowen Cooke, Churchward, Earle-Marsh, and Henry Fowler, not to mention Aspinall, who was in the chair, there was no senior representative from the North Eastern Railway, otherwise one can be fairly sure Hughes' remarks about compounding on passenger engines would not have passed unchallenged. The full story of how W.M. Smith's two masterpieces, the 4-cylinder compound Atlantics Nos 730 and 731, came to be built at Gateshead, in 1906, is told in the later chapter dealing particularly with 'Atlantic' engines in general; but in dynamometer car tests carried out between York and Newcastle in 1906 the relative capacity of the four

Type	4-4-0	4-6-0	4-4-2	4-4-2
Class	'R'	'S1'	V	4CC
Description	Inside cylinder piston valves	1900 build. Outside cylinders	2-cylinder outside cylinders 1903	Smith compound
Relative capacity	100	105	128	145
Drawbar pull at 55 mph (tons)	1.3	1.38	1.66	1.88

principal express locomotive classes on the North Eastern Railway were evaluated as shown in the table above. The figures speak for themselves.

By the year 1910, when Hughes read his paper to the 'Mechanicals' there were still many who were urging the use of compound expansion, to secure greater economy in fuel consumption; but, by that time, the claims of superheating, as an alternative, were being advanced. Among the leading British engineers of the day it did not seem to be a clear cut issue. With the prospect of having to pay royalties for proprietary design there is no doubt that some of them were looking over their shoulders to try and discern the attitude of the top management of their respective companies. Few locomotive engineers of the early 1900s had as free a hand to try out new ideas as Churchward, on the Great Western.

In technical gatherings, the advantages of eliminating condensation in the cylinders and the increased fluidity of superheated steam in passing through the valves, were weighed against the need to have more sophisticated means of lubrication, to cope with the dry searing effect of the steam on all internal parts. But the overriding fundamental fact was that of the greatly increased volume of steam produced by superheating. Whereas a pound of dry saturated steam at a boiler pressure of 160 lb per square inch has a volume of 2.6 cubic feet, with a temperature of formation of 370 degrees F, if it is superheated to 600 degrees its volume becomes 3.5 cubic feet, and one has, from the same boiler an increase of nearly 35 per cent, in the volume of steam available for doing work.

Some engineers took advantage of this characteristic to reduce the boiler pressure, and thus lessen their maintenance charges. Whereas working pressures in the majority of British locomotives using saturated steam in the early 1900s were 175 to 180 lb per square inch, when superheating was applied experimentally to existing engines, the pressure was reduced to 150 or 160 lb. On the North Eastern Railway, where Wilson Worsdell had advanced to no less than 225 lb per square inch for his big 'R1' 4-4-0 of 1908, the pressure was reduced to 170. At first it was only on the London and North Western Railway that the increased volume of steam available from superheating was utilised to provide increased tractive power. In building a superheated version of the already very successful 'Precursor' Class 4-4-0, C.J. Bowen Cooke kept the boiler pressure at 175 lb per square inch and increased the cylinder diameter from 19 to 20½ inches, a 12 per cent increase in volume. But in actual effect the improvement was much greater, as was reflected in the tonnage limits laid down on the fastest express trains south of Liverpool and Manchester—350 tons for a 'Precursor', 400 for a superheated engine.

Comparative tests on the LNWR showed not only a notable increase in haulage capacity, due to the larger cylinders, but a striking reduction in coal consumption by no less than 25 per cent. This was enough to outweigh by far all other disadvantages, and the cost of royalties on the Schmidt type of superheater, and the equipment thereafter became standard on all new LNWR express passenger locomotives from 1911. On the Great Western, however, having fitted up one engine with the Schmidt superheater, and tried an American apparatus of the Cole type, Churchward developed a type of his own. The Schmidt, which produced steam temperatures of more than 600 degrees, tended to result in there being a little superheat remaining in the steam when it was exhausted, and thus some heat was thrown away. In Churchward's 'Swindon' superheater the aim was to impart to the steam entering the cylinders just enough superheat to ensure that there was none left, as it were, when the steam had been expanded, done its work, and was exhausted. It involved a delicate balance of all the factors involved in the generation of the steam and its usage, and required the maintenance of the rated boiler pressure constantly throughout the journey; otherwise, some condensation could take place in the cylinders at the end of each piston stroke.

Reference to expansion of steam in the cylinders leads on to the question of valve gears, about which there have probably been more misconceptions and more jumping to conclusions than about any other part of the steam locomotive. It is true that the valve gear in combination with the design of the steam ports and passages in the valves can make all the difference between a free-running engine and a sluggard: one that does its work easily and economically, and one that needs to be pounded, on a heavy coal consumption to make its scheduled running speed.

Theoretically, the steam should be used as expansively as possible, using a wide open regulator, so that the steam enters the cylinders at a pressure little below that in the boiler, and that the valve gear should be so adjusted as to make the point of 'cut-off' as early as possible in the piston stroke. But in practice, even with the most recently designed engines certain factors supervene—or perhaps I should say contravene!—to make this ideal undesirable. Drivers, as practical men, would instinctively find the best way to make their engines run freely, and the result did not always agree with theory! Many thousands of miles on the footplate, and experience with a great variety of locomotives, British and otherwise, have convinced me that one cannot lay down any hard and fast rules of procedure, even for individual locomotives of the same class; and to attempt to judge the working efficiency solely by the point of steam 'cut-off' in the piston stroke would give the most fallacious impressions.

In the early 1900s by far the most common form of valve gear in Britain was the Stephenson link motion. It fitted in ideally with the traditional British inside cylinder design, neatly contained between the frames, leaving an absolute minimum of 'works' to be seen outside. The gear for each

cylinder required two eccentrics for its actuation, and these were mounted on the driving axle. Although the working parts were inclined to be heavy it was a simple mechanism, and favoured for its general reliability. A variant greatly favoured at one time in Scotland, and used on the celebrated 'Precedent' and 'Whitworth' Classes of 2-4-0 on the LNWR, was the Allan straight link motion, the difference between it and the Stephenson 'curved link' type can be seen from the accompanying drawings (below and top right). The Allan gear had gone out of use for new construction in the 19th century except on the Highland Railway, for which six new locomotives were built incorporating it as late as 1917. This gear required eccentrics on the driving axle as in the Stephenson.

It was in March 1879 that the celebrated inventor, David Joy, had patented his radial valve gear. It provided a very accurate and advantageous distribution of steam, but it had also the attractive feature of needing no eccentrics. The required oscillating and rotational motion was obtained by a link attached to the connecting rod, at almost the midpoint between the big-end and the gudgeon pin. The connecting rod had to be enlarged in section in the vicinity of the pin joint to compensate for the loss in cross-sectional area that would otherwise have resulted; but this pin joint was a feature to which certain engineers took exception. Not so the redoubtable F.W. Webb, Chief Mechanical Engineer of the LNWR, who adopted it first on his '18 inch' 0-6-0 express goods engines of 1880 and

Diagram of Stephenson's 'curved link' motion.

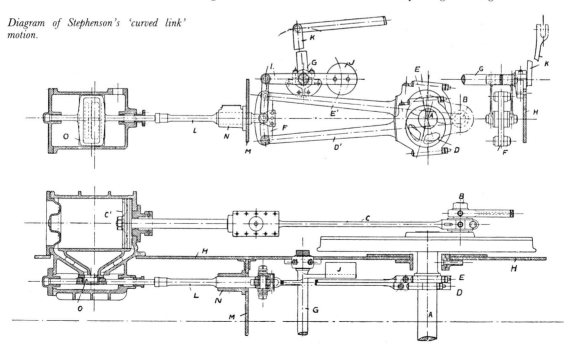

Diagram of Allan's 'straight link' motion.

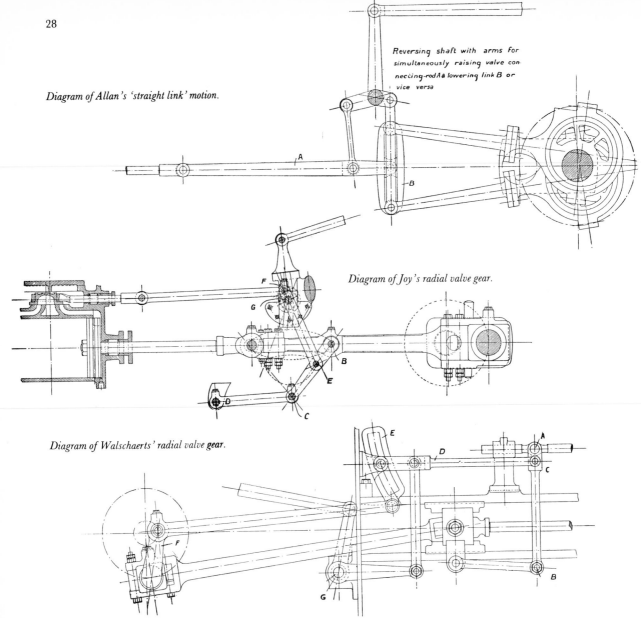

Reversing shaft with arms for
simultaneously raising valve con-
necting-rod A & lowering link B or
vice versa

A

B

Diagram of Joy's radial valve gear.

F

G

B

E

D

C

Diagram of Walschaerts' radial valve gear.

E

D

A

C

F

B

G

used nothing else afterwards. Its use was continued by his successors, except on the 4-cylinder 4-6-0s of C.J. Bowen Cooke, which had the Walschaerts radial gear. The Joy valve gear was also used on the Lancashire and Yorkshire Railway, as standard, by Aspinall, Hoy, and Hughes. In the early Grouping days, when engine maintenance was not at its previous standard the Joy valve gear earned a certain degree of disrepute through one or two breakages of connecting rods at the point of attachment to the valve link; but these failures could be attributed to arrears in maintenance, rather than to any inherent defect in the valve gear itself. The enormous train mileage accrued by 220 modern 4-4-0s built since 1904, and 350 contemporary 4-6-0s working the heaviest passenger traffic in Great Britain, (much of it at very high power output, without a single case of connecting rod failure), is testimony enough to the reliability of the gear.

The fourth valve gear to be increasingly used in Great Britain was the Walschaerts. This, like the Joy, is of the radial type and needed only one eccentric. It became popular for outside cylindered engines, because it could conveniently be mounted outside, and on locomotives with no more than two cylinders it allowed the entire space between the frames to be clear of all machinery. Everything could be got at from outside. There was no need to place an engine over a pit for the machinery to be examined or serviced. With the advantage of hindsight, however, one cannot say that any of the four valve gears referred to, the Stephenson, Allan, Joy or Walschaerts, was fundamentally better than the rest. The design of the valves themselves, slide or piston, the proportions of the port opening and the settings to determine the technical quantities in the valve movement known as the 'lap' and the 'lead' can exert a vastly greater effect on the performance of the locomotive than any differences in the mechanism for actuating the valves, as evidenced by the obvious differences between, for example, the Stephenson and the Walschaerts. The basic necessity was to provide for free entry to and free exhaust from the cylinders in all conditions of running; and there were many instances with the Stephenson, the Joy, and the Walschaerts where the detail design did not permit this.

A feature of design in British locomotives as the power and the weight of moving parts increased was the method of balancing. In a 2-cylinder engine the cranks were set at 90 degrees to each other, and it does not need much reflection to appreciate that the reciprocating and revolving action of the pistons, connecting rods and cranks resulted in some fairly large unbalanced forces. There are two aspects in the problem of balancing these forces, firstly to add balance weights at appropriate points in the wheels to ensure a smooth riding engine in itself; but secondly and at the same time, to avoid, as far as

Walschaerts radial valve gear: the apparently complicated machinery of this gear is not really so in actuality because it eliminated the heavy links and eccentrics. It is here seen on the French-built de Glehn 4-cylinder compound 4-4-2 purchased by the GWR in 1903 (British Railways).

possible, transmitting unbalanced forces to the track in the form of what are known as hammer blows. The latter can, in certain conditions, greatly increase the load the track has to carry. Much work had been done, even before the end of the 19th century, to balance the locomotive itself, notably by my old teacher Professor W.E. Dalby, Dean of the City and Guilds Engineering College, when he was in the service of the Great Eastern Railway; but the origins and effects of hammer-blow were not generally understood in the early years of the 20th century. With the increase in size and weight of locomotives, hammer-blow became critical. The general policy until then had been to balance the whole of the revolving parts, and two-thirds of the reciprocating parts by casting weights into the driving wheels of the locomotive.

The dynamics of a locomotive at speed were not appreciated by civil engineers and in the early 1900s the only criterion on which a locomotive was judged to be acceptable, or not, to run over a particular length of line, including underline bridges, was the dead weight on the axle. Two classic cases, one on the LNWR and one on the Highland, will illustrate the situation as it then existed. On the former the superheater 4-4-0s of the 'George the Fifth' Class had a maximum axle-load of 19.15 tons; but at a speed of 80 mph the hammer-blow due to the balance weights was 12 tons, so that the maximum combined load was no less than 31 tons. Then when Bowen Cooke was planning his big 4-cylinder 4-6-0 in 1911, he appreciated that by making all four cylinders drive on to the leading coupled axle, with the four crank positions quartering the circle, there would be no hammer blow at all. With a large boiler and firebox the maximum in axle load exceeded 20 tons, but this the civil engineer would not accept, even though there was no augmentation of this weight by hammer blow. Apparently he was deaf to all arguments that existing engines were imposing a maximum combined load of more than 30 tons upon the underline structures. A maximum of 20 tons per axle was the maximum dead load that he

would accept. And while the drawing office at Crewe was working out a revised design of boiler for the new 4-cylinder engines, he accepted the weight diagram for a new batch of 2-cylinder 4-6-0s, 'Prince of Wales' Class, which had a maximum axle load of 18.25 tons, to which a hammer blow of 11.4 tons was added at 80 mph.

The Highland case was tragic, as much in its story of difficult and intransigent personalities, as in its engineering sequel. At the beginning of the First World War F.G. Smith was Locomotive Superintendent. New and more powerful engines were needed, but while technically he was one of the ablest men of the day, and well liked by his own staff, he had a high handed way of dealing with his fellow officers which had already brought him into collision with the Chief Engineer, Alexander Newlands. When he received authority to design and have built six powerful new 4-6-0s for the heavy main line traffic of war-time, confident in his own technology he evidently thought it unnecessary to

submit a weight diagram to the Chief Engineer. Although the new engines were to be much heavier than anything that had previously run on the Highland, with an adhesion weight of 52½ tons, against 44¾ tons on the 'Castle', by reducing the amount of reciprocating balance below the traditional 'two-thirds' the maximum combined axle-load (including hammer blow) at 60 mph was actually less than that of the 'Castle'.

It is said that the first the Chief Engineer heard about the new engines was when the first two of them arrived at Perth from the builders. While officially this may have been so I find it hard to believe that news had not previously reached him, through the 'grape-vine' and that he was prepared to damn the engines out of hand. When Smith eventually produced the weight diagram, Newlands forbade their use, and Smith was given a week to resign or else be sacked. He resigned. The sequel to this unfortunate affair is told in a later chapter of this book.

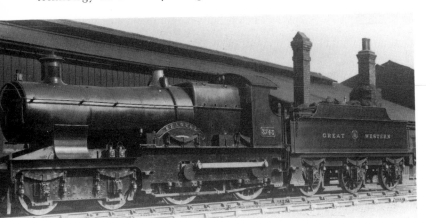

Left *The continuance of double-framing into the 20th century: one of the later examples of the 'Bulldog' Class 4-4-0s, as fitted with Churchward's taper boiler and top feed apparatus (the late W.J. Reynolds).*

Left *Great Eastern Railway: the* Claud Hamilton *4-4-0 of 1900, forerunner of a series of more than a hundred very simple and successful express locomotives (the late K.A.C.R. Nunn).*

Top right *A larger version of the LSWR 'T9' 4-4-0, the 'L12', which shows clearly the casing on the side of the firebox for accommodating the Drummond cross-watertubes (The Locomotive Publishing Company).*

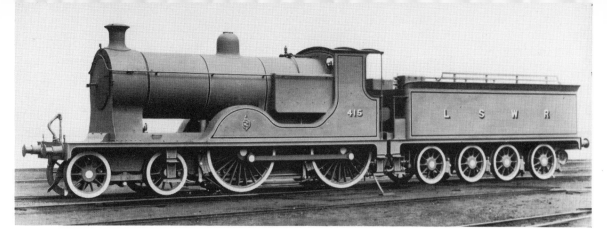

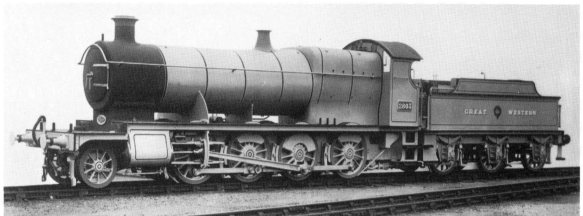

Above *The half-cone taper boiler applied to one of the earliest heavy freight locomotives of the GWR, No 2803, of the 2-8-0 type* (British Railways).

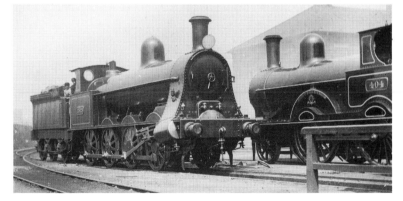

Right *One of the 3-cylinder Webb compound 0-8-0 mineral engines of the LNWR. The front casing of the one huge low pressure cylinder can be seen behind the buffer beam* (The Locomotive Publishing Company).

Right *LNWR: the difference at the front end between the 3-cylinder and the 4-cylinder mineral engines can be seen in the casing over the inside (low pressure) cylinders in this picture.*

Above *Midland Railway: one of the first two of the celebrated Johnson 3-cylinder compound 4-4-0s of 1902, forerunners of the series of LMS compound 4-4-0s* (British Railways).

Below *London and North Western Railway: classic usage of the Allan straight link valve gear on the record breaking 'Precedent' Class 2-4-0, No 790,* Hardwicke *(now preserved), which ran the Scottish racing train in 1895 from Crewe to Carlisle at an average speed of 67 mph* (British Railways).

Bottom *Lancashire and Yorkshire Railway: the first 2-4-2 passenger tank (by J.A.F. Aspinall) which was the progenitor of a large family of these engines, fitted with the Joy radial valve, also favoured on the LNWR* (British Railways).

3. 4-4-0 The British passenger locomotive

It is indeed remarkable to recall the extraordinary variety of styling, and still more so the sartorial elegance in which the basic British inside-cylinder 4-4-0 was clothed in the early years of the 20th century. Of 14 main line railways that used this simplest of passenger locomotive, all equipped with the Stephenson link motion, there was little difference in the ultimate purpose of the design. While those intended for the fastest express work had coupled wheels from 6 feet 6 inches to 7 feet diameter, the cylinder diameters varied between 18 and 19 inches, and boiler pressures mostly between 165 and 180 lb per square inch. Yet if one excepts the London and South Western 'T9', and the Highland 'Small Ben', which were so alike as to appear as close variants of the same design—which of course they actually were—the variation in appearance and colour was so great that the connoisseur might well scrutinise their outward form to try and discern some subtle reasons underlying it. It may, however, be perhaps an over simplification to suggest that one could take any of them and apply them to the work of any other railway, and achieve complete success, once the enginemen had become acclimatised. The basic dimensions of these 14 classes are set out in the table overleaf.

Some lines, like the North Eastern and the Midland had already begun to venture, in small numbers into larger and more elaborate designs; but taken all round the engines shown in the table were, in 1900-3, the principal main line passenger power of each of the lines concerned. To carry the theme of colour and variety still further one could, by 1910, add the 4-4-0s introduced on certain lesser railways of the same general design; while to complete the picture, 4-4-0s of two other railways that were not of a top-link passenger character can be included in this supplementary table, to present a grand total of no fewer than 20 inside cylinder 4-4-0s, all with Stephenson link motion. Of the smaller railways the North Staffordshire and the Hull and Barnsley were introducing the 4-4-0 for the first time in 1910. On the Great Northern, H.A. Ivatt was using the 4-4-0 as an intermediate general purpose passenger type, while continuing to use the Stirling 'singles', often in pairs, for the fastest express work while his famous 'Atlantic' design was being developed. On the Glasgow and South Western James Manson had introduced 4-6-0s for

London and South Western Railway: W. Adams' 7 foot 4-4-0 express locomotive.

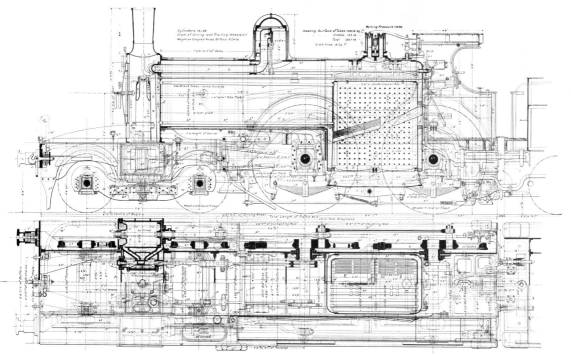

Inside-cylinder 4-4-0s of 1900-4 with Stephenson's Link Motion

Ref no	1	2	3	4	5	6	7
Railway	L & SWR	LBSCR	SE & CR	GER	Midland	GCR	NER
Class (designer)	Drummond 'T9'	Billinton 'B4'	Wainwright 'D'	Claud Hamilton	'Belpaire'	Robinson	'R'
Cylinders diameter × stroke (inches)	18½ × 26	19 × 26	19 × 26	19 × 26	19½ × 26	18½ × 26	19 × 26
Coupled wheel diameter (feet/inches)	6 7	6 9	6 8	7 0	6 9	6 9	6 10
Boiler pressure (lb per square inch)	175	170	175	180	180	180	200
Colour	Light Green	Yellow*	Bright Green	Royal Blue	Crimson Lake	Dark Green	Leaf (Spring) Green

Ref no	8	9	10	11	12	13	14
Railway	Furness	S & DJR	Cambrian	Caledonian	North British	GN of S	Highland
Class (designer)	Pettigrew '126'	'71' Class	Jones '94'	Dunalastair III	Holmes 317	Pickersgill 'T'	Small Ben
Cylinders diameter × stroke (inches)	18 × 16	18 × 26	18½ × 26	19 × 26	19 × 26	18 × 26	18½ × 26
Coupled wheel diameter (feet/inches)	6 6	6 0	6 0	6 6	6 6	6 1	6 0
Boiler pressure (lb per square inch)	160	175	170	180	200	165	175
Colour	Iron-Ore Red	Blue (purplish)	Black	Prussian Blue†	Brown (amber)	Blue Green	Moss Green

Inside cylinder 4-4-0s: Subsidiary table with Stephenson's Link Motion

Ref no	15	16	17	18	19	20
Railway	G & SWR	GNR	Midland & SW Junction	Midland & GN Junction	Hull & Barnsley	North Staffordshire
Class (designer)	Manson '240'	H.A. Ivatt	No 1 class	W. Marriott	M. Stirling	J.H. Adams
Cylinders diameter × stroke (inches)	18¼ × 26	17½ × 26	18 × 26	18½ × 26	18½ × 26	18½ × 26
Coupled wheel diameter (feet/inches)	6 6	6 7½	5 9	6 6	6 6	6 0
Boiler pressure (lb per square inch)	165	170	175	175	170	175
Colour	Blue-green	Medium green	Crimson Lake	Orange-brown	Black‡	Red-brown

*Later Vandyke Brown.   †Later, with white mixed, Sky Blue.   ‡Known officially as 'Invisible Green'. It looked black.

the principal Anglo-Scottish services, and his '240' Class was a larger boilered version of a 19th century design, for intermediate duties. The Midland and Great Northern Joint example was one of William Marriott's rebuilds of the standard Johnson Midland type, specially for the arduous double-home turns from Yarmouth to Leicester. The North Staffordshire 4-4-0s were used on certain summer holiday workings between Stoke-on-Trent and Llandudno, on which the NSR locomotives worked through.

Reverting to the engines in the larger table, by far the hardest all-the-year-round work fell to the Caledonian 'Dunalastairs' and the North Eastern 'R' Class, though at summer holiday periods the Great Eastern 'Claud Hamilton' Class were set some very heavy tasks. On the Highland, although the 'Small Bens' represented the avowed policy of Peter Drummond, in following his elder brother's practice on the London and South Western, the Highland enginemen retained a great affection for the practice of his predecessor, David Jones, and as 4-4-0s went preferred the outside cylindered 'Loch' Class of 1896 to the 'Small Bens'. It is significant that, in 1916 when additional engines were needed for working the heavy war-time traffic over the Dingwall and Skye line, where 4-6-0s were not then permitted, the Highland ordered three more engines of the 'Loch' Class from the North British Locomotive Company, rather than the more recent 'Small Bens', both of which had previously been built by that great firm. The three 'Loch' Class engines, in 1917 were the last to be built for service in Great Britain with the **Allan straight** link motion. It was somewhat significant of the sentiments then

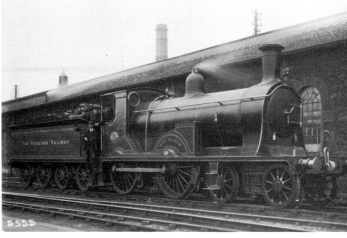

prevailing on the Highland Railway that when new engines were needed for the mail trains on the 'Farther North' main line from Inverness to Wick that these also were built with outside cylinders, though this is carrying the story into superheater days.

The other railway on which outside-cylinder 4-4-0s, using single expansion, were much in evidence in the early 1900s was the London and South Western. Dugald Drummond's predecessor as Locomotive Superintendent, William Adams, had introduced two classes of outside cylinder 4-4-0s, one with 7 foot 1 inch coupled wheels and the other, for the more heavily graded line between Salisbury and Exeter, with 6 foot 7 inch wheels. These truly splendid engines were built at intervals between

Above right *Highland Railway: Peter Drummond's 'small Ben' Class 4-4-0, No 10,* Ben Slioch. *Note the extreme similarity to the LSWR 'T9' Class (the late W.J. Reynolds).*

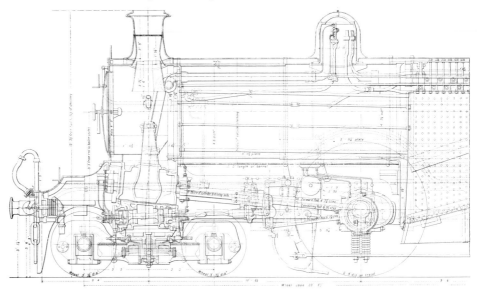

Right *Midland Railway: front-end of S.W. Johnson's 4-4-0 non-compound express locomotive, with piston valves. Note the arrangement of 'petticoats' on the chimney interior.*

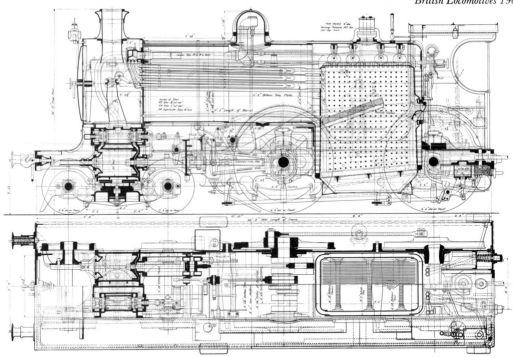

*Caledonian Railway: the ultimate development of the 'Dunalastair':
the superheated No IV Class, with indirect valve motion, 8 inch
diameter piston valves and Schmidt superheater.*

1890 and 1896, the last 20 of which were actually
completed at Nine Elms Works and put into traffic
after Adams had retired, and his place had been
taken by Dugald Drummond. At the time of their
introduction W.F. Pettigrew, who subsequently
became Locomotive, Carriage and Wagon
Superintendent of the Furness Railway, was Works
Manager at Nine Elms, and in his classic work, *A
Manual of Locomotive Engineering*, published in 1899,
he refers to the Adams 4-4-0s as probably the most
powerful, and certainly the most efficient locomotives in the world, at that time.

W.F. Pettigrew was joint author, with Adams, of
a notable paper read before the Institution of Civil
Engineers in 1895, describing trials with one of
these engines, and the coal consumptions, of
between 1.98 and 2.61 lb per indicated horsepower
hour, were not surpassed by any British locomotives
until the 1920s. The Drummond 'T9' Class built to
succeed them, and which earned such a
distinguished reputation, were slightly *less* powerful,
on a tractive effort basis, because the Adams engines
had cylinders of 19 inch diameter against 18½
inches. The Drummond engines had a much larger
firebox with a grate area of 24 square feet against 18
square feet in the Adams; but the results of the very

comprehensive trials described in the 1895 paper at
the 'Civils' showed that the combustion in the older
engine was of high efficiency.

The next grouping of inside-cylinder 4-4-0
designs was of those using the Joy radial valve gear.
These were mostly on the London and North
Western, and Lancashire and Yorkshire Railways,
though the latter dated from the 1890s, and the
former originated in 1904. The passenger
locomotives of the LNWR were about the hardest
worked of any in Great Britain, both in respect of
the power output regularly and continuously
obtained from them, and from the exceptional
weekly mileages that so many of them worked. Ever
since the first use of the Joy valve gear by F.W.
Webb (on the '18 inch' express goods engines of
1880) a centre bearing for the driving axle had been
inserted wherever possible; the only exceptions
during the later years of the Webb regime had been
the 3-cylinder compounds. Although the use of
bearings at three points on the driving axle called
for accurate aligning the supreme craftsmanship
tradition of Crewe found no difficulties in this, and
the increased bearing area made an important
contribution to the troublefree service rendered by
the 'Precursor' Class 4-4-0 under such arduous
utilisation. These engines had the traditional basic
dimensions of the early 1900s namely 19 inch by 26
inch cylinders, 6 foot 9 inch coupled wheels and a
boiler pressure of 175 lb per square inch; but a large

free-steaming boiler, backed up by the accurate and efficacious distribution of steam by the Joy valve gear, made possible an output of power, higher and longer sustained than was possible from any of the contemporary 4-4-0s with the Stephenson link motion.

At a period roughly 20 years after that of which I am now writing certain self-styled pundits on the subject of locomotive working used to aver that it was only by the use of long valve travels and piston valves that efficient performance and speedy running could be ensured, looking particularly to the maximum valve travels of 6½ inches on modern Great Western engines. But in studying the table of inside cylinder 4-4-0 locomotives on page 34 it is interesting to recall that many of these successful designs had gears providing no more than 4 inches maximum valve travel, and that the outside cylindered London and South Western 4-4-0 of William Adams, which gave so high a thermal efficiency in the tests reported in 1895, had a maximum valve travel of only 3¾ inches.

And so far as high speed was concerned, the first authenticated instance anywhere in the world of a maximum speed of 100 mph—probably just a shade over—came in 1904 from a Great Western 4-4-0, the *City of Truro*, having 18 inch by 26 inch cylinders, and balanced slide valves with a maximum travel of 4⅛ inches. These engines, like the preceeding 4-4-0s of the 'Atbara' Class, had double frames, and lay somewhat outside the general style of the locomotives tabulated on page 34. The same 'pundits' were equally inclined to emphasise that it was not possible to get expansive working of the steam with anything but long travel valves; but the tests of the Adams 4-4-0s, reported in the 1895 paper before the Institution of Civil Engineers shows that the normal point of cut-off of steam in the cylinders was at 17 per cent of the piston stroke, which was actually *earlier* than that usually worked on modern Great Western two-cylinder engines having a maximum valve travel of 6¼ inches. These latter were rarely pulled up shorter than about 22 per cent. The point of emphasis at this stage is that it was just not possible to pontificate as to the likely

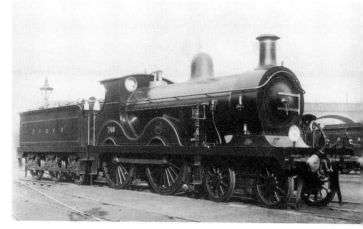

Top *South Eastern & Chatham Railway: the 'D' Class 4-4-0 introduced by H.S. Wainwright* (The Locomotive Publishing Company).

Above *Midland Railway: the Johnson 'Belpaire' 4-4-0 as subsequently modernised by superheating* (the late W.J. Reynolds).

Below *Great Central Railway: J.G. Robinson's express passenger 4-4-0 for the London Extension (1901)* (North British Locomotive Company).

Top *One of the Robinson 4-4-0s as superheated and running in early LNER days (1926)* (P. Ransome-Wallis).

Above *One of the first Great Western 4-4-0s to have a domeless boiler was No 3310,* Waterford, *which had a parallel boiler and high raised Belpaire firebox* (The Locomotive Publishing Company).

Below *The subsequent development, with taper boiler and straight outside frames, was the 'City' Class of 1903, one of which—the* City of Truro—*attained a maximum speed of 100 mph (or a shade over) with an Ocean Mail special in 1904* (P.J.T. Reed).

performance or efficiency of a locomotive, purely from the most comprehensive details of dimensions.

Among the 2-cylinder 4-4-0s of the early 1900s, albeit having the Stephenson link motion, the Great Western 'County' Class stood out from all the rest. Superficially one could class them with the Adams 4-4-0s of the LSWR and with the Highland 'Loch' Class; but actually they revealed far more of the American influence to which G.J. Churchward was very much subject at the time. One of the troubles experienced in some British outside cylindered locomotives was of a weakness developing in the attachment of the cylinders to the frames, with the cylinders working loose.

In the American practice that Churchward copied and standardised on all his 2-cylinder engines, the front end consisted of two castings only, each incorporating one cylinder and its valve chest, and half the smokebox saddle. The two castings were bolted together on the centre line of the locomotive. While adopting this commendable feature of American practice Churchward differed from it in the frame construction. The rear part carrying the coupled wheel axlebox guides were of plate, in the traditional British style, while at the front end each consisted of a thick rectangular slab attached to the buffer beam at the front end. The back end had to be splayed out to a reduced thickness to suit the depth of the main frame plate, and a joint between the front and main frame was made immediately behind the cylinders. The cylinder blocks were the same on both sides of the engine, and standard for all Churchward's range of locomotives having outside 18 inch by 30 inch cylinders.

The remaining 4-4-0s of those early years of the century were the compounds of the London and North Western, and of the Midland. The origin of both these large and powerful designs was referred to in the previous chapter, and both underwent some significant changes before many years had passed. On the former railway, after George Whale had succeeded F.W. Webb as Chief Mechanical Engineer, in 1903, he made an important and salutary alteration to the 'Alfred the Great' Class of compound express engines by fitting a second set of Joy valve gear to permit independent adjustment of the high pressure and low pressure valve gear. The original restriction caused by simultaneous notching up of both gears was eliminated by leaving the low pressure valves in full gear all the time, and notching up only the high pressure as required. Tests made in September 1903 with engine No 1952, *Benbow*, the first to be altered, showed that in working a heavy train of 372 tons between Crewe and Stafford the following comparative results were obtained:

LNWR Engine No 1952, 'Benbow':
Crewe-Stafford & Return: 24.5 miles

Direction	South-bound	South-bound	North-bound	North-bound
Gear	Original	Altered	Original	Altered
Time (minutes)	38½	34¼	34	30
Average speed (mph)	37.79	44.09	42.79	48.5
Maximum IHP	814.8	940.7	756.4	949.2

On the Midland, S.W. Johnson's successor, R.M. Deeley, did exactly the reverse when building additional engines of the 3-cylinder compound type, dispensing with the change-valve included in the Smith-Johnson compounds, which gave such a remarkable degree of flexibility in starting. It was felt that this device, together with the facility for independent control of the high and low pressure valve gear, was too complicated for the average engineman to use to the best advantage, and Deeley designed a regulator valve which was extremely simple to operate. When starting, the regulator handle was moved gradually to a position about half

Midland Railway: R.M. Deeley's modified form of the original 3-cylinder compound, with combined reversing gear control for high and low pressure cylinders.

way over on the quadrant plate, working the engine as a 2-cylinder simple, up to a speed of about 10 mph. Then the handle was pushed hard over to the full open position, and compound working began. Once full speed was attained the regulator could be eased back as required, but compound working continued. One could not revert to starting conditions, and 'simple' working unless the regulator was completely closed, and opened again. Apart from introduction of his special regulator valve, Deeley made certain alterations to the boiler proportions including a notably increased grate area, from 26 to 28.4 square feet and an increase in boiler pressure from 195 to 220 lb per square inch. This was before the addition of superheating.

With the rapid multiplication of the LNWR 'Precursor' Class, the building of more Midland compounds up to a total of 45, of many more 'Claud Hamilton' Class 4-4-0s on the Great Eastern, and of the Great Western 'County' Class, it began to look as though these successful designs marked the culmination of the type, and that future development would be in the form of 'Atlantics' and 4-6-0s. Two new designs introduced in 1907-8 did indeed represent the climax of the non-superheater 4-4-0 in Great Britain. On the Midland it would seem that Deeley was not entirely sure of his compounds, and in 1907 he built a simple 4-4-0 with 19 inch by 26 inch cylinders having the same boiler and firebox

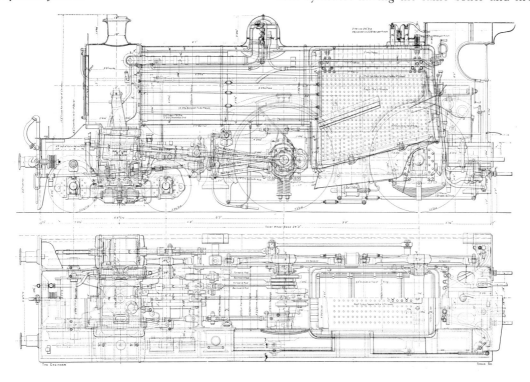

and high working pressure as the compound namely 220 lb per square inch. This was engine No 999, the first of a class of 10, that eventually became the mainstay of the express service between Leeds and Carlisle. These engines took the road just at the time when responsibility for locomotive running had been transferred from Deeley to the operating department, under the dynamic Cecil W. Paget, and with this change the era of rigid limitation of engine loads on the Midland Railway began. The '999' series of 4-4-0s were placed in No 3 Class, with the Johnson 'Belpaire' type, although the newer engines, despite smaller cylinders, had a higher tractive effort because of their higher boiler pressure. This was later reduced to 200 lb per square inch.

The most interesting feature of the '999' Class, as originally built, was their valve gear. No eccentrics were used. The valve movement was taken from the crosshead by means of a rod connected to the expansion link, and the travel for lead by means of a pendulum link. The crank on the crosshead of one side of the motion followed the driving crank and the crank oscillating the expansion link of the other motion would be leading the driving crank, so that in either fore or back gear one die was at the top of

the expansion link while the other was at the bottom. It was, in effect, a modification of the Walschaerts gear in which the crosshead of one cylinder was used to provide the equivalent of the eccentric for the other. It is understood that Deeley had designed such a gear when he was assistant to S.W. Johnson, but the latter would have nothing to do with it. When he had succeeded to the Chair at Derby, on August 11 1905 he applied for a patent for it. The date is important, because the gear became the cause of an almighty row between Deeley and Churchward. In June 1905 W.H. Pearce, a leading draughtsman at Swindon specialising in valve gears, had completed and shown to Churchward a wooden model of an almost identical gear, which was immediately adopted for the pioneer 4-cylinder simple 4-4-2 *North Star*. This engine was completed, and incorporated what was known at Swindon as the 'scissors gear', before Deeley's patent application was granted. Understandably, perhaps, Deeley was furious; but there was nothing he could do about it. The completion of Pearce's model preceded his patent application.

The climax in grace and majesty, quite apart from sheer size in non-superheater 4-4-0 design was reached in the 'R1' Class of Wilson Worsdell on the North Eastern Railway, at the end of 1908, and built at Darlington Works. While these great engines could be regarded as an enlargement of the very successful 'R' Class introduced nine years

Midland Railway: the superheated '999' Class '4P' with Fowler's parallel bore chimney and the Deeley 'Scissors' valve gear, requiring no eccentrics.

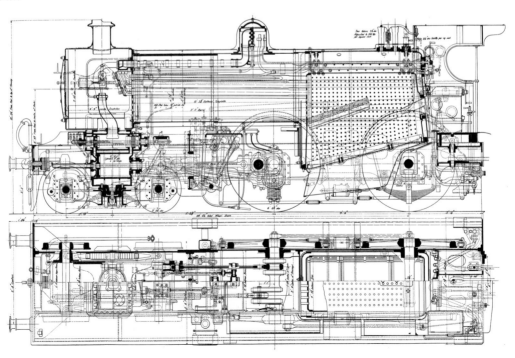

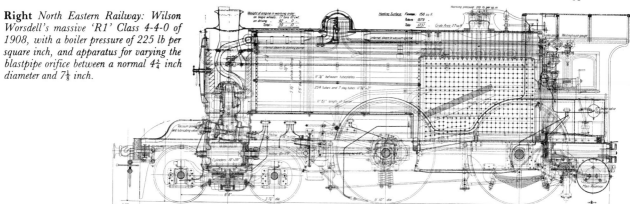

Right *North Eastern Railway: Wilson Worsdell's massive 'R1' Class 4-4-0 of 1908, with a boiler pressure of 225 lb per square inch, and apparatus for varying the blastpipe orifice between a normal 4¼ inch diameter and 7⅛ inch.*

earlier they were interesting as evidence of a return to the 4-4-0 type, albeit no more than temporarily, after experience with very large engines of the 'Atlantic' type—10 2-cylinder simples and two 4-cylinder compounds. On going into traffic the 10 engines of the 'R1' Class very largely monopolised the principal East Coast express passenger duties between York and Edinburgh, as far as their numbers permitted, taking the heaviest trains without difficulty. The cylinders and motion were the same as on the 'R' Class but, with a much larger boiler and a working pressure of no less than 225 lb per square inch, they were by a considerable margin the most powerful 4-4-0s yet seen in Great Britain. The tractive effort, at 85 per cent boiler pressure was no less than 22,000 lb, and this was amply supported by an adhesion weight of no less than 42 tons.

The building of 4-4-0 locomotives of a new design, which had languished somewhat after the year 1905, enjoyed a remarkable revival from 1910 onwards. This, of course, was due to the adoption of super-heating, with outstanding success, on the London and North Western Railway. The catalyst that sparked off this development did not originate at Crewe but, surprisingly perhaps, on the London Brighton and South Coast Railway. Apart from the Swindon apparatus that was coming into use on Great Western locomotives the only reliable equipment then available was that of Schmidt, and its use involved the payment of royalties in respect of patents on the various features of the design and its accessories in addition to the purchase price of the apparatus. In 1909, when Bowen Cooke

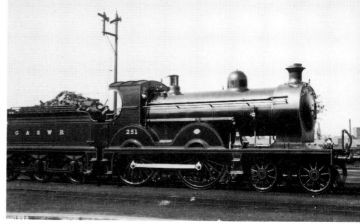

Above right *Caledonian Railway: the third version of the famous 'Dunalastair' series, by J. F. McIntosh (British Railways).*

Right *Glasgow and South Western Railway: James Manson's 4-4-0 express locomotive of 1904 which was used for intermediate duties (The Locomotive Publishing Company).*

succeeded Whale as Chief Mechanical Engineer of the LNWR, the Running Department was in a very healthy state. The engines introduced since 1904 were very much masters of the work; double-heading, which in Webb's last years was almost universal, had been reduced to minimal proportions, with an appropriate reduction in running costs, and to the Locomotive Committee of the Board there was no immediate need for larger or more powerful locomotives. Indeed, just before Bowne Cooke took office in 1909 an order for no fewer than 60 additional engines of the 4-6-0 'Experiment' Class had been placed on Crewe. They were certainly about the simplest and cheapest 4-6-0 passenger engines ever built.

Nevertheless, as a running man himself Bowen Cooke would have known that there were times when the willing and reliable Whale engines were stretched almost to their limit. The 4-4-0 'Precursors', as well as the six-coupled 'Experiments', were frequently called upon to haul loads of 400 tons on schedules demanding a start-to-stop average speed of 54 to 55 mph south of Crewe. Nothing approaching such performance was being attempted with emgines of comparable dimensions at that time elsewhere in Great Britain. At a time when there was a rather astonishing degree of parochialism in locomotive engineering circles, Bowen Cooke was about the last man to whom such a criticism could be applied; and he saw clearly that the way to future development in locomotive design lay in superheating, and the sooner Crewe got with it the better. The problem was to convince the Locomotive Committee of the Board. It was then that a fortuitous situation presented itself.

Four years previously Douglas Earle-Marsh had succeeded Billinton as Locomotive, Carriage and Wagon Superintendent of the London Brighton and South Coast Railway. The topline express passenger engines were then the excellent 'B4' 4-4-0s, but coming from Doncaster, where, as Works Manager, he had been very much involved with the building of the first of Ivatt's famous 'Atlantics', Earle-Marsh took the design to the Brighton, and before the year 1905 was out he had put on the road five engines so similar to the '251' Class of the Great Northern as to leave no doubt of where the inspiration came from. Then he set the drawing office to work on a tank engine version of the 'B4' with the 4-4-2 wheel arrangement.

A vigorous personality, anxious to put the Brighton in the forefront, he arranged for the first two engines of the express tank class to be built for a comparison: superheater versus non-superheater, and the two engines went into traffic late in 1908. By that time the North Western and Brighton were running the highly successful 'Sunny South Special' service between Liverpool and Manchester on the one hand, and Eastbourne. In the ordinary way engines were changed at Willesden Junction, but in July 1909 an interchange working was arranged by which one engine worked through between Rugby and Brighton, with North Western and Brighton engines on alternate days, and in this way it was possible to make direct comparison between an LNWR 4-4-0 of the 'Precursor' Class, and one of Earle-Marsh's superheater 4-4-2 tank engines.

From the tractive effort point of view the haulage of a train of around 250 tons on such pedestrian schedules would have been a mere holiday outing for the LNWR engine *Titan*. The train was allowed 87 minutes non-stop for the 77.2 miles between Willesden and Rugby, the same timing as the famous 2 pm West Coast Corridor train, on which the 'Precursors' were scheduled to take 420 tons before a pilot could be claimed; and, on the Brighton line, for the 40.4 miles non-stop from East Croydon—52 minutes. These timings do not bear

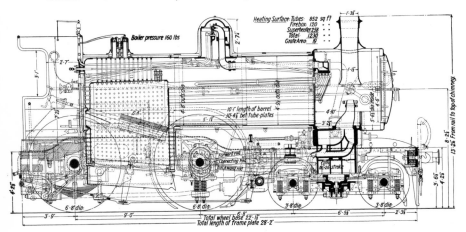

Great Northern Railway: superheater 4-4-0 express locomotive by H.A. Ivatt (Schmidt type with piston valves).

Right *North British Railway: Matthew Holmes' final 4-4-0 design, Class K, of 1903, in LNER colours* (P. Ransome-Wallis).

Below *Great North of Scotland Railway: this railway used the 4-4-0 for all main line duties, passenger and goods alike. One of the latest superheated series of 1920 was No 6850, Hatton Castle* (P. Ransome-Wallis).

Bottom *LB & SCR: one of the Billinton 'Grasshopper' 4-4-0s, rebuilt with a larger boiler as Class 'B2X', hauling the southbound Sunny South Express (LNWR coaches and dining car) at Tooting Common* (the late F.E. Mackay).

Somerset & Dorset Joint Railway: 4-4-0, locomotive No 78, generally of Midland design, and one of two built at Derby in 1907 (British Railways).

out the claim made by some writers that very hard running was required from both the competing engines; but the Brighton 4-4-2 tank and its crew were faced with a task requiring some first class enginemanship.

From the Brighton side it was stipulated that the round trip of 264 miles, covering two days, should be made on one heaped-up bunkerful of coal, 3¼ tons; and there was no facility for taking water on the 77.2 mile non-stop runs between Willesden and Rugby. To work the trains on the exiguous amounts of coal and water involved a maximum consumption of 27 lb and 22 gallons per mile, and these were satisfactorily accomplished. Such a performance gave Bowen Cooke just the demonstration he needed to secure authorisation to spend the extra required to build *one* superheater 4-4-0 engine for trial. The man who drove *Titan* during the interchange, P. Clow of Rugby shed, would have been well known personally to Bowen Cooke because, during the race of 1895, he was driving the Webb 3-cylinder compound *Adriatic*, non-stop between Euston and Crewe with the 8 pm Tourist express, and at that time Bowen Cooke was based at Rugby, as Running Superintendent.

In July 1910 two new 4-4-0 engines were completed at Crewe Works, Nos 2663 and 2664, named respectively *George the Fifth* and *Queen Mary*. They were almost identical except that the first was superheated and the second was not. The *Queen Mary* had the same sized cylinders as the 'Precursors', namely 19 inch, while the *George the Fifth*, in anticipation of the greater volume of steam from superheating, had 20 inch cylinders. By the end of October each had run about 40,000 miles on identical duties between Euston and Crewe and, with a close check being kept on the coal consumption, the superheater engine was showing an advantage of no less than 26 per cent. More top

line passenger engines were needed at once, and an order for nine more 'Queen Marys' was completed at Crewe in October. But so convincing already were the results from the superheated *George the Fifth* that an order was given to carry straight on with nine more of these latter immediately the 'Queen Mary' order was completed.

Shortly after its construction in July a dynamometer car test run had been made with the *George the Fifth*, hauling a load of 357 tons behind the tender, from Crewe to Euston and back, 158 miles each way with the following results:

Direction	Southbound	Northbound
Average speed		
(mph)	60.5	64.2
Coal consumption		
(lb per train mile)	39.6	45.7
(lb per ton mile)	0.0875	0.099

The ton-mile figure is based on the total weight of the train, engine and coaches together. When the 'George the Fifth' Class engines were in general service it was revealed to ordinary travellers, who took detailed and accurate notes of locomotive performance, that the test run of July 1910 was by no means an exceptional effort. I have before me details of 21 runs on top-line express trains northbound from Euston made in the years 1911-1915, and I have made an analysis of the uphill running (14.2 miles) between Watford and Tring where the gradient is rising mainly at about 1 in 335. On the test run of July 1910 the average speed on this length was 55.9 mph with a trailing load of 357 tons. On these 21 runs the average load was 402 tons and the average speed was 56 mph. On the test run the equivalent drawbar horsepower was 857, and this was surpassed on 16 of the other runs, with an average for the whole 21 of 930 building up to the remarkable maximum effort on which an average of 61.1 mph was made with a load of 435 tons, involving an output of 1,170 drawbar horsepower. Nothing approaching it had previously been seen in the performance of 4-4-0 locomotives. It was

Above *LNWR: one of the Webb 4-cylinder compound 4-4-0s fitted with independent valve gears by G. Whale in 1904. (Compare this with the photograph of the original type on page 24, Chapter Two)* (British Railways).

Right *LNWR: one of the celebrated 'Precursor' Class of 1904, No 2585, Watt, but fitted temporarily with oil-firing equipment during one of several coal strikes* (British Railways).

certainly a triumph for Mr Bowen Cooke and for the staff of the locomotive department of the LNWR.

From a paper presented to the Institution of Civil Engineers in 1914 by Henry Fowler (afterwards Sir Henry), Chief Mechanical Engineer of the Midland Railway, and from the discussion that followed, it was evident that on certain other British railways, which were feeling their way rather more gradually towards superheating, that similar economies in coal consumption were being realised. Some of the most interesting results came from the Midland itself, on which one of the Deeley 3-cylinder

compounds had been converted. On certain coal trials between St Pancras and Leeds the results shown in the table below had been obtained, a distance of 200 miles each way. Unlike the LNWR test of July 1910, the Midland tests were undirectional on each day: up one day, and down the next.

These might appear remarkable, especially for the superheater compound; but, of course, the loads were very light compared to those of the London and North Western Railway. They were just within the 230-ton maximum for Class 4 engines on 'Special Limit' trains. But they were enough to set the Midland Railway on a course of fitting super-

Engine no	**992**	**998**	**1039**	**1040**
Type	Simple non-superheater	Simple superheater	Compound non-superheater	Compound superheater
Trailing load (tons)	183	187	218	225
Average speed (mph)	51.5	51.5	51.5	51.5
Coal per train mile (lb)	31.3	24.3	29.4	22.3
Coal per gross ton-mile (lb)	0.109	0.083	0.0916	0.0679

heaters to many existing types of passenger locomotives, using the Schmidt apparatus. While the 2-cylinder simple engines on the Midland had piston valves, the 3-cylinder compounds, when superheated, retained slide valves for the low pressure cylinders.

Since the opening of the London Extension the Great Central Railway had built, for its fast express train services, large 'Atlantic' and 4-6-0 locomotives, culminating, in 1912, with the 'Sir Sam Fay' Class of 4-6-0 with inside cylinders no less than 21½ inches diameter. But there seems little doubt that these large engines were built as much for prestige purposes as in hopeful anticipation of increased traffic; because the train loads remained very light, compared to those of the London and North Western Railway. Although they may have been likened to those of the Midland Railway, the Great Central tonnages were certainly not the result of any limitations imposed by the operating department; it was simply lack of business. There can be little doubt that the outstanding success of the LNWR 'George the Fifth' Class had some

influence on the Great Central, and in 1913 J.G. Robinson introduced his well-known 'Director' Class 4-4-0, a superheated engine with 20 inch by 26 inch cylinders, and carrying a boiler pressure of 180 lb per square inch. These engines were soon doing good work on the fast trains between Marylebone, Leicester and Nottingham, and it is interesting to recall that their design and prowess caught the attention of the distinguished American technical journal *Railway Mechanical Engineer*, to such an extent that, in August 1916, they included a three-page article, with large-scale drawings, and a generally very enthusiastic write-up under the heading: 'An eight-wheel English locomotive'. The engines had 10 inch diameter piston valves driven by direct acting Stephenson's link motion, providing a maximum travel of 4⅛ inches.

This American article included the following observation in its introductory remarks: 'The advent of the superheater has perhaps been responsible as much as, if not more than anything else, for the retention of the 4-4-0 type locomotive in the front rank. The use of superheated steam in

Left *Midland Railway: one of R.M. Deeley's standard 3-cylinder compounds incorporating certain significant modifications from the Johnson type of 1902* (British Railways).

Below *Midland Railway: Deeley's non-compound competitor to the compound in 1908 was the '999' Class 4-4-0. It is seen here as originally built, non-superheated* (British Railways).

Above right *Great Western Railway: the Churchward standard principles— boiler, outside cylinders, link motion with long-lap and long-travel valves—applied to the 4-4-0 'County' Class the* County of Radnor (British Railways).

large cylinders and in conjunction with a boiler designed with ample heating surface and a sufficient capacity has resulted in largely increasing the scope of a locomotive planned on the 4-4-0 wheel arrangement and, although the type has receded in other countries, its position seems to be assured on British railways for some time to come where the principal main line passenger service is concerned'.

In the American article an instance was quoted of where a 'Director' Class engine hauled a train of 203 tons over the 103.1 miles from Leicester to Marylebone in 104 minutes start to stop, the actual schedule time being 110 minutes. In more recent times I have known equally fast time made with loads up to nearly 300 tons. Comparisons are not always strictly fair, but daily tasks set to 4-4-0 loco-movive just prior to the First World War may be quoted, thus:

Railway	LNWR	Midland	Great Central
Route	Euston-Crewe	St Pancras-Leicester	Marylebone-Leicester
Miles	158	99	103.1
Schedule time (minutes)	171	105	109
Average speed (mph)	55.5	56.4	56.6
Trailing load (tons)	400	230	200

The loads quoted in the first two cases are the scheduled maxima, for 4-4-0 engines, whereas in the Great Central case it is about the maximum then worked.

Another interesting case of a 4-4-0 revival was on the London and South Western Railway. Having, since 1905, built very large 4-cylinder 4-6-0 locomotives, with varying success, Dugald Drummond reverted to the 4-4-0 type in 1912 for what proved to be his last design. This was the large and handsome 'D15' Class, numbered 463 to 472. In accordance with previous practice these engines

were not superheated, but had Drummond's 'steam dryer' in the smokebox, and firebox water tubes. But they also had Walschaerts valve gear, an unusual provision on a British inside-cylinder engine. The 'D15' has been claimed as a 'masterly design'; but within three years of Drummond's tragic death, which occurred before the last of these engines had gone into traffic, his successor and former Works Manager, R.W. Urie, had taken out the steam dryers and cross-water tubes and put in his own version of the Schmidt superheater, which he called the 'Eastleigh'. The year being 1915 there was no question of paying any royalties to Germany! The 'D15' had been good engines from the start, but in their superheated form they were excellent, and put in many years of hard work. I rode on the footplate of one of them, on a Portsmouth-Bristol express as recently as 1950.

Before closing this chapter mention must be made of two distinctive Scottish designs. Having transferred from the Highland to the Glasgow and South Western, Peter Drummond continued to follow his brother's practice, and his big 4-4-0s of 1913, except in the matter of the coupled wheel diameter, included all the features of the LSWR 'D15' Class, with 19½ inch by 26 inch cylinders, steam dryer, feed water heater, and Walschaerts valve gear. Except for a brief trial, however, on a Highland 0-6-0, he did not use cross-water tubes in the firebox. The G & SW engines were intended for the hilly roads to the Clyde coast and had 6 foot instead of 6 foot 7 inch wheels. Drummond himself built a superheated version later, that was very successful and economical. The second design was that of Christopher Cumming, for the Farther North section of the Highland. This was a simple straight-forward outside-cylinder job with Walschaerts valve gear, 20 inch by 26 inch cylinders, and 6 foot 3 inch coupled wheels. The boiler pressure was originally specified at 160 lb per square inch but this was subsequently raised to 175. The two engines of this class, *Snaigow* and *Durn*, could very well put in a claim to be the handsomest ever of British 4-4-0s.

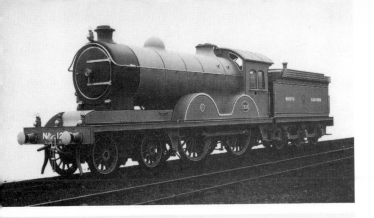

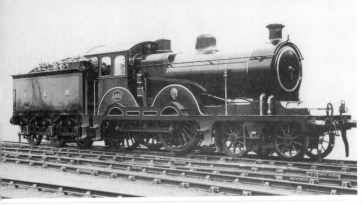

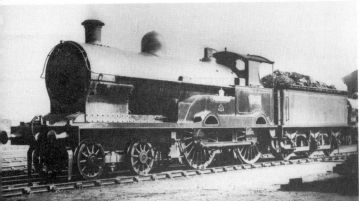

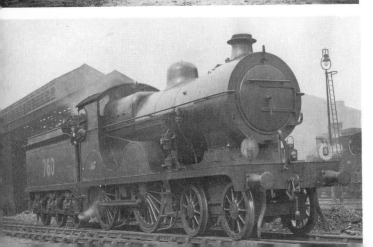

This page, top to bottom

North Eastern Railway: Wilson Worsdell's impressive 1908 development of his successful 'R' Class 4-4-0 was the 'R1' which carried a boiler pressure of 225 lb per square inch (British Railways).

Great Eastern Railway: a later member of James Holden's 'Claud Hamilton' Class, fitted with a Belpaire firebox (The Locomotive Publishing Company).

London and North Western Railway: the Coronation *engine of 1911, one of the brilliantly successful 'George the Fifth' Class of superheater 4-4-0s, built at Crewe from 1910 onwards* (the late W.J. Reynolds).

South Eastern and Chatham Railway: one of the 'L' Class 4-4-0s introduced in 1914, shortly after R.E.L. Maunsell had become Chief Mechanical Engineer (the late W.J. Reynolds).

Opposite page, top to bottom

Highland Railway: Peter Drummond's large boilered version of his 'Ben' Class No 60, Ben Bhreac Mhor (North British Locomotive Company).

Lancashire and Yorkshire Railway: one of the Aspinall 4-4-0s of 1891 as rebuilt with a superheater by G. Hughes in 1908 (British Railways).

Furness Railway: a 4-4-0 passenger engine by W.F. Pettigrew which was introduced in 1914 (North British Locomotive Company).

Midland Railway: an earlier 4-4-0 rebuilt with large non-superheated boiler and Belpaire firebox, conforming to Class '2' power classification (British Railways).

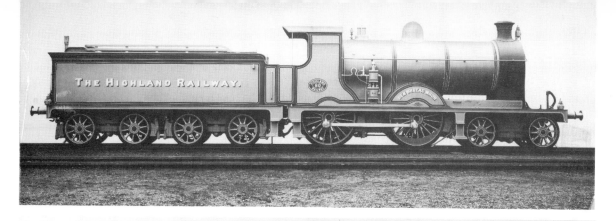

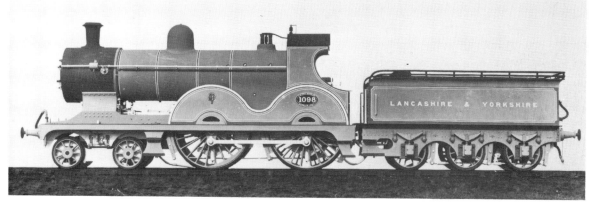

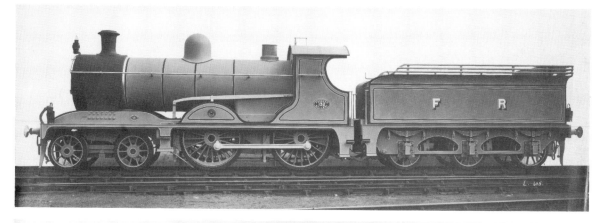

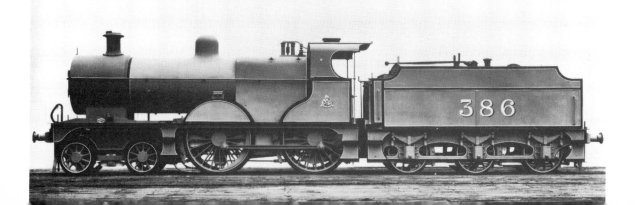

Opposite page, top to bottom

Midland Railway: a special example of the Class '2' superheated 4-4-0 by Henry Fowler which is decorated with a royal cipher on the cabside for a Royal Train assignment (British Railways).

Great Central Railway: one of the post-war examples of the 'Director' Class, here seen in LNER colours, No 5504, Jutland.

London and South Western Railway: one of the Drummond 'D 15' Class 4-4-0s (rebuilt and superheated by R.W. Urie) leaving Waterloo (P. Ransome Wallis).

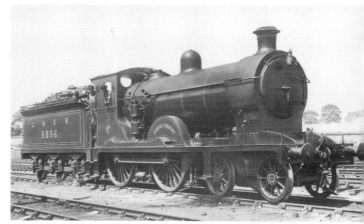

This page, top to bottom

Caledonian Railway: the final development of the 'Dunalastair' series of 4-4-0s, the superheated No 1V Class (British Railways).

North British Railway: the 'Scott' Class 4-4-0 by W.P. Reid, one of the first and non-superheated series of 1909, included the Dandie Dinmont, *here seen in LNER colours* (P. Ransome-Wallis).

North British Railway: the highly successful smaller wheeled version of the 'Scott' Class, used mainly on the West Highland line, and named after Glens. Here the Glen Dochart *at Fort William is seen heading an express for Glasgow.*

A very successful Brighton modernisation: the 'B4' of R.J. Billinton which was rebuilt and superheated to form Class 'B4X' in 1921. Here it is in Southern Railway colours (P. Ransome-Wallis).

4. The 0-6-0 tender engines

At the turn of the century, when there were some 20,000 locomotives in service in Great Britain, more than one third of this total was of the 0-6-0 tender type; and, although some of the railways carrying the heaviest traffic were already beginning to replace the older units with 0-8-0s and 2-8-0s, the vogue of the 0-6-0 as a general service goods and mixed traffic engine continued unabated. The London and North Western Railway, at the end of 1899, had a swarm of nearly 1,200 of them, in no more than three classes: the Special 'DX' (vacuum fitted), the 17 inch coal engine, and the celebrated 18 inch 'Cauliflowers'. Construction of the last named was still in full swing at Crewe and 140 of them were added to the stock in the first three years of the new century.

The Lancashire and Yorkshire had standardised on Aspinall's excellent design, with 18 inch by 26 inch cylinders and Joy valve gear, dating from 1889. There were eventually 484 of these engines, of which 60 were built between 1900 and 1909. The last 10, added to the stock of 1917-8, were built in unusual circumstances which will be related afterwards. On the Great Western, construction of the well-known 'Dean Goods', or '2301' Class, up to a total of 280 was completed; but although no further 0-6-0 tenders were built for the GWR until the Collett era, the '2301' Class was destined to play a remarkable part in British locomotive history in the 1950s.

The Midland, as befitted its rôle as a great mineral carrier, had about 1,000 engines of the 0-6-0 type, half of which were of the picturesque Kirtley double-framed type. Unlike the other great lines, however, the Midland continued to use nothing larger than 0-6-0s for the rest of its independent existence. The standard goods of 1900 was still S.W. Johnson's traditional design first introduced in 1878, of slender proportions, having 18 inch by 26 inch cylinders, 5 foot 2½ inch wheels, and at first a boiler carrying no more than 140 lb per square inch pressure. But in later batches this was gradually increased to 160, though the grate area remained at 17.5 square feet. Just at the very end of his career, when he had already introduced his 'Belpaire' 4-4-0s and the first 3-cylinder compounds he designed an enlarged boiler for the standard goods 0-6-0, of such proportions that it could be fitted, when necessary, not only to his earlier standard goods, but also to the Kirtley veterans. This boiler first appeared on a batch of new 0-6-0s built at Derby early in 1903, while Johnson was still in office.

In contemporary literature the boiler was described as similar to that of the Belpaire 4-4-0s, but with a round topped firebox. Actually it was a new design, having a grate area of 21.1 square feet and carrying a pressure of 175 lb per square inch. Rebuilding of the small boilered Johnson 0-6-0s began in 1904, and, before the end of the year, more than 100 of them had been so treated, while Derby Works was turning out new engines of the same design. The same boiler was also being used for rebuilding many of the Johnson 6 foot 6 inch 4-4-0s.

While this work was started after Deeley had

Above right *Midland Railway: the '4F' superheater 0-6-0 goods—later an LMS standard.*

Below *London and North Western Railway: one of the Webb '18 inch' express goods 0-6-0s (Cauliflowers), the first engines to have the Joy valve gear.*

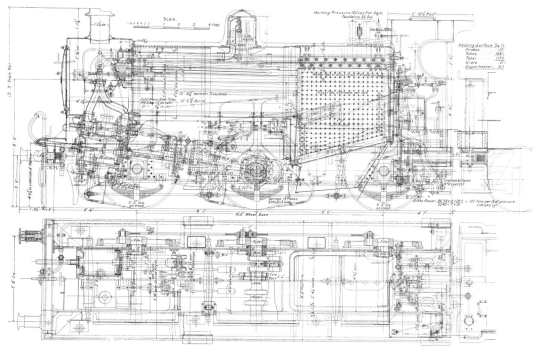

become Locomotive, Carriage and Wagon Superintendent, the design of these rebuilt 4-4-0s was due to Johnson, who in November 1903, not long before he retired, had used his enlarged 0-6-0 goods boiler on three 4-4-0 passenger engines built at Derby for the Somerset and Dorset Joint Railway. These were exactly the same as the Midland 6 foot 6 inch rebuilds, except that the coupled wheels were 6 foot diameter. There were eventually 482 of the Johnson-Deeley '18½ inch' 0-6-0s, later Midland Railway Class 3. At this point it may be mentioned

that, all through the year 1900, delivery was continuing to be taken from contractors of new 0-6-0s of the small boilered Johnson type though, of course, by that time some of the earliest engines of the class were then more than 20 years old.

The year 1900 was notable for the introduction of a number of interesting new designs of 0-6-0, outline details of which are tabulated below for ready reference.

In the last years of the 19th century the North Eastern had two relatively modern classes of 0-6-0

0-6-0 Tender engines of 1900

Railway	North Eastern	Highland	SE & CR	Hull & Barnsley	Great Eastern
Locomotive superintendent	W. Worsdell	P. Drummond	Wainwright	M. Stirling	J. Holden
Coupled wheel diameter (feet/inches)	4 6	5 0	5 2	5 0	4 11
Cylinders Diameter (inches)	18¼	18¼	18½	18	19
Stroke (inches)	26	26	26	26	26
Boiler pressure (lb per square inch)	175	175	160	170	180

goods engine. The first, dating from 1886 had 5 foot wheels, and was a long-lived and highly successful design of general service character; the second was built more particularly for the short-haul heavy mineral runs conveying coal from the Northumberland pits to the North Sea ports, where the colliers were loaded by tipplers from the high galleries, or staithes. The details tabulated relate to an enlarged version of the original Class 'P' of 1894, but still having wheels of only 4 foot 6 inch diameter. These engines, Class 'P1', were the predecessors of the much larger 'P2' and 'P3' Classes, of 1904 and 1906, having the same size of cylinders and motion, but with a huge boiler no less than 5 feet 6 inches in diameter. Construction of Class 'P3' continued down to the year 1923. It is certainly appropriate that one of these hard-slogging unobtrusive work-horses should be preserved and occasionally released from her show-place in the National Railway Museum at York, for some running on the North Yorkshire Moors preserved railway.

The Highland 0-6-0s, of the class affectionately known as the Barney, were almost identical to the contemporary design of elder brother Dugald, on the London and South Western Railway, except that Peter, in purchasing his engines from Dübs & Co, in Glasgow, included one of the family specialities that his brother did not apply to a goods engine, namely an 8-wheeled bogie tender, with inside bearings, as used on the 'Castle' Class 4-6-0 engines. A second batch of four of the engines, built by Dübs & Co, in 1902, had cross-water tubes in the firebox, again a feature that Dugald Drummond himself did not use on goods engines. In later years, when the characteristic lock-up safety valves on the dome had been replaced by valves in the more usual place over the firebox, the 'Barneys' became almost indistinguishable from the '709' Class 0-6-0s of the Caledonian, when both were in LMS black. The latter were built at St Rollox in 1895-7 to a total number of 83. On the 'Barneys' the wheel spacing from driving to trailing was 9 feet, against 8 feet 9 inches on the Caledonians, in order to accommodate a larger firebox with a grate area of 20.37 square feet; but in LMS days, when new boilers were needed the Caledonian '709' type was fitted to the former Highland engines. This latter boiler had a grate area of 19.5 square feet.

The Wainwright 'C' Class 0-6-0 was one of the first locomotive designs prepared after the formation of the Managing Committee for the South Eastern and the Chatham railways, and was a neat and simple machine, strong and reliable in service, and, until war conditions from 1914 onwards made it inappropriate, most gorgeously

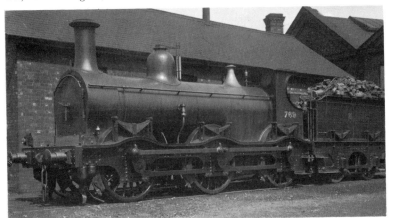

Left *One of the picturesque double-framed Kirtley 0-6-0s of the Midland which were regularly used on the coal trains until the 1920s* (The Locomotive Publishing Company).

Below *The standard Midland 0-6-0 goods engine of the late 1890s, by S. W. Johnson: an example built in 1902 for the Somerset & Dorset Joint Railway* (British Railways).

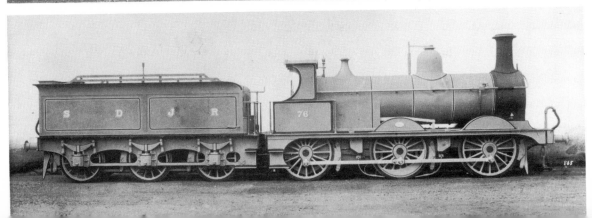

SECTION ON AA

SECTION ON BB.

SECTION ON CC.

SECTION ON DD

SECTION ON E E

SECTION ON F F

Great Western Railway: the standard cylinder arrangement for engines having two inside cylinders, 18 inches by 26 inches ('Bulldogs, 'Aberdare' goods).

having boilers with the largest diameter of barrel that had yet been seen in Great Britain, namely 4 feet 10¾ inches, though this, of course, was soon to be exceeded. Matthew Stirling's appointment, dating from 1885 when he was no more than 29 years of age, followed training on the Great Northern, under his father, Patrick, and then of various divisional duties on that railway. Throughout his long tenure of office at Hull he was very faithful to the precepts of his father and of his uncle in never building an engine with a domed boiler; and for some time he maintained the family tradition in his use of the cut-away roof of the cab. Although the basic colour of all his engines was 'invisible green', which looked black, the lining out was colourful, consisting of a bright blue band edged with red on both sides. In other respects the new Hull and Barnsley 0-6-0, which was an enlargement of Mr Stirling's first design of 1889, was traditional in its machinery.

The Great Eastern certainly steamed into the new century with a flourish. Following the production of the splendid 'Claud Hamilton' Class of express passenger 4-4-0s, the first of which took the road in March, there came a batch of 10 massive 0-6-0 goods engines of comparable proportions. Although the Great Eastern itself serves a region that was then almost entirely agricultural in its produce, there was

arrayed in the full passenger style, with a profusion of polished brass and copper work. The lining out on the tender, cab and boiler bands also was most elaborate, with a green of a lighter shade than the rich basic colour of the engine itself edged at one side with red and on the other yellow. A welcome feature of James Stirling's practice was retained in his excellent steam reverser. The steam and cataract cylinders of this were mounted vertically on the running plate, and might at first glance be mistaken for a Westinghouse donkey pump. Unlike some other apparatus I could name the Stirling steam reverser was simplicity itself to operate, as I found many years later when driving an ex-SE & CR 4-4-0 locomotive.

From this appreciative mention of James Stirling, who by 1900 was living in retirement, it is fitting to pass on to the work of his nephew, Matthew, who was then locomotive superintendent of the Hull and Barnsley Railway. His new 0-6-0 goods engines of 1900, built by Kitsons, of Leeds, were notable in

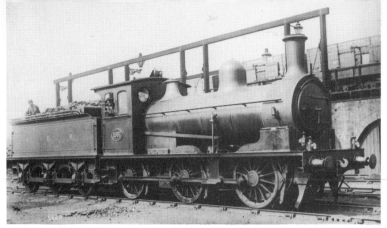

also a heavy coal traffic received off the Great Northern, both at Peterborough and down the Lincolnshire Joint Line. There was ample justification for larger and more powerful freight locomotives; at the time of their construction, indeed, they were the largest 0-6-0s in the country. The boiler, cylinders and motion were the same as those of the 'Claud Hamilton' 4-4-0s and, as in the case of the passenger engines, construction of them on a production-line basis began at once.

By the end of 1903 there were 60 of them in traffic, numbered from 1150 to 1209. One of them, however, was an odd engine, No 1189, and a very important one at that, because it was Stratford's first trial of a Belpaire firebox. But although it was at first fitted to only one 0-6-0, James Holden seemed fairly sure of it because, in the autumn of 1902, he began rebuilding his own very handsome 7 foot 2-4-0 express engines with much larger boilers which, apart from a shorter barrel, were the same as that fitted to the 0-6-0 goods engine No 1189. It must have been the largest diameter boiler ever fitted to a 2-4-0 engine, and gave such a massive appearance that the 21 engines so treated were nicknamed the 'Humpty Dumptys'.

Building of the Belpaire 0-6-0s began in 1905. These powerful engines were needed primarily for the coal trains but there was a multiplicity of goods train duties all over East Anglia; and although the Great Eastern had a fleet of more than 200 of the smaller Holden 0-6-0s, developed from Worsdell's design, and having 17¼ inch by 24 inch cylinders, the traffic people wanted still more, and in 1906 building of these smaller 0-6-0s began again. The last batch, numbered from 562 to 571, was turned out in 1912, and it is the first of these that has been preserved, and is working on the North Norfolk Railway between Sheringham and Weybourne. It was in 1912 also that the first of the Belpaire '1150' Class to be superheated was put into traffic. While reference to these is stepping a little out of chronological order, the details of the four varieties of 0-6-0 may conveniently be tabulated at this stage.

GER 0-6-0 goods: 1900-1912, all 4 foot 11 inch diameter wheels

Date	1900	1902*	1906	1912
Cylinders				
Diameter (inches)	19	19	17½	20
Stroke (inches)	26	26	24	28
Heating surfaces				
Tubes (square feet)	1,516.5	1,588.9	1,098.6	874.7
Firebox (square feet)	114	117.7	100.9	117.7
Superheater (square feet)	—	—	—	226
Grate area (square feet)	21.3	21.6	18.0	21.6
Boiler pressure (lb per square inch)	180	180	180	160

*Engine 1189 only in this year. Further 'Belpaires' in 1905.

A class of 0-6-0 introduced in 1901 as a run-of-the-mill goods engine, and soon completely eclipsed in popular acclaim by the larger and more spectacular types that followed it, was the 973-1012 series built by Neilson, Reid & Co for the Great Central. These engines were multiplied exceedingly beyond the original 40 built in 1901, until there were 174 in service by 1907, doing a great amount of hard, unobtrusive work on the line. Like most of J.G. Robinson's engines they were massively built, and had an excellent record from the maintenance viewpoint. All were still in service in the middle of the Second World War when Edward Thompson succeeded Sir Nigel Gresley as Chief Mechanical Engineer at the LNER. It was then that Class 'J11', as they were then designated, was, to most people's surprise, chosen as a future LNER standard, and designs were worked out for modernising them by fitting superheaters and piston valves, with long travel. Although this process began as early as 1942, only 30 of them had been so treated by 1951. Nevertheless all the remaining 144 of the original

class were at that time still in service. More of that, however, in a later chapter.

As originally built they could have been easily passed over as 'just another 0-6-0', of the conventional British design; but in view of the way they stayed the course, and of their selection for standardisation 41 years after their first introduction, they are worthy of more detailed notice. Quite apart from that, in the smart goods engine livery of black, picked out with red panel bands and white lines, and the graceful outline characteristic of all J.G. Robinson's engines, they were particularly pleasing to the eye. The basic dimensions were quite conventional, with cylinders 18½ inches diameter by 26 inches stroke, wheels 5 feet 1 inch diameter and a boiler pressure of 180 lb per square inch. The boiler was large, with a barrel 5 foot diameter, and the Belpaire firebox had a grate area of 19½ square feet. The total heating surface of 1,424 square feet was also large for that period. These excellent engines gained the nickname of 'Pompoms', why, I have never been able to find out. There may have been a story behind the name similar to that which led to Robinson's beautiful 'Atlantic' engines being known as the 'Jersey Lillies'.

Before passing on to the main line of development, four designs of what can be called the conventional type, but for the lesser railways, deserve mention, all dating from the 1907-1910 period. All were admirable examples of construction, and beautifully and colourfully finished in the passenger liveries of their respective companies (see table below).

I should add that the engines (below) of the Furness Railway were classed as 'mixed traffic' and in my own experience did a good deal of work on stopping passenger trains. Mr Pettigrew had a class with similar proportions but with 4 foot 8 inch wheels for the heavy mineral traffic. These dated from 1898.

An interesting development in freight train

motive power began on the Great Northern Railway in 1908. Certainly there had been several earlier instances of 0-6-0 tender engines designated 'express goods', notably the celebrated Webb '18 inch' Class on the London and North Western; but never previously had a wheel diameter so large as 5 feet 8 inches been used on a 0-6-0. This was symptomatic of the growing awareness of the need to speed up the more important through goods services. The railways of Britain had not yet begun to feel the effects of long-distance road haulage which, at that time, had scarcely got off the ground; but the Great Northern was in the forefront of the freight acceleration movement. Apart from the size of their coupled wheels the new engines were of conventional design, having wheels, cylinders and motion interchangeable with Mr Ivatt's 0-6-2 suburban tank engines: 18 inch by 26 inch cylinders, with slide valves actuated by Stephenson link motion. The boiler had an outside diameter of 4 feet 8 inches and with the firebox provided a total heating surface of 1,250 square feet. The grate area was 19 square feet.

On the Great Northern these express goods engines were Class 'J21', though this may have led to some confusion later, when the all-line classification for LNER locomotives was established and they

0-6-0s of secondary railways

Railway	Cambrian	Furness	Maryport & Carlisle	North Staffordshire
Wheel diameter (feet/inches)	5 1 ½	5 1	5 1 ½	5 0
Cylinders Diameter (inches)	18	18	18	18 ½
Stroke (inches)	26	26	26	26
Total heating surface (square feet)	1,283	1,134	1,139.5	1,120
Boiler pressure (lb per square inch)	170	160	150	175

Highland Railway: one of Peter Drummond's 0-6-0 goods engines, built in 1902, originally with cross-watertubes, here seen attached to one of the large snow ploughs at Blair Atholl.

became 'J1'. In pre-grouping days they were more familiarly known as the 'No 1 Class'. The first batch turned out in 1908 were numbered 1 to 9. Numbers 1 to 8 had previously been borne by Stirling single wheelers—4 and 6 by 7 foot 2-2-2s and the others by the famous 8 foot 4-2-2s. The pioneer engine of this latter class, the very celebrated 'No 1', had been withdrawn from ordinary traffic in September 1907 and set aside for preservation. Of the new 'No 1' Class there were 15 in all. These latter were followed in 1909-1910 by GNR—Class 'J22', the same as 'J21' except that they had 5 foot 2 inch, instead of 5 foot 8 inch wheels. Because of the smaller wheels they did not need to have the running plate raised to clear the coupling rods, and looked neater in consequence. There were 20 of the 5 foot 2 inch series, numbered 21 to 40. After grouping they became LNER Class 'J5'.

At the opposite end of the East Coast main line a new design of 0-6-0 had been introduced on the North British Railway in 1906 by W.P. Reid, who had been appointed Locomotive Superintendent after the death of Matthew Holmes in 1903. One of the major tasks for freight engines on the North British was the haulage of locomotive coal to Aberdeen from the Fife coalfields, and the sharp gradients of the main line north of Arbroath demanded a powerful locomotive. Except for use of a higher boiler pressure of 180 instead of 160 lb per square inch the new engines bore a remarkable

resemblance to the McIntosh '812' Class of the Caledonian introduced in 1899, both having 18½ inch by 26 inch cylinders and 5 foot wheels. The comparative boiler proportions were thus:

Scottish 0-6-0 boilers

Railway	Caledonian	North British
Heating surfaces (square feet)		
Tubes	1,284.45	1,462
Firebox	118.78	143
Grate area (square feet)	20.63	19.8
Working pressure (lb per square inch)	160	180

The Caledonian built a further series of these engines in 1908-9, bringing the total up to 96. Of these 17 were fitted with the Westinghouse brake for use on Clyde coast passenger trains, and painted blue; but the remainder were finished in 'Goods black'. All the North British 0-6-0s of 1906 were fitted with the Westinghouse brake, so making them available for passenger service when needed.

Turning now to the vital matter of superheating, which dominated the second decade of the 20th century, prominence must first be given to George Hughes, Chief Mechanical Engineer of the Lancashire and Yorkshire Railway who, at the end of 1906, built two more of the already numerous Aspinall standard 0-6-0 goods engines with Schmidt superheaters and piston valves. The accompanying cross-sectional drawing shows the general arrangement of these notable locomotives, from which it will be seen that the Joy valve gear was used. The following table shows the differences at the front end between the superheater and non-superheater members of this class:

L & YR 0-6-0 goods locomotives

	Non-super-heater	Super-heater
Diameter of cylinders (inches)	18	20
Stroke of piston (inches)	26	26
Length of ports (inches)	12½	19¼
Width of steamports (inches)	$1\frac{5}{8}$	1¼
Width of exhaust ports (inches)	3½	3
Area of steam port passages (square inches)	21.0	21.0
Area of steam ports (square inches)	19.7	23.9
Area of exhaust ports (square inches)	43.9	67.5
Lap of valve (inches)	1	$1\frac{3}{16}$
Lead of valve (inches)	$\frac{3}{16}$	$\frac{3}{16}$
Travel of valve (inches)	5	4¼

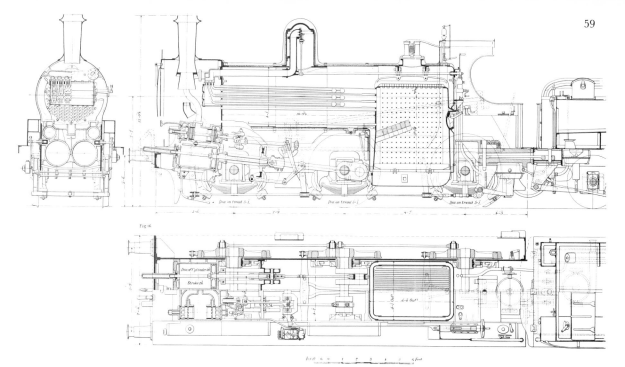

Fig 16

Lancashire and Yorkshire Railway: 6-wheeled fast goods engine with Schmidt superheater and Joy valve gear.

The two superheater engines were put into service in the ordinary links, and at the end of 10 months working it was reported that these engines could haul loads 10 per cent heavier than the non-superheater engines; and, as these results were confirmed by a further six months of running, authority was given for a further 20 superheater goods engines to be built. These were turned out from Horwich Works between April and November 1909, all at first retaining the round-topped type of firebox as on the original Aspinal design. A final batch built at Horwich in 1912 had Belpaire fireboxes. These superheater 0-6-0s, which carried the same boiler pressure as their non-superheated predecessors, 180 lb per square inch, showed not only enhanced haulage capacity but an economy in coal consumption of about 12½ per cent. It was not to be expected, perhaps, that an ordinary goods engine would show such a spectacular improvement as that of a top-link express passenger unit, as in the case of the 'George the Fifth' Class 4-4-0s of the LNWR instanced in the preceding chapter of this book. From the foregoing table it will be seen that although the maximum travel of the valves was *reduced* in the superheater LYR goods engines, the area of the ports, and particularly those of the exhaust, were notably increased.

At seasonal holiday periods, such as 'wakes weeks', every LYR engine that could turn a wheel was pressed into excursion passenger traffic, and it was then found that the superheater 0-6-0s had a good turn of speed, although having wheels no larger than 5 foot 1 inch diameter. But it was not only on occasional duties that these engines showed their speed. In August 1931 I was travelling from Manchester to Carlisle, and for a change elected to go via the Midland route, by the through express leaving Manchester Victoria for Glasgow St Enoch, at 9.20 am. The train was not unduly heavy, about 280 tons, but I was pleased to find that our engine was one of the big 4-cylinder 4-6-4 tanks of Hughes' design. We did not do anything very special over the heavily graded section between Bolton and Darwen and at Blackburn, to my surprise, the 4-6-4 came off, and was replaced by a superheater 0-6-0, one of the Belpaire batch built in 1912. She began rather laboriously, not accelerating to more than 30 mph up the 1 in 127-152 gradient to Wilpshire; but, once having topped the summit, she went tearing down the bank to Whalley in tremendous style, reaching 65 mph before easing to 53 mph over the viaduct at the foot of the bank. After the stop at Clitheroe it is hard climbing for most of the way to Hellifield, and we did well to pass Newisholme, 9.0 miles from the restart in 15¼ minutes before a signal delayed finish to the L & Y part of the journey.

Having arrived in Midland territory it is natural

Left *One of the very similar Caledonian 0-6-0s; here engaged on express passenger work piloting one of the 'Clan' 4-6-0s on the Callander and Oban line at Balquidder in 1937 (see page 58).*
Below left *Great Central Railway: one of the handsome Robinson 0-6-0s (nicknamed 'Poms-Poms' in LNER days) in heavy freight service.*
Below right *Great Eastern Railway: the ultimate development of the Stratford 0-6-0 family, the big superheated freight engine using the same boiler as the 4-6-0 express locomotives (British Railways).*
Bottom right *Furness Railway: a heavy mineral 0-6-0 of the 4 foot 8 inch class, introduced by W.F. Pettigrew in 1914 (North British Locomotive Company).*

Nottingham and Melton Mowbray, instead of the shorter route via Leicester.

The tests in question, made in 1913, were not exactly fair, as the competing non-superheater engine was a Deeley Class '3'. Conditions were to some extent balanced, because the superheater Class '4', No 3835 had a boiler pressure of only 160 lb per square inch, against 175. Both engines took trailing loads of around 615 tons southbound, returning northbound on the following day with 495 tons. Six return trips were made with each engine, and the coal consumption per ton mile showed, as would be expected, a marked advantage in favour of the superheater engine thus:

Engine no	**3815**	**3835**
Class	3 (non-superheated)	4 (superheated)
Gross weight* (tons)		
Southbound	712	700.7
Northbound	573.6	573.1
Coal per ton mile (lb)		
Southbound	0.0785	0.0673
Northbound	0.1234	0.1012

*Including engine and tender: 86.3 tons for No 3815 and 88.1 tons for No 3835.

Despite these favourable results the Midland Railway was in no hurry to build superheater goods engines. It is true that the Class '4F', as originally built and having a tractive effort of only 22,400 lb against 21,000 lb for the non-superheated Class '3', could have made little impression on the mineral train working as a whole. It was remarkable that the Midland Railway, one of the richest of all the British companies and carrying an enormous goods traffic, should have been content to work it with a swarm of undersized 0-6-0 engines, always double-headed; and as the war situation developed the pilots on the Toton-Brent coal trains were often Class '2' passenger 4-4-0s. Not infrequently one saw two 4-4-0s struggling with an enormous coal train!

to pass on to what, to readers of a later generation, are perhaps the best known of all British superheater 0-6-0s, the Fowler '4F', of which the first example, No 3835, was completed at Derby in 1911. This eventually very numerous class had a peculiarly undistinguished start. Although it had the publicity of a fully detailed cross-sectional and plan drawing in *The Engineer* in December 1911, only two engines were at first built, one with the Schmidt, and one with the Swindon superheater, and Fowler himself seemed quite lukewarm as to the advantages to be derived. In a paper presented to the Institution of Civil Engineers early in 1914 he said: 'The employment of superheated steam in goods engines is not so general as it is in passenger engines, either in this country or elsewhere, although in the United States a number of yard shunting engines have been fitted, it is said, with satisfactory results. On the Midland Railway little has been done towards superheating goods locomotives, but a couple of engines for coal traffic have been so fitted. This traffic is usually a one-direction one, and tests have been carried out between Toton and Brent sidings, which lie 126¾ miles apart by the route taken'. This latter was via

When it was found that the Tilbury 4-6-4 tanks could not be used for the duties they were designed for they were transferred to Wellingborough to help with the coal traffic, though their limited fuel capacity was a constant handicap. No doubt Midland managerial policy precluded the designing of larger engines; for although Fowler himself was away for much of the war period, on duties at the Ministry of Munitions that gained for him a KBE, he had a very able assistant in his chief draughtsman at Derby, S.J. Symes. In the event, multiplication of the '4F' 0-6-0 did not begin until 1917.

Three interesting Scottish designs must next be noticed. The Caledonian '30' Class, of no more than four engines, built in 1912, were used as mixed traffic engines on the Clyde coast passenger service, where the heavy gradients of the Wemyss Bay line needed some augmentation of power. They had superheater boilers similar to, though rather smaller than, the 'Dunalastair IV' Class 4-4-0s, and in consideration of their use on passenger trains they were painted in the delightful blue livery. Their stay on the Clyde Coast trains was not very long, however, because they were displaced by the Pickersgill 4-6-2 tanks that were introduced in 1917. Their Glasgow and South Western contemporaries, designed by Peter Drummond, and built by the North British Locomotive Company in 1913, were

the heaviest engines ever put on six wheels in this country, or anywhere else in all probability. Whereas the Midland '4F' weighed 48¾ tons, the G & SW '300' Class turned the scale at 57¾ tons, and they had attached to them an enormous tender, weighing another 47 tons. The 15 engines of this class were designed for the main line goods trains down to Carlisle, on which they were rostered to take 50 loaded wagons without assistance; with such massive proportions they should have done it easily enough, but at that stage Peter Drummond was experimenting with superheating, and these engines got his late brother's steam dryer. There must also have been something wrong with the valve setting because, although they had 10 inch diameter piston valves, they were sluggish and burned a quite inordinate amount of coal. Another trouble came from the introduction for the first time on the G & SWR of the marine type of big-end, and there were frequent cases of overheating. There were some dour struggles with these engines on the Carlisle road, highlighted all the more vividly when their superheated successors of the 2-6-0 type took over, and were as easy and economical as the 0-6-0s were a sore trial.

The third Scottish class was the superheated version of W.P. Reid's excellent Class 'B' on the North British introduced in 1906, and referred to

earlier in this chapter. By the year 1913 a total of 76 had been built, and in the following year the Class 'S' superheater development came. These two classes subsequently became LNER 'J35' and 'J37'. The superheater 0-6-0s were splendid engines not only doing a vast amount of heavy goods and mineral work on the East Coast main line, but also working very successfully on intermediate passenger duties, notably on the West Highland line. When I first visited that area in 1932 the entire service on the Mallaig Extension, passenger and freight alike, was being run by the 'J37s'. These three Scottish 0-6-0 classes provide a classic case of where basic dimensions give no clue as to the effectiveness of the engines in service; but for the record I have tabulated them below.

The last group of designs requiring special mention in this chapter are the superheated developments of both H.A. Ivatt and Gresley on the Great Northern. Reference has already been made to the 'No 1' Class, and its 5 foot 2 inch equivalent, and a superheated development of the latter was built at Doncaster in 1911. It took the road just after Mr Ivatt's retirement, and had larger cylinders, and a lower working pressure of 160 lb per square inch. They were followed in 1912 by the superheated version of the No 1 Class. But as on the Caledonian and on the Glasgow and South Western these latter big 0-6-0s were but a stepping stone to the adoption of the 2-6-0 type for mixed traffic. So, while the superheated 5 foot 2 inch 0-6-0s (later LNER Class 'J6') were multiplied up to an eventual total of 110, only 10 of the 5 foot 8 inch superheated 0-6-0s were built; and before that same year of 1912 Gresley had brought out the first of his 2-6-0s. The superheater 0-6-0s of both the 5 foot 2 inch and 5 foot 8 inch

classes had 19 inch by 26 inch cylinders and a pressure of 160 lb per square inch. The boilers were the same in both classes. The dimensions of the superheated and non-superheated varieties were:

Great Northern 0-6-0 boilers, 1908-12

	Non-superheated	Superheated
Barrel diameter (feet/inches)	4 8	4 8
Heating surface (square feet)		
Tubes	1,130	852
Firebox	120	120
Superheater	—	258
Total	1,250	1,230
Grate area (square feet)	19	19
Boiler pressure (lb per square inch)	170	160

In 1899 the last engines of the celebrated '2301', or 'Dean Goods' type of 0-6-0 were completed at Swindon bringing the total for the class up to 280. Apart from 20 of them that were converted into 2-6-2 tanks in 1907-10, few of them had been withdrawn by the time of the Grouping in 1923, and an important process of modernisation was applied during Collett's time at Swindon: so much so, that rebuilt, and mostly fitted with superheaters, there were still 179 in service in April 1939. In this, their rejuvenated form, they came to play an important part in British locomotive development, belonging to the second and third periods of its history, to be told later in this work.

Scottish 0-6-0s of 1912-1914

Railway	Caledonian	G & SWR	North British
Designer	J.F. McIntosh	P. Drummond	W.P. Reid
Wheel diameter (feet/inches)	5 0	5 0	5 0
Cylinders			
Diameter (inches)	19½	19½	19½
Stroke (inches)	26	26	26
Total heating surface (feet/inches)	1,457	1,784*	1,419.72
Boiler pressure (lb per square inch)	160	180	180†
Weight engine only (tons)	51.1	57.8	54.7
Weight tender (tons)	37.8	47.3	41.0
Number built	4	15	104

*Not superheated.   †When first built 165 lb per square inch.

North British Railway: W.P. Reid's superheater 0-6-0 of 1914 hauling a north-bound goods train near Stonehaven.

North British line: an unusual duty for a Reid 0-6-0 in 1925, hauling two newly completed 'King Arthur' Class 4-6-0s from the North British Locomotive Company's works en route for the Southern Railway (P. Ransome-Wallis).

Lancashire and Yorkshire Railway: the development of the Aspinall standard 0-6-0, Engine No 662, one of the original design, built at Horwich 1898 (Real Photographs).

LYR No 1, originally built in 1896, but here shown as rebuilt in 1911 with a Belpaire firebox and Schmidt superheater and ready to work a return excursion train from Blackpool (the late J.M. Tomlinson).

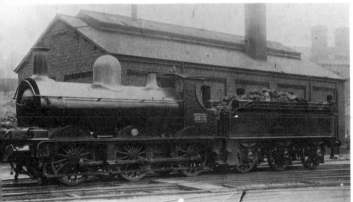

This page, top to bottom

Midland Railway: one of the Class '3' 0-6-0s on a typical duty on a loaded coal train near Shireoaks West Junction (P. Ransome-Wallis).

Great Western Railway: the celebrated 'Dean Goods' 0-6-0, as running in 1900, with polished brass dome and safety valve cover (British Railway).

Many years later, one of the reboilered examples of the same class ran a single empty coach train on the Lambourne branch. It is seen here near Newbury (M.W. Earley).

Opposite page, top to bottom

Glasgow and South Western Railway: one of the massive 0-6-0s introduced by Peter Drummond in 1913, the heaviest engines ever put on to six wheels, weighing 57¾ tons (North British Locomotive Company).

An ex-LSWR Drummond 0-6-0 as fitted with Maunsell superheater in 1926 (the late W.J. Reynolds).

GNR/LNER: One of the Ivatt 'No 1' Class express goods 0-6-0s—No 3004 in LNER colours.

GNR/LNER: one of the Gresley superheater express goods 0-6-0s in LNER colours.

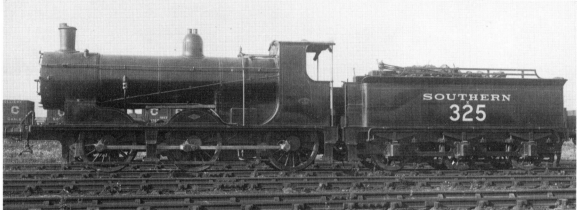

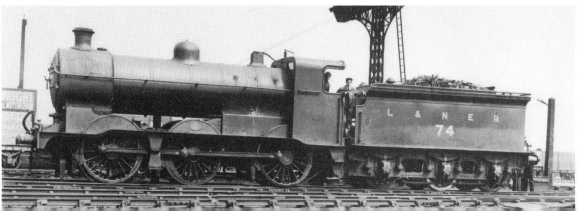

5. Tank engines: 8-wheeled or less

The above heading covers locomotives engaged in an immense variety of work, from high-stepping passenger runs into what could be called the 'stock-broker belts' of large cities, to the remorseless grind of heavy mineral hauls in the Welsh mining valleys. So, in discussing some of the more interesting designs of the period I have thought it best to group the engines by duties rather than wheel arrangements, for by so doing the merits of a great variety of classes can be laid alongside on a better comparable basis. First then can be taken the engines of the humble commuter trains: nothing very glamorous from the stop-watcher's viewpoint, but vital enough in carrying what used to be called the 'breadwinners' on their daily journeys to and from work. In London the companies most heavily engaged were the Brighton, the South Eastern and Chatham, and the Great Eastern, with the London and South Western poised half way between these three and those with a commuter business more of a longer distance residential nature like the Great Western, North Western and the Midland. One must certainly include the North London among the more intensive lines, but its activities were on a smaller scale than those of the Brighton or the Great Eastern.

At the turn of the century all three of the Southern lines were fairly well furnished with motive power for commuter trains. All were looking towards electrification, and no very significant additions were made in the ensuing 20 years. Both the Chatham and the South Eastern constituents of the SE & CR had excellent 0-4-4 tanks from the designs of Kirtley and James Stirling, and in the days of the Managing Committee H.S. Wainwright added 66, built to the design of Robert Surtees, his chief draughtsman. They were very similar to his Chatham engines, but larger and more powerful. The four varieties of 0-4-4 tank are shown below.

The Wainwright engines of 1904 were very similar in outward appearance to the Kirtley's, while the Stirling engines originally with domeless boilers were subsequently rebuilt to look, at a casual glance, almost identical to the Wainwrights. On the Brighton the only new passenger tank engine design for suburban, or inner residential, working was the 5 foot 6 inch Billinton 'radial' 0-6-2 tank, dating from 1902, and taking the road in the 'yellow' era. The first engine was No 567 *Freshwater*. These engines were used on the longer distance residential trains. They were handsomely proportioned, like all the Brighton engines and, needless to say, immaculately finished.

On the London and South Western, in 1897, Dugald Drummond had put the first of his notable 'M7' Class of 0-4-4 tank engines into service, and construction of this standard type continued until 1911, by which time there were 105 in service. These engines were a development of the Adams 'T1' Class of 1888-96, and had 5 foot 7 inch coupled wheels and cylinders 18½ inches by 26 inches. They were very fast and free-running engines, and when my family lived at Hurst, in 1914, I used to see them tearing through on the Reading to Waterloo semi-fasts in gallant style. I must also inject two other memories of them. When I was doing a good deal of footplate work from Stewarts Lane, Battersea, in the early 1950s the empty stock trains into and out of Victoria (Eastern) were worked by 0-4-4 tank engines, and I was interested to learn that the local men preferred the ex-SE & CR Wainwright 'H' Class to an 'M7', always averring that the former had got more 'guts'. But of footplate work I shall never forget a ride I had on No 670, light engine, from Barnstaple to Ilfracombe one Sunday morning in 1945. We skated along beside the Taw estuary rounding curve after curve at a merry 55 mph. She rode superbly, and as we 'floated' round those curves without a suspicion of a jolt or the merest beginnings of a roll, I could not help recalling William Stroudley's notable exposition of his idea in giving the famous 'Gladstone' 0-4-2s of the

LC & D, SER, and SE & CR 0-4-4 tanks

Railway	LC & D	LC & D	SER	SE & CR
Date	1875	1891	1888	1904
Designer	Kirtley	Kirtley	Stirling	Wainwright
Coupled wheel diameter (feet/inches)	5 3	5 6	5 6	5 6
Cylinders	17½ × 26	17 × 24	18 × 26	18 × 26
Boiler pressure	150	150	140	160
Number in class	36	33	118	66

Brighton large front-coupled driving wheels. Old 670 was 48 years old when I made that trip!

In London some 80 years ago there was a piece of child-like doggerel that ran:

'In 1900 we'd enough
Of smoky trains that went puff puff.
Now we have perfection found,
The bright electric Underground'.

Even then the advocates of electrification were many and vociferous, clearly having no conception of the implications of the capital investment required. It must be admitted that there was plenty of smoke around the big London stations, and I am old enough to remember the terrible fogs we sometimes had to endure, in the 1920s, in winter when the weather was calm. One of the points claimed for electric traction was that a train of 300 tons trailing load could be accelerated to 30 mph in 30 seconds from a dead start. No existing British suburban tank engine could approach that, on a level track. On the Great Eastern, however, they had at Stratford Works a chief draughtsman of highly imaginative and dynamic personality, in F.V. Russell—he who had prepared the detailed design of the splendid 'Claud Hamilton' Class 4-4-0s; and he, with the approbation of the distinguished Locomotive Superintendent, James Holden, worked out the design of a tank engine that would satisfy the 30 mph—30 seconds norm. Construction of one such engine, for trial purposes, was authorised, and so in December 1902 there emerged from Stratford Works the sensation of the day, the 'Decapod'.

As the name suggests it had 10 coupled wheels of 4 foot 6 inch diameter, with three cylinders 18½ inches by 24 inches stroke, and with a boiler pressure of 200 lb per square inch the tractive effort, at 85 per cent, working pressure, was no less than 43,000 lb. To make such a figure realistic an enormous boiler was designed, with an exceptionally wide firebox, having a grate area of 42 square feet. The general proportions of the boiler can be studied from the accompanying drawing. The total weight of the engine in working order was 80 tons. It might, of course, seem that reference to this remarkable machine is out of place in a chapter dealing with tank engines of no more than eight wheels; but the construction of the 'Decapod' was so closely entwined in the inner-suburban traffic problem of the Great Eastern, and the method of its ultimate solution by F.V. Russell, as to make its inclusion here germane enough. A section of the up fast line near Chadwell Heath was equipped with special electrical recording gear and a number of tests were carried out in March and April 1903, not only with the 'Decapod', but also with various standard Great Eastern locomotives for comparative purposes. Mr Holden gave some interesting details of the results obtained in a discussion on 'Large Locomotive Boilers', at the Institution of Mechanical Engineers in March 1906, following a paper by G.J. Churchward.

Mr Holden said: 'In all cases engines started from rest and pulled a load in addition to themselves of about 250 tons, and were worked with regulator full open and in full forward gear'. The results obtained are tabulated overleaf.

On another occasion it was reported that the 'Decapod' attained a speed of 28.7 mph in 30 seconds from rest, with a trailing load of 335 tons. It was said that the short life of this big engine was due to the damage it did to the track; for although its all-up weight of 80 tons was spread over five axles, 16 tons apiece, the concentration of weight in a total wheelbase of only 19 feet 8 inches was greater than on any other Great Eastern locomotive of that time. Contemporary journals wrote of the service improvements that were likely when more of the type had been built and were in traffic; but having proved the point that an acceleration of 1.46 feet per second per second with a 300-ton train could be achieved with steam, and at an infinitely smaller capital outlay than by electrification, the experiment

Great Eastern Railway: the boiler of the 'Decapod'.

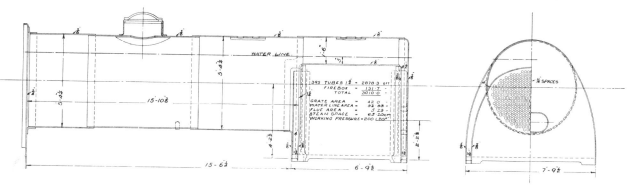

GER acceleration trials—1903 on level track

Engine type	0-10-0	0-6-0	4-4-0	2-4-0
Class	Decapod	'1151'	'Claud Hamilton'	'Humpty Dumpty'
Time in seconds				
Rest to 0.125 mile	30	36.3	43.5	49.6
Rest to 0.256 mile	46	54.3	65.4	72.5
Average speed over 0.131 mile (mph)	29.6	26.2	21.6	20.4
Boiler pressure				
Start	203	195	185	175
0.256 mile	175	165	175	170

was over. There was no use for the 'Decapod' in ordinary service and it was entirely rebuilt as an 0-8-0 tender engine, which did not last very long either.

For some 20 years after this notable experiment the Great Eastern worked its extremely intense inner suburban service with a swarm of 0-6-0 tank engines of little more than half the weight of the 'Decapod'. It is true that in 1914 A.J. Hill, who had succeeded James Holden's son as Locomotive Superintendent two years earlier, had produced a powerful new 0-6-2 tank engine; but it was not until 1921 that additions were made to the two original engines, Nos 1000 and 1001, only one of which had been superheated. The Hill 0-6-2s, however, which were the first of the subsequently numerous 'N7' Class of the LNER, were destined to play a vital part in suburban traffic working in East London in the grouping era. Until then the entire burden was carried by the series of 0-6-0 tank engines that originated from James Holden's class (LNER J66) of 1886, which had 4 foot wheels, and believe it or not, cylinders no larger than 16½ inches by 22 inches. The boiler pressure was 160 lb per square inch at first, but raised in the batch built in 1902-4 to 180. Enthusiasts whose sentiments lie south of the Thames are inclined to place the little Stroudley 'Terrier' 0-6-0 tanks of the Brighton on a special

pinnacle of fame; but when one recalls that these Holden 0-6-0s were the only tools F.V. Russell had when he completely reorganised the Great Eastern suburban service in 1920, on a basis of intensity unprecedented with steam traction, one salutes not only the design, but the maintenance that kept the engines in a condition able to continue indefinitely in this hard work.

That it worked so well can be related to the very important change in the locomotive organisation that was made in 1915, one of the reforms initiated by that great General Manager, Henry W. Thornton. Following the precedent set by Guy Granet on the Midland, eight years earlier, he decided to separate the responsibility for running the trains, and all the work-force concerned, from those of designing, building and repairing locomotives, carriages and wagon. He created a new post, Superintendent of Operation, and as Granet had done on the Midland he chose a locomotive engineer for the job, none other than F.V. Russell. Although reporting to the Chief Traffic Manager of the railway, Russell was given supreme responsibility for everything appertaining to the movement of traffic, even to the compilation of timetables, and his staff included shed, station and yard personnel, as well as all the enginemen, guards and signalmen. It was a unique opportunity

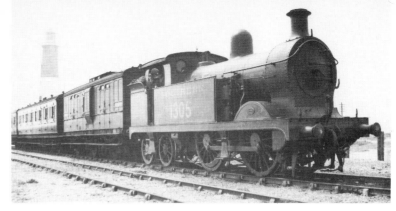

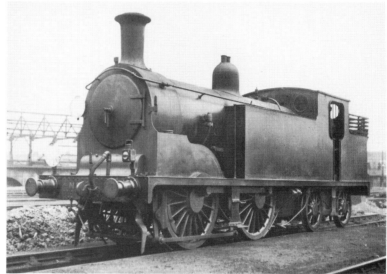

Below left *London Brighton & South Coast Railway: a delightful period scene around 1900 with one of the yellow-painted Stroudley 0-4-2 tank engines,* Maresfield, *with a train of 4-wheeled coaches, on the light, crudely-ballasted track of the day.*

Above right *South Eastern and Chatham 0-4-4, tank No 1305, in Southern days at Dungeness. (Note the lighthouse in the background.)*

Right *LSWR: the first of Dugald Drummond's 'M7' 0-4-4 express tank engines of 1897* (P. Ransome-Wallis).

for a master co-ordinating brain, and Russell was pre-eminently the man for the job. Although this is a book about locomotives, one cannot entirely divorce technicalities from the personalities of the men concerned; and on the Great Eastern, particularly from 1912 onwards, personalities loomed large.

In what were aptly called the 'Crush' hours the suburban trains were made up to 16 close-coupled four-wheelers, seating six aside, on bare boards, in the thirds; and the standard make-up on the Chingford and Enfield lines was 8 thirds, 6 seconds, and 2 firsts. Although the design of the game little engines that hauled these trains dates back to 1886 they were so indispensably a part of the Great Eastern motive power stud, for the rest of the company's separate existence, as to be regarded as 20th century machines. The original batch was actually intended for shunting and local goods work, and they were not fitted with the Westinghouse brake. They had cast iron wheels, steam brakes, and lever reverse. Following the fitting up of one of them as a passenger engine, and trials on the

Enfield branch, it was decided to adopt the type as a suburban train standard and, from 1890, construction began and was continued over 11 years of a batch that eventually numbered 100 engines. These were similar to the 1886 shunters, but had cast steel wheels, Westinghouse brake and screw reverse. In the same period a further 40 were built for goods and shunting work, and these like the 1886 originals had cast iron wheels, lever reverse, and no automatic continuous brake. Both varieties had boilers with a tube heating surface of 881.2 square feet, firebox 78 square feet and a grate area of 12.4 square feet. The working pressure was 160 lb per square inch. A later batch of 20, built in 1904, had larger boilers and fireboxes, and a pressure of 180 lb per square inch. A final 10, built in 1912 in Hill's time, were distinguished by having copper capped chimneys in place of the traditional Great Eastern stovepipe, and higher cabs, with side windows.

Before standardising on the 0-6-0 type for the inner suburban traffic, and using wheels as small as 4 foot diameter, the Great Eastern had used the 2-4-2

Left *Midland Railway: the Johnson version of the popular 0-4-4 tank type, here seen in LMS days, but otherwise in original condition* (P. Ransome-Wallis).

Left *North Eastern Railway: Wilson Worsdell's 'O' Class 0-4-4 used extensively in the north-east of England* (The Locomotive Publishing Company).

Left *Caledonian Railway: although this railway had a large class of passenger tank engines with 5 foot 9 inch coupled wheels, the one illustrated, with 4 foot 6 inch coupled wheels, was designed for rapid acceleration between the closely spaced stations of the Cathcart Circle Line in South Glasgow* (British Railways).

Above right *One of James Stirling's domeless boilered 0-4-4 tanks on the South Eastern and Chatham Railway* (British Railways).

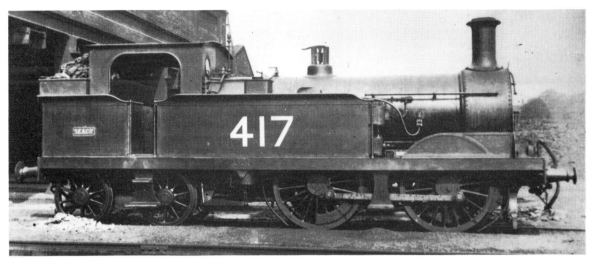

type of tank engine, with 5 foot 4 inch coupled wheels. The original design was by T.W. Worsdell, before he went to the North Eastern; but James Holden followed it up, with a development of his own, using Stephenson link motion, instead of Joy's radial gear. They were intended for the longer residential runs, with a minimum of stops in the inner suburban area, and 120 of them were built between 1903 and 1909. They had larger boilers than the 0-6-0 tanks, and were naturally adapted to faster running. Even before the end of the 19th century, however, James Holden had built a further class of 2-4-2 tanks, 50 in all, with 5 foot 8 inch coupled wheels with a total heating surface of 1,217 square feet and a grate area of 18 square feet. These were used on the longest of the commuter runs, to Southend, Witham and Bishops Stortford. They were built at Stratford between 1893 and 1902. Though they had speedier engines the passengers were still conveyed in 4-wheeled 'dog boxes'!

Hill's 0-6-2 tanks, completed at the end of 1914, were potentially much more powerful machines, for the inner suburban services. Of the two originals, No 1000 used saturated steam, and No 1001 the Robinson superheater. The coupled wheel diameter was 4 foot 10 inches, a kind of half-way house between the 4 feet of the 0-6-0s and the 5 feet 4 inches of the 2-4-2s; but an interesting development for the Great Eastern was the use of inside Walschaerts valve gear. Although it was reported that the two new engines had shown high accelerative capacity one wonders if they might not have been better still with the Stephenson link motion, and Churchward's setting, with negative lap on the valves in full gear. Nos 1000 and 1001 were gorgeously finished in all the current Great Eastern finery of the day, with copper capped

chimney, polished brass band at the joint of the boiler barrel and smokebox, and the profusion of red lining out, including red coupling rods. They proved to be the only 'N7' tank engines to be so adorned; for when multiplication of the class began in 1921 all Great Eastern engines were in 'battleship grey', with the numbers in large white figures on the tank sides.

The Great Northern also had a suburban traffic problem in the London area, though not approaching the intensity of that endured by the Great Eastern. The problem was rather that of awkward gradients, in working over the Inner Circle lines of the Metropolitan where the exhaust had to be condensed, and in climbing the steep banks of the High Barnet and Enfield branches. The Stirling 0-4-4 tanks were doing good work on these duties, and H.A. Ivatt's first essay towards the problem, was in the form of small 4-4-2 tank engines, not unlike those he had introduced on the Great Southern and Western in Ireland; these engines never seemed to have the 'guts' of the Stirling 0-4-4s, and did not supersede them and, in 1907, a powerful new 0-6-2 tank, No 190, was put into traffic. After extensive trials production began in the following year, with a series having smaller side tanks. Engine No 190 was the prototype of a very fine 'Gauge One' model by Bassett-Lowke. Construction of these engines continued up to 1912, by which time there were 54 of them in service.

Moving away now from the London area, reference must next be made to the numerous and remarkably successful 2-4-2 tank engine family on the Lancashire and Yorkshire Railway. As with the Great Eastern classes discussed earlier the saga began in the 19th century, in 1889, when the first engine to be completed in the newly constructed

Horwich Works was the pioneer 2-4-2 tank No 1008, now happily preserved. It was yet another of J.A.F. Aspinall's designs that was 'right from the word go', and there were eventually no fewer than 300 of the type in service on the Lancashire and Yorkshire Railway. By the end of the century 230 of them had been built, all at Horwich and, apart from the fitting of larger coal bunkers from October 1898 onwards, the original design was unchanged, and continued so up to February 1901. The first development from Aspinall's basic design came in 1905 when George Hughes built 20 additional engines of the class with Belpaire, instead of round topped, fireboxes and followed this, in 1910, with a further 20 of the same design. At that later time he was very much involved with superheating and, in 1911, when a further batch of 20 was authorised, they were built with Schmidt superheaters, and back-to-back balanced slide valves.

This provided no half-hearted advance in capacity or speed-worthiness; because the boiler pressure was kept at 180 lb per square inch, and cylinder diameter increased from 18 to 20½ inches. The result was the highest tractive effort of any four-coupled engine in the country, no less than 24,584 lb. Of the first 10 engines of the series, one was stationed at Colne for working over the heavy gradients of the East Lancashire line; six went to Newton Heath and the remaining three to Blackpool. The running staff at these two latter sheds soon realised that they had a very powerful and free running engine, and began to put them on to what were really unsuitable turns—for a tank engine with a leading radial axle; and, on June 21 1912, when working an express booked non-stop from Rochdale to Halifax, one of them took the Charlestown curve, near Hebden Bridge, at somewhat excessive speed, and forced the track between 3 and 5½ inches out of alignment for about 175 yards. The speed was estimated at about 60 mph instead of the stipulated 45, and the engine with all seven coaches of the train was derailed, with some loss of life.

Although the 30 chain curve was led into by an accurately laid transition, and had a superelevation of 5 inches, the Inspecting Officer of the Board of Trade, enquiring into the circumstances of this alarming accident, drew particular attention to the strain thrown upon the track by this heavy tank engine at speed. The weight distribution, as compared to that of the original Aspinall 2-4-2s, is of interest in this connection. Both varieties had radial axles both front and rear of the coupled wheels.

L & YR 2-4-2 tanks: Weight distribution

Axle	Aspinall		Hughes (superheated)	
	(ton)	(cwt)	(ton)	(cwt)
Leading radial	13	10	12	16
Driving	16	12	19	11
Trailing coupled	15	2	19	14
Trailing radial	10	15	14	8

The Hughes engines had larger coal bunkers, which accounts for the increased weight on the trailing radial axle. As a result of the accident all the superheated 2-4-2 tank engines were taken off main line expresses.

At the time these engines were built, Hughes' developments with superheaters had not progressed beyond use of the Schmidt type but, like other British engineers, he was seeking ways of avoiding the payment of royalties in respect of the German patents, and in the discussion following the presentation of Fowler's paper to the Institution of Civil Engineers, in the early spring of 1914, he described the two 'Horwich' types of superheater that he was then installing in the large 0-8-0 coal engines referred to in a later chapter of this book. They were called the 'plug' type, and the 'top and bottom header'. A smaller version of the latter, referred to sometimes as the 'T & B', was fitted to four of the Aspinall 2-4-2 tanks as early as 1915, after a number of them had been rebuilt, from 1914, with the Schmidt type; but, from 1918

Below left *Great Eastern Railway: the remarkable 0-10-0 experimental tank engine, the 'Decapod', built to demonstrate the power of acceleration with steam* (British Railways).

Above right *LB & SCR: one of the Billinton 'radial' 0-6-2 tanks, so called because of the mountings of the trailing axle which allowed a radial movement on curves.*

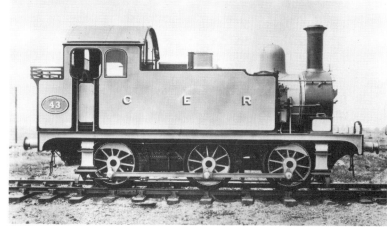

Right *Great Eastern Railway: the final version of the Holden 0-6-0 suburban tank engine, as turned out by A. J. Hill in 1912* (British Railways).

onwards, many more of the older 2-4-2 tanks were rebuilt with the 'T & B' type; even down to the year 1926.

To those with vivid memories of the later days of steam in Great Britain, and the efforts of the design staff of the nationalised British Railways to evolve an outward style that would be distinctive, and instantly recognisable as that of 'BR', different from that of all its predecessors, it is equally remarkable how the old railways of the early 1900s themselves contrived to achieve individuality and distinction, even with the humblest of motive power. It was not only with the great companies, like the London and North Western, and the Midland; and it is in studying in particular the 0-6-2 tank engine designs of the period that this characteristic of British practice generally becomes evident. On the big lines it cannot be said that the 0-6-2 was one of the most popular tank engine types. Admittedly the North Western had plenty of them, 380 in two varieties, both precise tank engine equivalents of the famous Webb '17 inch coal', and '18 inch express goods' 0-6-0 tender engines; but it was on the smaller lines that the greatest individuality of design styles was to be seen—using the word

'design' in this sense as that of plastic form, rather than of engineering technology.

The case may be noticed of two designs of the 0-6-2 tank type introduced within a few months of each other, in 1903-4, on the North Staffordshire, and on the Furness Railway. They might conceivably have been thought to have a family connection, because the former was designed by J.H. Adams, a son of William Adams, the former and very distinguished Locomotive Superintendent of the London and South Western Railway, while W.F. Pettigrew of the Furness had been Works Manager of the LSWR at Nine Elms before he went to Barrow. But though both were neat and compact engines in a painting style that was very similar in colour, one could see marked differences in the boiler mountings. On the North Staffordshire engine the shapely chimney savoured of Robinson's style on the Great Central, while the safety valve casing was something quite original. For engines designed essentially for mixed traffic, both classes were beautifully finished, carrying the company's coat of arms, and whereas the Furness engine had the initials FR in large shaded letters on the side tanks, its counterpart had the full name, no more than slightly abbreviated to 'North Stafford' with the words on either side of the coat of arms. An artistic touch on the bunker sides was to incorporate the number within the entwinings of the traditional Staffordshire Knot. The engines had three-figure numbers and this could be neatly arranged on a cast brass plate. This latter was, however, not a feature perpetuated on subsequent North Staffordshire locomotives of J.H. Adams' design.

Both classes in their several ways earned distinction in later years. The Furness engines became very familiar to me from 1916 onwards. In his book on the *History of the Furness Railway* McGowan Gradon refers to them as 'banking engines'; but I remember them doing a great deal of stopping train passenger work on the main line, both north and south of Barrow, and also on the branches to Coniston and Lakeside (Windermere). The North Staffordshire Class had one moment of glory that brought engine No 158 into the limelight of 'British Locomotive Practice and Performance', in *The Railway Magazine*. Before the grouping of 1923, the 12.5 pm from Manchester to Euston, running via Stoke-on-Trent, was always worked by a North Staffordshire engine as far as Stoke. This train was usually worked by one of the powerful superheated 0-6-4 tanks, built at Stoke in 1916; but, on this occasion in 1921, when it was fortunate that Cecil J. Allen was a passenger, one of the big engines was not available, and one of the 0-6-2 tanks of 1903 was put on to the job. As Allen wrote afterwards of his experience: 'This little engine No 158, was faced with the haulage at express speed of a corridor train consisting of seven large 8-wheeled vehicles and two 12-wheeled dining cars, weighing 298 tons empty and 310 tons full'. He went on to tell how the 19.9 miles from Macclesfield to Stoke were covered in 28 minutes 35 seconds, only 1½ minutes more than schedule, and that a speed of 53½ mph

was sustained on level track. This was certainly quite a feat from an engine with coupled wheels no larger than 5 foot diameter, with a heating surface of 1,011.7 square feet and a grate area of 17.8 square feet. I never noticed anything to compare remotely with this with the Furness 0-6-2s, though I must add that in my experience no such opportunity to shine forth came to them.

It was on the local railways of South Wales that the 0-6-2 tank type came to reign supreme. It was ideal for the mineral hauls, and for the local passenger work alike, and it was only in the rather special operating conditions of the Barry Railway that the 0-6-2 did not become an all-purpose standard. Working on the Taff Vale was perhaps the most severe of any, and there Tom Hurry Riches was Locomotive Superintendent from 1873 until his death in 1910. In 1907 he achieved the honour of Presidency of the Institution of Mechanical Engineers. After use of the 4-4-0 and 4-4-2 type for passenger working he turned, in 1891, to the 0-6-2 as an all purpose design and, except for some 0-6-0s with saddle tanks for dock working, he used no other type for the rest of his career. Neither did his successor, J. Cameron. Of the 20th century varieties of 0-6-2, the successive developments of the '0' Class of 1894 are important. By 1902 Riches had got to Class '03'. Like its predecessors it had 17½ inch by 26 inch cylinders, and 5 foot 3 inch coupled wheels, while pressure had been increased stage by stage from the original 150 lb per square inch to 170. In his Presidential Address to the Mechanicals, in April 1907, the references to his own work on the Taff Vale were modest in the extreme, and he illustrated his 4-4-2 tank of 1888, and his '01' Class 0-6-2 tank of 1896; and, when he granted an illustrated interview to the Editor of *The Railway Magazine* in January 1902, it was the '02' that formed the subject of one of the

fine lithographed colour plates. The '03' came later in 1902, with boiler pressure increased to 170 lb per square inch. The boiler dimensions for all four of the '0' Classes were the same, except that some necessary strengthening was embodied in the later varieties, to take the higher pressure.

It was in the year of his Presidency of the Mechanics that his last 0-6-2 tank engine design was introduced, the '04'. This was not really in the same line of development for, while having the same cylinders as previously, the boiler was much larger with a total heating surface of 1,321 square feet against 1,002; a working pressure of 175 lb per square inch and a larger grate area, 21¾ square feet against 19. The coupled wheels were only 4 feet 6½ inches. In consequence the nominal tractive effort of Class '04' was 21,750 lb against 17,200 lb for '03'. In view of subsequent developments on the Taff Vale perhaps the most significant change was the marked increase in grate area. Before proceeding to the final period, under Cameron, it is interesting to compare progress with that of its great neighbour, and one time rival, the Rhymney Railway. In 1904 the legendary Cornelius Lundie, having reached the age of 89(!) retired from the dual post of Traffic Manager and Engineer. The latter title also included responsibility for the Locomotive department. In the 42 years he had held this office, the Rhymney Railway had prospered exceedingly. The dividend on the ordinary shares had often been up to 10 per cent, and in the year of his retirement it was 8½. Lundie's engines were all saddle tanks, with outside frames, and he had introduced the 0-6-2 type in 1890. They proved excellent engines, and construction of them continued until 1900, by which time there were 47 of them in traffic.

Lundie had as his assistant for many years an able man in Richard Jenkins, who in most matters had carried the responsibilities of the department. He was appointed Locomotive Superintendent in 1905, but was in office for less than a year; for, in January 1906, C.T. Hurry Riches, son of the Taff Vale

chief, was appointed to succeed him. In the short interregnum between the Lundie and the Riches eras Jenkins introduced a more powerful design of 0-6-2 tank that was as conventional in outward appearance as its predecessors had been otherwise. Riches held office at Caerphilly for the rest of the independent existence of the Rhymney Railway, and he put another 53 0-6-2 tank engines on the road. There were three varieties, all carrying a boiler pressure of 175 lb per square inch, as under:

Rhymney railway 0-6-2 tanks

Class	A	R	P
Cylinders			
Diameter (inches)	18	18½	18
Stroke (inches)	26	26	26
Coupled wheel diameter			
(feet/inches)	4 4½	4 6	5 0
Total weight			
(tons)	64	67	61

The 'P' Class were designed for passenger service and the other two were freight haulers.

Left *Great Northern Railway: H.A. Ivatt's 0-6-2 suburban tank engine of 1910. Although designed for the residential trains travelling to stations on the 'Northern Heights' of London, these engines had apparatus for condensing the exhaust steam when working in the underground tunnels to Moorgate (the late W.J. Reynolds).*

Above right *Great Eastern Railway: the longer-distance suburban tank, 2-4-2 type, used on London-Southend and similar runs (British Railways).*

Right *The forerunner of a long and successful series of LNER 0-6-2 tanks, A.J. Hill's No 1000 of 1914, fitted with shelters for men taking indicator diagrams, prior to the introduction of the intense new suburban service of 1920 (K.A.C.R. Nunn).*

There was a significant change in the engines that C.T. Hurry Riches began to introduce in 1907, though it could not well be appreciated from outward appearances. The 0-6-2 tanks purchased in the short spell of Richard Jenkins' tenure of office had relatively large grates of 21.6 square feet in area, while Riches went back to even smaller grates than those traditionally being used on the Taff Vale. On the latter line Cameron went even smaller on his very fine 'A' Class of 1914. The particular conditions of working in the Welsh valleys need to be emphasised, in order to appreciate the reasons for an unusually small grate area. Contrary to what might at first imagine, the hardest work is with the *empty* trains; but these have to be worked up the valleys, against the grade, and the loading for empty mineral trains was then 50 to 55 wagons, to be hauled at 17 to 20 mph. With the loaded trains, which were, of course, much heavier, the engines had to do a great deal of coasting; and the small grate area was found to result in a lower coal consumption per trip, when coal would otherwise be burnt just in keeping the firebars covered. The grate

area of the very handsome Taff Vale 'A' Class 0-6-2s of 1914 was only 18 square feet.

The Brecon and Merthyr was in a different category to the Taff Vale and the Rhymney railways, in that it had a long main line extending northward into the heart of the mountains, far beyond the coal measures. Southwards from Brecon one had to climb the fearsome Talybont incline, of 1 in 38 for 7 miles to Torpantau tunnel, and although there was never any case of hauling maximum load coal trains over such a line, one needed a boiler capable of hard continuous steaming. The Brecon and Merthyr had two distinct varieties in its modern 0-6-2 tank engine power. One was a massive looking, very handsome class of eight, introduced in

1910, with the kind of proportions one would expect for a mountain climbing engine, while the later one, dating from 1915, was designed more in the style of the Taff Vale and Rhymney, with a small grate area, for working loaded coal trains down to Newport docks. The respective proportions, in the table below, will make the difference between the two designs clear:

North Staffordshire Railway: an Adams 0-6-2 tank engine of 1903 design, a preserved example of a design once familiar in the Potteries (British Railways).

Brecon & Merthyr 0-6-2 tanks

	1910	1915
Cylinders (inches)	18½ × 26	18 × 26
Coupled wheel diameter (feet/inches)	4 6	5 0
Total heating surface (square feet)	1,419.5	1,327
Grate area (square feet)	21.5	18
Working pressure (lb per square inch)	175	175
Total weight (tons)	67	61

The Barry Railway was one of the latest to be opened in the South Wales coalfield, and its varied stock of locomotives were built almost entirely between 1888 and 1900. There was no question of having general purpose tank engines. The Barry used 0-4-4 and 2-4-2 for passenger, and notably 0-8-2 tanks for freight, although there were some 0-6-2s. The passenger locomotives had to work fast trains between Cardiff and Barry, over a road that permitted the nearest approach to express running on the local railways in South Wales. These trains included the 'Ports-to-Ports Express', a through restaurant train which ran between Barry and Newcastle-on-Tyne and was hauled by a Barry Railway locomotive as far as Cardiff.

Last among the South Wales to be mentioned is the Rhondda and Swansea Bay, not opened throughout until the 1890s, and included the 2-mile long tunnel by which it obtained access to the Rhondda Valley. The little company opened for business with five 0-6-0 tanks, and three 2-4-2 tanks for passenger service; but again, the mainstay of the locomotive department was the 0-6-2 tank, of which there were 22 by 1904. The 2-4-2 and 0-6-2s alike had 4 feet 6 inch coupled wheels, while some of the 0-6-2s had fireboxes with grates as large as 21 square feet. They were mostly built by Kitsons, of Leeds, and had the unmistakable 'look' of that firm's products about them. It was a pleasant little railway not least in its dramatic start, from the head of the Rhondda Valley, where it makes a bee-line for the great mountain that lies in the direct line ahead, and dives clean underneath it.

Finally, the apropos of mountain climbing, there were the 0-6-2 tank engines designed for the Glasgow and South Western Railway, in 1916, by Peter Drummond. When he was on the Highland Railway he had introduced an 0-6-4 tank engine, primarily for banking on the long ascent from Blair Atholl up to Druimuachdar summit, and sometimes for double-heading trains to the same point from Aviemore. On the Glasgow and South Western the steeply graded branches from the Ayrshire coast needed augmented power, and Drummond took his Highland 0-6-4, fitted a shorter bunker, and produced instead an 0-6-2, which had the same design of boiler, cylinders and motion. Its basic dimensions were conventional, with a much larger firegrate than customary in South Wales, namely 22.43 square feet, and it proved an excellent engine, of which 18 were built. Oddly enough, in LMS days two of them were transferred from G & SW territory to Blair Atholl, to work as bankers on 'The Hill', in place of some of the ex-Highland 0-6-4 tanks which had then been withdrawn.

Left *London and North Western Railways: one of F. W. Webb's tank engine versions of the '18-inch' express goods 0-6-0s, as seen here in LMS days. They originally worked on the fast residential trains from Euston and Broad Street.*

Left *Taff Vale Railway: one of the 0-6-2 series developed by T. Hurry Riches. Engine No 195, illustrated here, was one of a batch built in 1896 by the Vulcan Foundry Ltd* (The Locomotive Publishing Company).

Below *Furness Railway: W.F. Pettigrew's 0-6-2 tank, one of a class originating in 1904 and used for stopping passenger, freight, and rear-end banking duties* (North British Locomotive Company).

Right *One of the later 0-6-2 tanks of the Taff Vale Railway 'A' Class, here seen as modernised after the amalgamation of 1923 with a Great Western type taper boiler and Belpaire firebox (British Railways).*

Right *Great Northern Railway: H.N. Gresley's superheated 0-6-2 condensing suburban tank engine, later to become LNER Class 'N2' (the late W.J. Reynolds).*

Below *Great Western Railway: the post-amalgamation standardised 0-6-2 tank engine for South Wales, using a chassis of Rhymney Railway proportions and standard Swindon boiler and motion (British Railways).*

6. The 'Atlantics'

There is a 'something' about a locomotive having a pair of carrying wheels beneath the firebox that adds a touch of elegance to any design. It was very evident in the many 4-2-2 bogie 'singles' that graced the British railways in the latter part of the 19th century; but I think it rose to perhaps its highest expression in the various designs of 'Atlantic' engines that took the road from 1898 onwards. Many of these looked, and proved, veritable aristocrats among engines; and it is remarkable that most of them survived to do unquestionably their finest work in the years between the two World Wars. It was a changing world into which the first-ever British 'Atlantic' was out-shopped at the Doncaster Plant in the early summer of 1898 and, reading contemporary literature one rather gains the impression that the world of railway enthusiasts was not sure whether to applaud, or not.

When the news came of No 990's completion, Swindon was still building the Dean 7 foot 8 inch 4-4-2s, including the immortal 3065 *Duke of Connaught*; Crewe was turning out 3-cylinder 2-2-2-2 compounds of the 'John Hick' Class and, in Scotland, the second 'Dunalastairs' were apostrophised as 'The New Caledonian Flyers'. Those who revered the memory of Patrick Stirling, on the Great Northern, did not know quite what to make of the huge grey giant, that began working from Grantham. *The Railway Magazine*, however, 'jumped the gun' as it were, and presented its readers with a truly magnificent colour plate 15¼ inches by 7½ inches showing the new engine in its running colours. It was the first of the series of lithographed plates from the firm of Alfred Cooke, of Leeds, and its colour rendering was superb—there is no other word for it. Unfortunately the plate was so large that it had to be folded to fit within the size of the magazine, and today it is a little marred by creases.

Colour plates apart, however, the building of No 990 was the beginning of a new era in British locomotive practice. Ivatt was a close personal friend of his fellow superintendents, John Aspinall, of the Lancashire and Yorkshire, and Wilson Worsdell, of the North Eastern, and in 1897 the three friends were all busy designing and building large new passenger engines; and, as the news became known, there was much speculation as to who would be first. Worsdell's engine turned out to be a 4-6-0, but intense interest was created, in a comparison of the Ivatt and Aspinall 'Atlantics'. The latter type had originated in the USA, and pedantic commentators argued that Aspinall's was not a true 'Atlantic', because it had inside cylinders, and because the drive was on the leading, and not the trailing coupled axle.

Ivatt won the 'race' by just over six months, because the first of the Aspinall engines was not completed until February 1899; but, as mentioned earlier in the book, Ivatt's '990' was by way of a prototype, not followed by a production batch until 1900, whereas by that time Aspinall had 20 of his famous 'Highflyers' in regular service. There was a great difference in the duties for which these big engines were intended. On the Great Northern the loads of the principal expresses were very much on the increase. Heavy corridor carriages, not to mention luxurious dining and sleeping cars, were being introduced on many of the crack trains and, after all the excitement of the Race to the North had

Great Northern Railway: a later example of the pioneer British 'Atlantic' design by H.A. Ivatt, No 259, temporarily equipped for oil firing (British Railways).

finally subsided, it was heavy pulling rather than high speed that was required.

Nevertheless the Great Northern was not by any means bereft of all competitive services in 1900. They had to reckon with the Midland, to Leeds and Bradford; and there was a very enterprising joint operation with the Great Central between London and Manchester. But the trains involved were not heavy, and they were frequently run by single-wheelers. The Lancashire and Yorkshire 'Atlantics', with their 7 foot 3 inch coupled wheels were intended for the highly competitive services striking out east and west from Manchester. To Liverpool the L & Y had two rivals, with the London and North Western using the historic pioneer route, opened with such pageantry in 1830, and the Cheshire Lines Committee going farther to the south, via Warrington. The Lancashire and Yorkshire were soon to run on equality in time with the North Western—40 minutes non-stop between the two cities—and for the L & Y it meant much harder running, because they had 5 miles farther to go, 36.4 against 31.4 miles, and had to average 54.6 mph start to stop. The North Western could include one intermediate stop within the 40-minute overall

timing. The Aspinall 'Atlantics' working west from Leeds, or York, would often shed a few coaches at Manchester, leaving a minimum load, sometimes of no more than three coaches, for the final dash to Liverpool.

Aspinall's 'Highflyer', of which the first order was for 20, was a beautifully designed engine. Externally the boiler looked very long, but the distance between the tube plates was no more than 15 feet because the smokebox was extended back into the barrel for about 2 feet at the front. The firebox was of the Belpaire type, deep and narrow, with the grate horizontal—the easiest of all grates to fire. The valve gear, as then standard on the L & YR was Joy's. Having settled the major points of design, Aspinall left the working out of it to his very able chief draughtsman, Zachariah Tetlow, and the front-end was generally the same as that of the 7 foot 3 inch 4-4-0s, which had been doing very good work. He kept the same design of bogie, with its rather short wheelbase of 5 feet 6 inches and with swing-link side control. The trailing axle had inside

Great Northern Railway: the large-boilered 'Atlantic' of 1902 in its non-superheated form.

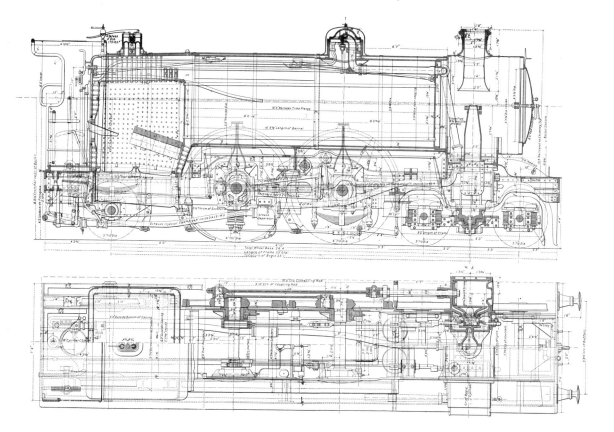

Top *Lancashire & Yorkshire Railway: a later example of the famous Aspinall 'Highflyers' with the short chimney and outside bearings to the trailing wheels (the late J.M. Tomlinson).*

Above *GNR: after successful trials of the pioneer large-boilered '251', production began in 1904 with No 171 illustrated here* (The Locomotive Publishing Company).

bearings with the axleboxes supported on coil springs.

Apart from a very few minor troubles, the only serious complaint about the great new engines was occasional rolling. This was cured by substituting the Adams spring-constrained type of bogie for the swing link type; while a further improvement made later, was to introduce an outside bearing for the trailing wheel. This was done after the second 20 engines of the class had been completed in 1902. Long before this, before even the first batch was in traffic, Aspinall himself was promoted from Chief Mechanical Engineer to the high office of General Manager; and moving residence from Horwich to Gledhill, Liverpool, he travelled to and from Manchester each way on the 40-minute flyers—not infrequently on the footplate. He would thus have been well placed to appreciate any tendency to rough riding, and to urge his successor in the CME's department to do something about it.

In reviewing the work of these large and impressive engines it must be pointed out that they were surprisingly light, quite apart from their very small tenders. The all-up weight of the engine only was slightly *less* than that of an LNWR 'Precursor' class 4-4-0, 58¾ tons against 59; and the adhesion weight was only 35 tons. With 19 inch by 26 inch cylinders and those huge 7 foot 3 inch coupled wheels the tractive effort was considerably less than that of a 'Precursor', which had 38 tons of adhesion weight, and was in any case inherently more sure-footed than an 'Atlantic'. The Aspinall 'Highflyers' had to be handled on a very light rein, to avoid slipping when starting away, and I have often thought how completely misleading was the caption to the frontispiece in the late Eric Mason's otherwise admirable book* on the L & YR; for a painting of No 1419, leaving Poulton-le-Fylde with a

The Lancashire & Yorkshire Railway in the Twentieth Century.

Manchester express, is captioned 'Sound and Fury: No 1419 storming away . . .'. No driver, with anything of a load would attempt to 'storm away' from a station stop.

During the First World War, when the unreliability of the Hughes 4-6-0s, and their non-availability, was throwing almost the entire burden of the express traffic on to the 'Atlantics', it was found necessary to provide pilot assistance for them on the steep initial gradients eastbound from Manchester when the loads of the Yorkshire expresses much exceeded about 200 tons. The pilots were usually taken as far as Todmorden. These 'Atlantic' engines were disappearing from main line work by the time I had begun my own stop watching and of course there was no use for such machines on branch and secondary work. I used to travel occasionally by the Blackpool-Manchester express that left Preston at 2.59 pm and one day, in June 1927, we had No 1411, then numbered 10326 in LMS stock. The train had the generous allowance of 51 minutes non-stop for the 30.3 miles from Preston to Salford, and with a 260-ton train we had no difficulty in gaining 2 minutes on schedule, despite two signal checks. Six months later the engine was withdrawn for scrapping. The last time I saw one of them was in 1932 at Liverpool Exchange station. This time it was No 10307 which was scrapped in the following year.

While the Lancashire and Yorkshire 'Atlantics' could not well be developed to meet modern conditions it was far otherwise with their contemporaries on the Great Northern; yet the process of evolution at Doncaster, looked at some 80 years later, seems a little odd at times. The pioneer engine of 1898, No 990, named *Henry Oakley*, although having a nominal tractive effort *less* than that of the final batch of Stirling 8 foot bogie singles, proved satisfactory in heavy main line work. The boiler steamed well and, while the cylinder volume was relatively small, the valve design was good and permitted large volumes of steam to be passed through freely; and in 1900 a further 10 locomotives of the class were built at Doncaster.

Then, in 1902, Ivatt began to experiment, first with a similar engine to the '990' Class but with four cylinders, all driving on to the leading coupled axle. As in the case of No 990, the cylinder volume was kept low in relation to boiler capacity, though not to the same extent; and to do this the cylinders were of 15 inches diameter, with the very short stroke of 20 inches. The layout of the machinery no doubt made for a smooth riding engine, but it

would seem that the experiment otherwise did not yield any very positive results because, in 1904, the engine was altered to have Walschaerts valve gear outside, instead of the inside Stephenson's link motion originally fitted.

Then, at the end of 1902, Ivatt built another 'Atlantic' engine, identical to No 990 so far as wheelbase, cylinders and motion were concerned, but with an enormously enlarged boiler, having a total heating surface of 2,500 square feet, against 1,442, and with the wide Wootten type firebox spreading out widthwise across the frames. This was the ever-famous 251. But what astonished the connoisseurs of the day, and even now causes a few eyebrows to be raised, was why such an enormous boiler should have been placed upon a locomotive having a tractive effort of no more than 15,670 lb. That this engine had potentialities for an astonishing development later was certainly not appreciated at the time. The basic proportions certainly look rather strange when set alongside those of contemporary British 'Atlantic' engines,

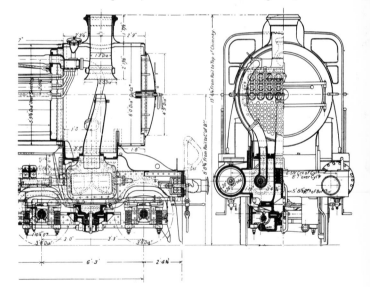

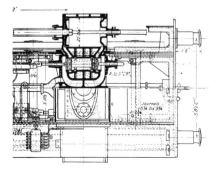

GNR: part section showing modification of smokebox and front end to accommodate 32-element superheater and piston valves.

though not so in comparison with American practice of the day. Yet whereas Ivatt seemed to be heading for the opposite extreme from the precepts of his predecessor at Doncaster, his colleague on the North Eastern Railway, recently returned from a visit to the USA and tremendously impressed by the performance of 'Atlantic' engines on the Pennsylvania and the Reading Railroads, designed the large engine in column 5 of the table, the very impressive Class 'V'.

The similarity between this engine and the Great Northern No 251 was confined to the diameter of the boiler, which was 5 feet 6 inches; for the North Eastern engine had a deep, narrow firebox, and very large cylinders. These, together with the boiler pressure of 200 lb per square inch gave the Class 'V' a tractive effort 50 per cent higher than that of No 251. The first of the new NER engines, No 532, was completed at Gateshead Works in November 1903, and the authorisation was for 10 of the class. The last two engines were completed in October 1904. There is an amusing story to be told about the designing of these very handsome engines. Wilson Worsdell, the Chief Mechanical Engineer, had been one of a party of senior NER officers visiting the USA under the leadership of the General Manager,

George S. Gibb. When they returned it was to find that his Chief Draughtsman, the redoubtable Walter Mackersie Smith, was ill. Worsdell immediately set the Gateshead drawing office on the design of the big 'V' Class 'Atlantic' and Gibb, having seen what was going on in America, readily gave authority to build 10. The story goes that, when Smith returned after his illness, he was furious that such an epoch-marking design had been put in hand, behind his back, as it were. Wilson Worsdell had some awkward moments with his chief draughtsman, who was pacified only by the promise that two 'Atlantics' of his own design should also be built. As early as March 1904 *The Locomotive Magazine* carried a note: 'Two new locomotives of the 'Atlantic' type, Class 'V', are to be built as four-cylinder compounds on Smith's patent system'. Unfortunately these two magnificent engines had barely been completed in the spring of 1906 before their designer was seized by an illness that proved fatal, and he was not to witness their triumphs.

The next 'Atlantic' to be completed in 1903 was for the Great Central Railway, which company was displaying an abounding enterprise in every one of its multifarious activities. With the stimulus of competition on every hand some very fast express train services had been put on; but the loading was still very light, and most trains could be readily handled by J.G. Robinson's 4-4-0s of the 'Sir Alexander' Class, if not even by the Pollitt 4-2-2 'Singles'. But authority was forthcoming to prepare for bigger things, and in 1903 orders were placed on Beyer, Peacock & Co, for four 10-wheeled express passenger engines, alike except that two were to be 'Atlantics', and the other two 4-6-0s. They were, without question, among the most beautiful 10-

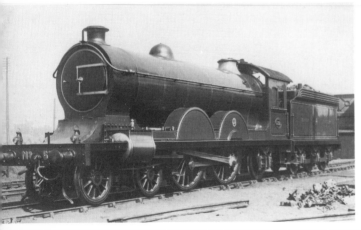

Left *North Eastern Railway: the outcome of Wilson Worsdell's visit to the USA was the first 'Atlantic' from Gateshead Works, No 532, in November 1903* (British Railways).
Below *Great Central Railway: one of the very handsome 'Jersey Lillies', Robinson's 'Atlantic', for high speed service* (Beyer, Peacock & Company).

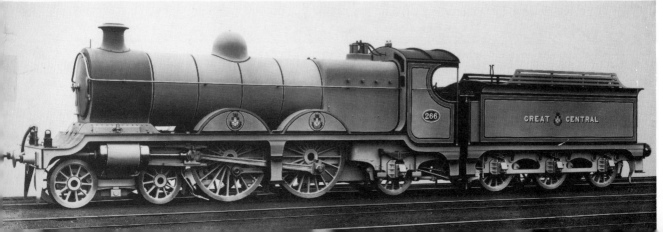

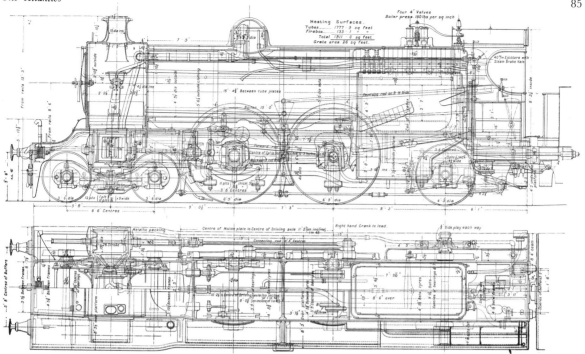

Heating Surfaces.
Tubes___ 1777·3 sq feet
Firebox___ 133·1 "
Total 1311·0 sq feet.
Grate area 26 sq feet.

Great Central Railway: 'Atlantic' engine as originally built, non-superheated, and with slide valves.

wheeled engines that have ever run in this country, 4-4-2 and 4-6-0 alike. Apart, however, from their very pleasing outward appearance they were the most balanced of the earlier 'Atlantics' and 4-6-0s, in that their boiler proportions were more equally matched to the cylinder capacity, as can be seen from a study of their basic dimensions in the table on page 89. Their performance was as good as their handsome looks, though for many years the demands put upon their tractive abilities were slight. In a later chapter of this book will be recounted some stirring feats of haulage and speed in the 1930s.

I must add a note at this point as to how it was that the Great Central 'Atlantics' got their celebrated nickname of the 'Jersey Lillies'. At the time of their introduction the actress, Lilly Langtry, was one of the great beauties of the day, and by some who heard the nickname of the GCR engines in more recent times it was imagined to have been a tribute to their graceful and shapely appearance. Actually it was far otherwise. At one of the local 'pubs' near Gorton works there had been on exhibition an extremely fat woman reputedly weighing 32 stone, and sarcastically advertised as the 'Jersey Lilly', as Lilly Langtry was popularly known. Well, when the first of the new 'Atlantics' arrived from Beyer, Peacock's works nearby, its enormous size, compared to that of the older GC engines, and particularly the girth of the boiler led to some wag

dubbing it the 'Jersey Lilly', after the fat woman in the pub; and for good or ill the Great Central 'Atlantics' were known as the 'Jersey Lillies' ever after!

In Chapter Three of this book I have told how Douglas Earle-Marsh came from Doncaster to succeed R.J. Billinton as Locomotive Carriage and Wagon Superintendent of the Brighton Railway, and how he brought with him the design of the Ivatt large-boiler 'Atlantic' engine, of which there were 21 in service by the end of the year 1904. Although service requirements on the Brighton line were somewhat different from those on the Great Northern, he obtained five 'Atlantics' from Kitson's of Leeds which were very similar in appearance to those that he, as Works Manager at Doncaster, had already built. The boilers and fireboxes were almost identical, except that the pressure was 200 lb per square inch and Marsh used a more conventional piston stroke of 26 inches. On the Brighton line the tasks awaiting them were not unduly onerous. The really prestige job was to take the 'Stockbrokers' Express'—nickname of the 8.45 am up—from Brighton to London Bridge, and then go 'light engine', tender first, round the South London line to Victoria to be ready for the 11 am

'Southern Belle'. The 8.45 am up was usually the heavier train, with a high proportion of first class accommodation, while at that time the 'Belle' had a standard load of seven first class Pullmans.

When the North British found it necessary to introduce larger express engines than 4-4-0s there was some surprise that they too should have chosen the 'Atlantic' type rather than the 4-6-0, in view of the heavy gradients on both the East Coast main line north of Edinburgh and on the Waverley route, on neither of which was there much opportunity for sustained fast running. On the one NBR route where the terrain was suitable, the Edinburgh-Glasgow line, the loads were relatively light and the timetables undemanding. Furthermore one gains the impression that W.P. Reid's massively impressive 'Atlantics' did not get off to a very good start. There were complaints of excessive coal consumption, some of which reached Board level, though at that time in locomotive history allegations of that nature were apt to be made on the most superficial of evidence. Nevertheless, the Chairman, William Whitelaw, who always seemed to enjoy the prospect of comparative trials, arranged with the LNWR for a one-day test between Carlisle and Preston, in which one of the 'Atlantics' was matched against an 'Experiment' Class 4-6-0. As was so often the case, however, the comparison proved to be one of the driver's expertise rather than of locomotive design.

On the Sunday in question the regular driver of the North British 'Atlantic' No 881, *Borderer*, was not available, and the substitute was not one of the best. It was once, unkindly perhaps, said of him that he could not drive a horse and cart, let alone a locomotive! In any event, in relation to the power output on that trip from Carlisle to Preston and back, the coal consumption was astronomical, and

the figures were not made public until some 20 years later. The futility of the exercise seems to have been realised in high circles on the NBR because, in no more than a few months after the conclusion of the Carlisle-Preston test, an order was placed with Robert Stephenson & Co for six more 'Atlantics' of identical design.

Apart from the pioneer Great Northern 'Atlantic' No 990, *Henry Oakley*, and one of the Brighton engines named *La France*, used for special trains conveying French dignitaries on official visits, and travelling via Newhaven, none of the 'Atlantics' featured in the table on page 89 were named until the introduction of the Reid engines on the North British; and with them systematic naming of all new express passenger locomotives on the line began. One can certainly hold up the North British 'Atlantics' as a class distinguished by interesting, appropriate, and indeed glamorous names. Of course, there were not too many of them, so that the system of nomenclature did not have to be carried to the absurd extent that one became all too familiar with in later years. The complete list, including the six additional engines of 1911, is worth quoting, thus:

868	Aberdonian	875	Midlothian
869	Bonnie Dundee	876	Waverley
870	Bon Accord	877	Liddesdale
871	Thane of Fife	878	Hazeldean
872	Auld Reekie	879	Abbotsford
873	St Mungo	880	Tweeddale
874	Dunedin	881	Borderer
1911 Batch			
901	St Johnston	904	Holyrood
902	Highland Chief	905	Teribus
903	Cock O' the North	906	Buccleugh

These engines, like those of the Great Central, did

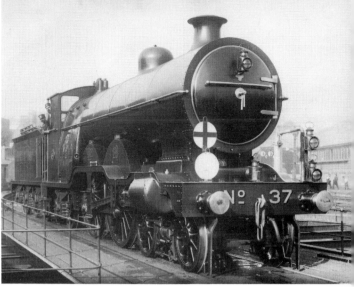

all their finest work in the years between the two world wars. My recollection of many journeys enjoyed on their footplates, and when travelling behind them must be held over for a later chapter.

The 'Atlantic' era on the Great Western was something quite apart from the general line of development in Great Britain. Churchward more than once stated that he thought the modern locomotive problem was that of the boiler; and in his work at Swindon he established principles of boiler construction that were to stand for the remaining 60 years of the life of the steam locomotives on British metals. It is true that inattention to details of design can involve heavy maintenance charges, even though the boiler itself may be free enough in steaming on its best days, but Churchward also wanted more power and more speed. Great Western locomotives of the early 1900s were notably free running, one has only to utter the words *City of Truro* in support of this! But high power was needed as well and, in view of the laudatory reports of the work of the Du Bousquet—De Glehn compound 'Atlantics' on the Northern Railway of France, he determined to give one of them a trial. This was not an interchange in the accepted sense. The Nord engines as they were would not clear the English loading gauge and so a separate engine, identical to the French so far as its machinery was concerned, but with boiler mountings suitably attenuated, was purchased from Alfred de Glehn's works, in Belfort. The proportions of this engine are discussed later, together with those of the other British compound 'Atlantics'; at the particular moment, the important point was that, to ensure the closest possible comparison with his own 2-cylinder simple 10-wheeler, Churchward altered this latter to an 'Atlantic', by taking off the rear pair of coupled wheels and substituting a pair of trailing carrying wheels.

This engine, No 171, *Albion*, ran in competition with the French compound, the *La France*, and both did first class work. Although the use of 'Atlantics' in the heavy main line traffic of the Great Western, and particularly in view of the very severe gradients west of Newton Abbot, was rather against Churchward's inclinations, he determined to make an extended trial of 4-4-2 *versus* 4-6-0, and in 1905 he built 13 more 'Atlantics', and six more 4-6-0s.

There was an amusing contretemps over the new 'Atlantics', the first of which were sent to the new Old Oak Common shed. They would not steam! Stanier was then London Divisional Superintendent and he was summoned to Swindon to meet a very irate Churchward, who wanted to know just 'what the Hell's the matter with them'. Stanier had very carefully compared the new engines with the converted *Albion* and said that the only difference he could see was in the ashpan. On the former 4-6-0 it was shaped to clear the rearmost coupled axle, and this shape had not been changed when the engine was converted. On the new engines the ashpan was straight. Churchward said: 'I think you've hit it. We've restricted the air flow'. One of the new engines was altered and all was well; and incidentally, of course, no further change was needed to the ashpan when the 'Atlantics' were eventually converted to 4-6-0s, in 1912.

The new constructional programme at Swindon in 1905 began in February with the 'Atlantic' No 172, which was named *Quicksilver*; then followed five 4-6-0s, similar to the original *Albion*, after which came 12 more 'Atlantics' Nos 179 to 190, the last two of which were outshopped in September. Of these No 179 was named *Magnet* but the remainder were at first not named. It was not until the end of 1906 that naming began in earnest, with titles associated with the 'Waverley' novels of Sir Walter Scott, and then with Nos 171, 172 and 179 renamed as below, the 14 'Atlantics' became:

171 The Pirate	184 Guy Mannering
172 The Abbot	185 Peveril of the Peak
179 Quentin Durward	186 Robin Hood
180 Coeur de Lion	187 Bride of Lammermoor
181 Ivanhoe	188 Rob Roy
182 Lalla Rookh	189 Talisman
183 Redgauntlet	190 Waverley

The principal differences between these engines and those included in the table on page 89 lay in the special form of coned boiler developed at Swindon by Churchward, and the American style of front-end with the cylinders, valve chests and smokebox saddle incorporated in two identical castings bolted together on the centre line of the engine. The piston valves were provided with long laps, and long travel, and actuated by the special setting of the Stephenson link motion designed by W.H. Pearce, the senior draughtsman specialising in this work. These engines provided one example of where the 'basic' dimensions did not give a true impression of the potentialities. The cylinders were 18 inch diameter by 30 inch stroke; the total heating surface of the half-cone taper boiler first used on these engines was 2,143 square feet, and the grate area 27 square feet. The working pressure was 225 lb per square inch. The nominal tractive effort was 23,090 lb.

In June 1905 comparative tests, with the dynamometer car, were carried out on the severely graded stretch of the line between Newton Abbot and Plymouth between one of the new 'Atlantics', No 172 then *Quicksilver*, and a 4-6-0 No 178, *Kirkland*, each hauling a train of 217 tons. From a close study of the dynamometer car rolls it is clear that there was nothing to choose between the climbing ability of the two engines, and no evidence of any tendency to slip by the 'Atlantic'. In the case of the eastbound run, this latter engine was checked near Plympton, and so began the ascent of the Hemerdon bank at no more than 46 mph, where the 4-6-0 was doing 55 mph; but the 'Atlantic' climbed that dreaded 2¼ miles at 1 in 42 without difficulty. From these tests there was no hesitation in using 'Atlantic' engines on the through Paddington-Plymouth rosters then coming into use. All these engines were converted into 4-6-0s in 1912. (See table opposite.)

The use of 'Atlantics' on the Great Western had arisen from Churchward's desire to make the fairest possible comparison between his own 10-wheelers and the French-built de Glehn compounds, and this leads on to a study of the various compound 'Atlantic' engines introduced on this, and other British railways in 1903-8. Dimensional details of the seven varieties are tabulated opposite. The Great Central engines, of which there were eventually four, had exactly the same cylinder dimensions as the Smith-Johnson 4-4-0 compounds of the Midland Railway, and they took the road at almost the same time as the Deeley development of the latter engines. They were powerful, reliable and long lived machines, all in service, still as compounds, at the end of the *Second* World War, though never showing any advantage over the standard two-cylinder simple 4-4-2s of Robinson's design. The French built engines on the Great Western had similar proportions to those of the Northern Railway of France, for No 102, and of the Paris-Orleans Railway for Nos 103 and 104.

The Great Northern compounds were an oddly assorted lot. Engine No 1300, built by the Vulcan Foundry, was of the de Glehn type, very similar in its proportions to those working on the Great Western, but No 292, although having the huge '251' Class boiler had such tiny cylinders as to have a tractive effort, when working compound, of no more than 8,994 lb. In 1906 a series of trials were conducted between Kings Cross and Doncaster on the compound engines 292 and 1300, and a standard 2-cylinder simple 'Atlantic', No 294, on which the boiler pressure was raised, specially for the tests, from 180 to 200 lb per square inch, to

North British Railway: one of the handsome Reid 'Atlantics' in its original non-superheated form, Aberdonian, *(North British Locomotive Company).*

'Atlantics': the first phase

Ref no	1	2	3	4	5	6	7	8
Railway	GNR	LYR	GNR	GNR	NER	GCR	LBSC	NBR
Date	1898	1899	1902	1902	1903	1903	1905	1906
Cylinders (number of)	2	2	4	2	2	2	2	2
Diameter (inches)	18¾	19	15	18¾	20	19½	18½	20
Stroke (inches)	24	26	20	24	26	26	26	28
Coupled wheel diameter (feet/inches)	6 8	7 3	6 8	6 8	6 10	6 9	6 8	6 9
Total heating surface (square feet)	1,442	2,052.8	1,303	2,500	2,456	1,911	2,459	2,256
Grate area (square feet)	26.75	26.05	24.5	30.9	27	26	30.9	28.5
Boiler pressure (lb per square inch)	175	175	175	175	200	180	200	180
Adhesion weight (tons)	31	35	32.7	37	39.0	37.0	37.0	40
Total weight (tons) engine only	58	58.7	58.7	68½	72.0	68.3	67.0	74.4
Nom tractive effort (lb)	15,670	16,050	16,700	15,670	23,250	18,750	18,930	21,170

Compound 'Atlantic' engines

Ref no	1	2	3	4	5	6	7
Railway	GWR	GWR	GCR	GNR	GNR	GNR	NER
Engine no	102	103-4	258-9	292	1300	1421	730-1
No of cylinders	4	4	3	4	4	4	4
Cylinders							
Diameter HP (inches)	$13\frac{3}{8}$	$14\frac{3}{16}$	19	13	14	13	14¼
Diameter LP (inches)	$22\frac{1}{16}$	$23\frac{3}{8}$	21	16	23	18	22
Stroke HP (inches)	$25\frac{3}{16}$	$25\frac{3}{16}$	26	20	26	20	26
Stroke LP (inches)	$25\frac{3}{16}$	$25\frac{3}{16}$	26	26	26	26	26
Coupled wheel diameter (feet/inches)	6 8½	6 8½	6 9	6 8	6 8	6 8	7 1
Total heating surface (square feet)	2,455.7	2,755.7	1,911	2,500	2,514	2,351.8	2,096
Grate area (square feet)	29.5	33.4	26	31	31	31	29
Boiler pressure (lb per square inch)	227	227	180	200	200	200	225

equal that of the two compounds. The average weight of the trains hauled by the three engines was very light, varying between 230 and 238 tons, and at average speeds between 49 and 50 mph. Three sets of enginemen were selected, and each set ran each engine for three weeks on the same group of trains, so that the tests lasted for nine weeks in all. The result to all intents and purposes was a dead heat. Ivatt published the full results in a short paper presented to the institution of Mechanical Engineers in May 1907, of which the following is a brief extract.

GNR 'Atlantic' engine trials, 1906

Engine no	292	1300	294
Total miles run, train	11,415	11,045	11,415
Average load (tons)	238.03	229.98	234.29
Average speed (mph)	49.9	49.02	49.58
Coal per train mile (lb)	43.98	45.84	45.31
Cost of repairs per engine mile (pence)	0.45	0.56	0.37
Total cost per engine mile (pence)	2.91	3.125	2.88

The only significant result to emerge was that the repair costs were lowest with the simple engine, No 294, as one might expect from its having only two cylinders as against four.

In 1908 Ivatt built a second compound engine of his own design at Doncaster, No 1421, reference 6 in the table. It differed from No 292 in having larger low pressure cylinders, and a boiler shortened by having the smokebox extended backwards into the barrel, instead of ahead of the chimney. I came across the only details I have ever seen about the working of this engine quite accidentally, in the Darlington drawing office of the former North Eastern Railway. In 1953 I was browsing through some tests made in pre-grouping days with the NER dynamometer car, (now in the National Railway Museum at York) and came across a test made in 1909 with the new East Coast Royal Train, prior to a visit to Edinburgh by King Edward VII, and it began at Doncaster. The test was primarily to record the rolling resistance of the new train, and so did not include any details of the engine working. This was unfortunate, for the GNR locomotive was No 1421 and the performance was spectacular to a degree. The load was 302 tons behind the tender, and with this a speed of 60 mph was attained in 4¾ miles from the start; and then, gradually working up to a sustained speed of 73 mph on the level the train passed Selby, 18.4 miles, in the unprecedented time, for that period of 19½ minutes. Checks spoiled the continuation of the run to York, where the North Eastern Railway took over the haulage.

So we come to the last of the British compound 'Atlantics', reference 7 in the table on page 89, and justly regarded as W.M. Smith's masterpieces, a four-cylinder development of his famous three-cylinder system which did so well for both the Midland and the Great Central Railways. The two North Eastern compound 'Atlantics' No 730-1 had all the simplicity of control that characterised Smith's work, and their performance in traffic was outstanding. It is interesting to speculate as to what the future of North Eastern locomotive practice might have been, had not Smith himself died just at the time these two engines were completed. There is no doubt that on many points he did not see eye to eye with the chief, and Wilson Worsdell cannot have been very pleased when dynamometer car test runs showed, without any question, that the Smith compounds were greatly superior in haulage

Below *Great Western Railway: the first French built de Glehn compound 'Atlantic', No 102,* La France *(British Railways).*

Bottom *GWR: one of the competing 2-cylinder simple 'Atlantics', No 181,* Ivanhoe, *which formed part of Churchward's historic development at Swindon (British Railways).*

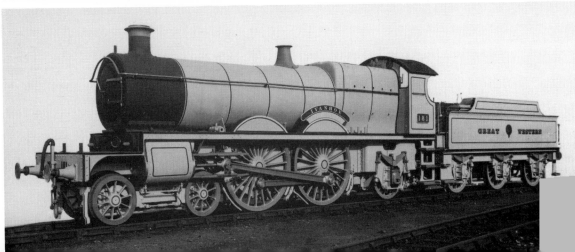

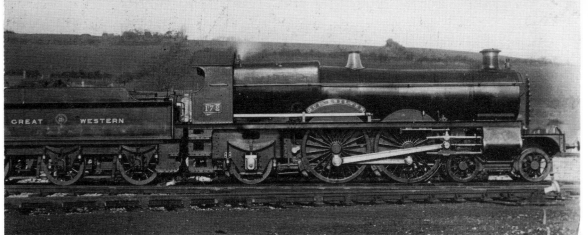

GWR: the 'Atlantic' engine, Quicksilver, *at Laira sheds, Plymouth, at the time of the 4-6-0 versus 4-4-2 trials in June 1905* (the late W.A. Dunn).

capacity to the large 'Atlantics' he built in 1903 when Smith was away ill. These tests established the relative capacities of the four classes of NER express passenger engines thus:

Class	R	S1	V	4CC
Type	4-4-0	4-6-0	4-4-2	4-4-2
Relative capacity	100	105	128	145
Drawbar pull at 55 mph (tons)	1.3	1.38	1.66	1.88

Driving practice on the North Eastern Railway in the early 1900s was to make very vigorous starts from rest, to obviate the need for high sustained speed afterwards. For example, when the 5.30 pm from Kings Cross was first given a timing of 44 minutes, start-to-stop for the 44.1 miles from York to Darlington, the 'R' Class 4-4-0s used to be pounded away from York to cover the initial 5.5 miles to Beningbrough in little more than 7 minutes, with their loads of 150 tons; and after this a steady rate of about 65 mph was all that was subsequently necessary to keep time. During the dynamometer car tests of 1906 the compound 'Atlantic' No 730 had a load specially made up to 475 tons, on the down 'Flying Scotsman', and passed Beningbrough in 8 minutes 2 seconds—an incredible feat. After such a start she sailed placidly along at 53 to 58 mph on level track. Another fine performance was to haul a test load of 455 tons from Darlington to York in 45½ minutes start to stop.

One can form the impression that the achievements of these two engines were regarded with a little jealousy at Gateshead; and, inview of their remarkable achievements, the record of the locomotive department in the ensuing few years seemed to indicated a lack of direction. In 1908, as recorded in Chapter Three of this book, Wilson Worsdell produced the 'R1' Class of 4-4-0, and followed it, in 1910, with a considerably less powerful version of his 'Atlantic' of 1903. Class 'V1' had 19½ instead of 20 inch diameter cylinders and a boiler pressure of only 180 lb per square inch. The latter was indeed strange, seeing that the 'R1' 4-4-0s, like the '4CC' compound 'Atlantics', used 225 lb per square inch. But, by the time the 'V1' Atlantics took the road, Wilson Worsdell had retired, and been succeeded by Vincent L. Raven. More top-line express passenger engines were needed, and a review of the existing stud showed that the four-cylinder compounds stood supreme on almost every count. How their maintenance charges compared with the 'V' and 'V1' 'Atlantics' I cannot say; it is understood that at the end of 1910 an order was placed for 10 more compounds, though rescinded at the last minute. Raven had been very impressed with the smooth starting from rest, with heavy loads, of the 3-cylinder 4-8-0 shunting engines used in the Erimus marshalling yard, Middlesbrough, and instead of more compounds he decided upon a three-cylinder simple express 'Atlantic' locomotive. Orders were placed with the North British Locomotive Company for 20, 10 to use saturated steam, and 10 to be superheated. These engines went into traffic in 1911-12.

It was a time when much experimenting with superheater locomotives was in progress, and on no railway was the issue so quickly and decisively resolved, as had been the case on the London and North Western, as instanced by the 'George the Fifth' 4-4-0s and related in Chapter Three. On the North Eastern, Raven, like Ivatt on the Great Northern, at first took superheating as an opportunity to reduce boiler pressure, and so reduce maintenance costs; and the new 3-cylinder 'Atlantics' used 180 lb per square inch on the saturators, and 160 on the superheated. Apparently there was no question at first of increasing power, because the tractive effort of the new engines was actually *less* than that of the 'V1' Atlantics. The comparative cylinder dimensions of the four classes of non-compound Atlantics on the NER were:

Class	V	V1	Z	Z1
Cylinders				
Number	2	2	3	3
Diameter (inches)	20	19½	15½	16½
Stroke (inches)	28	28	26	26
Coupled wheel				
diameter (feet/				
inches)	6 10	6 10	6 10	6 10
Boiler pressure				
(lb per square				
inch)	200	180	180	160
Tractive effort (lb)	23,250	19,900	17,550	17,650

In view of the developing trends of the day it was rather surprising that in its issue of January 1912 *The Locomotive Magazine* published as a supplement a fully detailed general arrangement drawing of the *non*-superheated version of the new NER three-cylinder 'Atlantics'. Perhaps it was because of the considerable uncertainty shown in the boiler proportions of the superheated version. The first details that I can trace were contained in an apparently fully authoritative article in *The Railway Magazine* in February 1915 from the pen of the Editor himself, J.F. Gairns, in which it appears that by that time all the engines originally built as 'saturators' had been converted. It also revealed that, in a new batch of these engines built in 1914, there had been a remarkable change in the heating surface proportions. In the original 'Z1' Class, in which a superheat temperature of around 650 degrees had been aimed at, the tubes appear to have been unduly crowded. In the discussion following Henry Fowler's paper to the Institution of Civil Engineers in 1914, Raven said that they had not been getting the superheat they hoped for, and that

things had been much improved by blocking up a number of the small flue tubes. Furthermore, the crowding of the small tubes had led to the cracking of the tube plates, due to the narrowness of the bridges between the tubes. The result was seen in the reduction of the tube heating surface in the 1914 batch of 'Z' Atlantics from 1,798.9 square feet to 1,295.8 entirely by reducing the number of small tubes from 149 to 90.

The Schmidt superheaters in these engines were always of 24 elements, in 5¼ inch flue tubes. Originally the elements were carried almost to the rearmost limit because a superheating surface of 530.1 square feet was very large for a 24-element apparatus. After some years of experience, and trouble with burning of the elements at the forward end, the length was reduced. On some engines of the class the heating surface was cut back to 392 square feet. While on others it was 437 square feet. In later engines of the class the boiler pressure was raised to 175 lb per square inch, bringing the tractive effort up to 19,300 lb. When the North Eastern Railway became part of the LNER in 1923 it was evident that changes in the boiler design of the 'Zs' was even yet not finished. On the official diagram published in a series of articles in *The Railway Gazette* in 1935 showed that the number of small tubes was 134; so that the four stages of boiler development on these engines can be shown thus:

Boilers: Class 'Z' 4-4-2s

Approximate date	1911	1916	1922	1935
Large tubes	24	24	24	24
Small tubes	149	90	90	134
Heating surfaces				
(square feet)				
Small tubes	1,267	764	764	1,140.6
Large tubes	531.9	531.9	531.9	531.9
Superheater elements	530.1	530.1	392	437

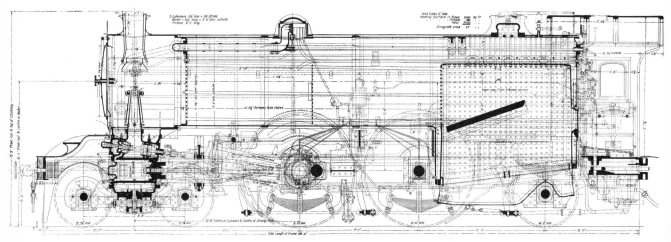

Below left *North Eastern Railway: Class 'Z' 3-cylinder 'Atlantic' non-superheated.*

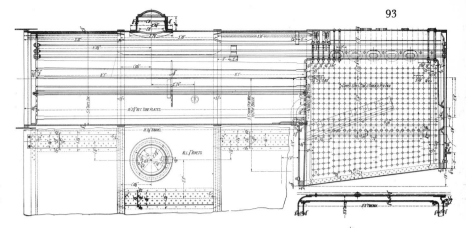

Right *NER: the superheated boiler, later fitted to all 50 engines of the 'Z' Class—general arrangement and cross-sections.*

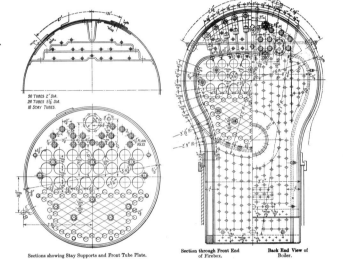

Sections showing Stay Supports and Front Tube Plate.

Section through Front End of Firebox.

Back End View of Boiler.

Although the superheating of the **Great Northern** 'Atlantics' belongs mainly to a later period to that of which I am now writing, the first stages in what was to develop into a most brilliant success may be mentioned at this stage, and with it the collateral development of what can be termed their 'first cousins', on the Brighton railway.

Ivatt–Marsh large boilered Atlantics

Date	1902	1910	1905	1911
Railway	**GNR**	**GNR**	**LBSC**	**LBSC**
Engine no	251	1452	37	421
Cylinders				
Diameter (inches)	18¾	20	18½	21
Stroke (inches)	24	24	26	26
Heating surface (square feet)				
Tubes	2,359	1,909.5	2,337.1	1,895
Firebox	141	143.5	136.4	136.5
Superheater	—	343	—	460
Boiler pressure (lb per square inch)	175	150	200	170

On both railways one saw the opportunity taken to reduce boiler pressure and increase cylinder volume; but, whereas the Brighton did not proceed any further with the 'Atlantic' type on the Great Northern, the building of the 10 new engines, 1452-1461, was only the beginning of an entirely new era.

Looking back to the spacious age that ended in August 1914, when 'Atlantics' on most railways ran lightly loaded trains at average speed of around 55 mph and when even on the East Coast main line the day Anglo-Scottish expresses rarely loaded to much above 300 tons, it is equally remarkable to recall what those same engines were daily called upon to do before the war was over, admittedly on timings that had been very much eased out. At the end of

1918, for example, the 6.25 pm express from York to Newcastle was recorded on six successive occasions as loading to 560, 615, 600, 510, 465 and 625 tons, and double heading was unheard of with the 'Z' Class 'Atlantics'.

On the Great Northern, towards the end of the war a concession was made in allowing the large Ivatt 'Atlantics' to be piloted out of Kings Cross as far as Potters Bar, to obviate the inconvenience and delay that would be caused if the train engine stalled in one of the tunnels on the steep gradient out of the terminus. The Ivatt 4-4-0s were used for assisting, but a pilot could not be claimed unless the train consisted of 70 axles, or more, about 550 tons! The time between Kings Cross and Peterborough, 76.4 miles, was then 103 minutes, an average of 44.5 mph, inclusive of the time to put off the pilot engine at Potters Bar.

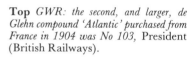

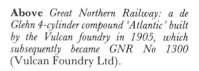

Top *GWR: the second, and larger, de Glehn compound 'Atlantic' purchased from France in 1904 was No 103,* President *(British Railways).*

Above *Great Northern Railway: a de Glehn 4-cylinder compound 'Atlantic' built by the Vulcan foundry in 1905, which subsequently became GNR No 1300 (Vulcan Foundry Ltd).*

Above left and left *Two experimental 4-cylinder compound 'Atlantics', built at Doncaster by the GNR No 292 in 1906 (Lens of Sutton) and No 1421 in 1907 (the late W.J. Reynolds).*

Right *NER: Wilson Worsdell's last design, the 'V1 Atlantic' of 1910, which was completed after his retirement. They were powerful engines and were still in main line service in the 1930s, as shown here at Darlington.*

Right *LB & SCR: the superheated development of the Earle-Marsh 'Atlantic', No 421* (British Railways).

Right *GNR: one of the Ivatt non-super-heated 'Atlantics', No 1440, on the 2.20 pm Anglo-Scottish express near Potters Bar* (the late C. Laundy).

Below *GNR: one of the first superheated 'Atlantics', No 1460, just outside Kings Cross with the morning Leeds and Bradford express* (F.E. Mackay).

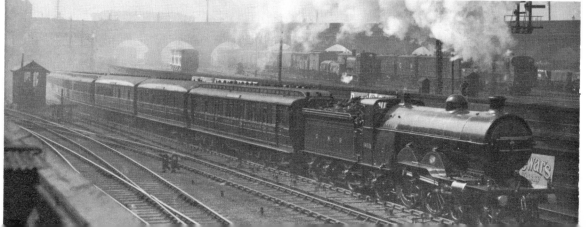

7. The 8-coupled freighters

Eighty years ago the major part of the revenue of all the north-going railways of England was derived from freight. It was the slow-moving goods trains rather than the glamorous 60 mph express that brought in the money and, at a time before the First World War, it is interesting to recall how freight predominated on six of the leading railways. The figures in the table below relate to the first six months in 1912. In Scotland, the figures for the Caledonian and the North British were both around the 60 per cent level.

Everywhere the tempo of operation was slow. Nevertheless, while the almost exclusive use of loose-coupled 4-wheeled wagons, without continuous brakes, on the heaviest mineral trains, gave the opportunity of taking up the load gradually when starting from rest, with trains of such weight there was ample need for the power and adhesion of an 8-coupled locomotive to maintain a reasonable commercial speed on level, and rising gradients. Apart from the special case of the Barry Railway which, in 1889, purchased from Sharp Stewart & Co two outside-cylindered 0-8-0s that had been built for a Scandinavian railway which could not pay for them, the London and North Western Railway was the first in Great Britain to introduce the 0-8-0 tender type for main line work, in 1892-3; and, after a trial of 'simple versus compound', F.W. Webb went ahead and built 110 more compounds of the three-cylinder type between 1893 and 1900. These latter were the standard heavy freight engines of the LNWR at the turn of the century. The kind of work they were then called upon to do was shown in the results of a dynamometer test run made over the steeply graded Stockport-Leeds main line, when the first of the compounds took a 50-wagon fully loaded goods train. The weight of the train, including the dynamometer car, was given as 369¾ tons tare; but as the train was heavily loaded an addition of at least 200 tons can be assumed, to make up the gross load behind the tender.

Between the start at Stockport, and the entrance to Diggle Tunnel, 15¼ miles, indicator diagrams were taken at 13 locations. Above Stalybridge the gradients vary between 1 in 125 and 1 in 175, with an average around 1 in 135, and here the engine maintained a steady speed of 21 to 23 mph with this heavy train, which can have been little short of 600 tons behind the tender. During this spell the indicated horsepower varied between 720 and 768. The accoustical accompaniment of this big effort must have been impressive to hear, with only the two mighty exhaust-beats per revolution at the slow speed of just over 20 mph and the engine being worked very hard. These engines worked not only throughout the main line, taking heavy freight trains over Shap, but also brought trainloads of coal northward from South Wales over the steep gradients from Abergavenny via Hereford and Shrewsbury.

With 110 of these locomotives in traffic Webb

Railway	LNWR	Great Western	Midland	North Eastern	Lancashire & Yorkshire	Great Central
Total revenue from passengers, mails and freight	£7,436,400	£6,526,758	£5,729,366	£4,521,867	£2,885,387	£1,931,370
Percentage of total derived from freight	59.2	55.8	68.7	67.4	59.2	69.5

Left *LNWR: a Webb 4-cylinder compound 0-8-0 hauling a 'Jellicoe special' (coal for the Grand Fleet in the First World War) climbing Shap with a bank engine at the rear* (F.E. Mackay).

Right *Lancashire and Yorkshire Railway: the first of the Aspinall 0-8-0s which were built at Horwich in 1900 using the same design of boiler as used on the 'Highflyer' 4-4-2s* (British Railways).

went on to produce a much enlarged design in 1901 with four cylinders, supplied by the largest boiler that had then been constructed at Crewe. They were without doubt the most successful compounds that Webb ever built, and fulfilled an important part in the motive power position of the LNWR for many years. In all, 170 of them were built, and although a number were subsequently converted into simples, no fewer than 60 remained as compounds when the LNWR was merged into the LMS system in January 1923. Comparative dimensions of the three- and four-cylinder compound 0-8-0s were as follows:

LNWR compound 0-8-0s

	3-cylinder	4-cylinder
Cylinders		
HP diameter (inches)	15	16
LP diameter (inches)	30 (1)	20½ (2)
Stroke (inches) (both)	24	24
Coupled wheel diameter (feet/inches)	4 10	4 10
Tubes (number of)	210	249
Outside diameter (inches)	$1\frac{7}{8}$	$1\frac{7}{8}$
Heating surface (square feet)	1,374.3	1,630
Length (feet/inches)	13 4	13 4
Firebox heating surface (square feet)	114.7	123
Grate area (square feet)	20.5	20.5
Boiler pressure (lb per square inch)	175	200

Between Crewe and Euston the 4-cylinder engines took loads of 900 tons single-handed; and, during the First World War when vast tonnages of Welsh coal had to be hauled up to Scotland for use of the Grand Fleet, based at Scapa Flow, they played an important part. F.E. Mackay secured a memorable photograph of one of them pounding up Shap with a load of 50 wagons piled high with coal, and banked in rear by an 0-6-0.

In the years 1900-2 four other English railways introduced powerful 0-8-0 locomotives for heavy freight and mineral haulage. All were 2-cylinder simples but, while there would probably have been little difference between them in their ability to handle the traffic, there were considerable variations in detail design and outward appearance. The Lancashire and Yorkshire design was Aspinall's last, before he moved up into the high management, and had a similar design of boiler to that of his 'Atlantics'. The drawing office, however, managed to work in larger cylinders, to great advantage to the engines. They were eventually used all over the system, but not before one of them had given all concerned a grievous shock. In March 1901 one of the new 0-8-0s, built no more than nine months earlier, was working a 52-wagon loaded coal train from Glasshoughton Colliery sidings to Goole docks, for export, and they had just passed east of Knottingley when the boiler exploded killing the driver and fireman instantly. Aspinall was very upset, and things were not made any better when his successor as CME, H.A. Hoy, suggested that it was the fault of the driver and fireman, by letting the water level in the boiler get dangerously low. The Board of Trade enquiry was conducted by Major Druitt, he who 14 years later had the gruesome task of enquiring into the causes of the terrible accident at Quintinshill, on the Caledonian Railway. In 1901 the Major completely exonerated the unfortunate driver and fireman, and proved that this alarming accident was due to faulty material in no fewer than 20 of the firebox stays.

This was a sad indictment of the standards of production then at Horwich, and Aspinall, who had done so much towards the building up of the tradition of that works, took it very much to heart. Although it was very much an isolated case it caused such a stir that Aspinall felt something special had got to be done about it, and he urged Hoy, his CME, to make a trial of a corrugated firebox, with a circular cross section. The idea was to give the firebox sufficient strength in itself to avoid the need for staying, at the same time to give increased water space between the firebox itself and the outer shell.

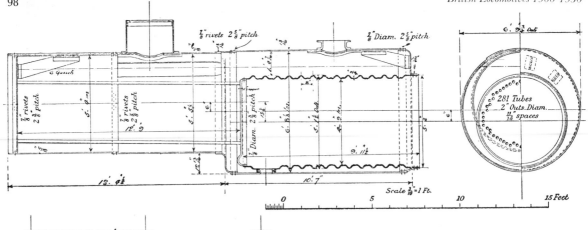

Above *LYR: boiler with corrugated firebox.*
Left *LYR: section of firebox corrugations.*

As can be seen from the accompanying drawing, this was also of circular cross-section and of no less than 6 feet 9¾ inches outside diameter. A subsidiary drawing shows a much enlarged cross-section of the corrugations. It will be appreciated that a boiler and firebox of these proportions could have been mounted only on a locomotive with small driving wheels.

Though sustaining the teething troubles that were inevitable with so radical a departure from established firebox design practice, the standard 0-8-0 that had been rebuilt thus gave sufficient evidence of future promise that construction of 20 similar engines was undertaken in 1903, and they were put into traffic, in the ordinary heavy freight links between March and August in that year. After Hoy's sudden departure in March 1904 following an invitation to become Managing Director of Beyer, Peacock & Co, George Hughes, who was appointed to succeed him, had the job of nursing the 'corrugateds' along. He referred to them at some length in the discussion following Churchward's paper on *Large Locomotive Boilers* to the Institution of Mechanical Engineers in February 1906. After describing and illustrating their construction he concluded in these somewhat guarded terms:

'With regard to the general question of maintenance, he could not give figures because money had had to be spent on getting over difficulties of untried design, but it was an absolute fact that the engines with the corrugated boxes had taken their turn in their respective links with the ordinary engines and, when all factors were brought into line, he had no doubt that those with corrugated boxes would be somewhat more economical'.

What Hughes did not discourse about at the Institution of Mechanical Engineers was the incredible time it took to get up steam. If an engine was required for a train on Monday it had to be fired up early on the previous Saturday! There was much trouble with leaky tubes; the water circulation was bad, and even when steam was raised these engines were sadly addicted to priming. One can understand in view of all this that Hughes had been to some pains to assure the I Mech E that it was 'an absolute fact' that the engines had done some work in the ordinary links. They were all rebuilt with ordinary boilers in 1912-14. In the meantime the engines of Aspinall's original design continued to do steady reliable work.

Of the remaining three 0-8-0 designs of the 1900-2 period, the first of the North Eastern 'T' Class had W.M. Smith's type of segmental piston valves. There were 10 of these engines, and the valve, which was the same being currently used on the 'R' Class 4-4-0 express passenger locomotives, is shown in the drawing on page 20. Then in 1902 a further 10 of these engines were built, but with ordinary slide valves. Both varieties were put into service on the very heavy road across the Pennines, conveying loaded coke trains from West Auckland to Tebay, en route for Barrow-in-Furness. On this duty it was found that these 0-8-0 engines could take loads of 40 loaded coke wagons and two brake vans without assistance, on the lengthy adverse gradients

Right *LYR: a rear end view of a boiler with a corrugated firebox, designed after the disastrous boiler explosion near Knottingley in 1901* (British Railways).

Below *LYR: one of the 20 0-8-0s built with a corrugated firebox which also had a large 8-wheeled non-bogie tender* (the late J.M. Tomlinson).

of 1 in 70. The reversion to slide valves on the second batch of 0-8-0s caused some surprise because, at the summer meeting of the Institution of Mechanical Engineers in 1902, which was held in Newcastle, Smith read a paper strongly advocating the use of piston valves and quoting results from engines of the 4-4-0 'M' Class, which had so distinguished themselves in the Race to the North in 1895, showing how much better piston valves were in respect of coal consumption.

This was not all. The time for discussion of Smith's paper was relatively short, but one of the speakers was Charles Baister, then locomotive running superintendent of the North Eastern Railway, and said he, 'thought that slide-valves were one of the most fruitful sources of engine failure. Frequently the flat valves were broken in various ways, especially those on the top of the cylinder. He did not remember one single case of an

engine failure resulting from a piston valve since they were first adopted'. Nevertheless it will be appreciated from the drawing that Smith's segmental type of piston valve was a complicated thing. In 1902 they had not been long in service, either on passenger or freight locomotives and, by the time of Smith's untimely death in 1906, there were evidently some second thoughts in the Locomotive Department.

In that same year Wilson Worsdell put the experimental department of his drawing office on to dynamometer car tests between West Auckland and Tebay, in which a piston valve 0-8-0 was matched against one of those with slide valves. While both engines handled the test loads with equal facility, the slide-valve engine showed a pronounced superiority in coal consumption. Very great care was taken before the tests started to ensure that both engines were in a strictly comparable state of

repair—very good—and yet whereas the piston valve engine used 81 lb of coal per mile, the slide valve engine used no more than 73 lb. The result was that 20 more of the slide valve type were built in 1907-8, and a further 20 in 1911.

The Great Northern 0-8-0s in 1901, were introduced to cope with two very heavy traffics: coal originating from the Nottinghamshire pits, and concentrated for onwards conveyance at Colwick, and the traffic in bricks, from the yards beside the line at Fletton just south of Peterborough. Southwards to the London area the standard loads were those of 55 loaded wagons of coal, or 50 of bricks, together with a 20-ton brake van. These represented a gross load of 800 tons in each case, though on a special test with 65 loaded wagons of brick, 1,050 tons, no difficulty was experienced in keeping the standard timing for these heavy trains. Forty of these powerful engines had been built by the end of 1904, and further small batches brought the total up to 50 by mid-1909. The boiler was the same as that of the '990' Class 'Atlantics' and steam distribution was by balanced slide valves on the top of the cylinders actuated by Stephenson's link motion, through rocking shafts. A number of these engines were stationed at Colwick for working the coal trains to Peterborough. They went by the nickname of the 'Long Toms'. One of these engines, No 417, was chosen for a trial of the Schmidt superheater, in 1908.

The Great Central also had a very onerous task in mineral train haulage, from the Wath concentration yards, near Barnsley, where coal from the South Yorkshire pits was collected, and thence over the Pennines to destinations in Lancashire and Cheshire. Passengers by the old Great Central route from Sheffield to Manchester will have been well enough aware of the heavy climbing involved throughout to the eastern portal of Woodhead Tunnel; but the work facing the locomotives of passenger trains in steam days was a mere nothing compared to the job of getting the loaded coal trains as far as Penistone. For the way up from Wath concentration yard included the fearsome Worsborough Incline, with its 2½ miles of 1 in 40. To get the maximum load trains, about 1,000 tons, up this terror of a bank needed the efforts of four 8-coupled engines—one in front and three pushing in rear. The Great Central was greatly developing this traffic in the early 1900s, and Robinson's 0-8-0 mineral engines of 1902 were appropriately the largest that had yet been introduced on that railway. As will be seen from the table on page 102 they were, by a considerable margin, the heaviest of all the early 2-cylinder simple 0-8-0s. Robinson's locomotives were distinguished by their massive frame construction, and this stood them in good stead for the severe work they were called upon to do.

Great Northern Railway: Ivatt 0-8-0 Mineral engine, with Schmidt superheater and piston valves.

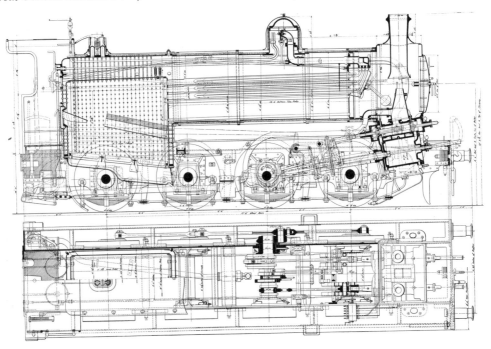

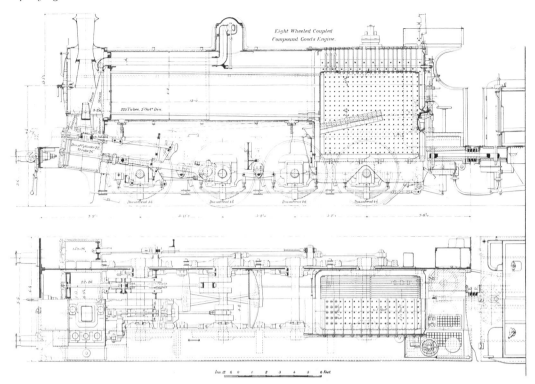

Eight Wheeled Coupled Compound Goods Engine.

Lancashire & Yorkshire Railway: a 4-cylinder compound mineral 0-8-0.

Two more non-superheated 0-8-0s may be mentioned at this stage, though neither were very numerous. In 1901-3 the Caledonian built eight very powerful engines for hauling the heavy mineral trains in the Lanarkshire colliers area. The Locomotive Superintendent, J.F. McIntosh, had built a number of 30-ton high capacity bogie open wagons for this traffic and these big engines, which had 21 inch by 26 inch cylinders, 4 foot 6 inch coupled wheels and a boiler pressure of 175 lb per square inch were found capable of hauling *60* loaded wagons of this type. To facilitate control of such enormously heavy trains, both engines and wagons were fitted with the Westinghouse brake. The second design, built for the South Yorkshire coal traffic, but routed in the opposite direction to the major hauls of the Great Central, was Matthew Stirling's 0-8-0 for the Hull and Barnsley, introduced in 1907. These engines of which there were eventually 15, were of his characteristic domeless boiler type. The cylinders were 19 inch diameter by 26 inch stroke, with valves actuated by the Allan straight link motion. The boiler was large, with a Belpaire firebox, and a total heating surface of 1,859 square feet with a boiler pressure of 200 lb per square inch. The total weight of the engine alone in working order was 61½ tons.

Before passing on to the rather complicated development from the Webb compound types on the London and North Western Railway, there is another interesting compound goods 0-8-0 which requires consideration, that of the Lancashire and Yorkshire Railway, designed by G. Hughes. This particular enterprise began in 1904 with the rebuilding of one of the standard Aspinall coal engines as a 4-cylinder compound. The general layout, as shown in the accompanying drawing, followed that of Webb's on the LNWR, except that the disposition of the cylinders and the intermediate receivers was neater and more compact, and avoided the overhanging appearance on the front-end in the Webb engines. Comparative tests on the L & YR seemed to establish the superiority of the compound, and in 1907 10 more were built at Horwich. In his paper, read to the Institution of Mechanical Engineers in 1910 *Compounding and Superheating in Horwich Locomotives*, Hughes gave some interesting results from a comparison of the overall performance of the 11 compounds with 11 standard simple 0-8-0s over 24 months, ending at November 30 1909.

The interesting point revealed by this very exhaustive comparison is of the very low mileage run for every hour the locomotives were in traffic. The utilisation, taken over two years was thus:

24 months LYR 0-8-0 engine working

Type	Compound	Simple
Total engine hours	54,846	61,991
Total engine miles	441,811	472,083
Miles: Percentage utilisation		
Train	67.5	63.7
Assisting	0.2	0.3
Light engine	7.0	6.8
Ballasting	nil	nil
Shunting	25.3	29.2

The total hours in 24 months is 8,760, or 96,520 for each group of 11 engines, so that the engine hours for each represent 57 per cent of total time for the compounds and 64 per cent, for the simples. The relative coal consumptions in tons were:

	Compound	Simple
Per train mile	86.75	95.27
Per engine mile	59.25	60.67
Per ton mile	0.185	0.205

Hughes made a very thorough analysis of all the figures and came to the conclusion that in coal the compounds showed a saving of 4.9 per cent. But, of course, this did not tell the whole story, which would require to include the maintenance costs. The speeds were very slow, amounting on average to around 8 miles for every hour in traffic, while it may, or may not be significant that the compounds were in traffic for only 90 per cent of the time clocked up by the simples. Despite Hughes' obvious enthusiasm for compounds, evidenced at the 1910 meeting of the Institution of Mechanical Engineers, no more of them were built for the Lancashire and Yorkshire Railway.

In the meantime their larger neighbour, the London and North Western, was busy converting many of the Webb compounds to simples. To make clear the nature of the conversions, references must first be made to the Class 'D' and 'G' boilers designed for use on the 0-8-0 simple engines. These were a variant of those used on the 'Experiment' Class 4-6-0, but with a longer barrel, of 14 feet 6 inches against 13 feet and a smaller grate area 23.6 square feet against 25. The 'D' carried a pressure of 175 lb per square inch. By the end of 1911 all except three of the Webb 3-cylinder compounds had been converted into simple engines, and they were of three classes, two of which carried the original boilers. It will be recalled that before embarking on the compound 0-8-0 programme Webb had built a simple engine, No 2524, for comparative purposes. This engine had never been converted, and the first rebuildings of the 3-cylinder compounds brought them into line with this original 0-8-0, having 19½ inch by 24 inch cylinders. A total of 15 were converted thus and became known as Class 'C'. In practice it was found that the 19½ inch cylinders were on the large size for the original boiler, and a further 31 engines were rebuilt with 18½ inch cylinders. These were Class 'C1'. Then, in 1906, the Class 'D' boilers was designed, and this was used on further conversions, on which the cylinders were 19½ inches by 24 inches, and the pressure 175

English 0-8-0 freight locomotives of 1900-2

Railway	Lancashire & Yorkshire	North Eastern	Great Northern	Great Central
Date first built	1900	1901	1901	1902
Engineer	Aspinall	Worsdell	Ivatt	Robinson
Cylinders (position)	inside	outside	inside	outside
Diameter (inches)	20	20	19¾	19½
Stroke (inches)	26	26	26	26
Wheel diameter (feet/inches)	4 6	4 7½	4 8	4 7
Valve gear	Joy	Stephenson	Stephenson	Stephenson
Total heating surface (square feet)	2,152	1,675	1,438.8	1,785
Grate area (square feet)	23	21.5	24.5	23.6
Boiler pressure	180	200	175	180
Total engine weight (tons)	53¾	52¼	54.6	63¾
Number built	108	90	50	89

Right *LYR: the first Aspinall 0-8-0 as rebuilt by G. Hughes with large boilers. This formed the basic design for many more superheated 0-8-0s which continued to be constructed until 1920* (Real Photographs).

Below *North Eastern Railway: Wilson Worsdell's 'T' Class 0-8-0 of 1900, built with W.M. Smith's segmental ring piston valves* (British Railways).

Bottom *Great Central Railway: Robinson's 0-8-0 heavy mineral engine of 1902 which was used for the trans-Pennine coal hauls* (British Railways).

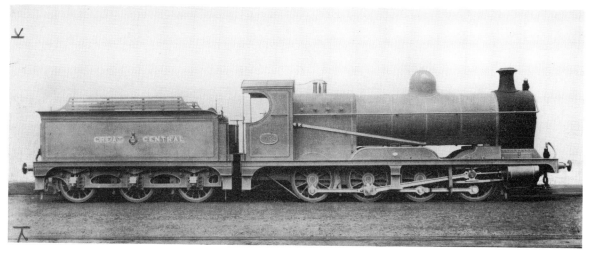

lb per square inch. In due course, the remaining 70 three-cylinder compounds were rebuilt into Class 'D'.

The 4-cylinder compound 0-8-0s were being built new at Crewe Works until August 1904 and, as previously mentioned, were proving satisfactory; but the appearance of overhang at the front end gave the impression of excessive weight on the leading coupled axle, although the actual distribution that Horwich used in their compound 0-8-0s was much the same. To appease the doubters Whale rebuilt some of the Webb engines as 2-8-0s, and the resulting distribution, as compared to that of the L & Y compounds, was as under:

4-cylinder compound 8-coupleds

Railway	LNWR		LNWR		LYR	
Type	0-8-0		2-8-0		0-8-0	
Weights:	Ton	Cwt	Ton	Cwt	Ton	Cwt
Leading radial	—		9	19	—	
Leading coupled	13	16	7	10	14	05
Driving	17	04	13	01	16	13
Intermediate	13	00	13	01	16	09
Trailing	9	10	12	19	14	09
Adhesion	53	10	46	11	60	16
Total, engine only	53	10	56	10	60	16

When the conversion of the 4-cylinder compounds to simple engines began, the procedure was much simpler than with the 3-cylinder class. The outside cylinders were taken off, and the 20½ inches inside cylinders were left *in situ*. The 'D' Class boiler was fitted to all the 4-cylinder compound conversions, and to distinguish them from the earlier rebuilds with large boilers they were classified 'G'. The difference between the two was that 'D' had 19½ inch and 'G' 20½ inch diameter cylinders. At the

same time 12 of the compound 2-8-0s were rebuilt with 'G' Class boilers. The 'G' Class simple 0-8-0s were very successful and became a new standard class. Additional engines were built new at Crewe from 1910 onwards, until, in 1912, the superheated version was introduced, Class 'G1'. On the line these locomotives were colloquially known as the 'Super Ds'. The comparative boiler proportions were:

LNWR 0-8-0 large boilers

Engine classes	4-cylinder compounds	'D', 'G' and 'G1'
Heating surface (square feet)		
Small tubes	2,034	1,160.9
Large tubes	—	464.8
Firebox	146.6	146.6
Superheater	—	378.6
Grate area (square feet)	23.6	23.6
Boiler pressure (lb per square inch)	175	160

The weight distribution on the four axles of the superheater engines from front to rear was 15, 17½, 15¼ and 12½ tons. These engines must be reckoned among the most successful of all 0-8-0s, because many of the final development, with a boiler pressure of 175 lb per square inch, Class G2', lasted until the final days of steam on the nationalised British Railways.

On the Lancashire and Yorkshire, following the

Below LNWR: one of the 2-cylinder 0-8-0s converted from Webb's 3-cylinder compound design (British Railways).

Above right LNWR: a large-boilered development of the same process of conversion, carried out in 1907 (British Railways).

construction of the 4-cylinder compounds a final batch of the Aspinall standard 0-8-0s, 20 in all, was built at Horwich in 1907-8. By that time Hughes was thinking in terms of much larger boilers, and the first of his ill-starred 4-cylinder 4-6-0 passenger engines took the road in June 1908. The first of the large boilered 0-8-0s, non-superheated, came just two years later, and a disproportioned thing it was. It was evidently intended to do harder work than the standard Aspinalls; but the cylinders, motion and frames were the same, although the links of the Joy valve gear were made much heavier, as if to anticipate possible trouble from fracturing of the links. The boiler was very large, with a total heating surface of 2,416 square feet, not quite so large as that of the 4-6-0s, and the pressure remained at 180 lb per square inch. Twenty of these large engines were built and then, from the end of 1912, Hughes produced his superheated version, with cylinders increased to 21½ inches diameter and boiler pressure retained at 180 lb per square inch. These powerful engines, of which 115 were built new at Horwich between November 1912 and 1920, weighed 66½ tons without their tenders. Many of the older 0-8-0s were rebuilt with the larger boilers, some superheated and some saturated; but the majority were scrapped in the 1930s. Only 33 of those built new from 1910 onwards survived the Second World War. Like most of the larger Lancashire and Yorkshire engines they suffered much from maintenance troubles, particularly with the types of superheater Hughes designed to avoid the Schmidt patents, and with driving axlebox breakages, which were distressingly frequent.

In 1913, under Vincent L. Raven's superintendence, the North Eastern Railway produced the superheated version of the very successful 'T1' 0-8-0. The new engines were designed to be driven 'all-out' for indefinite periods at anything up to maximum mineral train speeds. The boilers were the same as those used on the superheated 'Z'

Atlantics, described in the preceeding chapter, and retaining the original 160 lb pressure. Working in 72 per cent cut-off, full forward gear, and a wide open regulator these remarkable engines developed 1,000 drawbar horsepower at 19 mph. Quite apart from any finer points of technicalities it was their almost unfailing reliability that so endeared them to the running department. They were ruggedly built; could stand any amount of hard thrashing, and would steam freely under any conditions. Furthermore, the massive proportions of their machinery made them as free from incidental defects as any running superintendent could wish. A first batch of 30 of them was built at Darlington in 1913; 40 more followed to help with the heavy wartime traffic; 19 in 1917, 8 in 1918, and 13 in 1919. After the war an order for a further 50 was placed with Armstrong-Whitworth & Co, and the entire stud of 120 was still going strong when the London and North Eastern Railway passed into national ownership in 1948. One of the running inspectors at York in the early 1950s once described them to me as, 'the engines that won the war!'. They were no Rolls-Royce's to ride on, but by thunder they did the job. In the later batches the boiler pressure was raised to 180 lb per square inch, and this gave them a nominal tractive effort of 28,800 lb.

Reverting to the time of the First World War the entire stud of 'T1' 0-8-0s, the 50 non-superheated class with slide valves, was loaned to the Railway Operating Division of the British Army for service in France; and there they won golden opinions from all who had to deal with them. They too had a tractive effort of 28,000 lb, using 175 lb per square inch, and their solid reliability and willingness in standing up to merciless thrashing on heavy gradients, made them one of the most valuable groups of locomotives in the war zone. It should be added that although the North Eastern Railway itself was carrying an unprecedented volume of freight traffic in the war emergency, the motive power situation on one of the most heavily worked lines had been helped by the electrification between Newport and Shildon.

While the 0-8-0 type, exemplified particularly by the constructional strength and longevity of the 'G1' and 'G2' Classes on the London and North Western, and by the 'T2' on the North Eastern, could be regarded as the ideal wheel arrangement for a hard slogging, low speed, freight hauler, there is no doubt that the addition of a pony, or radial truck at the front end made for a better 'vehicle', that was kinder to the permanent way, and gave the enginemen a more comfortable ride. In later years the 2-8-0 became the standard heavy freight type in Great Britain. In the period 1900 to 1920, however, apart from the relatively few 4-cylinder compound conversions on the LNWR, only three of the main line companies were using the type.

The Great Western was the first to introduce the 2-8-0, and it was included in the range of future standard designs, all with two outside cylinders, proposed by Churchward in 1901, a year before he succeeded Dean in the Chair at Swindon. The prototype engine, No 97, was built in 1903, and it included one feature of Churchward's future practice that could be called a fetish. He could not tolerate the sight of inclined outside cylinders, and with the standard coupled wheel diameter of 4 feet 7½ inches for heavy freight engines, the centre line of the cylinders, if extended to pass through the driving centre of the wheels, would have meant that the cylinders covers would not clear the loading gauge, allowing for worn tyres and axlebox crowns. So the centre line of the cylinders was raised 2½ inches. The remarkable thing is that, although there was ample clearance on the larger wheeled engines, he incorporated this 2½ inch offset in all of them in the cause of standardisation.

Engine No 97 had originally the half-cone taper boiler, representing an early stage in Churchward's general development of Swindon designs; but the intention was to make it standard with that of the 4-6-0 express passenger engines. When quantity production of the 2-8-0s began in 1905, they too had the short-cone taper boiler that was then being used. Later batches, however, had the well-known long-cone 'No 1' standard. These engines were, with one exception, turned out in all the glory of the full passenger livery, with its profusion of polished brass and copper work. This was suppressed in the First World War, and never revived for freight engines. The '28XX' Class was very successful, and very many additions to the class were made. They had Churchward's particular setting of the Stephenson link motion, and when superheated the moderate degree of superheat that was customary on all Great Western engines until after the Second World War. The 2-8-0s were not altered afterwards, but when the newly appointed Railway Executive carried out interchange trials in 1948, and one of the later 2-8-0s, No 3803, was matched against recently designed engines of other companies, the basic coal consumption in very heavy freight service of this design of 1903, showed up very favourably thus:

Engine class	GWR '28XX'	LNER '01'	LMS '8F'	War department 2-8-0	2-10-0
Coal per DHP hour average (lb)	3.41	3.39	3.51	3.81	3.49

One could truthfully say that taking account of all factors that could affect road trials with the dynamometer car there was nothing in it between the five classes.

The next 2-8-0 to have a distinguished history is that of the Great Central introduced in 1911, by one prototype built at Gorton works, No 966. This was a superheated development of the Robinson 0-8-0 mineral engine, in fact it had the same coupled wheels, axleboxes and motion. The cylinders were 21 inches by 26 inches with 10 inch diameter piston valves. After successful trials of the one engine, orders were placed for considerable numbers of these engines, and a total of 127 more were built for the Great Central Railway itself. In the later stages of the First World War, when Sir Sam Fay, General Manager of the Great Central, was Director of Movements at the War Office, it was no doubt through his influence that the GCR 2-8-0 was chosen as the standard freight engine for military railways in France, and more than 500 of them were built by various contractors. The principal difference between these and the standard GCR engines was the fitting of the Westinghouse instead of the automatic vacuum brake. On the Great Central itself, in 1918, Robinson built 15 additional engines of the type, with larger boilers, carrying a pressure of 200 lb per square inch. Dimensional details of these engines are shown in the table on page 108.

The Great Northern 2-8-0s introduced by Gresley in 1913 were built with the Peterborough-London coal traffic in view, the loading of which was at times taxing the Ivatt 'Long Toms' almost to their limit. Five 2-8-0s were built for trial purposes and stationed at New England shed, Peterborough. The dimensional details are given in the table on page 108 relate to the second batch of these engines, 15 in all, built by the North British Locomotive Company in 1918. The original Doncaster engines, Nos 456-460, had a slightly larger tube heating surface of 1,922 square feet, and the working pressure was 170 lb per square inch. Between the Doncaster and the NBL batches was an isolated engine, No 461, which was a veritable milestone in East Coast locomotive history; for it was the first to have three cylinders with the conjugated valve gear that played so important a part in subsequent Doncaster practice. This development, however, belongs so essentially to the period between the wars that consideration of the design of No 461 is deferred to a later chapter of this book.

The last 2-8-0 to be mentioned at the present stage, reference 5 in the table, is that built at Derby in 1914 for the Somerset and Dorset Joint Railway. At first glance their very high tractive effort was quite belied by their slender appearance; and in fact the boiler was interchangeable with that used on the standard Midland superheater compounds, with the boiler pressure reduced, as it was also on these latter engines during the First World War from 220 to 190 lb per square inch. The six engines built in 1914, Nos 80-85, were extremely successful. It is probable that the Somerset and Dorset drivers did not attempt to make full use of their high tractive effort in climbing the fearsome 1 in 50 gradients between Bath and Evercreech Junction, because their limited adhesion weight of only 56 tons would have made them a prey to slipping. But in the last years of the line, when at summer weekends there was often a

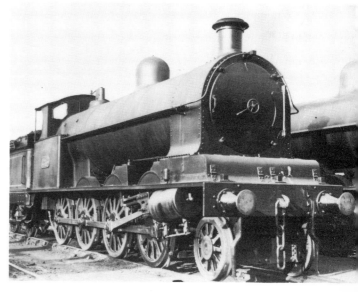

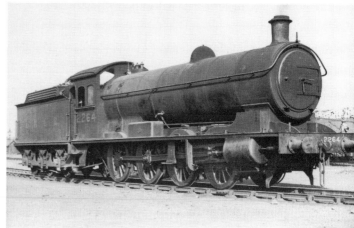

Above right *LNWR: a 4-cylinder compound converted to the 2-8-0 type and fitted with a large boiler* (the late W.H. Whitworth).

Right *North Eastern Railway: V.L. Raven's superheated 'T2' Class 0-8-0 of which 120 were built, here seen in the LNER style of painting* (P. Ransome-Wallis).

Below *Great Western Railway: one of the Churchward standard heavy freight 2-8-0s in the elaborate painting style used for all engines before the First World War* (British Railways).

2-8-0 Superheater mineral locomotives

Ref no	1	2	3	4	5
Railway	**GWR**	**GCR**	**GNR**	**GCR**	**SDJR**
Engineer	Churchward	Robinson	Gresley	Robinson	Fowler
Cylinders					
Diameter (inches)	18½	21	21	21	21
Stroke (inches)	30	26	28	26	28
Coupled wheel diameter (feet/inches)	4 7½	4 8	4 8	4 8	4 7½
Heating surfaces (square feet)					
Tubes	1,686.6	1,348	1,862	1,641	1,170
Firebox	154.78	153	162	174	151
Superheater	262.62	255	570	308	360
Total	2,104.0	1,756	2,594	2,123	1,681
Grate area (square feet)	27.1	26	27	26	28.4
Boiler pressure (lb per square inch)	225	180	180	200	190
Tractive effort (lb)	35,380	31,300	33,800	34,750	35,932

desperate shortage of engines, the 2-8-0s were pressed into passenger service, and were found capable of taking 10 bogie corridor coaches unassisted over the Mendips, whereas the Stanier 'Black Five' 4-6-0s, and the capricious Bulleid 'Pacifics' had to be limited to eight.

So far as 8-coupled tank engines are concerned, those that were no more than tank equivalents of the standard 8-coupled mineral engines can be passed with little more than a reference in the dimensional table. The Great Northern 0-8-2 was not primarily intended as a freight shunter, and short distance engine. The pioneer unit, No 116, was the Great Northern equivalent of the Great Eastern 'Decapod', designed as a rapid acceleration suburban tank engine, and equipped with condensing apparatus to enable it to work to Moorgate Street from Kings Cross over the City Widened Lines. But it proved too heavy, and it was modified by reduction in size of the side tanks, and after further trials the 0-6-2 type was adopted for the London suburban work and No 116 was transferred to Colwick, for shunting and short distance runs with the coal trains. A further 40 engines of the class were built. The Great Western 2-8-0 tank, introduced in 1910, was the short-distance equivalent of the 2-8-0 tender engine having the same cylinders, wheels and motion, but with a smaller standard taper boiler, working at a pressure of 200 lb per square inch. Large numbers of these engines were built primarily for use in South Wales. They were the only engines of those in the table above that were superheated from the start, though some of the GNR 0-8-2Ts were afterwards equipped.

The need for a heavy and powerful shunting engine for the special conditions developing in large mechanised hump marshalling yards led to the introduction of two designs which, between them, were to have a considerable influence on future locomotive practice in the country, far beyond the menial task of humping wagons. In the early 1900s it was characteristic of the Great Central to do things in a big way, and the construction of the new concentration yard for westbound coal traffic at Wath, beside the main line between Mexborough and Barnsley, was typical. No less typical was the provision of four enormous 0-8-4 tank engines for propelling of coal trains up to 1,000 tons in gross weight over the hump. A locomotive of exceptional power was needed, and J.G. Robinson provided it with three cylinders, 18 inches diameter by 26 inches stroke. The cranks were arranged at 120 degrees and, with six exhausts per revolution instead of the usual four, the turning moment applied to the driving wheels is even, and minimises the risk of slipping. For these great engines had a tractive effort of 34,523 lb. The boiler and firebox were the same as those of the main line 2-8-0 mineral engines. Because the demand for steam was intermittent there was no need to have a boiler commensurate with the greatly increased tractive effort. These engines were very successful, and two additional engines were built in 1932, as will be described later in this book.

This innovation was followed two years later by Wilson Worsdell, on the North Eastern Railway, who produced a 3-cylinder 4-8-0 for hump shunting in the Erimus Yards, beside the River Tees, near

Standard 8-coupled freight tanks

Railway	GNR	LNWR	GWR	Caledonian	LYR	Barry
Type	0-8-2	0-8-2	2-8-0	0-8-0	0-8-2	0-8-2
Cylinders						
Diameter (inches)	18	20½	19	19	21½	20
Stroke (inches)	26	24	30	26	26	26
Coupled wheel diameter (feet/inches)	4 8	4 3	4 7½	4 6	4 6	4 3
Boiler pressure (lb per square inch)	175	175	200	175	180	150
Number built	41	30	160	6	5	7
Notes:	Colwick shunters and trip coal trains	Tank equivalent of Class 'G' 0-8-0	South Wales coal engine	Lanarkshire coal shunter	Banking engines	First ever British 0-8-2T; introduced 1896

Hump shunting 8-coupleds

Railway	Great Central	North Eastern	L & SWR
Date	1907	1909	1921
Engineer	J.G. Robinson	Wilson Worsdell	R.W. Urie
Type	0-8-4	4-8-0	4-8-0
Cylinders no	3	3	2
Diameter (inches)	18	18	22
Stroke (inches)	26	26	28
Coupled wheel diameter (feet/inches)	4 8	4 7	5 1
Heating surface (square feet)			
Tubes	1,818	1,169	1,267
Firebox	154	141	139
Superheater	—	—	231
Total	1,972	1,310	1,637
Grate area (square feet)	26	23.6	27
Boiler pressure (lb per square inch)	180	175	180
Adhesion weight (tons)	75.6	67.6	72.9
Tractive effort (lb)	34,523	34,100	33,990

Middlesbrough. These also had cylinders of 18 inch diameter by 26 inch stroke; but use of the 4-8-0 wheel arrangement did not give such a tremendous impression of size as did the Great Central 0-8-4s. Actually there was very little difference in tractive effort, as the table of comparative dimensions shows. Ten of these very successful engines were built in 1909-10, and a further five were added by the LNER in 1925. An important construction feature was that the three cylinders and their associated valve chests were embodied in a single steel casting, thus foreshadowing the 'monobloc'

form of construction used in some of the later three-cylinder locomotives of the LNER. It was the success of these 4-8-0 hump engines that inspired locomotive development of the North Eastern in the Raven period. In the accompanying table I have added details of the 4-8-0 hump shunting tank engines designed by R.W. Urie for the Feltham yard of the London and South Western Railway, in 1921, though these were 2-cylinder machines. As will be told later in the chapter dealing with 4-6-0 locomotives, Urie could not abide having any machinery between the frames.

Left *Great Central Railway: a Robinson 2-8-0 of the excellent design adopted for war service by the Railway Operating Division of the British Army, here seen on a freight train near Retford* (P. Ransome-Wallis).

Below *Somerset and Dorset Joint Railway: the largest tender locomotive built by the Midland Railway at Derby, the first of six powerful 2-8-0s for the very severe gradients across the Mendips* (British Railways).

Bottom *Great Central Railway: the huge 3-cylinder 0-8-4 tank used for shunting in the hump marshalling yard at Wath near Barnsley.*

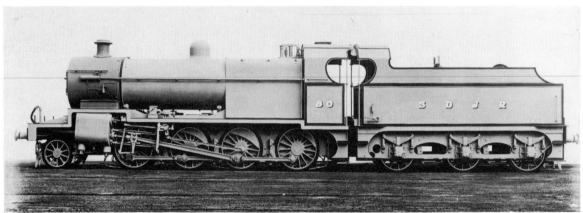

North Eastern Railway: a 3-cylinder 4-8-0 tank engine for hump shunting at Erimus yard, on Tees-side, near Middlesbrough (The Locomotive Publishing Company).

LNWR: a tank engine equivalent, 0-8-2 type, of the standard non-superheated 0-8-0 illustrated by engine No 1866 on page 105 (British Railways).

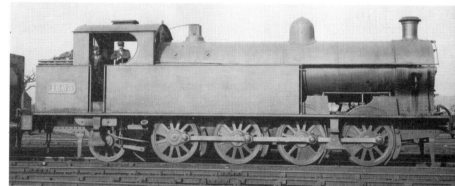

Great Western Railway: the Churchward standard 2-8-0 tank engine for short-haul coal trains in South Wales (British Railways).

Lancashire & Yorkshire Railway: one of a class of five 0-8-2s designed (by G. Hughes in 1908) for banking duties on steep inclines. They were not superheated (British Railways).

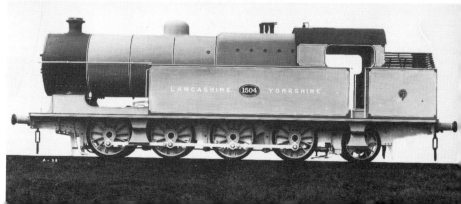

8. The large express and mineral tank engines

In the last two decades of the pre-grouping era, and in particular during the years before the outbreak of war in 1914, the British railway scene, colourful and diverse as it was in its equipment and working methods, moved on to touch the heights in the proliferation of tank engines which were introduced. A cynical historian might say that it was diversity for diversity's sake, and that one or two basic designs could have done the work of all of them. But in writing of British railway history, and particularly of its locomotives, there is no room for cynicism; and, in recalling these fine engineering productions of that age, we can delight in their colours, their sturdy achievements on the road, and in the almost loving care with which they were cleaned and groomed. Just imagine, for one example, a time when a hard worked express tank engine would be taken out of traffic for a day to have the paint touched up!

No one would, of course, pretend that all the tank engine classes introduced in those years were uniformly good. Some of them, indeed, did no credit at all to their sponsors, however impressive or striking they may have looked. But performance apart, if one could group together a collection of scale models, or of coloured picture postcards in the 'F. Moore' style, what a galaxy they would present! There is not space to discuss all the tank engines of 10 wheels and upwards that were produced; but it is hoped that the tabulations will help to fill in something of the overall picture.

Turning now to the table of passenger 4-4-2 tank engines on page 116, those of the London Tilbury and Southend were among the most handsome and hard working of any that have ever run the rails. Their artistic finish may be studied and enjoyed from a beautiful colour plate published in the *Locomotive Magazine* in January 1908, or alternatively from the fine model of the first of the 4-6-4 tanks in the Science Museum in London. Dimensionally even the '79' Class of 1909 were the least powerful of all the designs tabulated; but none had to work harder, or run so fast, in their ordinary workaday duties. At the peak hours on the Southend express trains, the coach formations were regularly made up to the maximum that could be accommodated in the platforms in the Great Eastern terminus at Fenchurch Street, into which the 'Tilbury' worked by running powers. Thirteen bogie coaches could be worked, but not 14; so the most heavily patronised trains were made up to 13 plus one 6-wheeler. The coaches were all non-corridor, and had a tare weight of 325 tons but, when crowded with passengers in the 'crush' hours, the gross load to be hauled would be about 400 tons. On the favourable stretches of line east of Barking, maximum speeds approaching 70 mph were frequently attained with these heavy trains.

The Great Central engines, reference 2 in the table, were designed by J.G. Robinson primarily to develop the London suburban service of the newly opened railway. Like all his engines they were beautifully proportioned, but the traffic did not extend them to any extent. They had an easy mastery over the very light trains which were at first adequate, even over the steep gradients of the joint line with the Metropolitan, where it passed through the beautiful, but very hilly, country of the Chiltern

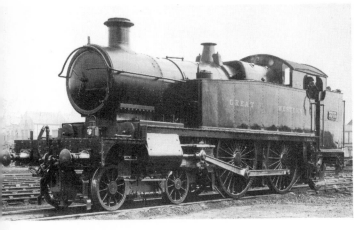

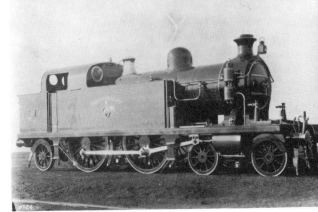

hills between Rickmansworth and Aylesbury. The Great Western 'County tanks', reference 3, were intended for the fast outer residential services to Reading, and beyond. They were introduced in the first wave of standardisation inaugurated by G.J. Churchward, and were at first non-superheated. They later had the moderate degree of superheat adopted on the GWR, but no change was made to the cylinder diameter or boiler pressure. As a boy I travelled behind them between Mortimer and Reading West, on my way to school, by a train that originated at Basingstoke, and ran fast from Reading to Paddington. The 2-6-2 tanks that afterwards took over such duties have not been included in the table because their development and extensive use belongs to the inter-war period.

The London and North Western 'Precursor tank', as its name suggests, was a tank engine version of the celebrated 'Precursor' express passenger 4-4-0, and had the same relatively large boiler. The coupled wheels, however, were 6 feet 3 inches against 6 feet 9 inches, thus providing a still higher tractive effort. From their introduction in 1906 these powerful engines had a monopoly of the London suburban services from Euston for about 25 years. They used to work down the main line as far as Bletchley, sometimes beyond, and had a good turn of speed. They were still on the job when I began commuting daily between Bushey and Euston in 1931. In their early days they worked on the residential expresses between Manchester and Buxton; and, after they were displaced by more modern engines on the London suburban services in the 1930s, some of them were moved north to Oxenholme for local workings and piloting duties over Shap.

The Brighton 'I3' Class was only one of several 4-4-2 tank designs introduced by Douglas Earle-Marsh. The 'I1s' were rather feeble little things,

very likely inspired by their designer's acquaintance with the Ivatt 4-4-2 tanks, which did not have a very distinguished record on the London suburban services of the Great Northern Railway. The 'I2s', with slightly larger boilers, were not much better but, as Earle-Marsh's latest short-distance tank engines, they *had* to be used to haul the Royal Train when King Edward VII went to the 'Derby'. With an 'I1' in 1907 and an 'I2' in 1908 there were some anxious moments in getting the heavy and luxurious 5-coach train up the 1 in 86 gradient between Mitcham and Sutton, and the still more severe length of the branch terminating at Epsom Downs, because those 4-4-2 tanks would not steam freely! On each occasion Earle-Marsh himself rode on the footplate, but history does not record whether or not he wore a silk hat, as did George Hughes on the Lancashire and Yorkshire, when one of his 4-6-0s had to work the Royal Train to Blackpool.

Whatever the shortcomings of the 'I1' and 'I2' Classes may have been, the superheated version of

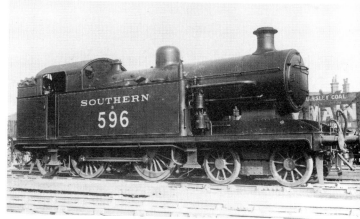

Far left *Great Western Railway: one of the Churchward standards, a 4-4-2 express tank engine with 6 foot 8½ inch coupled wheels* (the late W.J. Reynolds).

Left *London, Tilbury & Southend Railway: the large boilered express 4-4-2 tank engine,* Thundersley (The Locomotive Publishing Company).

Above right *London and North Western Railway: the 'Precursor' 4-4-2 tank for the fast London suburban services.*

Right *LB & SCR: a latter day rebuild by Maunsell of the Earle-Marsh 'I1' Class 4-4-2 tank with a larger and more effective boiler* (the late W.J. Reynolds).

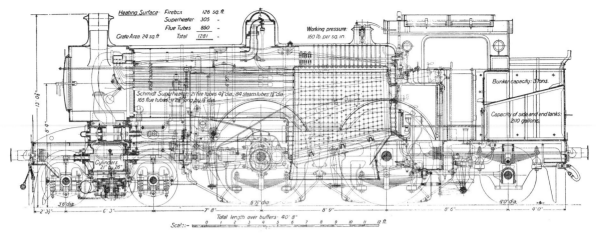

London Brighton & South Coast Railway: Class 'I3' superheater 4-4-2 express tank engine.

the 'I3', details of which are tabulated, were excellent engines and reference to them has already been made in Chapter 3 of this book, and of their influence on future London and North Western practice. The non-superheated version had 19 inch by 26 inch cylinders and 180 lb per square inch pressure. Even so, the 'I3' superheaters, good as they were, were not intended to be more than a stepping stone to future practice on the Brighton railway. As explained later in this chapter dealing with 4-6-2 tank engines, Earle-Marsh himself was intending to develop the 4-6-2; but, because of his ill-health and early retirement, this did not happen, and his successor, needing more engines, quickly added another 10 'I3s', bringing the total up to the 21 tabulated. In later years the 'I3s' which had been built as 'saturators' were superheated. In 1948, just 40 years after their first introduction, I did some footplate work on these engines and found them as sound and reliable as ever.

The North Staffordshire Railway, which remained independent until the time of grouping in 1923, was in an interesting position, both geographically and strategically, in that it controlled one section of one of the most important and profitable routes from London to Manchester. Certain London and North Western expresses were routed via Stoke-on-Trent and, for 38¾ miles, from Colwich to Macclesfield, they passed over North Staffordshire metals. Colwich not being an appropriate place to change over the haulage, the arrangement was for the North Staffordshire engines to work these trains between Stoke and Manchester, a distance of 37½ miles, and a roughly equal mileage to that of the NSR track ownership and maintenance. The 12.10 pm express from

Manchester to Euston was a prestige job for both engines and men, because it conveyed a minimum load of 330 tons and, in view of such a regular assignment, it seems surprising that the 4-4-2 tank engines built expressly for the job had such small boilers. They were in very strong contrast to the North Western's own 4-4-2 tanks with more than double the tube heating surface. The train in question was allowed 18 minutes start to stop for the 11¾ miles from Stockport to Macclesfield, and then 27 minutes for the ensuing 20 miles onward to Stoke.

The second section was the easier of the two; because although there is a hard initial pull at 1 in 102 up to Macclesfield Moss Box, rear-end banking assistance was always provided with heavy trains, and after that it is downhill or level for the remaining 17½ miles to Stoke. The really hard part of the run, for the unassisted engine, comes after leaving the Manchester-Crewe main line at Cheadle Hulme, where speed had to be much reduced for the junction. This slowing was followed by a continuous rise on gradients varying between 1 in 277 and 1 in 137 right into Macclesfield. Yet on one recorded occasion when the load was two coaches above normal, about 380 tons, engine No 55 ran from Stockport to Macclesfield in 18¼ minutes. Then, after the usual assistance up to the Moss box, the 4-4-2 engine ran well, sustaining 60 mph on level track with this big train. It was, however, not always possible to maintain this standard of performance with engines having such small boilers and, in 1913, designs were in hand for an 0-6-4 tank engine. As related afterwards in this chapter, its production was delayed by the onset of war.

The North British engine, reference 8 in the table, was a superheated version of a class produced only a few years previously. While not called upon for heavy express work of the foregoing kind, these

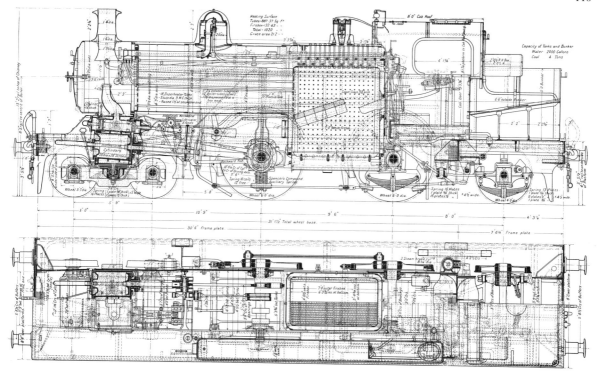

North Staffordshire Railway: 4-4-2 superheater tank engine.

engines did some smart running with the Clyde Coast trains between Glasgow and Helensburgh, also on the faster suburban runs from Edinburgh and on the branch line services in Fife. Some of them were used on the local service worked over the West Highland line between Craigendoran and Arrochar. It was all work of a light and intermediate character and this was reflected in the relatively small fireboxes, in relation to the tractive effort. Providing that the demands for steam are not continuous, a small firegrate enables the coal consumption to be kept small. These engines were notably economical. At the end of the table have been added the dimensions of the Furness Railway tank engines used for the Lakeside and Coniston branches. They were handsome little engines and did much smart work with light trains.

Passing now to tank engines of the 4-6-2 type, the London and North Western and the Great Central turned out powerful superheated examples within a few months of each other, in 1910-11, but for rather different assignments. The Great Central was introducing the massive new Robinson elliptical roofed coaches (providing the greatest luxury that had yet been seen for London commuter traffic) at a time, incidentally, when the Great Eastern still sat its

third class passengers on bare boards! Something more powerful was needed than the handsome 4-4-2 tanks of 1903, and Robinson duly provided it in his massive 4-6-2 tanks of 1911.

The lavish provision of coal and water capacity (4 tons and 2,330 gallons) and the high raised boiler gave the impression of a very large engine, while actually the boiler was that of the 'Sir Alexander' Class of 4-4-0 express locomotive, fitted with a superheater. The construction, however, was on the usual Gorton 'battleship' style and the adhesion weight of 54 tons made them sure-footed and reliable when rapid acceleration was needed. Despite having coupled wheels no larger than 5 feet 7 inches diameter, they ran freely. I have a note of a smart run from Harrow into Marylebone with engine No 169 hauling five of the heaviest GCR non-corridor carriages, on which Finchley Road, 7.3 miles, was passed in 8 minutes 50 seconds from the start after a maximum speed of 67 mph had been attained at Neasden. When first introduced, although based in London, some of them worked as far north as Leicester on intermediate trains, and for this class of work they were fitted with water pick-up apparatus.

The first of the London and North Western 4-6-2 tanks was completed at Crewe just at the end of 1910. It was at the time when superheating had

4-4-2 Passenger tank engines

Ref no	1	2	3	4	5	6	7	8	9
Railway	LT &SR	GCR	GWR	LNWR	LBSC	LT & SR	NSR	NBR	Furness
Engine class	'51'	'9K'	County tank*	Precursor tank	'I3'	'79'†	'8'	'L'	—
Engineer	White-legg	Robinson	Church-ward	Whale	Earle-Marsh	White-legg	Adams	W.P. Reid	Pettigrew
Date introduced	1900	1903	1905	1906	1908	1909	1911	1915	1915
Cylinders									
Diameter (inches)	18	18	18	19	21	19	20	19	17½
Stroke (inches)	26	26	30	26	26	26	26	26	24
Coupled wheel diameter	6 6	5 7	6 8½	6 3	6 7½	6 6	6 0	5 9	5 8
Heating surface (square feet)									
Tubes	920	1,033	1,396.6	1,848.4	1,126	992	887	930	1,039
Firebox	107	110	121.3	161.3	120	107	133	95	88
Superheater	—	—	—	—	254	—	261	220	—
Grate area (square feet)	19.77	19.85	20.4	22.4	23.75	19.77	21	16.6	15.4
Boiler pressure (lb per square inch)	170	180	195	175	160	170	160	165	160
Tractive effort (lb)	15,600	19,250	20,010	18,650	19,630	17,400	19,760	19.060	14,700
Number in class	18	52	30	50	21	16	7	21	4

*Later superheated: total heating surface 1,373.75 square feet. †Total includes 12 rebuilds of earlier engines.

barely passed beyond its trial stages, and construction of non-superheater 4-4-0 express engines of the 'Queen Mary' Class had only recently finished. Of the first 20 of the new 4-6-2 tanks, 10 were built non-superheated, and the first one to appear, No 2665, was one of these. The new engines were, however, intended for a wide range of activities, and few of them were put on to purely suburban duties, on which latter the 'Precursor' 4-4-2 tanks were doing admirable work. The new 4-6-2s, although having a considerably smaller coal and water capacity than their Great Central counterparts, were intended for a wider range of activities, one of which was that of working the heavily graded Central Wales line, from Shrewsbury via Llandrindod Wells through to Swansea, a run of 115 miles. Although the loads were not heavy by LNWR main line standards, it was something of a marathon run for a tank engine.

A typical duty for one of the London based engines was a round trip of 165 miles to Rugby and back, on a 'diagram' involving a mixture of fast, and stopping, trains: semi-fast Euston to Watford, then all stations forward to Bletchley; a wait of just over an hour, and another train, all stations to Rugby. The return trip was by an express, calling only at Northampton, Bletchley and Willesden Junction, and requiring some fast running, with a load of about 300 tons. To equip them for long through workings, these engines were fitted with two water scoops, for picking up at speed, whether travelling chimney or bunker first. They continued as excellent performers for many years. I had a run behind one of them in 1929 on the 5.25 pm express from Shrewsbury to Crewe, conveying a load of no less than 397 tons *tare*—at least 420 tons with passengers and luggage. We passed Nantwich Junction, 29.8 miles, in 37¼ minutes, in good trim for an arrival at Crewe in 43 minutes, but we were stopped by a signal outside. The maximum speed attained was 69 mph. The engine concerned was the second one built, in 1910, No 2666, then non-super-heated, but subsequently made standard with the rest of the class.

Opposite page, top to bottom

Great Northern Railway: H.A. Ivatt's earlier form of suburban tank engine for the London area with condensing apparatus for use in the Underground tunnels. It was built in 1899 (British Railways).

Furness Railway: W.F. Pettigrew's 4-4-2 tank for passenger traffic on Lakeland branch lines, built in 1915 (Kitson & Company).

London and North Western Railway: a 4-6-2 express tank engine of 1910, one of the earliest of the class which was built non-super-heated (British Railways).

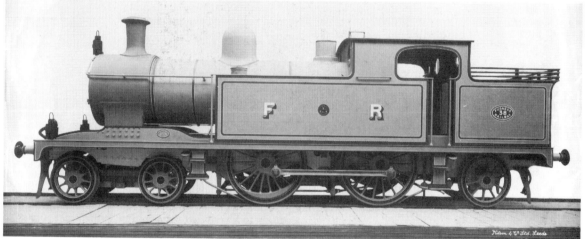

In the last years before the First World War the London Brighton and South Coast Railway continued to be a delight to the enthusiast fraternity; for, although the yellow engine livery of Stroudley had been superseded by the more workmanlike, yet still very handsome dark brown of Earle-Marsh, there had arisen a surprising lack of standardisation in the express locomotive designs introduced since 1905. The onlookers were certainly kept guessing as to what would come next. There had been the GN-like tender 'Atlantics' of 1905; the 'I3' superheater 4-4-2 tanks; the ineffective 'Grasshoppers', Class 'B2' that were then being rebuilt with larger boilers and, while Brighton Works was getting ready to build six superheater 'Atlantic' tender engines, there emerged, fully lined out in photographic grey, the magnificent 4-6-2 tank No 325, *Abergavenny*, just at the end of 1910. Unlike its contemporaries on the Great Central and the LNWR, the new Brighton engine was intended for top line express passenger working and accordingly had 6 foot 7½ inch coupled wheels. The tractive effort of 19,570 lb was actually less than that of the superheater 'Atlantics' which came out in 1911; because, while the cylinder and coupled wheel dimensions were the same, *Abergavenny* carried a boiler pressure of 160 lb per square inch at first, as against 170 on the 'Atlantics'. The big tank engine had, of course, the advantage of a greater adhesion weight of 54½ tons.

It is interesting to set alongside, at this stage, the basic dimensions of the three classes of superheater express locomotives on the Brighton railway in 1911, thus:

Type	4-4-2T	4-6-2T	4-4-2
Cylinders			
Diameter (inches)	21	21	21
Stroke (inches)	26	26	26
Coupled wheel diameter (feet/inches)	6 7½	6 7½	6 7½
Heating surfaces (square feet)			
Tubes	1,126	1,462	1,913
Firebox	120	124	136.7
Superheater	254	357	461
Grate area (square feet)	23.75	25.16	31.0
Boiler pressure (lb per square inch)	160	160	170

An engineer looking in at Brighton affairs at that time may have felt that Earle-Marsh, and to some extent B.K. Field (the power behind the throne), had been caught in a fog of uncertainty, revealed to the outside world by the lack of any settled policy of locomotive design practice. There is evidence to suggest that the 4-6-2 tank engine, *Abergavenny*, Earle-Marsh's pride and joy, was hoped to be the standard passenger engine of the future. It was certainly the only design for which he could claim complete originality, for the 'Atlantic' tender engines were clearly derived from Doncaster, and the 'I3' tanks were a direct tank-engine derivative from the very successful Billinton 'B4' 4-4-0.

In 1911 a second 4-6-2 tank was on the drawing boards, with sufficient differences in design for comparisons of detail to be made. Unhappily, however, Earle-Marsh did not stay to see this second 4-6-2 completed. He was stricken by an illness of such a nature that he was compelled to resign; and, when the second engine did take the road, early in 1912, one could not be sure which of the various differences in design could be attributed to Earle-Marsh himself, or to his successor, Colonel L.B. Billinton. On No 326, *Bessborough*, the most obvious difference was the use of Walschaerts radial valve gear in place of the traditional Stephenson's link motion. The names, blazoned on the side tanks in a revival of the Stroudley tradition, were in honour of the Marquis of Abergavenny, a director, and of the Earl of Bessborough, the Chairman of the company.

Both 325 and 326 proved very good engines, though it was generally considered that 326 with the Walschaerts gear was, if anything, the better of the two. This second engine also carried a higher boiler pressure of 170 lb per square inch. The one-time intention to make the 4-6-2 tank a future standard was killed early in 1912, when an urgent call from the traffic department for more passenger engines was met by building 10 more 'I3' 4-4-2 tanks. It is nevertheless remarkable that in the age of standardisation which followed the formation of the Southern Railway in 1923, that the two 4-6-2 tanks remained unaltered save for the trimming down of their boiler mountings and cabs to suit the composite loading gauge of the new group. In 1947-8 both of them were stationed at Tunbridge Wells, and working regularly on the heavy and popular residential trains, both from London Bridge and Victoria via the severely graded Oxted line. I rode down from Victoria one day on the footplate of the erstwhile Abergavenny, then No 2325 and unnamed, and found her still an excellent engine.

When William Pickersgill, of the Great North of Scotland, was appointed to succeed J.F. McIntosh (as Locomotive Superintendent of the Caledonian) this quiet, scholarly, but rather indecisive man began to make alterations in the hitherto settled design policy of the line. When Dugald Drummond went south to become Chief Mechanical Engineer of the London and South Western Railway, some of the best men from the St Rollox drawing office went to join him and, by the time McIntosh retired, John Barr, the Running Superintendent, had become the power behind the throne on the Caledonian. Then Pickersgill began changing things by introducing outside cylinders, and it will be told in the next chapter how strangely the valve gear on the 4-6-0 passenger engines got mixed up. But the 4-6-2 tanks that Pickersgill specified for the Clyde Coast services were built by the North British Locomotive Company and, whatever suggestions may have come from St Rollox, the experienced drawing office staff at Hyde Park did not mince matters. The 4-6-2 tanks were excellent engines. I travelled many times behind them between Glasgow and Wemyss Bay, and they ran freely on the level, and climbed sturdily on the severe gradients of the branch.

Before passing on to other arrangements I must briefly mention three other classes of 4-6-2 tank, dimensional details of which are tabulated, but which could not be classed as 'fast train' engines. The North Eastern 'W' Class, which were originally built as 4-6-0s, and known as the Whitby tanks', were intended as general service engines for the sharply curved and steeply graded coastal route

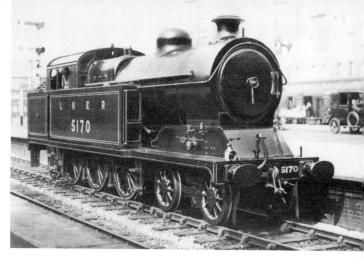

Above right *Great Central Railway: J.G. Robinson's massive 4-6-2 tank for the outer London residential trains, here seen in LNER colours* (P. Ransome-Wallis).

Right *Caledonian Railway: one of the Pickersgill 4-6-2 tanks in drab LMS finish* (P. Ransome-Wallis).

Below *London, Brighton & South-Coast Railway: Earle-Marsh's masterpiece, the 4-6-2 express tank engine,* Bessborough, *of 1911* (British Railways).

from Saltburn down to Scarborough. They were used on passenger and goods trains alike, and even though the passenger trains generally consisted of only four or five non-corridor bogie carriages the engines had such an appetite for coal that after a time their bunkers had to be roughly doubled in size, and a radial trailing axle added to carry the additional weight. The 'Y' Class 3-cylinder 4-6-2 was a heavy mineral hauler, designed to take loads of 1,000 tons at 20 mph on level track. The London and South Western engines of 1921 were designed for heavy transfer freight trains across the western outskirts of London from the Willesden and Cricklewood yards to the new LSWR concentration yard at Feltham. The coupled wheel diameter of 5 feet 7 inches was rather large for such a duty, but the dimensions were standard with the 'S15' 4-6-0 tender engines.

The 0-6-4 tank type, next to be considered, can be regarded as a development of the 0-4-4. In passenger work it was not one of the most successful and while, when designed specifically for freight, like those of the Lancashire, Derbyshire and East Coast, and of the Barry, it rendered many years of admirable hard service, those of the Midland, the South Eastern and Chatham, and of the Metropolitan had a somewhat chequered existence. Actually, so far as British railways were concerned, the type originated on the Wirral Railway, as long ago as 1900, when two locomotives that proved an excellent investment were supplied by Beyer, Peacock & Co.

The Lancashire, Derbyshire and East Coast Railway or that part of it that was actually in operation in 1900, between Chesterfield and Lincoln, was only the central portion of a magnificent scheme for a line from Warrington to Sutton-on-Sea, which would pass through Macclesfield, Buxton, and some of the highest regions of the Peak District to reach Chesterfield; while from Lincoln it was to continue to the North Sea coast, where docks for coal exporting were proposed at Sutton. The Bill projecting the whole line, 170 miles long, was passed by Parliament in 1891; but the eastern and western sections were never built. From the engineering point of view this was a pity because the line westward from Chesterfield, through the Peak District, would have included some of the most spectacular structural works anywhere in Great Britain. Even so, the line, actually built with a ruling gradient of 1 in 100, involved some hard work in operating heavy coal trains. The six 0-6-4 tank engines introduced in 1904 were the most powerful of the type ever to run in Great Britain, and the company was taking delivery of a further three just at the time when the LD & EC itself was being incorporated in the Great Central in 1906. The original engines supplied by Kitsons, of Leeds, were distinctive, rather than handsome, having a rather ugly circular extension to the smokebox; but under Great Central ownership they were transformed, with J.G. Robinson's very shapely chimney.

Peter Drummond's banking engines for the Highland have been referred to in a previous chapter, when the general similarity of the design to his later 0-6-2 tanks on the Glasgow and South Western was commented upon. I had only one experience of an 0-6-4 on the Highland, and that was of no consequence, except that contrary to usual practice the banker was coupled ahead of the train engine, instead of pushing in rear. It was on the 6.25 am mail from Perth, 350 tons, which had been worked unassisted as far as Blair Atholl by one of the new LMS 'crab' 2-6-0s. Up 'The Hill' the two engines sustained a not very exciting 26 mph on the 1 in 70 gradient. The other purely freight 0-6-4 tank, that of the Barry Railway, was of another excellent design, due to John Auld, who had been appointed Locomotive Superintendent in 1909. After grouping in 1923 he was appointed Docks Engineer of the Great Western, but he was destined for still higher office; and when Stanier went to the LMS in 1932 he was appointed Principal Assistant to the Chief Mechanical Engineer, at Swindon. As might be imagined, the Barry 0-6-4 tanks, which had rendered such good service, did not fit in with the Great Western schemes for standardisation. They were no more than a small class, and although

North Eastern Railway: one of Wilson Worsdell's Class 'W', Whitby tanks, as originally built as 4-6-0s. They were subsequently enlarged to 4-6-2s (British Railways).

some were fitted with Great Western standard taper boilers, the general recession in the coal trade, after the lengthy strike of 1926, reduced the need for them and they were withdrawn and scrapped in that same year. Those that were rebuilt looked very smart with their taper boilers, top feed, and Belpaire fireboxes, but very *un*-Great Western below the waistline!

Except in the case of the North Staffordshire the railways that built 0-6-4 tanks for passenger service intended them as a follow up on duties hitherto successfully worked by 0-4-4s, superficially a natural development where extra adhesion was desirable. But in practice it did work out that way. A front-coupled engine may have been a smooth riding 'vehicle' in the manner so brilliantly postulated by Stroudley in his 'Gladstone' Class 0-4-2s on the Brighton railway; and in an earlier chapter of this book I have written enthusiastically of my own footplate experience on one of the Drummond 'M7' 0-4-4 tanks on the LSWR. When, however, the traction unit, unguided by any radial or bogie wheels, was enlarged from 4- to 6-coupled wheels and surmounted, moreover, by greatly enlarged side tanks, the result was often a very unsteady engine at anything approaching express speed. On the Midland engines the tanks were extended to the very front of the smokebox, and had between the two a capacity of 2,250 gallons. There was no waiting until a prototype had been tried out. With the mixture of self-confidence and ineptitude that unhappily characterised the locomotive department of the Midland, in what Hamilton Ellis has so poignantly described as 'The Troubled Years', Derby swung at once into quantity-production with a vigour that for a time promised to match the greatest days of Crewe, and in record time the Running Department had not only a prototype of a rather doubtful and bad riding tank engine, but 39 more of them! The whole class was turned out in 1907.

The men nicknamed them the 'flat-irons'. They were put on to the suburban services around Manchester and Birmingham, and then, after the 'take-over' of 1912, six of them were tried on the hardest express workings of the Tilbury line, with near-disastrous results. Otherwise, they were not often seen in the London district, nor at Leeds, where the 0-4-4 tanks continued to skip merrily along with the London expresses between there and Bradford. After they were equipped with superheaters a few of them were on the St Pancras locals. Around 1925 I was occasionally using the 1.7 pm (Saturdays) to St Albans, and one day we had the pioneer engine, No 2000, then superheated, to haul a load of about 195 tons gross. The running as far as our first stop at Radlett was not exactly heroic, but as it is the only record I have ever seen of the work of one of these engines the details are appended herewith. The climbing through the tunnels to Finchley Road was laborious, on 1 in 182; the sharp descent from Cricklewood to Welsh Harp took us

4-6-2 Tank engines: passenger and goods

Railway	Great Central	LNWR	LBSC	North Eastern	North Eastern	Caledonian	LSWR
Service	Passenger	Passenger	Passenger	Mixed	Mineral	Passenger	Goods
Engineer	Robinson	Bowen Cooke	Earle-Marsh	W. Worsdell	V.L. Raven	Pickersgill	R.W. Urie
Date introduced	1910-11	1910-11	1910	1907	1910	1917	1921
Cylinders (number of)	2	2	2	2	3	2	2
Diameter (inches)	20	20	21	19	16½	19½	21
Stroke (inches)	26	26	26	26	26	26	28
Coupled wheel diameter (feet/inches)	5 7	5 8½	6 7½	5 1	4 7½	5 9	5 7
Heating surface (square feet)							
Tubes	1,139	947.4	1,462	1,182	1,508	1,395	1,267
Firebox	141	138	124	130	140	121	139
Superheater	214	248	357	—	—	220	231
Grate area (square feet)	21.2	23.9	25.2	23	23	21.5	27
Boiler pressure (lb per square feet)	180	175	170*	170	180	170	180
Tractive effort (lb)	23,743	21,950	20,800	21,720	29,400	20,150	29,300
Number in class	21†	47	2	10	20	12	5

*First engine 160 lb per square inch.   †10 more added in 1923.

up to no more than 56 mph and after the rise to Elstree, mostly at 1 in 176, there was a last minute 'dash' up to 60 mph before we slowed down for Radlett.

Distance (miles)		Time m s	Speeds mph
0.0	St Pancras	0 00	
1.5	Kentish Town	4 55	
3.4	Finchley Road	8 25	35
5.2	Cricklewood	11 05	40¼
6.9	Hendon	13 10	56
12.4	Elstree	20 00	45
			60 (max)
15.2	Radlett	23 20	

The South Eastern and Chatham introduction of the 0-6-4 tank type came just at the end of the Wainwright period, and only five were built. What the intentions were for the type it is hard to say but no more were built. It is reported that they too suffered from unsteady riding. There was, however, every justification for larger locomotives on the country extension line of the Metropolitan Railway, and the 0-6-4 tanks put on the road at the end of 1915 came as a welcome supplement to the 0-4-4 tanks that had so far done all the passenger working north of Harrow. The greater adhesion weight and higher tractive effort was welcome for climbing the severe gradients of the line through the Chiltern Hills, between Rickmansworth and Aylesbury. These engines cannot, nevertheless, have been an unqualified success, for at the end of the First World War when more large engines were required, Mr Jones changed surprisingly to the 4-4-4 type. On the 0-6-4 tanks, for the first and only time with Metropolitan Railway steam locomotives, names were

bestowed upon them. Who chose the names I do not know, but it was certainly unusual in those days for an engine to be named after its own designer while he was still in office. The four engines were named *Lord Aberconway* (Chairman of the company); *Robert H. Selbie* (General Manager); *Charles Jones*, and *Brill*.

Earlier in this chapter I referred to the fine work done by the North Staffordshire 4-4-2 tanks in hauling certain of the Euston-Manchester expresses on the section north of Stoke-on-Trent. As early as 1913 Mr J.H. Adams had prepared designs for a more powerful tank engine of the 0-6-4 type, and a line diagram of this engine was included in a lavishly illustrated article describing the locomotive works at Stoke in *The Railway Magazine*, for November 1913. Due to war conditions, however, the first engines of the new class were not completed until 1917, some little time after Mr Adams' death. Although, like the ill-starred Midland 'flat-irons', they had a total tank capacity of 2,250 gallons, the proportions were more agreeably arranged; and the North Staffordshire 0-6-4s put in many years of hard work on express trains, until re-arrangements of the locomotive workings consequent upon grouping, ended the arrangements by which ex-NSR engines took a share in the haulage of those London–Manchester expresses that ran via Stoke.

The 4-4-4 type of tank engine originated, surprisingly enough, on the Wirral Railway. It is remarkable that this little railway with no more than 14 miles of route, and which remained independent until the grouping of 1923, should have been the first to use not only the 4-4-4, but also, as related earlier, the 0-6-4 tank type. The 4-4-4s of which there were three, belong to a period earlier than that covered by this book; and they, like those that were purchased a little later by the Midland and South Western Junction Railway had no influence towards subsequent practice. Both the Wirral engines of 1896, and the M & SWJ of 1897 had 17 inch by 24 inch inside cylinders; coupled wheels of 5

Highland Railway: one of Peter Drummond's 0-6-4 tank engines for banking duties on heavy gradients, built in 1909 and here seen in LMS colours (P. Ransome-Wallis).

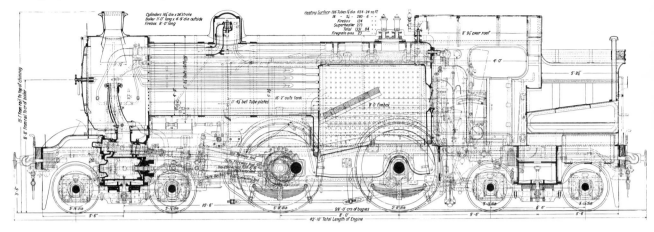

North Eastern Railway: Raven 3-cylinder 4-4-4 express tank engine.

foot 2 inch diameter and carried a boiler pressure of 160 lb per square inch. The real 20th century development began in 1913, with the introduction of Vincent L. Raven's 3-cylinder 'D' Class on the North Eastern, which eventually numbered 45 engines. Their cylinders were 16½ by 26 inches, coupled wheels were 5 feet 9 inches in diameter, and boiler pressure 160 lb per square inch.

When they first came out, the earliest batches were based on Tees-side, and there was talk of their being used also on the heavily graded cross-country line from Darlington to Tebay. But there, the vintage 2-4-0s of the Fletcher and Tennant classes remained in undisturbed possession of the passenger services for many years to come. The 'D' Class tanks were smooth riding and free running engines. They were used on the 'local' express trains between Tees-side and York, and used to make fast time with trains of 150 to 200 tons on the level stretches of line south of Northallerton, attaining speeds of between 65 and 70 mph. They used also to work on the longer distance residential trains from Leeds on the Harrogate line; but my own clearest recollection of them is at Whitby, where one of them used to arrive by the coastal route from Saltburn each afternoon. Being of the 4-4-4 type they ran equally sweetly both chimney and bunker first, and the contrast between them and the cumbersome 4-6-2 tanks of the 'W' Class was absolute. In 1920-2 a further 25 were added, all built at Darlington Works.

In 1920 some surprise was caused when the Metropolitan Railway, having previously introduced the 0-6-4 tank type for the heavier passenger services through the Chiltern Hills, adopted instead the 4-4-4 type. Here again, no

doubt, it was the 'double-ended' feature that governed the decision to change, because the 4-4-4 rode equally well when running chimney or bunker first. The new Metropolitan tanks were extremely handsome engines, and while the change to outside cylinders was something new in the current age they were nothing new on the Metropolitan. In 1920 in fact, the survivors of the famous Beyer, Peacock 4-4-0 tanks with which the railway opened for business on the Inner Circle in 1863, still formed the most numerous class on the line, mustering 13. After them the eight new 4-4-4 tanks were the most of any one wheel arrangement. The new engines were built by Kerr, Stuart & Co of Stoke-on-Trent. They made an interesting contrast dimensionally to the North Eastern 'D' Class, like which they were excellent workers. When they were first introduced the line was not electrified north of Harrow, and there traction changed to steam.

4-4-4 Express tank engine

Railway	North Eastern	Metropolitan
Engineer	V.L. Raven	C. Jones
Cylinders (number of)	3	2
Diameter (inches)	16½	19
Stroke (inches)	26	26
Coupled wheel diameter		
(feet/inches)	5 9	5 9
Heating surfaces (square feet)		
Tubes	934.8	1,046
Firebox	124	132
Superheater	273	268
Grate area (square feet)	23	21.4
Boiler pressure (lb per		
square inch)	160	160
Tractive effort (lb)	21,000	18,550

In the 1920s the 2-6-2 and 2-6-4 types both came

Above *Great Western Railway: one of the former Barry Railway 0-6-4 tanks, as rebuilt with a standard GWR boiler* (British Railways).

Left *North Staffordshire Railway: an Adams 0-6-4 tank which was used on the heaviest expresses between Stoke-on-Trent and Manchester.*

into prominence as express tank engines, and their prowess will be discussed later in this book. There were one or two examples in service prior to 1914, but of these only one was in regular passenger service, and that not of a very distinguished kind. These were the 20 Lancashire and Yorkshire 2-6-2 tanks built at Horwich during the time when H.A. Hoy was Chief Mechanical Engineer, in 1903-4. They were huge looking, ungainly things, and I am sure that the majority of L & Y men who had anything to do with them, whether in the shops, in the sheds, or on the footplate, would agree that the less said about them the better! They rode badly; they spread the road, they derailed themselves, and, in the shops, were a maintenance man's nightmare. They were taken off passenger work altogether in 1913.

The last express tank type to be discussed is the 4-6-4, two varieties of which were introduced before the First World War and two just afterwards. In 1911 Robert H. Whitelegg succeeded his father as Locomotive Engineer of the London, Tilbury and Southend Railway, and he immediately began to make preparations for the larger engines that were becoming necessary. Hitherto it had always the practice to turn the 4-4-2 express tank engines at Plaistow or Shoeburyness so as to have them chimney first on the hard jobs, and Whitelegg chose the 4-6-4 type for his new engines, instead of the 4-6-2 to obviate the need for turning. At the London end, engines had to go 'light engine' from the Fenchurch Street terminus for 5 miles, to Plaistow sheds for turning. Whitelegg's new express tank was to be a monster, weighing 94 tons in working order. A.L. Stride was then Chairman of the company, and to him, as a former civil engineer, Whitelegg showed the weight diagram. The engine was so much bigger and heavier than anything previously used that he needed confirmation, because the last 2.7 miles into the London terminus were owned by the Great Eastern Railway, and the Tilbury worked over them by means of running powers. Stride was delighted with the great engine. The Tilbury line was his pride and joy, and he seemed to relish the prestige that would accrue from having the largest tank engines in the country. So the order was passed to Beyer, Peacock & Co, to build eight of them.

It was not, apparently, until the first few engines were nearing completion in Manchester, that news of their size and weight reached the civil engineers of the Great Eastern, and only then, it seems, through the 'grape-vine'. At once an embargo was put on their use between Gas Factory Junction and Fenchurch Street. This meant that they could not be used on any of the hardest Tilbury jobs; but worse than that came the news that the railway itself was to be taken over, not by the Great Eastern as might have been expected, but by the Midland, of all railways! Of course this take-over was quite in keeping with the expansionist policy of Sir Guy Granet the General Manager of the Midland, but so far as locomotives were concerned it meant that when the big 4-6-4s arrived from Manchester, late in 1912, they were painted in the Midland colours and numbered 2100-2107.

Whitelegg did not stay long after he had taken

these remarkable engines through their trial trips, and nursed them clear of teething troubles. An autocrat by nature it was not likely that he would knuckle under as a mere divisional chief, dictated to at every end and turn by the pundits of Derby—for that is what divisional officers had to endure on the Midland of those days. He resigned, and with the onset of war soon found an outlet in military service. In the meantime his 4-6-4s, deprived of the duties for which they were designed, were transferred to Wellingborough to work coal trains on the Midland main line. Those who would see what their designer intended may gaze in delight at the magnificent scale model of the first of them in Tilbury colours, and named *Arthur Lewis Stride*, in the Science Museum, at South Kensington.

The second British 4-6-4 tank was that of the Brighton, on which railway Earle-Marsh's concept of a stud of 22 express tank engines of the 4-6-2 type languished after his resignation in 1911. His successor, Colonel L.B. Billinton, wanted a still bigger engine, and he turned to the 4-6-4 type,

Right *Midland Railway: one of the Deeley 0-6-4 passenger tanks, nicknamed the 'Flat-irons'* (British Railways).

Below *Lancashire and Yorkshire Railway: one of the huge, but somewhat ineffective, 2-6-2 tanks introduced by H.A. Hoy in 1903. They were taken off passenger work in 1913* (Real Photographs).

Glasgow & South Western Railway: the huge Whitelegg 4-6-4 express tank engine.

building two engines for trial. At the time it was announced that there would be seven of these engines; but the trials of the pioneer engine No 327 named *Charles C. Macrae* (after one of the directors of the company) had barely been concluded when war came in August 1914, and the remaining five engines were not built until 1921-2. Water surging around in the tanks was one of the main troubles initially, leading to dangerously bad riding. Each of the side tanks had a capacity of 1,350 gallons, and when the insertion of baffle plates had failed to cure the trouble, the capacity of the tanks was halved, though without altering the external appearance; and this deficiency was made up by a well-tank slung below the boiler barrel. The Brighton 4-6-4 tanks were splendid looking engines—'every inch a racer', as one of their many admirers put it. But in actual service they had such an amount of power in hand, even with the heaviest trains, that they could climb the gradients of the main line at such speeds as made very high downhill maxima unnecessary. The second engine, No 328, was not named.

The Furness engines, the only ones of the type to have inside cylinders, were built to provide increased tractive power for the increasingly heavy trains making a number of intermediate stops on the short runs between Barrow and Carnforth, Barrow and Whitehaven. And because of the shortness of the runs it was not considered necessary for them to be superheated. They made easy work of the sharply graded sections of the line, but were never called upon to make any appreciable speed. It was noticeable that after the grouping of 1923, when ageing non-superheater 4-4-0s from certain of the constituent companies of the LMS were drafted on to the Furness line, the 4-6-4s generally showed to advantage uphill, but the older 4-4-0s, with larger coupled wheels, made the faster running elsewhere.

The last of the 4-6-4 tanks to be built by one of the pre-grouping companies appeared in 1922 on the Glasgow and South Western. It was perhaps natural for Robert Whitelegg, thwarted in two ways in his attempt to introduce the type for the heavily worked commuter services of the Tilbury, to have seen in the Clyde Coast services of the G & SWR and their heavy summer loads an opportunity to introduce the type again, to the advantage of his new company. Every detail of the new engines was worked out with the greatest care and, as the table at top right shows, the result was a very powerful engine, and an impressively massive, and handsome one. The men were equally impressed by its ability to get away with a load. But it seemed that Whitelegg was fated not to follow through the

4-6-4 Passenger tank engines

Railway	LT & S (Midland)	LBSC	Furness	G & SW
Date	1912	1914	1920	1922
Engineer	R. Whitelegg	L. Billinton	E. Sharples	R. Whitelegg
Cylinders				
Diameter (inches)	20	22	19¼	22
Stroke (inches)	26	28	26	26
Coupled wheel diameter (feet/inches)	6 3	6 9	5 8	6 0
Heating surfaces (square feet)				
Tubes	1,155	1,535	1,850	1,574
Firebox	141	152	153	156
Superheater	319	383	—	255
Grate area (square feet)	·25	26.7	26	30
Boiler pressure (lb per square inch)	160	170	170	180
Tractive effort (lb)	19,930	25,550	21,700	27,200
Number built	8	7	5	6

0-6-4 Tank engines

Ref no	1	2	3	4	5	6	7	8
Railway	Wirral	Great Central (ex LD & EC)	Midland	Highland	SE & CR	Barry	Metro-politan	North Stafford
Service	Goods	Mineral	Passenger	Banking	Passenger	Mineral	Passenger	Passenger
Engineer	E.G. Barker	C.P. Markham	Deeley	P. Drummond	Wainwright	J. Auld	C. Jones	J.H. Adams
Date introduced	1900	1904	1907	1908	1913	1914	1915	1917
Cylinders								
Diameter (inches)	18	19	18½	18½	19½	18½	20	20
Stroke (inches)	26	26	26	26	26	26	26	26
Coupled wheel diameter (feet/inches)	5 2	4 9	5 7	5 0	5 6	4 7	5 9	5 6
Heating surfaces (square feet)								
Tubes	1,063	1,366	1,206	1,144	999	1,372	1,046	887
Firebox	111	124	125	110		123.5	132	129
Superheater	—	—	—	—	234	—	268	258
Grate area square feet	21.5	21.75	21.1	22.5	17.6	22	21.4	21.2
Boiler pressure (lb per square inch)	170	180	175	180	160	180	160	160
Tractive effort (lb)	18.550	23,800	18,650	22,082	18,920	23,400	19,730	20,620
Number built	2	9	40	8	5	10	4	16

introduction of his fine engines. Again it was a 'take-over', this time by the inclusion of the G & SWR in the vast LMS Group. He stayed long enough to be designated Mechanical Engineer, Kilmarnock, but after only two months he left to become General Manager of Beyer, Peacock & Co. Very many years later I had the honour of meeting him. He had long retired, but was still as keenly interested in locomotives, retaining much of that forthright personality that in Tilbury days earned him the nickname of 'Robert the Devil'.

In this chapter I have not dealt with the tank engines of the 2-6-2 and 2-6-4 types that were already in use because the major development and utilisation of both was yet to come at the time of grouping. But in concluding these notes on the express tank engines of the pre-grouping era, one cannot but appreciate how especially those huge, portentous monsters of the 4-6-4 type, in all their distinctive colours and impeccable finish, epitomised the railways of Britain in the age that was to slip away so quickly after the year 1923.

Left *London Brighton & South Coast Railway: the first post-war example of L.B. Billinton's 4-6-4 express tank engine, a type first introduced in 1914 (the late Lord Monkswell).*

Left *Great Central Railway: one of the earliest British examples of the 2-6-4 type which was introduced in 1914 for short-haul coal traffic (British Railways).*

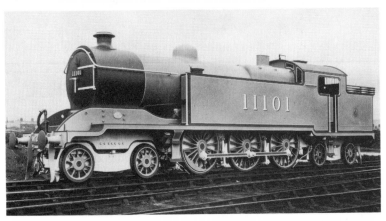

Left *Furness Railway: the handsome non-superheated 4-6-4 tank of 1920, here seen in LMS colours (British Railways).*

Below *London Tilbury and Southend Railway: R.H. Whitelegg's impressive 4-6-4 tank completed by Beyer, Peacock & Company just at the time of the Midland take-over in 1912. It is seen here in Midland colours (Beyer, Peacock & Company).*

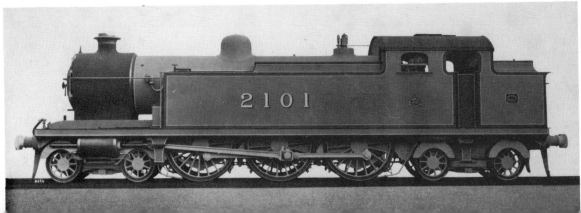

9. 4-6-0: the emergent premier locomotive type—I

At the end of the 19th century there were only 22 locomotives of the 4-6-0 type in service in Great Britain, and 15 of these were of the celebrated pioneer British class with this wheel arrangement, the 'Jones Goods' on the Highland. Five others, the beginning of a considerable fleet of mixed traffic engines were on the North Eastern, and the remaining two were experimental units—very much so!—on the Great Western. Twenty years later the total, taken at the end of November 1919, had gone up to 976; and of this increase very nearly half, 482 had been on only one railway, the London and North Western. The other totals then quoted were Caledonian 53; Glasgow and South Western 19; Great Central 55; Great Eastern 40; Great Western 138; Highland 46; Lancashire and Yorkshire 20; London and South Western 46, and North Eastern 70. Having these totals in mind it is interesting to study the circumstances in which the 4-6-0 type was first introduced, and then developed. The lack of any policy of standardisation becomes remarkably apparent in some administrations.

Rather than attempting to chronicle successive additions in strict historical sequence, a clearer picture is likely to emerge by recording events company by company. There was little if any connection between collateral developments, if anything rather the reverse, where the individuality of the senior engineering executives involved sometimes seemed to weigh more heavily than the actual needs of the traffic.

On the Highland Railway, where the type originated in Great Britain, the situation was straightforward enough until the disgraceful affair of the 'River' Class engines in 1915. Before the accident on the footplate that led to his premature retirement, David Jones had prepared the design for a passenger equivalent of his famous and outstandingly successful 'big goods' of 1894 and, when he took over at Inverness, Peter Drummond was content to leave the basic design unchanged, merely putting on boiler mountings in the family style, and using his brother's huge double-bogie tender, with inside bearings. Dubs & Co delivered the first six engines of the 'Castle' Class in June 1900; they were an immediate success and delivery was taken of four more of them in July 1902. Two more, to the original Jones/Drummond design were added in 1910-11, and after F.G. Smith had been appointed Locomotive Superintendent, in 1912, another four, to a slightly modified design, were built by the North British Locomotive Company in 1913. The most noticeable changes were the provision of a slightly extended smokebox, thought to make provision for a superheater at some future time, and solid, instead of marine big-ends. The last three, built in 1917 after the 'River' Class 'incident', had coupled wheels of 6 feet diameter, instead of 5 feet 9 inches. It was with one of the 1917 batch, *Darnaway Castle*, that I clocked the highest speed I ever noted with a Highland 4-6-0 engine, 67 mph; but a more rousing memory is that of a run on the footplate of *Beaufort Castle*, one of the 1902 batch, as leading engine of the down Mail in a January blizzard, climbing from Aviemore to Slochd summit, when at one time, snow was driving horizontally, clean through the cab!

How the Highland Railway came to be deprived of the use of six of the finest engines ever to run in Scotland came about thus. F.G. Smith, who succeeded Peter Drummond as Locomotive Superintendent, was one of the most advanced thinkers of the day in locomotive design, and he was aware that it was not so much the dead weight per axle of a locomotive that affected the track and underline

Highland Railway: 4-6-0, No 146, Skibo Castle, *at Perth, coaled up ready for the run to Inverness* (R.D. Stephen).

structures, as what is termed the dynamic augment, or the hammer blow effect caused by the unbalanced forces arising from the rotation and oscillation of heavy parts at speed. Smith designed the 'River' Class 4-6-0s so that although the dead weight on their driving axles was greater than that of Drummond's 'Castles' the balancing was so arranged that at express speed the total effect was less. Unfortunately Smith had a rather high handed way of dealing with his colleagues in other departments. He had already upset the civil engineer over another matter, and when the Board authorised the purchase of the six engines of the 'River' Class he did not submit the weight diagram. When the first two engines arrived at Perth from the builders the civil engineer was there to meet them; and after a week-end of traumatic calculation and consultation

he forbade their use. He was quite deaf to the argument about dynamic augment. The engines were sold to the Caledonian, and Smith was given a week to resign, or be dismissed. He resigned. The irony of the whole affair is that the 'Clan' Class engines, designed by his successor, had a considerably worse effect on the track—dead weight plus dynamic augment; but because they had a lighter axle load the civil engineer accepted them without question!

The North Eastern Railway was the first to introduce the 4-6-0 type ostensibly as an express passenger engine; but although the subsequent line of development and its ultimate results were entirely successful, they were not, one would imagine, what Wilson Worsdell originally intended. The first five 4-6-0s built at Gateshead in 1899 were designed to

Left *Highland Railway: one of the 'River' Class 4-6-0s which was returned to the work originally intended for them, after 12 years' banishment on the Caledonian (British Railways).*

Below *North Eastern Railway: the 'S1' Class of express passenger 4-6-0s, built in 1901 (The Locomotive Publishing Company).*

eliminate double-heading on the heavy East Coast expresses between Newcastle and Edinburgh; but they gave a lot of trouble mechanically. To cope with the severe gradients north of Berwick they had coupled wheels of 6 feet 1 inch diameter and, while these did not prevent running fast on occasions, heating troubles were frequent and in 1901 a further batch of five was built with 6 foot 8 inch coupled wheels. But the new 'R' Class 4-4-0s were doing such excellent work that plans for further 10-wheeled engines were held in abeyance. It was then that Wilson Worsdell accompanied the General Manager's party on its tour of American railways, and he came back so impressed with what he saw of 'Atlantic' engine performance that the idea of using 4-6-0 locomotives on the principal East Coast expresses lapsed, and was never revived. In the meantime, however, the 10 original 6 foot 1 inch 4-6-0s, Nos 2001-10, had been found so useful on express goods trains that the traffic department asked for more, and construction of another 30 was authorised in 1906-9.

In 1911, when Raven had succeeded Wilson Worsdell as Chief Mechanical Engineer, construction of a further 20 mixed traffic 4-6-0s was authorised; these were generally similar to Class 'S', but with 5 foot 6 inch diameter boilers, and superheated. They were very successful, and worked regular rosters that included express passenger, and fully-fitted express goods trains. They were classed 'S2', and could be regarded as something of a forerunner to the famous 'Black Five' 4-6-0s of Stanier's day on the LMS. There was one important difference. Throughout his career on the North Eastern Railway, Raven remained unshakeably devoted to the Stephenson link motion, between the frames, even after he was building few except 3-cylinder engines, with three sets of valve gear. His engines, good though they were, did not fulfil the post-grouping requirement that everything should be 'get-at-able'. On the North Eastern there had nevertheless been a notable continuity of development with the 4-6-0 type, and the process was consummated with Raven's three-cylinder 'S3' Class in 1919, of which more will be written later.

When Great Central locomotive history is studied one can be faintly surprised that an engineer of such ability as J.G. Robinson appeared to be so undecided as to what his standard mixed traffic locomotive should be. Without knowing exactly what was in his mind it would be unfair to suggest that he was designing new engines for the sheer delight of doing so; but in contrast to the record of production of heavy freight and express passenger engines, at any rate up to the year 1914, the rapid succession of dissimilar mixed traffic designs was really rather extraordinary. The situation as it developed up to 1918 is shown in the table below. Classes 1, 2, 3 and 4 all had the characteristically handsome Robinson 'look' about them. They were beautifully styled, and all did excellent work. But was it really necessary to have so many different wheel diameters? One can appreciate that the two 6 foot 9 inch engines were needed for direct comparison with the first 'Atlantics', but would not 6 feet and 6 feet 9 inch have been enough? Again one is curious to know why the 5 foot 3 inch engines of

Great Central 4-6-0s 1902-1918

Ref no	1	2	3	4	5	6	7	8
Date introduced	1902	1903	1906	1906	1912	1913	1917	1918
Class	'Fish'	'196'	'Imming-ham'	5 ft 3 in	'Sir Sam Fay'	'Glen-almond'	'Lord Faringdon'	'53'
Service	Mixed	Passenger	Passenger	Fast goods	Passenger	Mixed	Passenger	Mixed
Number built	14	2	10	10	6	11	6	3
Coupled wheel diameter (feet/inches)	6 0	6 9	6 6	5 3	6 9	5 7	6 9	5 8
Cylinders position	outside	outside	outside	outside	inside	inside	out & in	outside
Diameter (inches)	19	19	19½	19½	21½	21½	16 (4)	21
Stroke (inches)	26	26	26	26	26	26	26	26
Heating surface (square feet)								
Tubes	1,622	1,778	1,778	1,778	2,219.9	2,219.9	1,881	1,641
Firebox	126	133	153	131.6	167	167	159	174
Superheater	—	—	—	—	430	430	343	308
Grate area (square feet)	23	26	26	23.4	26	26	26	26
Boiler pressure (lb per square inch)	180	180	200	200	160	160	180	180
Tractive effort (lb)	19,150	17,700	21,550	26,700	20,200	24,400	25,145	25,850

1906 had smaller fireboxes, which hardly matched their very high nominal tractive effort.

In Great Central days all these engines, except the 'Fays' and the 'Faringdons' were painted in 'goods black', smartly lined out in red, with the coat of arms on the tenders and coupled wheel splashers. On the LNER in the economy days of 1928 and after, when the 'Atlantics' and 'Directors' went into black, some quirk of administration decreed that the 'Imminghams', and the two 6 foot 9 inch 4-6-0s should remain in green in keeping with the 'Fays' and 'Faringdons'. In the late 1920s some of the 'Imminghams' were transferred to Copley Hill, Leeds, Great Northern shed, and they worked on the London expresses as far as Doncaster. Twice, when travelling by the 5.30 pm to Kings Cross, we had the ex-GCR engines and their work was quite thrilling. They were piloted up the steep climb to Ardsley but from Wakefield they were on their own. The downhill start to Sandal gave some opportunity to take a run at the 1 in 150 bank that extends for 3½ miles to Nostell, and after that it is downhill to Carcroft. The two runs, with heavy trains, are well worth setting on record.

Great Central Railway: 'Sir Sam Fay' Class inside-cylinder superheater 4-6-0 of 1912.

LNER 5.30 pm Leeds to Kings Cross

Engine ex-GCR 4-6-0 No	**6099**		**6102**	
Load tons E/F	313/340		343/365	
Distance	**Time**	**Speeds**	**Time**	**Speeds**
(miles)	m s	mph	m s	mph
0.0 Wakefield	0 00	—	0 00	—
1.7 Sandal	3 10	51	3 00	48
5.5 Nostell	8 05	43	8 10	41
8.0 Hemsworth	11 05	60	11 10	61
11.2 South Elmsall	14 05	71 ½	14 00	74
13.3 Hampole	15 55	72	15 55	69
15.9 Carcroft	18 00	—	18 10	66
		sig stops		sig stops
19.9 Doncaster	34 05	—	28 00	—

The time allowance was 24 minutes, and both engines would have kept it comfortably but for the final checks.

In 1912 the 'big engine' era began on the Great Central, with the huge-boilered 'Sir Sam Fay' Class. They were so well proportioned, however, that one did not appreciate their vast bulk until one

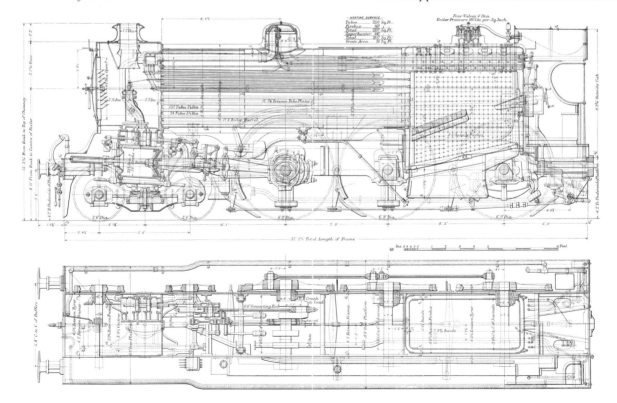

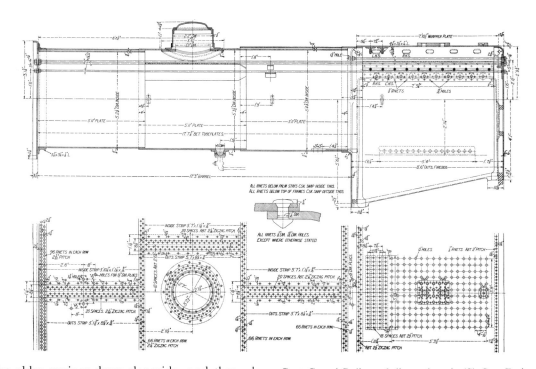

Great Central Railway: boiler used on the 'Sir Sam Fay' and on the later 4-cylinder express and mixed traffic 4-6-0s.

of the older engines drew alongside, and then—! Looking at the dimensions on the last four engines in the table, although the boiler barrels of the 'Fay' and the 'Faringdon' were the same, it would seem that the tubes on the former were found to be too crowded. Great Central engines of the second decade of the century have been criticised for having inadequate grate area. If they had been called upon for a continuously high output of maximum power I would agree; but with the relatively light loads of most Great Central expresses, the demand for high power was at the most, intermittent, and a moderate sized grate, combined with high storage volume for steam in the boiler, can be the most economical proportions for minimum coal consumption. So far as engine design is concerned one is inclined to think that Robinson changed from the relatively simple *Sir Sam Fay* to the much complicated and expensive 'Faringdon' for prestige purposes—'Keeping up with the Jones's', of Crewe and Swindon! But the real curiosity in the table is No 8. Why, when one had the 'Glenalmond' Class, build a new outside cylinder class of only three engines, which would involve new patterns, new tooling and much else besides?

Nevertheless, I cannot end the story of the Great Central 4-6-0s down to 1920 without referring once again to their magnificent 'presence' and always superb turnout. I cannot remember *ever* having seen one of them that was not immaculate. Robinson and his drawing office at Gorton touched the heights in

attaining what Henry Maxwell once called 'a balanced plastic symmetry' in the outline of their engines. While the saga of the Great Central was not to be ended when grouping came, the appearance of the engines became a travesty of their former glory, as will be told later, although Gresley had a marked affection for them. It was largely through Robinson that he was appointed Chief Mechanical Engineer of the LNER and several times, when new engines were wanted in quicker time than was available to prepare new designs, Gresley turned to Great Central classes to fill the breach.

In pre-grouping days the rivals of the Great Central engines for sheer beauty of line were those of the Caledonian, and the first introduction of the 4-6-0 type came in 1902. Until then the Callander and Oban line, with its mountainous gradients and severe curvature, had been worked by a class of 10 outside-cylinder 4-4-0s, designed specially for it by W. Brittain and built by Dübs & Co, in 1882. They were sturdy little things with 18 inch by 24 inch cylinders, and 5 foot 2 inch coupled wheels and they had done the job well for 20 years; but the tourist traffic was increasing, and when it came to adding heavy through carriages from farther afield, and

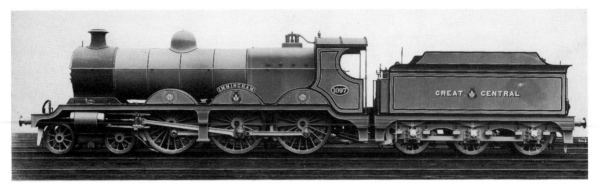

slogging it out on lengthy inclines of 1 in 55 and 1 in 60, it was clear that something larger than 4-4-0s of 1882 vintage was needed. So J.F. McIntosh, using even smaller coupled wheels than on the Brittain 4-4-0s, 5 foot diameter, and the well tried 'Dunalastair II' front end, boiler and firebox, produced a very powerful engine of 23,269 lb tractive effort. Although the gradients were very severe the demands for steam were intermittent, and no difficulties arose from using a longer boiler barrel than on the 'Dunalastair II', the periods of all-out effort were not more than of about 20 minutes duration, followed by spells of downhill coasting. The 'Oban bogies' were a great success, and the nine engines of the class handled the increasing traffic for some 25 years.

Before the second batch of these engines had left the erecting shop at St Rollox in 1903 some vastly greater 4-6-0s were in hand. The increasing use of heavy corridor coaches, dining and sleeping cars on the principal expresses to and from England demanded larger engines than the admittedly powerful 'Dunalastair III' 4-4-0s, and there were no half measures about the way McIntosh responded to the call. What was perhaps remarkable was the astonishing grace and beauty of the huge 4-6-0 express engines that he produced. If it may be presumed to write so, they seemed a little out of character with the man himself. Without going to the extreme of describing him as a 'rough diamond', this bluff, one-armed, one-time shed foreman, who had risen to such heights, still had a style of conversation that was more appropriate to the drawing office than to the drawing room; and it is said of him that he entertained King Edward VII mightily on journeys with the Royal Train with his fund of blue stories! When it came to locomotives, from his long experience in the running department he had no hesitation in laying down the essential basic proportions of a design; but how did they come to be clothed in such elegance?

In his old age, when he used to write amusing

letters to *The Railway Gazette*, that fiery Scots advocate, Norman Doran Macdonald (whose active railway enthusiasm went back to the racing days of 1895, and earlier) had a way of claiming something of the credit for himself. Certainly on his own confession he plagued not only McIntosh, but Wilson Worsdell and others besides with his ideas and recommendations—often made in the most forthright language! He could tell a good story against himself. Writing to *The Railway Gazette* on Christmas Day 1936; of his encounters with McIntosh, he continues: '. . . One day after I had given him two months respite I walked into his room. He was surrounded by a galaxy from the drawing office. He looked up and shouted: "Hullo, Maister Macdonald, how have you escaped from your assielum?"'! Joking apart, the end result on the big express passenger 4-6-0s was superb, and the first two, introduced in 1903, and the subsequent five, with modified dimensions, became a legend in their day. All of them were allocated to specific duties, which they worked month in, month out, with the same crews.

The stately goings and comings of these engines, no less than the chronometer-like punctuality that they maintained, sent the prestige of the Caledonian sky high in the pre-1914 era. The first two engines, Nos 49 and 50, were turned out in the 'official' dark Prussian blue livery, duly signalised by a splendid example of the lithographed colour plates celebrated in the early days of *The Railway Magazine*. No 50, named after the General Manager of the Caledonian, Sir James Thompson, was at once assigned to the duty on which the first of the second batch, No 903, *Cardean*, afterwards became a positive institution: the 2 pm 'Corridor', from Glasgow down to Carlisle, returning with the corresponding northbound train leaving Carlisle at 8.13 pm. One of the objects of designing such big engines was to eliminate the need for rear-end banking assistance from Beattock up to Summit, and No 50 had not been on the job for long before

Charles Rous-Marten went north to record the performance. His opening words catch the spirit of the occasion: 'At Carlisle, Mr MacIntosh's Caledonian colossus, No 50, came on under the admiring gaze of a large crowd of eyes, there being quite a big assemblage of spectators kept within bounds by a policeman. The vast size and magnificent appearance of the new engine was very striking, especially in comparison with the relatively small engines of the six other railway companies that run into Carlisle . . .'. It may be added that his train was hauled from Crewe to Carlisle by a pair of 6 foot 6 inch 'Jumbo' 2-4-0s of the LNWR!

On that occasion a load of 330 tons behind that great tender was taken without any rear-end assistance up the Beattock bank, and the summit, 49¾ miles from Carlisle and 1,015 feet above sea level, was passed in 66 minutes. But on the following day, with the load increased to 395 tons, a bank engine was taken. The initial 39¾ miles to the stop at Beattock station took 44½ minutes, and, with assistance from a 0-4-4 tank engine, the 10-mile climb, mostly at 1 in 75, took 18½ minutes, and the summit was passed in 65½ minutes from the start at Carlisle. Rous-Marten's other runs showed also that No 50 could run very fast on favourable stretches of line, and he clocked several instances of maximum speeds between 75 and 79 mph.

Before leaving those pioneer McIntosh express 4-6-0s, I must also remark upon how superbly matched their great tenders were to the engines. While the provision of a very large tender may suggest an inordinate appetite for coal it must be remembered that there were then no water troughs on the Caledonian, and water was not taken intermediately in the 102 miles between Glasgow and Carlisle. The tender carried 5,000 gallons, and five

Above left *Great Central Railway: express passenger 4-6-0, No 1097,* Immingham, *with 6 foot 6 inch coupled wheels* (Beyer, Peacock & Company).

Right *Great Central Railway: one of the Robinson 5 foot 3 inch 4-6-0s of 1906, sometimes known as the 'fish engines' because of their use on fish specials, seen here in LNER colours* (P. Ransome-Wallis).

Below *Great Central Railway: one of the large boilered inside-cylinder fast goods and mixed traffic engines of 1913* (British Railways).

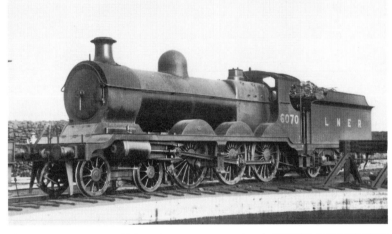

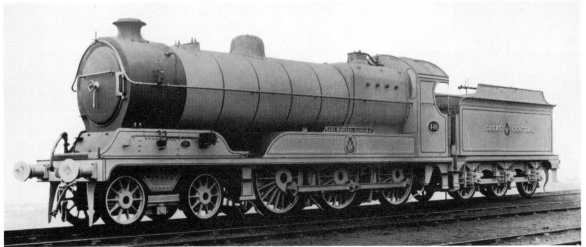

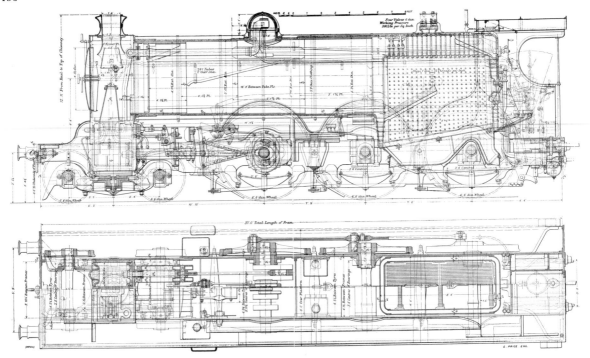

Caledonian Railway: the legendary '903' or 'Cardean' Class 4-6-0 of 1906, by J.F. McIntosh.

tons of coal, and the latter was expected to suffice for the round trip from Glasgow to Carlisle and back. This provided for a consumption of 50 lb per mile, which was not excessive in view of the loads regularly hauled.

The second batch of large express 4-6-0s, built in 1906, were better known than the first two, largely through the unbroken association of No 903 *Cardean* with the 'Corridor' for about 10 years. The minimum load of the down train was that of seven 12-wheelers of the beautiful WCJS stock, about 305 tons; but it was very frequently exceeded, and details of a series of seven runs published in *The Railway Magazine* in 1914, showed the loads as being 305, 320, 335, 360 and 390 tons. As a provision against the effects of inclement weather on Beattock bank the schedule allowed for a stop to take a bank engine, which was usually taken. Otherwise it meant hard work, with 44 minutes for the initial 39¾ mile run from Carlisle; 2 minutes for attaching the bank engine, and then 20 minutes up to Summit. The downhill allowance of 23 minutes for the 23¼ miles down the Clyde Valley to Strawfrank Junction, where the Edinburgh portion was detached, gave something of a recovery margin; and the record of punctuality was very high. The

table of dimensions on page 142 shows the boiler proportions both before and after superheating, the modification having taken place in 1911-2.

Cardean herself was the only engine of the class regularly stationed in Glasgow. Engines 904 and 905 were at Perth, for working on the Aberdeen road, and 906 and 907 were at Carlisle. The normal duties of these latter engines were the 'midnight' from Euston: the heavy sleeping car express to Glasgow, making the fastest run of the 24-hours, and secondly the Glasgow portion of the 10 am from Euston. The return trips were on the 10 am up from Glasgow and on the 10.45 pm sleeper. When 907 was in the Quintinshill catastrophe of 1915, and so badly damaged that she was subsequently scrapped, she was not on her regular duty but working a 'running-in' turn when newly returned after a general overhaul at St Rollox.

I shall never forget my first sight of one of them, at Glasgow Central. It was 1923, after the grouping, but in August of that year no Caledonian engines were as yet painted anything but blue. We were bound for Wemyss Bay, and while we waited, the engine for the 3.50 pm Liverpool and Manchester express backed down. It was No 50, so immaculately clean against the drab background as to be a positive apparition. I thought of this occasion when another railway littérateur likened the idea of a Caledonian express engine in red to a jazz version of *The Immortal Hour*! Even that was better than the miserable unlined black in which No 49 (as LMS 14750) was clad when I travelled behind her in 1930.

Two further 4-6-0 Classes were introduced on the Caledonian in 1906. The '908' was a smaller wheeled version of the 'Cardeans', designed for rapid acceleration with the Clyde Coast expresses and for the Glasgow-Perth section of the north main line. The '918' Class, was a large-boilered version of the 'Oban bogies', having the same wheel base, but a larger diameter boiler. It was primarily a main line express goods engine. The '908' and '918' Class 4-6-0s both had 6-wheeled tenders. Neither class was subsequently superheated; but just before his retirement, McIntosh introduced a powerful superheated version of the '908' Class, readily distinguishable from the earlier ones, and indeed from all other Caledonian 4-6-0s before or since, by having side windowed cabs, rather in the North Eastern style. They may have given better shelter for the men, but they did not improve the appearance of the engines.

It came as a surprise and a disappointment to the men of St Rollox when, after McIntosh's retirement early in 1914, one of their number was not promoted to succeed him. Instead, the Board brought in William Pickersgill, who for 20 years had been Locomotive, Carriage and Wagon Superintendent of the Great North of Scotland Railway. It was a tiny concern compared to the Caledonian with little more than 100 engines, and nothing larger than 4-4-0s, the most powerful of which had 18 inch by 26 inch cylinders, 6 foot 1 inch coupled wheels, and very small boilers. Pickersgill's early training and experience had all been in England on the Great Eastern Railway on which, as a lad of 15, he entered Stratford Works. He served under a succession of famous engineers: William Adams, Massey Bromley, Thos W. Worsdell and James Holden, and it was the last named who appointed him District Locomotive Superintendent at

Below *Great Central Railway: a post-war example,* Valour, *the GCR war memorial engine, of the 'Lord Faringdon' Class 4-cylinder 4-6-0 of 1917 (the late W.J. Reynolds).*

Bottom *GCR: the fast goods equivalent of the 'Faringdon' which was introduced in 1918.*

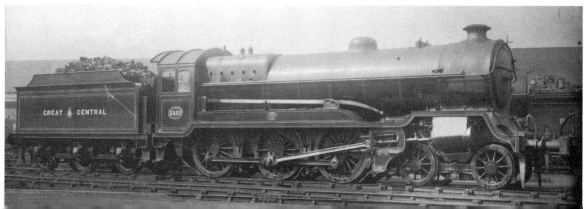

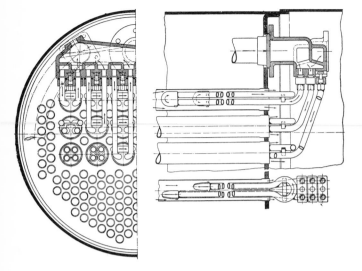

Left *The Schmidt superheater.*

Right *Lancashire & Yorkshire Railway: Hughes 4-cylinder 4-6-0, non-superheated, with Joy valve gear.*

Norwich in 1891, when he was 30 years of age. He secured the GNSR post three years later.

His record on the Caledonian was extraordinary in its ineffectiveness. At the moment I am concerned only with the '60' Class of outside cylinder 4-6-0s. They should have been splendid engines. They had a good boiler, though with a lower degree of superheat than previously used at St Rollox; they were massively built, but for some utterly inexplicable reason the Stephenson link motion was designed with crossed, instead of open eccentric rods. In consequence, the lead of the valves decreased, instead of increasing as the gear was notched up, and this made the engines the most awful sluggards. When they were first introduced, at the end of 1916, train services were being drastically decelerated, and their disabilities were not so apparent as they might otherwise have been. At the strong recommendation of W. Barr, who was running superintendent in Scotland after grouping, a further 20 of these engines were built in 1925-6, and one of them gave some interesting results in dynamometer car tests between Preston and Carlisle, in 1926. These are discussed in a later chapter.

In pre-grouping days there cannot have been two railways in more sustained and bitter rivalry than the Caledonian and the Glasgow and South Western. It extended to every facet of activity where their interests impinged; and, needless to say when the news got around in the railway world of Glasgow that the Caledonian was planning a monster 4-6-0 engine, the high management of the G & SWR authorised their own Locomotive Superintendent, James Manson, to go one better—if not in size, then certainly in scale of operations. And the frames of

the giant Caledonians 49 and 50 were scarcely laid down in St Rollox Works before the neighbouring North British Locomotive Company received an order for *10* large 4-6-0s, to Manson's design, to be built at their Atlas Works, the former Sharp, Stewart establishment. The race was on! Which of the arch-rivals would be first to steam the first big Scottish 4-6-0 express locomotive? The Caledonian were first, but by a mere two months; and they had just the two engines in regular service by the end of May 1903, while by mid-June the NBL had delivered all ten of the G & SWR '381' Class.

The tractive power of these latter engines was considerably less than that of the Caledonians; for not only were the cylinders of 20 inch diameter against 21 inch, but the boiler working pressure was no more than 180 lb per square inch. With outside cylinders driving on to the middle pair of coupled wheels they were comely, pleasing engines to look upon. No doubt to comply with weight restrictions imposed by the civil engineer they were not so robustly built as the massive Caledonians. It was fortunate that driving traditions on the G & SW were somewhat different from those of their rivals. The drivers tended to handle their engines on a light rein, taking them gently uphill, and letting them 'fly' on the favourable stretches. The Manson 4-6-0s proved to be very fast engines, and it was not until their years mounted up that the weaknesses in their frames, and construction at the front end began to become serious, with cylinders working loose, and frames cracking. The Midland Scotch Expresses were not generally heavy, and even in their prime these engines were not called for very hard work. It was perhaps just as well.

The Manson 4-6-0s had always been relatively light on coal; but, in 1911, when much attention in the locomotive world was being given to means of increasing thermal efficiency, two more 4-6-0s were ordered from NBL, fitted with Schmidt superheaters. These were engines Nos 128 and 129 and the second of them was equipped in addition with the Weir feed water heater, and pump. Theoretical considerations indicated that the thermal efficiency of an engine could be increased if the water fed into the boiler was hot. Several British engineers, notably Earle-Marsh on the Brighton, had been experimenting with 'hot feed', but it was the sustained development in this direction of the Glasgow firm of G & J Weir, that produced a reliable apparatus. In the Brighton case the storage

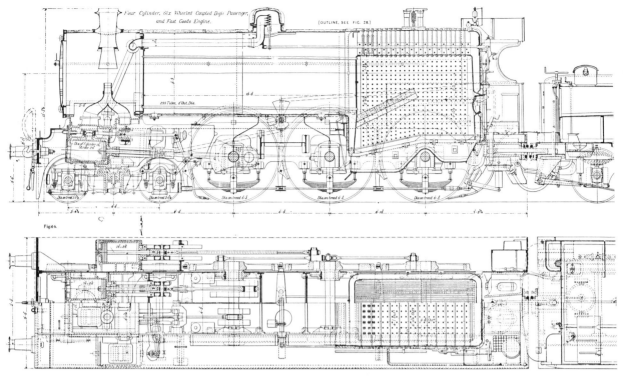

Four Cylinder, Six Wheeled Coupled Bogie Passenger, and Fast Goods Engine.

tank was mounted on the running plate, but on the G & SW No 129 it was mounted on top of the boiler, between the chimney and dome, and looked horrible! Looks apart however, No 129 did some very good work, though one would imagine maintenance costs of the apparatus tended to outweigh the savings achieved in fuel consumption. The Weir feed water heater was removed in 1919. After grouping, engines 128 and 129 worked for a time in composite link between Glasgow and Carlisle, outward via the Caledonian route and returning in the G & SW line. The work of these two superheater 4-6-0s compared reasonably well with that of Caledonian 4-4-0s; but as a nonstandard type they were scrapped in the early 1930s. For the record, they had 21 inch by 26 inch cylinders, 6 foot 6 inch coupled wheels, and the heating surfaces of tubes, firebox and superheater were 1,430, 130 and 445 square feet respectively. the grate area was 24.5 square feet and the boiler pressure 160 lb per square inch.

It was in June 1908 that George Hughes, Chief Mechanical Engineer of the Lancashire and Yorkshire Railway, completed the first two of his big 4-cylinder 4-6-0 passenger engines, of which there was a works order for 20. On paper they were immensely powerful engines, with cylinders 16 inch

by 26 inch; coupled wheels of 6 foot 3 inch diameter, and a boiler pressure of 180 lb per square inch. The tractive effort was 27,157 lb, and the enormous boiler, 5 foot 10 inch outside diameter, seemed ample enough to back up the needs of those four large cylinders. But to the non-technical members of the railway enthusiast fraternity they must have been one of the biggest locomotive enigmas of all time. In a paper read before the Institution of Mechanical Engineers in July 1909 Hughes himself said: 'This design was brought about by the further increased weight of trains and the necessity of accurate timekeeping with the accelerated train schedule of the Liverpool, Manchester and Hull expresses, the Leeds, Bradford and Fleetwood boat trains and to cope with gradients on the Bradford, Huddersfield and Sheffield sections'. It is curious he did not mention the Liverpool-Newcastle expresses because, judging from contemporary photographs, these were among the first on to which the new engines were allocated. In any case, however, the loads were trifling compared to those on the main lines of the London and North Western Railway.

From a study of Hughes' paper it is evident that an immense amount of thought was packed into the design of these engines. It would be a little unkind,

one feels, to suggest that it was all a monument of wasted effort; but all the same, taking the most charitable view of it they were little removed from the most complete failure seen in the British locomotive world for very many years. Everything conceivable that could go wrong did so. They were sluggish; their coal consumption, even when the cross-country corridor trains did not exceed seven or eight coaches, was astronomical, and mechanical faults put them out of traffic for weeks at a time.

In the day-to-day attention at sheds, which had to be done while an engine was in steam, they were a fitter's nightmare, especially when there were jobs to do between the frames. All the fittings were in a most inaccessible position, under the smokebox, with valve spindles, rocker arms, spindle guides and valve gear intermingled, and everything hot and greasy . . . There is no point in prolonging the miserable tale. At the end of the First World War, when less than half of them were serviceable, the decision was taken to withdraw the lot, and embark upon a thorough and expensive process of rebuilding. Their subsequent history is told in a later chapter.

Altogether contrasting is the story of the introduction of the 4-6-0 type on the Great Eastern Railway at the end of 1911. By that time James Holden had retired and his son was in the chair; but

Top *Caledonian Railway: one of the first of J.F. McIntosh's express passenger 4-6-0s, No 50,* Sir James Thompson, *built in 1903* (British Railways).

Above *Caledonian Railway: one of the 5 foot 9 inch superheated mixed traffic 4-6-0s of the '179' Class of 1913 in LMS colours* (British Railways).

he was a 'lightweight' and contributed little except securing the authorisation for the new engines. The designer was F.V. Russell, then Chief Draughtsman at Stratford, and like its 4-4-0 predecessor of 1900, the *Claud Hamilton*, the new 4-6-0, No 1500 was absolutely right from the outset and did very first class work. By reason of its very large cab the engine looked a good deal larger than it was really, scaling no more than 64 tons, with a maximum axle load of 16 tons, on the leading coupled axle, the success of these engines, of which many more were built, was a simple, and amply proportioned layout of machinery, and a free steaming boiler. The cylinders were 20 inches by 28 inches; coupled wheels of 6 foot 6 inch diameter, and heating surfaces in tubes, firebox and superheater of 1,489, 143.5 and 286.4 square feet respectively. The grate area was of 26.5 square feet and boiler pressure 180 lb per square inch. In the standard 'Royal Blue' livery of the Great Eastern, they looked superb.

I have left until last in this chapter the interesting

story of 4-6-0 development on the London and South Western Railway, because its culmination includes perhaps the most significant feature towards future practice of anything so far touched upon. But events must first be taken back to 1903 when, at J.F. McIntosh's invitation, the mighty Dugald Drummond paid a visit to St Rollox, the scene of his former labours, and was shown one of the two new express 4-6-0 engines. Apparently the dour old man was not particularly impressed, and went so far as to chide McIntosh for building such unnecessarily large engines. In after years the incident became one of the best of McIntosh's stories, for he told with a relish that, after seeing 49 and 50, Drummond went back to Nine Elms and immediately set his drawing office on to designing something even bigger—the enormous '330' Class of 4-cylinder 4-6-0!

Impressive though the appearance and dimensions of these latter engines might seem, their effectiveness as motive power units is lost in a fog of obscurity. The celebrated author, Charles Rous-Marten, who was then writing the monthly 'British Locomotive Practice and Performance' feature in *The Railway Magazine* usually went hot-foot after each new design, clocking up details of its running, usually with ready approbation of the railway authorities concerned. But about Nos 330-334 of the LSWR, and equally of the isolated 335 that followed in 1907, there is not a single mention, let alone any details of running!

There were probably good reasons for this, because from the little that South Western men have said one gathers they were not successful engines. Dugald Drummond was generous enough in the facilities he granted to those who wished to see his engines at work. In the year 1912 he gave Rous-

Marten's successor, the late Cecil J. Allen, an all-stations, all-trains, footplate pass for a month; but by that time there was no evidence of the '330s' on express trains. It has been suggested that the dissimilar valve gear on the outside and inside cylinders made them sluggish, yet the smaller boilered 'G14' Class that followed in 1908 had the same arrangements, and ran freely enough. For some years these latter were the regular engines on the sharply timed 3.30 pm ex-Waterloo, and in addition to putting in some good climbing performances, there are plenty of instances of maximum speeds between 75 and 80 mph with them.

In the last of his 4-cylinder 4-6-0s, the 'T14' Class, nicknamed the 'Paddleboats', because of their large, all-embracing coupled wheel splashers, Dugald Drummond altered the layout of the machinery. The outside cylinders were brought forward to a position in line with the inside, thus simplifying the internal pipework, while the valves of the inside cylinders were driven by rocker shafts taking the motion from the Walschaerts gear of the outside cylinders. The 'Paddleboats' were real flyers, attaining speeds of over 80 mph with ease.

The first four engines of the 'T14' Class used saturated steam but, on the remaining six, the Drummond steam dryer was fitted in the smokebox. The range of superheat did not exceed about 400 degrees, only about 20 degrees above the temperature of formation of steam at the pressure of 200 lb per square inch used in these engines. This almost minimal degree of superheat Drum-

London & South Western Railway: the 6 foot 7 inch 4-cylinder 4-6-0, fitted with Drummond steam dryer (nicknamed 'Paddleboats').

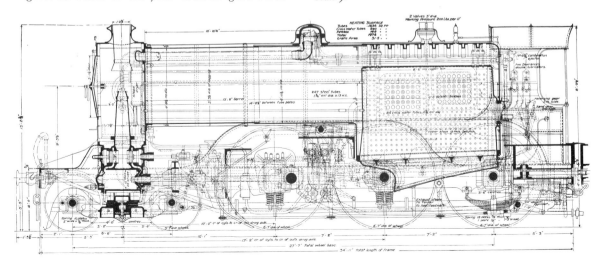

mond considered to be adequate for a high speed locomotive, and it enabled him to avoid the complication of having to provide dampers, or forced lubrication. All these 4-cylinder 4-6-0s had cross-water tubes in the firebox. Dugald Drummond, like David Jones on the Highland, was unfortunate in sustaining a serious accident while on the footplate. In Drummond's case the scalding he received was so serious as to compel amputation of his leg, and aged 72 he died from shock the following day. He was succeeded as Chief Mechanical Engineer of the LSWR by his Works Manager, Robert W. Urie, who had been Chief Draughtsman of the Caledonian in the early McIntosh days, and then Works Manager at St Rollox. He had come south to join the LSWR in 1897; and, having loyally supported Drummond for 15 momentous years, he then proceeded to design a range of locomotives that was not only entirely different in concept, but which was, in its layout of the machinery, the true prototype of the British steam locomotive in its most critical and final age.

In a batch of 10 powerful mixed traffic 4-6-0s, the first of which was completed in December 1913, Urie cleared the space between the main frames of all machinery. Henceforth all new LSWR locomotives would have two cylinders only, with outside Walschaerts gear, and large diameter piston valves. All the running gear was outside and readily accessible. There was no need to get an engine over a pit. The tenders also had outside bearings. So far as the boilers were concerned, he dispensed at once with cross water tubes, and steam dryers, and began to introduce a more orthodox form of superheating.

There was room to manoeuvre among the proprietary designs then in existence, and while at first four engines of this batch were fitted with the Schmidt and four with the Robinson, the remaining two used saturated steam.

In the meantime he was developing his own superheater, the 'Eastleigh' which was fitted to one of the hitherto saturated engines in 1917. The new engines, Class 'H15' although designated mixed traffic, proved fast runners, and were used on some of the principal express trains; but Urie's true express passenger engine, the 'N15', with 6 foot 7 inch coupled wheels did not appear until 1918. This, of course, was the fore-runner of the celebrated 'King Arthur', of Southern Railway days, just as his express goods 4-6-0 of 1920 sired the Southern version of the 'S15' Class.

Excellent as was the 'engine' design of the three successive Urie 4-6-0s on the London and South Western Railway, the boiler design was not entirely successful in meeting demands for continuous hard steaming. The formula for this had been found in Churchward's famous development on the Great Western, at the time when Dugald Drummond was in the throes of his complicated manoeuvre with big 4-6-0s on the LSWR. The introduction of the locomotive designs already mentioned in this chapter were to a very large extent false starts, or starts that led their originators into blind alleys. Fascinating as is the story of the 4-6-0 so far related, it must be emphasised that it covers no more than 303 locomotives, from seven different railways. In the next chapter the massive development on the other two is discussed.

North Eastern 4-6-0s

Class	S	S1	S2	S3
Date	1899	1900	1911	1919
Service	Mixed traffic	Passenger	Mixed traffic	Express Goods
Engineer	Worsdell	Worsdell	Raven	Raven
Cylinders (number of)	2	2	2	3
Diameter (inches)	20	20	20	18½
Stroke (inches)	26	26	26	26
Coupled wheel diameter (feet/inches)	6 0	6 8	6 0	5 8
Heating surfaces (square feet)				
Tubes	1,639	1,639	—	1,398
Firebox	130	130	—	166
Superheater	—	—	—	530
Grate area (square feet)	23	23	23	27
Boiler pressure (lb per square inch)	200	200	160	180
Tractive effort (lb)	—	—	—	—
Number built	40	5	20*	22†

*One engine, No 825, fitted with Stumpf uni-flow cylinders.   †48 more built 1921-4.

Highland Railway 4-6-0s

Ref no	1	2	3	4	5	6	7
Class	Jones Goods	Castle I	Castle II	River	Castle III	'Clan' Goods	'Clan'
Date	1894	1900	1913	1915	1917	1918	1919
Engineer	Jones	Jones/P. Drummond	F.G. Smith (Jones)	F.G. Smith	Cumming (Jones)	Cumming	Cumming
Cylinders							
Diameter (inches)	20	19½	19½	21	19½	20½	21
Stroke (inches)	26	26	26	28	26	26	26
Coupled wheel diameter (feet/ inches)	5 3½	5 9	5 9	6 0	6 0	5 3	6 0
Valve gear	Allan	Allan	Allan	Walschaerts	Allan	Walschaerts	Walschaerts
Heating surfaces (square feet)							
Tubes	1,559	1,916	1,916	1,460	1,916	1,069	1,328
Firebox	113	134	132	140	132	127	139
Superheater	—	—	—	350	—	241	256
Grate area (square feet)	22.6	26	25.5	25.3	25.5	22.75	25.5
Boiler pressure (lb per square inch)	175	180	180	160	180	160	170
Tractive effort (lb)	23,666	21,922	21,922	23,324	21,008	23,587	23,012
Number built	15	12	4	6	3	8	4*

*Another four built in 1921.

Caledonian 4-6-0s: 1902 to 1916

Class	'Oban'	49 and 50		'Cardean'		'908'	'918'	'179'	60*
Date	1902	1903-1911		1906-1911		1906	1906	1913	1916
		Saturated	Super-heated	Saturated	Super-heated				
Cylinders									
Diameter (inches)	19	21	20¾	20	20¾	19	19	19½	20
Stroke (inches)	26	26	26	26	26	26	26	26	26
Coupled wheel diameter (feet/inches)	5 0	6 6	6 6	6 6	6 6	5 9	5 0	5 9	6 1
Heating surfaces (square feet)									
Tubes	1,800	2,178	1,509.3	2,117.5	1,666	2,050	1,895	1,439	1,529
Firebox	105	145	145	148.3	148.3	128	128	128	146
Superheater	—	—	515.8	—	515.8	—	—	403	258
Grate area (square feet)	20.63	26	26	26	26	21	21	21	25.5
Boiler pressure (lb per square inch)	175	200	175	200	175	180	175	170	170
Tractive effort (lb)	23,269	24,990	21,348	22,667	21,348	20,812	23,269	20,704	20,620
Number built	9	2		5†		10	5	11	6

*Outside cylinders: Pickersgill type. 20 more built by LMS.   †One scrapped in 1916, after severe damage at Quintinshill.

London & South Western: 4-6-0s 1905-1920

Class	'330'	'335'	'G14'	'T14'	'H15'	'N15'	'S15'
Date introduced	1905	1907	1908	1911	1913	1918	1920
Cylinders (number of)	4	4	4	4	2	2	2
Diameter (inches)	16	16½	15	15	21	22	21
Stroke (inches)	24	26	26	26	28	28	28
Valve gear							
Outside	Walschaerts	Walschaerts	Walschaerts	Walschaerts	Walschaerts	Walschaerts	Walschaerts
Inside	Stephenson	Stephenson	Stephenson	(derived)	—	—	—
Coupled wheel diameter (feet/inches)	6 0	6 0	6 0	6 7	6 0	6 7	5 7
Heating surface (square feet)							
Tubes	2,210	2,210	1,580	1,636	1,716	1,716	1,716
Cross water tube	357	357	200	200	—	—	—
Firebox	160	160	149	140	167	162	162
Superheater	—	—	—	—	308*	308	308
Grate area (square feet)	31.5	31.5	31.5	31.5	30	30	30
Boiler pressure (lb per square inch)	175	175	175	200	180	180	180
Tractive effort (lb)	25,500	29,370	24,250	25,200	26,200	26,350	28,200
Number built	5**	1**	10	10	10‡	10†	20

*On 'H15' Class, originally; 4 with Schmidt (360 square feet), 4 with Robinson (333 square feet).
**Rebuilt to correspond with 'H15' Class later.   ‡12 additional engines built 1924.   †10 additional engines built 1922-3.

Below left *Caledonian Railway: a Pickersgill outside-cylinder 4-6-0 of the 1916 '60' Class* (National Railway Museum).

Right *Glasgow and South Western Railway: one of the two Manson superheated 4-6-0s, here seen in LMS 'red', leaving Glasgow St Enoch* (P. Ransome-Wallis).

Right *Lancashire and Yorkshire Railway: a Hughes 4-cylinder 4-6-0 as originally built, non-superheated, in 1908* (British Railways).

Right *Great Eastern Railway: the first of the very successful superheater 4-6-0s of 1911, here seen in LNER livery with the number changed from 1500 to 8500* (P. Ransome-Wallis).

Left *London and South Western Railway: one of Dugald Drummond's 4-cylinder 4-6-0s—No 335 of 1907, a very impressive but not very successful locomotive* (British Railways).

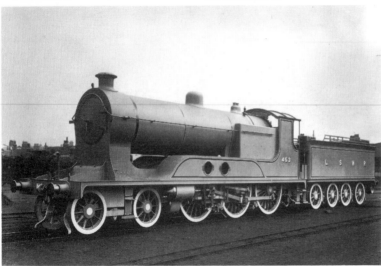

Left *LSWR: Drummond's smaller boilered 4-cylinder 4-6-0 (Class 'G14') used mainly between Salisbury and Exeter* (British Railways).

Below *LSWR: the most successful of the Drummond 4-cylinder 4-6-0s of the 'T14' Class, nicknamed 'Paddleboats'.*

Right *LSWR: R.W. Urie's 2-cylinder 4-6-0 (Class 'H15'), the forerunner of a notable series of Southern Railways 4-6-0s* (British Railways).

Right *Highland Railway: a 'Clan' Class 4-6-0, the* Clan Mackenzie, *on a Glasgow–Oban express in LMS days.*

Below *Glasgow & South Western Railway: James Manson's express passenger 4-6-0 of 1903* (North British Locomotive Company).

10. 4-6-0: the emergent premier locomotive type—II

It was appropriate to the very large volume of passenger, goods and mineral traffic carried over Britain's 'Premier Line', the LNWR, that a programme of large-scale standardisation of motive power should have been fairly consistently followed. In the 19th century it was only in the later stages of the 3-cylinder compound era that relatively small batches of successive express passenger classes should have been constructed. By the year 1902 the 4-cylinder compound had become the established form of propulsion for heavy main line power, and in 1903 the large 4-4-0 passenger and the 0-8-0 heavy mineral classes were joined by a 4-6-0 for mixed traffic and express goods. This proved to be F.W. Webb's last locomotive design. It became known, however, that he had no intention of retiring at midsummer in 1903, and that it had largely been forced upon him by the action of the Board. He was then 68 years of age, and proving an increasingly difficult colleague, among the senior officers of the company. The announcement of George Whale as his successor was taken by him as an affront, and he virtually walked out forthwith.

The 4-cylinder compound mixed traffic 4-6-0s were, at the time, described as 'a fitting triumph to the long and successful career that Mr Webb has enjoyed'. But from some contemporary comments it would seem that few in the Running Department of the LNWR would have agreed with such an appraisal. Why they should have gained the reputation of being such temperamental troublesome things is a little hard to imagine. Or were they really so bad? Their case history does not match up. The first engine, No 1400, was completed at Crewe in February 1903; the second, No 2033, followed in June, after Mr Webb had left. There was then ample time for testing and general appraisal before a further eight were built in November-December 1903.

At this stage it should be added that, in practically every respect except the wheels, they were duplicates of the 4-cylinder compound coal engines. The boilers, cylinders, and motion parts were the same; and the coupled wheels were 5 feet 9 inches in diameter, with the drive from all four cylinders on to the leading pair. The radial truck (not strictly a bogie) was the same as that of the compound express 4-4-0s, but with slightly smaller wheels. Now the Webb 4-cylinder compound coal engines were the most reliable and long lived of all his compounds, and although the building of compound express passenger engines at Crewe had ceased with the last of the 'Alfred the Great' Class in August 1903, capacity was found in the new-engine building programme for 10 more compound 4-6-0s in September-October 1904, and another 10 in January-February 1905, at a time when the Works was also building the new non-compound 'Precursor' Class 4-4-0s at an average output of five a week!

The new compound 4-6-0s were sometimes referred to as the '1400' Class, from the number of the first one built; but actually the numbers followed in the Crewe tradition of taking the first number on the capital list that was available, and in 1903 that could mean anything between 1 and 2,570! As things turned out, 14 out of the 30 took the numbers of Webb 3-cylinder compounds that were being

London and North Western Railway: a Webb 4-cylinder compound mixed traffic 4-6-0, No 1400 (British Railways).

scrapped at the time. It is indeed remarkable to reflect upon the situation at Crewe immediately after Webb's retirement, when one group of compounds were being scrapped, and another built simultaneously. For the record, and knowing the intense interest always shown in what might be called the *personnel* of the LNWR locomotive stud, the numbers of the 4-cylinder compound 4-6-0s and the identity of passenger engines they displaced are appended:

LNWR 4-cylinder compound 4-6-0s

Engine number	Date completed	Passenger engine replaced	
		Name	Class 3-cylinder compound
1400	Feb 1903		
2033	June 1903		
170	Nov 1903		
545	Nov 1903	*Tamerlane*	'Dreadnought'
695	Nov 1903		
1352	Nov 1903		
1429	Nov 1903		
1466	Dec 1903		
1567	Dec 1903		
1729	Dec 1903		
173	Sept 1904	*City of Manchester*	'Dreadnought'
504	Sept 1904	*Thunderer*	'Dreadnought'
511	Sept 1904	*Achilles*	'Dreadnought'
637	Sept 1904	*City of New York*	'Dreadnought'
1113	Sept 1904	*Hecate*	'Experiment'
1407	Sept 1904		
1414	Sept 1904		
1500	Oct 1904		
2063	Oct 1904	*Huskisson*	'Dreadnought'
2339	Sept 1904		
307	Feb 1905	*Victor*	'Experiment'
321	Jan 1905	*Servia*	'Experiment'
363	Feb 1905	*Aurania*	'Experiment'
606	Feb 1905		
610	Feb 1905		
1131	Feb 1905		
1379	Feb 1905	*Stork*	'Dreadnought'
2055	Feb 1905	*Dunrobin*	'Dreadnought'
2058	Feb 1905	*Medusa*	'Dreadnought'
2059	Mar 1905	*Greyhound*	'Dreadnought'

One notes that a 'Dreadnought' Class compound had been scrapped soon enough after Webb's retirement for a new engine to receive its number in November 1903; and there was a new 'Precursor' Class 4-4-0, named *Tamerlane*, completed at Crewe in March 1904. Note also, that in all three batches

of '1400' Class 4-6-0s the production rate at Crewe was eight per month.

Judging by their life-span alone, the '1400' Class cannot have been regarded as successful engines. When they first came out they did a good deal of hard work on express goods trains and, by the summer of 1905, they had sufficiently impressed the running department with their relatively free running that they attempted to use them on certain heavy express trains of an intermediate character in the Northern Division. At that time with all passenger engines except the new 'Precursors', and the few 4-cylinder compound 4-4-0s with altered valve gear (see Chapter 3) a pilot engine had to be provided for any load greater than 'equal to 17'. This rule was waived in the case of the '1400s'; but it was really expecting too much of any 4-6-0 of that era, with no more than 5 foot coupled wheels, to work punctually with heavy trains of more than 300 tons, requiring start-to-stop runs such as 31 minutes for the 27¼ miles from Preston to Carnforth, and Oxenholme to Penrith, 32 miles over Shap in 44 minutes. Somewhat naturally they failed to do this. With the introduction of many new mixed traffic non-compound 4-6-0s from 1906 onwards, the need for this relatively non-standard class receded and from 1913 onwards they were scrapped.

After the very successful introduction of the 'Precursor' Class express passenger 4-4-0s in 1904 George Whale laid down the specification for a generally similar engine, but of the 4-6-0 type, to cope with the heavy gradients of the Northern Division. The Crewe drawing office under the able direction of J.N. Jackson, Chief Draughtsman, and his leading hand, T. Sackfield, evolved a design that was to form the solid basis of a range of no fewer than 420 standard 4-6-0 locomotives. There was no question of building for prestige, or 'one-upmanship' against fellow chief mechanical engineers. Whale and his men produced a solid dividend earner, that had a very high route availability over the entire LNWR system. It was perhaps a little unfortunate at the outset that not only the number, but the name of one of Webb's least successful engines should have been chosen for the prototype, No 66 *Experiment*, because the very last things the new engines could be called were 'experiments'. They stemmed from a very soundly worked out design, so sound that it remained unchanged, save for the addition of superheaters and piston valves, for 17 years. Delivery of the last engines of the type was taken in April 1922. Yet, alongside the universal acclaim that greeted the introduction of the 4-4-0 'Precursors' in 1904, the advent of the 'Experiments' a year later was singularly lukewarm.

The first engine was completed at Crewe in April 1905, and a further four turned out in June of that year. During the heavy summer traffic the five 4-6-0 engines worked on the Carlisle road. One very critical and experienced observer, R.E. Charlewood, was not at all impressed. He used to contribute (to *The Railway Magazine* each year) an analysis of London and North Western express train working; and at the end of 1905 he wrote, 'It must be admitted that it was thanks to the fast downhill speed, rather than to any wonderful hill-climbing abilities, that the "Experiments" performed the most exacting of their tasks'. On the face of it this was surprising because with coupled wheels of the reduced size of 6 foot 3 inches one would have expected them to be good climbers. On the other hand they were proving exceptionally fast downhill and, in that first year of service a maximum of 93½ mph with one of them was clocked by C. Rous-Marten. Reading some contemporary comments on locomotive performance generally, it seemed that the writers took it for granted that plenty of steam would be available; but, with the larger boilers and fireboxes that were being introduced in those early years of the 20th century, this was not always the case.

The design of boilers, and their steaming qualities has been a perennial topic of discussion among locomotive engineers, though not so frequent have been the occasions when the reaction of the footplate staff to a new design has been voiced. There was a fundamental difference between the firebox design of the 'Precursor' and the 'Experiment'. That of the former was narrow and deep, and had a form with which generations of North Western men had been familiar with over the years. The 'Experiments' had a shallow, longer fire-grate, horizontal and clear of the middle coupled axle, and at first the firemen found difficulty in feeding that grate to the best advantage. It was not surprising, because it was something unlike anything they had previously worked on. They could not see what was happening at the front of the grate, and holes were allowed to develop in the hottest part of the fire. In due course they found that the most effective way of keeping a good even fire on the forward part of the grate was to shoot the coal so that it struck the firebox tubeplate, and fell back on to the grate.

This technique required a certain knack, and a former Crewe man who had much experience on the footplate once said this of it, to me: 'The shovel was a long narrow one, with a long handle, and the secret was to bang that shovel, held level, on the firebox doorplate, the while sliding the shank smartly through the guiding hand. Once this had been mastered there was nothing to fear'.

The locomotive inspectors had to acquire this knack, as much as the top-link firemen, so that the tradition could be passed on. With the intensive utilisation of engines on the LNWR, the crews might have an 'Experiment' one day and a 'Precursor' the next, and hence to adapt their firing technique accordingly; and, by the end of the year 1905, Whale and his senior assistants were evidently satisfied with the 'Experiments', for further production began.

With the four that had followed the prototype, in

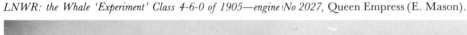

LNWR: the Whale 'Experiment' Class 4-6-0 of 1905—engine No 2027, Queen Empress (E. Mason).

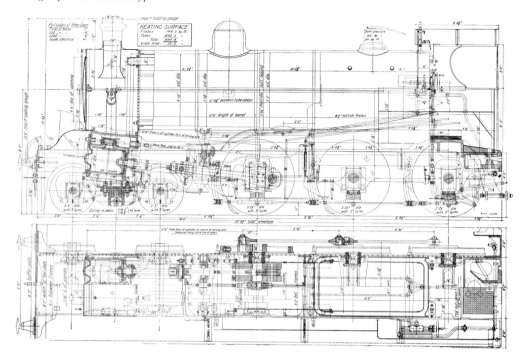

London and North Western Railway: the 19-inch mixed traffic 4-6-0.

June, the names had all been taken from recently scrapped 3-cylinder compounds. That on the first of these, No 306 *Autocrat*, might have in memory of Webb himself! The other three were *Britannic*, *Germanic* and *Sarmatian*. When, however, it came to the new batch of 10, completed at Crewe in January and February 1906, it did at first seem that at length the LNWR was going in for a systemised form of nomenclature; for they were all named after cities, albeit in perpetuation of names once carried by the short-lived 'Dreadnought' compounds. There had been 12 of the Webb engines named after cities, but in 1906 two were not revived, *City of Chicago* and *City of New York*. A further batch of 20, with all the old promiscuity of names, followed in September to December 1906, to be followed immediately by the mixed traffic version, usually known as the '19 inch Goods'.

The new mixed traffic engines, with 5 foot 2 inch coupled wheels, which were the natural follow-up to the '1400' Class 4-cylinder compounds, had the same coupled wheelbase as the 'Experiments' and the same boilers; but advantage was taken of the lower coupled axles to make the firebox a little deeper, and it had 144 square feet of heating surface, as against 133 on the 'Experiment'. When the '19 inch Goods' first came out the boiler pressure was

quoted as 185 lb per square inch, though this was subsequently reduced to the 175 usual on all the modern non-compound LNWR locomotives. The productivity of Crewe Works in the 12 months beginning on December 1 1906 was tremendous, as follows:

Month	Number of new engines	Classes
Dec 1906	7	2 'Experiments' 5 '19 inch'
Jan 1907	8	'19 inch Goods'
Feb 1907	7	'19 inch Goods'
Mar 1907	8	'Precursor Tank' 4-4-2
Apr 1907	8	2 'Precursor Tank' 6 '19 inch Goods'
May 1907	8	'19 inch Goods'
June 1907	10	5 '19 inch Goods' 5 'Precursor' 4-4-0s
July 1907	8	'Precursors'
Aug 1907	7	'Precursors'
Sept 1907	7	'Experiments'
Oct 1907	8	3 'Experiments' 5 '19 inch Goods'
Nov 1907	8	'19 inch Goods'
Total	94	Average 1.8 new engines a week

By the end of 1907 the '19 inch Goods' was as established a standard type as the 'Precursors' and 'Experiments' perhaps even more so than the latter, and construction continued rapidly afterwards. The last 20 were built in August-October 1909, bringing the total up to 170 engines of the class. By that time C.J. Bowen Cooke had succeeded George Whale as Chief Mechanical Engineer. Like Whale himself he was a 'running' rather than a drawing office or a 'works' man; but he was also a man of the broadest, indeed international, outlook and very much aware of current developments in Europe.

Largely through certain mis-informed comments at the time, the impression has unfortunately persisted in some quarters that the 'Experiment' Class were little short of failures, and Bowen Cooke has been blamed for allowing construction of a further 20 to go forward in November 1909 after the final batch of '19 inch Goods' had been completed. This is to ignore, or to be ignorant of, the facts of the situation. While it is true that trouble was experienced in steaming when the engines were first introduced, familiarity with the firebox had overcome these initial difficulties and the engines were doing excellent work in 1908-9, of which Bowen Cooke, as Running Superintendent of the Southern Division, would be able to appreciate well enough. Two runs from Rugby to Willesden are enough to show what they could do. Engine No 1534, *Westmorland*, hauling a load of 415 tons, ran this 77.2 miles in 81 minutes 54 seconds start to stop, and No 1987, *Glendower*, with 440 tons took 86 minutes in spite of two checks that cost 2¼ minutes between them. There were very few locomotives running in the country in the 1908-1910 period that could average 56.6 mph and 55.2 mph net with such loads as these.

The superheated version of the 'Experiment' Class came before it had originally been planned. Authorisation had been given in 1911 for 10 large 4-cylinder 4-6-0s, and an order had actually been placed on the works. But the civil engineer would not accept the original weight diagram, and while the drawing office was engaged upon a redesign of the boiler, the order on the works was changed to the superheater 'Experiment', which of course became the first batch of the very numerous and successful 'Prince of Wales' Class. The dimensions of the three classes of inside cylinder LNWR 4-6-0s are shown in the accompanying table. All had the Joy valve gear, but while the 'Experiments' and the '19 inch Goods' had slide valves, the 'Prince of Wales' Class had 8 inch diameter piston valves.

LNWR Inside cylinder 4-6-0s

Class	'Experiment'	'19 inch Goods'	'Prince of Wales'
Number built	105	170	245
Cylinders			
Diameter (inches)	19	19	20½
Stroke (inches)	26	26	26
Coupled wheel diameter (feet/inches)	6 3	5 2½	6 3
Heating surface (square feet)			
Tubes	1,908	1,840.5	1,375.8
Firebox	133	144.3	135.8
Superheater	—	—	304.4
Grate area (square feet)	25	25	25
Boiler pressure (lb per square inch)	175	175*	175
Tractive effort (lb)	18,630	22,390	21,750

*Originally quoted as 185 lb per square inch.

Below left *LNWR: in 1909 the 'pride of the line'—engine No 1987,* Glendower *was stationed at Camden. It was used daily on the 2 pm Scotch Corridor train to Crewe* (C.J. Barnard).

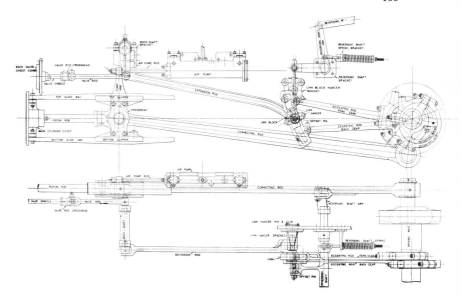

Right *Great Western Railway: standard arrangement of Stephenson link motion.*

The heating surfaces quoted are those given on the original drawings in each case. In LMS days there had been some slight modifications, chiefly through the use of boilers with fewer small tubes.

The 'Prince of Wales' Class, although an admirable general purpose passenger locomotive, never seemed to attain such high maximum speeds as the 'Experiments'. I have not seen a higher speed than 80 mph, whereas the older engines used occasionally to top 90. The piston valves of 8 inch diameter were, however, on the small side for 20½ inch, cylinders, and although having Trick ports, which acted as a kind of 'supercharger' at admission, they would not have helped the exhaust. The maximum travel of the valves like the slide valves of the 'Experiments' and the '19 inch Goods' was slightly greater than 5 inches, which was distinctly longer than customary elsewhere in Great Britain at that time, except on the Great Western. The question is sometimes asked as to why, in view of the success of the 'Prince of Wales' Class, no programme of adding superheaters to the 'Experiments' was undertaken, or for that matter to the '19 inch Goods'; but, with the introduction of many new superheater engines for the hardest main line duties, there was a wealth of secondary passenger work of a shorter distance character all over the system for which the non-superheated 4-6-0s were well suited.

Bowen Cooke's major express passenger 4-6-0 of the 'Claughton' Class was inhibited at the design stage by the refusal of the civil engineer to accept the original weight diagram. As comparison is often made between these engines and their Great Western counterparts of the 'Star' Class it is convenient at this stage to pause in the story of developments at Crewe, and trace events in the collateral development at Swindon, up to the year 1912. In Chapter 6, dealing with the 'Atlantic' type, reference was made to the extensive comparison of engines of otherwise identical proportions made between 4-4-2s and 4-6-0s on the Great Western Railway. At the time these comparisons were in progress the two salient features of the Swindon 2-cylinder design had been established, namely the tapered boiler using the high pressure of 225 lb per square inch, and Pearce's setting of the Stephenson link motion, with long valve travel, and a small amount of *negative* lead in full gear. The further refinements of a medium degree of superheating, and top feed had not been introduced by the end of 1905, when the 4-4-2 *versus* 4-6-0 comparisons were in full blast.

Churchward read his famous paper on 'Large Locomotive Boilers' to the Institution of Mechanical Engineers in February 1906. By that time he seemed to have settled—if he had ever personally had any doubts—for the 4-6-0 rather than the 4-4-2, and quantity production of the former had began in earnest, with the 2901-2910 series. While there is no doubt that all who had to deal with them would agree that they were real 'ladies' in the locomotive sense there was an intriguing touch of conceit in naming them after ladies of history, even though one or two of the characters concerned, *Lady Macbeth* in particular, were not exactly famed for ladylike behaviour!

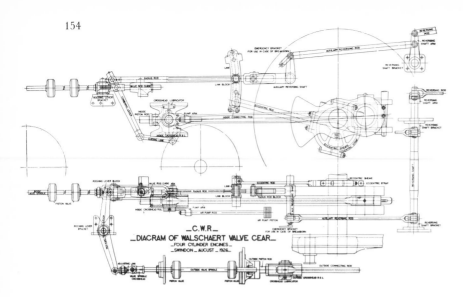

Left *GWR: diagram of Walschaerts valve gear on 4-cylinder engines.*

Below *LNWR: one of the '19-inch' mixed traffic 4-6-0s, No 2188 (the late W.J. Reynolds).*

Right *GWR: 4-cylinder 4-6-0 'Star' Class as originally built non-superheated.*

In 1907 Swindon went even better with a further batch of 20 of these 2-cylinder 4-6-0s naming them after saints, though curiously enough they did not have one named after the patron saint of travellers, Saint Christopher. The setting of the Stephenson link motion, with negative lead in full gear, made Churchward's 4-6-0 exceptionally strong in getting away with a load, and even when the gear was linked up and something approaching express speed had been attained, one could sometimes feel a slight fore and aft surging motion in the leading coaches of the train.

The French compounds, referred to previously in Chapter 6, had impressed everyone by their very smooth action, resulting from use of four cylinders and from the division of the drive between two axles. It seemed that while the 'Saints', as the 2-cylinder 4-6-0s became collectively known, could be regarded as the standard general purpose express locomotive of the line, there would be advantage in having a smooth riding 4-cylinder engine for the high-speed long non-stop runs and, in 1906,

Churchward built the *North Star*, as an Atlantic for direct comparison with the French compounds. Against two 18 inch (later increased to 18½) cylinders with 30 inch stroke, the *North Star* had four, 14¼ inches by 26 inches, giving an almost equal cylinder volume.

The drive was divided, as on the French engines, and in view of Churchward's abhorrence of outside valve gear, Pearce designed the very neat 'Scissors' gear, which caused such a rumpus with R.M. Deeley, of the Midland, as told in Chapter 3 of this book. The *North Star* was very successful, but when it came to building more 4-cylinder engines, in 1907, the 4-6-0 type was adopted as the future standard. They were also named after 'Stars'; but although they were 'star' engines in most other ways, the names were revivals of old broad gauge titles that dated back to 1839. Except for the last one, No 4010 *Western Star*, they were not super-heated, and by that time Churchward had begun his experiments with superheating apparatus.

The first superheater to be fitted to a Great

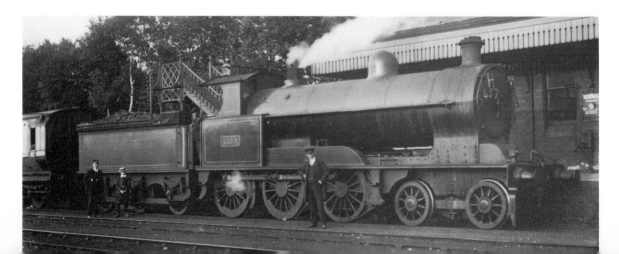

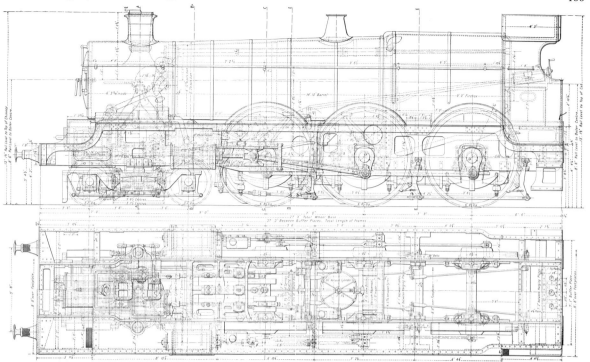

Western engine was of the Schmidt type to No 2901, *Lady Superior*, in 1906; but there were features of this apparatus that did not appeal to Churchward, and in any case its use at that time was generally governed by conditions involving the use of other Schmidt patent devices. Such constraints were not to Churchward's liking, and his first moves towards the general adoption of superheating were towards the circumventing of the Schmidt patents. The Cole superheater, as installed in No 4010, *Western Star*, was of an American design, and from this the Swindon development proceeded. It lasted in all over three years, during which time only four engines were fitted with successive versions of what was to be the standard Swindon type. There had been no particular hurry, because the new 4-6-0s of both 2- and 4-cylinder varieties were handling the traffic with ease; and by 1909, when the third and final version of the Swindon superheater was produced, Churchward had 30 'Saints' and 30 'Stars' in traffic, in addition to the 'Atlantics' and the comparative 4-6-0s and the three French compounds.

For the record, the engines fitted with the three types of Swindon superheater were No 4011, *Knight of the Garter*, and the giant 'Pacific' No 111, *The Great Bear*, of which much more in the next chapter, with the No 1; the two cylinder engine No 2922, *Saint*

Gabriel, had the No 2, and the No 3 and final, was fitted to No 4021, *King Edward*, in June 1909. After that the fitting of superheaters to the existing 4-6-0 locomotives proceeded apace, at a modest cost (so Churchward told the Institution of Civil Engineers, in 1914) of £90 per engine.

In the steam chest, just before entering the cylinders, the temperature of the steam was about 550 degrees F, as compared to 390 degrees of dry saturated steam at a pressure of 225 lb per square inch. On the London and North Western Railway with the Schmidt superheaters coming into standard use from 1910, the steam temperature was about 650 degrees F, as compared with 360 degrees, in non-superheater engines at 175 lb per square inch. The immediate problem, from the intense dryness of the steam, was that of lubrication, and while Bowen Cooke at once adopted as standard the Wakefield mechanical type of forced feed, Churchward had spent a considerable amount of time developing a hydrostatic device of his own. It was very successful and contributed not a little to the free running and modern Great Western locomotives. It was standard at Swindon until after the Second World War, when higher degrees of superheat compelled the use of a mechanical type.

The last major development of Great Western 4-6-0s in Churchward's time was the introduction of top feed. It was a time when many engineers had been experimenting with feed water heating, as a means of increasing the overall thermal efficiency of the engine, but the advantage of top feed is that the water is heated by contact with the steam before it makes contact with the metal of the boiler. In the Swindon system the feed water was delivered through clack boxes at each side of the safety valve on to sloping trays, which broke the feed into a fine spray and delivered it forward over a wide area. As usual with all Churchward's developments, the shape and slope of the trays was established only after careful and sustained experimenting. In this case the trials took place in the open yard at Swindon, with trays fed from a metered water supply quite apart from any locomotive. The first 4-6-0s to have the standard top feed apparatus were 20 of the 2-cylinder variety built in 1911. Swindon seemed to have run out of 'Ladies' and 'Saints' and turned to stately homes for names. It may well be that this suggestion came from Churchward himself, for although the 'Courts' were applied in alphabetical order, beginning with No 2931, *Arlington Court*, the engine chosen for the official photograph of the new class, circulated to all the railway and technical journals of the day was No 2934, *Butleigh Court*, a fine great house a few miles to the south of Glastonbury where Churchward was frequently the guest of Neville Grenville.

By the time the 'Court' series of GWR 4-6-0s were in traffic, Crewe was well advanced with the construction of the *Sir Gilbert Claughton,* the large 4-cylinder 4-6-0 on which Bowen Cooke had been hindered in the design stage by the intransigence of the civil engineer in refusing to accept the fact that the layout of the machinery, with all four cylinders driving on to the leading coupled axle, eliminating **hammer blow**. There was irony in the situation on

two separate accounts. The 'George the Fifth' and 'Prince of Wales' Classes, which the civil engineer had accepted without question, both had a very severe hammer blow effect at speed which were far more damaging to the track and underline structures than the 'Claughton' as originally proposed would have been, thus:

Class	Maximum axle load (tons)	Maximum hammer blow (tons)	Maximum combined axle load (tons)
'George the Fifth'	19.15	14.1	33.2
'Prince of Wales'	18.25	11.4	29.7
'Claughton' as actually built	19.75	Nil	19.75

Then, at the very time the first 'Claughton' weight diagram was being rejected, the civil engineering authorities of the Netherlands State Railways had advised the mechanical engineer that they were prepared to accept larger and heavier engines provided that the unbalanced centrifugal forces of balance weights in the wheels could be eliminated—in other words by doing exactly what Bowen Cooke did in the 'Claughtons', using four cylinders, all driving on the leading coupled axle. The detailed designing of the new Dutch engines was done in Manchester, by Beyer, Peacock & Co, and it became a State Railways standard for many years afterwards.

Even though he was somewhat hamstrung as to weight, Sackfield produced an excellent boiler for the 'Claughtons'. In the early days there were some

LNWR: 4-cylinder 4-6-0 'Claughton' Class.

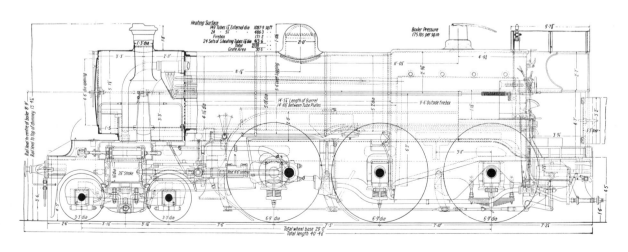

instances of poor steaming but, as in the case of the 'Experiments' eight years earlier, these could be traced to the inexperience of the firemen rather than to any shortcomings in the design. The relevant dimensions make an interesting comparison with those of the Great Western superheater 4-6-0 boilers, as used on both 'Saints' and 'Stars'.

	'Claughton'	GWR 4-6-0
Boiler pressure (lb per square inch)	175	225
Superheat temperature (degrees F)	650	550
Small tubes (number of)	159	176
Outside diameter (inches)	$1\frac{7}{8}$	2
Superheater flues (number of)	24	14
Outside diameter (inches)	$5\frac{1}{4}$	$5\frac{1}{8}$
Elements (number of)	96	84
Outside diameter (inches)	$1\frac{1}{2}$	1
Heating surfaces (square feet)		
Tubes	1,647.2	1,687
Firebox	171.2	155
Superheater	413.6	262
Distance between tubeplates (feet/inches)	14 10½	15 3
Grate area (square feet)	30.5	27.1
Free gas area as per cent of grate area	14.7	15.1

The higher degree of superheat in the LNWR engine would not only give a greater fluidity to the steam, and enable it to flow more freely through valves and ports but, although the working pressure was lower, the higher superheat would give a greater total energy to the steam. The respective values in lb calories per pound of steam would have been about 710 for the Great Western 4-6-0s and 745 for the 'Claughton'.

After the experience with the superheated 'Star' Class 4-6-0s, Churchward decided that he could increase the cylinder diameter to 15 inches, from the original 14¼ inches. This was done first on the series named after 'Princes' and built at Swindon in 1913, and it brought the tractive effort up to 27,800 lb. After some initial variations, the 'Claughton' cylinder diameter was fixed at 15¾ inches, and this gave a tractive effort of 24,000 lb.

Dimensional statistics apart, however, the 'Claughtons' soon showed that they were capable of higher power output at maximum speed. Some observers were inclined to regard the dynamometer car test runs of November 2 and 4 1913, details of which Bowen Cooke gave at a meeting of the Institution of Civil Engineers in 1914, as something

exceptional, not to be expected in ordinary service; but actually some extremely fine runs were made in ordinary service, on the Scotch expresses between Crewe and Carlisle, and particularly by the engine stationed at Edge Hill, and doing the 'single-home' round trip of 387 miles from Liverpool to Euston and back daily, for several months.

In developing his 4-6-0 locomotives on the Great Western, Churchward set a target of a drawbar pull of 2 tons at 70 mph and this the 'Star' Class engines came to surpass, on dynamometer car test runs, by small amounts, though it is probable that they were not extended to the same degree as with the LNWR engine, *Ralph Brocklebank*, in the tests in November 1913. In the data he presented to the Institution of Civil Engineers Bowen Cooke quoted the following instances of high power output:

Speed (mph)	Drawbar pull (tons)	Indicated horsepower
58	3.4	1,617
71	1.8	1,088
66	2.8	1,562
71½	2.3	1,314
66½	2.8	1,548
70½	1.8	1,222
69½	1.8	1,206
67	2.4	1,407
69	2.6	1,669

The overall results of the two tests were quoted thus:

Date	November 2	November 4
Route	Euston-Crewe	Crewe-Carlisle
Load behind tender (tons)	435	360
Average speed (mph)	62.3	59.4
Mean drawbar pull (tons)	2.4	1.83
Average IHP from all diagrams	1,358	1,387
No of points at which taken	25	17
Max IHP	1,617	1,669

On the second run the demands upon the tractive capacity of the locomotive virtually ceased when Shap Summit was passed, 31½ miles short of the journey's end. The drawbar pull was negligible in this last, downhill section, during which no indicator diagrams were taken. To the passing of Shap Summit, 109.7 miles from Crewe, the average speed had been 59.6 mph from the start.

It could be claimed, with some justification, that

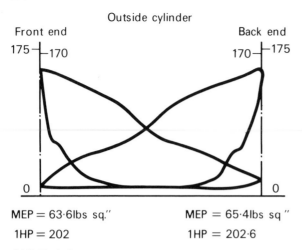

Outside cylinder

Front end   Back end
175—170   170—175

MEP = 63·6lbs sq."   MEP = 65·4lbs sq."
1HP = 202   1HP = 202·6

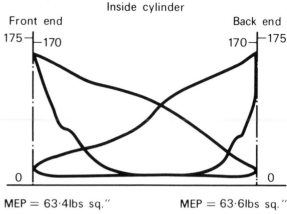

Inside cylinder

Front end   Back end
175—170   170—175

MEP = 63·4lbs sq."   MEP = 63·6lbs sq."
1HP = 201·4   1HP = 197

LNWR: indicator diagrams taken off 'Claughton' Class 4-6-0, Ralph Brocklebank, on high power test runs, November 1913.

in the 'Claughton' Class engines, Bowen Cooke had produced an express passenger class that was without question second to none in haulage capacity at high speed on the railways of Great Britain. It was shown later that its thermal efficiency was less than that of the Great Western 4-6-0s; but at the time it was first introduced the prime object of the 'Claughton' was to haul heavy loads without recourse to assistant engines, and, prior to the deceleration of service in the later years of the First World War, engines of the 'Claughton' Class took loads up to 420 tons tare, without assistance, over Shap Summit on the fastest schedules previously operating. The timing of the 1.12 pm express from Crewe to Carlisle, which allowed 159 minutes for the run of 141 miles, was planned originally for a load of about 200-250 tons, for haulage by 'Experiment' Class 4-6-0s. Details are available showing that the 'Claughtons' observed it with loads of 440 tons.

The early success with these engines justified the multiplication of the class, as additional maximum power locomotives were needed, and to cope with the exceptional demands put upon the London and North Western Railway in the war years, additional engines were built at Crewe bringing the total number of 'Claughtons' to 60 by the year 1917. The bulk building of a successful design was entirely in the Crewe and LNWR tradition and, at the end of the war when arrears of new locomotive construction had to be recovered, the building of a further 70 was authorised. So, when grouping came in 1923 there were no fewer than 130 'Claughtons' in addition to 245 'Prince of Wales' Class 4-6-0s in service in the

LNWR. The later engines of the 'Claughton' Class had one design change from the 60 built before 1917. In them Crewe dispensed with the one feature that might have been thought to be derived from Churchward's practice: the fire-grate, level at the back for about a third of its length, till it cleared the rearmost coupled axle, and then sloping downwards. Actually it was not quite the same as on the GWR 4-6-0s, on which latter the change from level to sloping came about halfway along its length. On the celebrated LNWR 4-6-0 No 1914 *Patriot*, the first of the post-war 'Claughtons', the grate was uniformly sloping throughout.

A change of a different kind was made on the last 90 engines of the 'Prince of Wales' Class. On the earlier engines of this class, as also on the 'George the Fifth' Class 4-4-0s, to obtain the maximum travel of the valves of $5\frac{3}{8}$ inches, a rocking lever had been introduced between the radius rod of the Joy valve gear and the valve spindle, involving three additional pin joints. With wear developing in these joints the valve events became erratic and, just after the end of the war, a direct actuation was tried, which would eliminate the three pin joints. Although the *maximum* travel of the valves was reduced to $4\frac{1}{2}$ inches, the port openings in the ordinary running positions of the gear were improved, in addition to lessening maintenance problems, at a time when they were beginning to loom larger than at any time previously, due to the labour situation in the country generally.

Maintenance could easily have become a very serious problem on the Great Western 4-6-0s, where Churchward's insistence on keeping all the valve gear out of sight, even when it involved a very inaccessible layout of the Walschaerts radial gear on the 4-cylindered engines, had presented the running and shed staffs with some problems at times. That those problems never rose above the level of things to be coped with in everyday work was due much more to the impress of personality and administrative efficiency than to actual engineering design.

As on the London and North Western Railway, the locomotive department of the Great Western, drawing office, works, running sheds and footplate staff were all under one control; and Churchward like Bowen Cooke, was a highly respected 'Chief'. At Swindon, and at all the out-stations, a tremendous sense of 'pride in the job' had been fostered and

sustained. It was a feeling that carried that very inaccessible valve gear triumphantly along, at a time when lack of care and diligence in the sheds could have been catastrophic. Both the Great Western and the London and North Western had greatly standardised their motive power since 1905, and on the eve of grouping, at the end of 1922, the former had built a further 12 'Stars', named after abbeys, bringing the total of the class up to 72, while by that time also the LNWR had 130 'Claughtons' in addition to the 245 'Prince of Wales' 4-6-0s.

Right *LNWR: one of the earliest batch of 'Prince of Wales' Class engines of 1911, No 2021,* Wolverine, *climbing Shap with the Glasgow portion of the 10 am express from Euston, later known as the Royal Scot* (F.E. Mackay).

Below *LNWR: the 'Prince of Wales' Class superheated 4-6-0 No 2520, G.P. Neele, which was named after the great 19th century Superintendent of the Line* (British Railways).

Bottom *Great Western Railway: the first express passenger 4-6-0 No 100, built at Swindon in 1902 with a domeless parallel boiler* (British Railways).

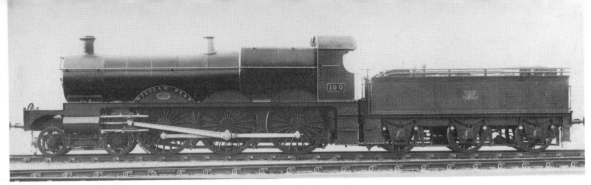

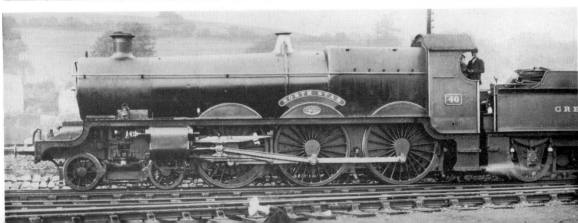

Opposite page, top to bottom

GWR: 4-6-0, No 100, as first rebuilt with 'half-cone' taper boiler and named William Dean *(British Railways).*

GWR: Churchward's standard 2-cylinder 4-6-0 before superheating, with a 'long-cone' taper boiler—No 2918, Saint Catherine *(P.J.T. Reed).*

GWR: the corresponding standard 4-cylinder 4-6-0, one of the series built in 1908, No 4016, Knight of the Golden Fleece *(British Railways).*

GWR: the pioneer 4-cylinder express engine. North Star, *originally built as an 'Atlantic', here seen with the later standard superheater boiler, top feed apparatus, but still carrying the original number, 40 (P.J.T. Reed).*

This page, top to bottom

GWR: one of the 2-cylinder 'Saint' Class 4-6-0s in the final superheated condition, and the plain green painting style of wartime, No 2903, Lady of Lyons.

One of the last of the 4-cylinder 'Star' Class locomotives, No 4038, Queen Berengaria, *built in 1911, here seen in British Railways colours in March 1952 (Kenneth H. Leech).*

LNWR: the first 4-cylinder 4-6-0, No 2222, Sir Gilbert Claughton, *when newly outstopped at Crewe in 1913. Sir Gilbert himself, chairman of the company, is at the regulator and the Chief Mechanical Engineer, C.J. Bowen Cooke, is on the footplate grasping the tender rail. Members of the Locomotive Committee of the board are grouped in front (British Railways).*

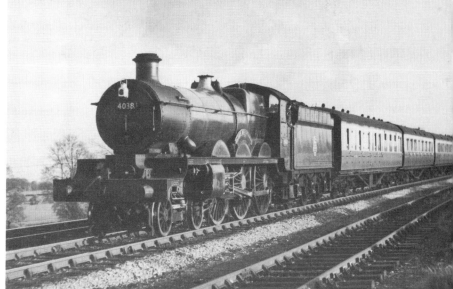

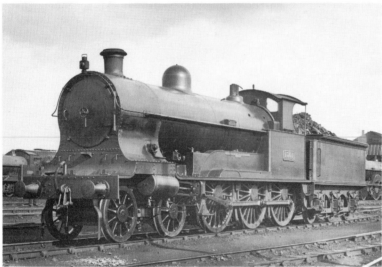

Above *LNWR: one of the first batch of 'Claughtons' of 1913, No 163,* Holland Hibbert, *named after the director who subsequently became Lord Knutsford* (British Railways).

Left *LNWR: an experimental rebuild of an 'Experiment' Class 4-6-0, No 1361,* Prospero, *with four cylinders arranged on the Dendy-Marshall system* (the late F.R. Hebron).

Below *LNWR: after his untimely death in 1920 one of the 'Claughton' Class 4-6-0s, hitherto unnamed, was named* C.J. Bowen Cooke *after him* (British Railways).

11. 'Pacific', 'Prairie', another 'Decapod' and 'Mogul'

Before passing on to the general line of historic development, in which for a time the 2-6-0 or 'Mogul' type, rather than the 4-6-0, seemed to be more generally favoured as the 'general utility' type of the future, there are three remarkable 'one-offs' that need much more than a passing mention; because in their several ways two of them, at any rate, bore evidence of scientific thinking far in advance of the actual requirements of the moment. The first of this trio was the first British 'Pacific', Churchward's huge *The Great Bear*. Reading contemporary literature there would seem to be some doubt as to when this engine was actually completed. The official booklet issued by the Great Western Railway in 1919 gives the date as June 1908; but the *Locomotive Magazine* of February in that year carries a full description and photograph, while no more than a month later there was a splendid colour plate reproduced from an oil painting by the publishers' artist, 'F. Moore'. It seems evident from this that the engine was completed and photographed in grey at just about the turn of the year. By the standards of the day it was, of course, enormous; and many times since, historians and connoisseurs of locomotive practice have questioned why it was ever built.

In later years, when F.W. Hawksworth was Chief Mechanical Engineer of the GWR, and also in his retirement, I had the pleasure of many talks with him; and learning that he had made the general arrangement drawing of the great engine, I put to

him the view I had formed, that *The Great Bear* was primarily an exercise in boiler design. I was interested to learn that he agreed, without any hesitation, and that Churchward was stepping well ahead of current requirements to be ready when the next advance in power was called for.

In the discussion at the Institution of Mechanical Engineers in March 1910 on George Hughes' paper 'Compounding and Superheating in Horwich Locomotives', with Aspinall in the chair, Churchward was reported saying: 'He did not think the author laid quite enough stress in reckoning the commercial advantages and disadvantages between the systems, upon the greater power and efficiency for the hauling of trains. As the efficiency of the locomotive was increased, more work could be done on trains, either passenger or goods, and if the author's experience on the Lancashire and Yorkshire Railway agreed—as he expected it did—with the speaker's on the Great Western Railway, he would find that every pound of efficiency that was put into the locomotive was immediately absorbed by the traffic department in giving the engine extra work by means of which the efficiency was swallowed up. Up to the present, even having *The Great Bear* in mind, on the Great Western

Great Western Railway: the magnificent 'Pacific' engine, No 111, The Great Bear, *built at Swindon in 1908 as an experiment in large boiler construction* (British Railways).

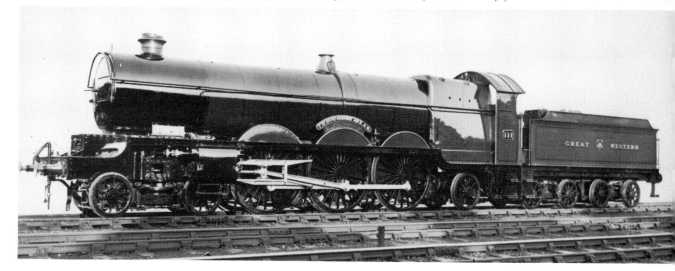

Railway at any rate, they had not yet arrived at the limit of the capacity of the traffic department in that particular respect'. In other words, he was expecting to have to haul still heavier trains, and in *The Great Bear* he was developing a boiler that would be as much in advance of future needs, as his 'Standard No 1' boiler was proving in current circumstances.

In 1910, the superheated 'Stars', as represented by the 'Queen' series, then in course of construction at Swindon, were the furthest advance in the development of the standard express passenger locomotives, and a comparison of their dimensions with those of the preceding non-superheated 'Stars', and with *The Great Bear* is revealing. In the design of the 'Pacific' Churchward could not accommodate larger cylinders than 15 inches without departing from standard details at the front end and from his resolute intention never to have anything but horizontal cylinders; and although the resulting cylinder volume bore no relation to the vast increase in heating surface and grate area, he was content, because, after all, the engine was primarily an exercise in boiler design.

Engine no	4001	4031	111
Engine name	Dog Star	Queen Mary	The Great Bear
Cylinders			
Diameter (inches)	14¼	14¼	15
Stroke (inches)	26	26	26
Heating surface (square feet)			
Tubes	1,989	1,687	2,674
Firebox	154	155	182*
Superheater	—	263	545
Grate area (square feet)	27.1	27.1	41.8

*Including 24 square feet from four arch tubes.

The Great Western, like the North Western but unlike almost every other British railway, did not reduce its standard boiler pressure with the intro-

Great Western Railway: an amusing juxtaposition of new and old engines. On the left is No 111, The Great Bear, in all its overpowering elegance, and on the right is the old 111, an Armstrong double-framed 2-4-0 with 17 inch by 24 inch cylinders, which hitherto worked between Chester and Birkenhead (British Railways).

duction of superheating; and so the tractive effort of the first superheated 'Stars' remained the same as those with saturated steam. But, as will be appreciated from the foregoing table, the tractive effort of *The Great Bear* bore no relation to the vastly, increased heating surface: 27,800 lb against the 25,090 of the 'Queens'. With the building of the 'Prince' series, with 15 inch cylinders the tractive effort of 4-6-2 and 4-6-0 became identical. One feature of *The Great Bear* that is a little difficult to understand from the firebox dimensions and the large grate area is the remarkably small firebox heating surface. When the Swindon No 3 type of boiler was substituted for the No 1, and the arch tubes were removed, this heating surface was only 159 square feet or little more than that of a 'Star', and considerably less than that of a North Western 'Claughton'. The first Gresley 'Pacifics', with a firegrate area of 41.25 square feet had 215 square feet of firebox heating surface.

There is no record of the boiler of *The Great Bear* being steamed to anywhere near its maximum capacity in the same way as was done many years later with the boilers of the large 4-cylinder 4-6-0s; but on the duties to which it was assigned it steamed freely enough. Teething troubles were mostly mechanical, from heating of the radial trailing axle. As can be imagined from the size of the boiler, the axle loading was heavier than on the 'Stars', and for that reason its route availability was limited to between Paddington and Bristol, and there was no opportunity of its working the hardest express duties. Before the war a frequent turn was on the 6.30 pm down express, returning in the night with a heavy express goods train. After the war it was often on the 10.45 am down from Paddington, a heavy but easily timed train, returning on a train arriving back in London at 4.10 pm. This ran non-stop from Bath and carried portions from Ilfracombe and Minehead, via Bristol. In the summer it was a very heavy train and, with 'Saint' Class engines, sometimes needed double-heading through the Box Tunnel. In 1924 the boiler of 'The Bear' needed heavy repairs and, in view of the limited route availability of the engine, Churchward's successor decided to scrap it and shorten the chassis to take a boiler of the 'Castle' type. 'The Bear' had certainly been an experiment, and a worthwhile one, even though the outward and visible results were negative.

The second 'one-off' to be recalled was very different, and was a 'brain child' of Cecil W. Paget, when Assistant Locomotive Superintendent of the Midland Railway at Derby in 1906. He was then 32 years of age; but three years earlier he had been confidently 'tipped' as the most likely successor to Samuel W. Johnson as Locomotive Superintendent —so much so indeed that the *Locomotive Magazine* in its issue of September 5 1903 announced that he had got the job. This of course, was incorrect and he remained assistant to R.M. Deeley.

However, Paget, son of Sir Ernest Paget, the Chairman of the company, was of an exceptionally original turn of mind, and entirely in his own time he conceived and worked out the design of a loco-

motive on what could be termed a 'uniflow' system. There were four cylinders, open at both ends, and each containing two pistons of the trunk type as used in automobile engines, so that in effect there were eight driving pistons. The locomotive itself was a 2-6-2 and the cylinders were mounted horizontally in line with the axles. The leading coupled axle was driven by two of the trunk pistons, and the rear axle likewise; while the central axle was driven by four pistons, two from ahead and two from the rear. The arrangement will be apparent from the accompanying drawing of this remarkable locomotive. It was a simple and potentially free running machine.

The valve gear, though just as brilliantly conceived, brought the great experiment to an end. Paget sought to eliminate as far as possible the friction inherent in the ordinary slide valves then in most common use on locomotives. Although the Midland Railway had used W.M. Smith's segmental form of piston valve this was not free of troubles and, in his experimental 2-6-2 locomotive Paget devised an ingenious rotary sleeve-valve mechanism which effected the distribution of the steam with a minimum of power needed to drive it. It was the most daring and revolutionary part of the whole conception, and one needing much

The 'Paget' locomotive: general arrangement drawing and plan.

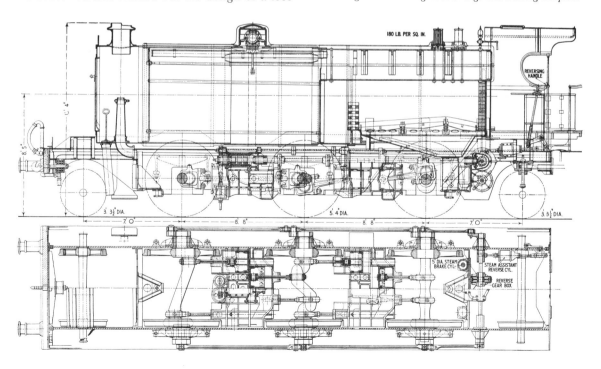

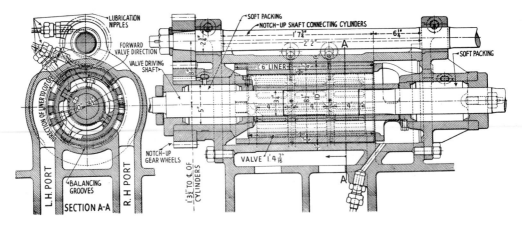

Above *'Paget': section through steam chest with valve and liner.*

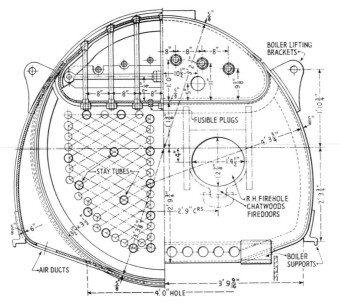

Left *'Paget': cross section and front view of firebox.*

Below *'Paget': arrangement of firebox brickwork and firebridge.*

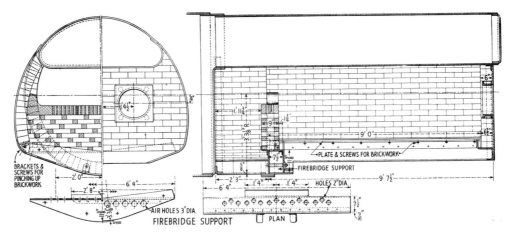

Midland Railway: the 'Paget' 2-6-2 locomotive, No 2299, of 1908 (British Railways).

development work to bring it to perfection. Unfortunately, in his freelance design, Paget was not carrying the boffins of Derby with him—very much the reverse. As details of it gradually became known there was increasing hostility, and there were snide remarks about *Paget's Folly,* or *Paget's Mistake.* The drawings were made privately by two men who subsequently rose high in the locomotive engineering world: James Clayton, who became Personal Assistant to R.E.L. Maunsell, first on the South Eastern and Chatham, and then on the Southern Railway; and Herbert Chambers, who afterwards became Chief Locomotive Draughtsman on the LMS.

When the drawings were finished it was reluctantly agreed that the engine should be constructed at Derby to Paget's private order. Unfortunately it cost a good deal more than was anticipated, and before it was finished he had run out of money. The Midland Railway finally agreed to complete it, but only on condition that all trials, and subsequent commissioning should be entirely in 'official', and not Paget's personal hands. After that, and for some years after his death in 1936, the whole affair was wrapped in some mystery. *The Locomotive Magazine* published a note in October 1908 reading: 'We have recently seen an entirely new type of locomotive on this railway which possesses many novelties of design. It bears No 2299 and is an 8-coupled tender engine having double frames and a large boiler with two firehole doors. There are eight single acting cylinders, with rotary valves and patent axles'.

Two months later this note, incorrect as far as the wheel arrangement was concerned, was followed by another: 'MIDLAND RAILWAY—No 2299, the new 8-cylinder engine, is of the 2-6-2 (Prairie) type with outside frames and inside cylinders placed in two groups between the coupled axles. Two cylinders in each series of four drive the leading and trailing coupled wheels respectively, whilst the other

four, two in front and two behind it, drive the middle coupled axle. Up to the present this engine has only reached the experimental stage, and we hope to give illustrations and further details later'. After that, the 'iron-curtain' of Derby descended, and nothing further was published about it until 1925, by which time the engine had been scrapped some 10 years previously.

Reverting, however, to the year 1906, when Sir Guy Granet became General Manager of the Midland Railway, freight train operating was in a state of almost chronic congestion. While the lightly loaded passenger trains were run briskly and punctually, mineral trains stood for hours upon end in loops awaiting line-clear, and in aggregate the total of unproductive engine and enginemen's hours was staggering. Whatever he may have thought of the 2-6-2 locomotive project, Granet quickly realised that he had, in Paget, a man of outstanding personality and drive, and with the power of highly original thinking; and in 1907 he detached him from the locomotive department to become the first General Superintendent. It was to become the 'key' executive post on the whole line beneath the General Manager himself, and into his new department Paget took responsibility for all train running and the men concerned with it. For the first time in British railway history the responsibility for the day-to-day working of the locomotives was taken away from the man who designed and built them, and Deeley's title was changed to Chief Mechanical Engineer, not at all to his liking!

Friction developed between the operating and the CME's departments. This was not exactly propitious for Paget's 2-6-2 locomotive, which Deeley's men had to test. Deeley himself was of an original turn of mind, and had plans for larger express passenger engines of his own. He was not an easy colleague, and had no exaggerated respect for the top management of the railway

What the exact chronological sequence of events was is not entirely clear; but, so far as Paget's 2-6-2 is concerned, after some preliminary runs on which the engine ran freely and very smoothly at speeds up to 80 mph on level track, there was a mishap with the rotary sleeve mechanism which caused a complete failure on the road. There are varying accounts of the extent of this, one saying that the mechanism seized up solid, and that the line was blocked, fortunately on a Sunday, for many hours. But in any case it was enough for Derby to terminate all work on the engine. It lay in the Works, sheeted over and occult from public gaze, until 1915, when advantage was taken of Paget's absence in France, on military service, for it to be quietly scrapped. Thus ended an experiment that in other circumstances might have yielded much more positive results. The story of it and its ultimate influence was by no means ended, however, as will be related in a later chapter of this book.

The third 'one-off' to be described now was also a Midland engine, and in the atmosphere that prevailed on the railway in the immediate post-war years it is difficult to imagine how this engine ever came to be authorised. The entire operating policy of the line seemed to be to run the trains, passenger and freight alike, with a swarm of little engines, nothing larger than 4-4-0s and 0-6-0s, and very few of those of maximum power for the respective types. On the West of England main line the Lickey Incline, with its two miles at 1 in 37.7 northwards from Bromsgrove, certainly presented a massive obstacle, and a stud of 0-6-0 tank engines was maintained there for the sole purpose of assisting trains up the bank. Even though northbound passenger and freight trains were frequently double-headed, two and sometimes three 0-6-0s buffered up in rear, to assist the train up to Blackwell. This was one of the busiest routes on the entire Midland Railway and, because of the close succession of trains at certain times of the day, anything up to 10 0-6-0 tank engines had to be kept constantly in steam.

In 1919 the Derby drawing office was launched into the design of an extraordinary engine, so utterly un-Midland as to be scarcely believable. This was the second English 'Decapod', a 4-cylinder 10-coupled banking engine, No 2290, specially for the Lickey, intended to do the work of two 0-6-0 tank engines. It had cylinders of 16¾ inches diameter by 28 inches stroke; wheels of 4 foot 7½ inch diameter, and carried a boiler pressure of 180 lb per square inch. The tractive effort was 43,312 lb. After grouping, although it remained a 'one-off' and non-standard in every way, it seemed to remain a pet of Derby. It was well maintained and was still at work on the Lickey after the *Second World War*.

I had a day out on the line in 1949, and rode on its footplate during banking operations; but, although handled by a pair of tough and resolute youngsters, whose combined ages incidentally did not add up to my own at that time (and that was more than 30 years ago!) the boiler could not produce enough steam to sustain an all-out effort for the eight minutes of ascent, banking a passenger train. From the initial 180 lb per square inch, on leaving Bromsgrove we were down to 135 on passing Blackwell, with the tractive effort reduced to about 33,000 lb. In my footplate work on express trains between Bristol and Birmingham I found that the main line drivers needing 'two-engine' assistance up the Lickey always preferred to have two 0-6-0s behind, rather than the unaided efforts of No 2290.

In passing on to the 2-6-0, or 'Mogul' type, the engines purchased from the USA around 1900, by

Midland Railway: the 4-cylinder 0-10-0 banking engine of 1919 (in LMS black) for the Lickey Incline (British Railways).

the Great Central, Great Northern and Midland railways are left out of consideration. They were relatively small power units imported when there was an exceptional need for locomotives which could not be met, either by the railway shops or by British manufacturers. None of the designs concerned had any influence upon the trend of locomotive practice on the home railways.

Twentieth century development of the 'Mogul' type began on the Great Western Railway in 1900 with the building of a prototype, No 33. Generically it was of the same design as that of the celebrated 'Atbara' Class of 4-4-0 express engines, with outside frames, inside cylinders, and a parallel domeless boiler. At the time William Dean was still in the chair at Swindon, and officially the design is attributed to him; though it is now known that this engine, like the 'Atbaras', was a product of the transition period in which Churchward was gradually assuming responsibility for the work to which he was formally appointed, in 1902.

As a heavy freight engine, having 4 foot 7½ inch coupled wheels, the prototype No 33 proved successful and quantity production of what became known as the 'Aberdare', or '2621' Class began in 1901; by midsummer the total in service, including No 33, was 20, with the numbers extending to 2639. They were mostly stationed in South Wales. In the fashion of the day they were finished in the full passenger livery, with red-brown underframes, decorative lining out, and a polished brass safety valve cover. There was a lithographed colour plate of No 33 in *The Railway Magazine* for July 1901.

More followed rapidly and, before the end of the year 1902, Swindon was engaged upon the final batch numbered 2661-2680. More important still, all except the first of this last 20 had taper boilers. Engine No 2662 was indeed a milestone in Great Western, and indeed British locomotive history, as **being the first 6-coupled engine to carry the type of boiler** that nearly 50 years later was to become the

standard form on the British nationalised railways. In its original non-superheated form it was used also on the 'City' and 'County' Class 4-4-0s, while the larger development of the half-cone type was used on the second express passenger 4-6-0 No 98, completed at Swindon early in 1903. The 'Aberdare' No 2662 was only the second engine ever to have Churchward's taper boiler. The prototype, fitted in September 1902, was on the 'Atbara' Class 4-4-0, *Mauritius*; but No 2662 had its fully developed form, with the sides of the firebox curved very slightly inwards towards the top, and the much larger radius in transition from the sides to the flat top. The accompanying drawing, which is taken from Churchward's paper, *Large Locomotive Boilers*, shows also how the top was not horizontal, but sloped down slightly towards the cab. The dimensions given for the boiler of the 'Aberdare', reference 1 in the table on page 175, are those of the tapered type first used on engine No 2662.

It was not until some eight years later that the next 'Mogul' design appeared, and then again it was on the Great Western. Churchward, looking far ahead of immediate requirements, wanted an engine that would be an eventual replacement for the various outside framed 4-4-0s, and ultimately the 'Aberdares' as well. With the building of the powerful new standard 4-6-0s the 4-4-0s were gradually passing on to secondary duties that did not require a really fast-running engine; and the conception developed of a locomotive in the standard range, with coupled wheels of 5 feet 8 inches diameter and the No 4 standard boiler, as used on the 'Cities' and 'Counties'.

The '43XX' Class of 1911 was a total synthesis of standard parts, using the outside cylinders of the 'Saint, the wheel of the '31XX' 2-6-2 tank, and the No 4 boiler, in its superheated form. The new engines became the first of a very large class, the

GWR: the No 4 standard taper boiler.

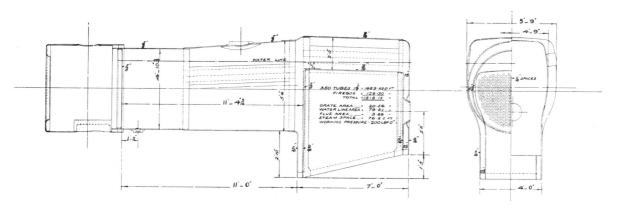

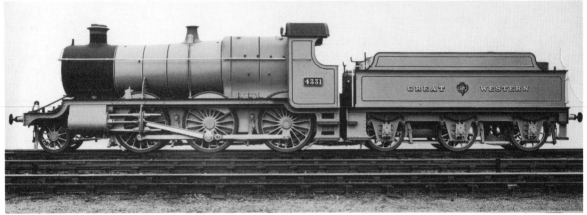

Top *Great Western Railway: an unsatisfactory start with the 2-6-0 in 1900, forerunner of the 'Aberdare' Class inside-cylinder design.*
Above *Great Western Railway: one of the Churchward standard 'Moguls', '43xx' Class, introduced in 1911* (British Railways).

utility of which can be assessed from a single instance: that in the early 1920s, with no more than a single exception, they operated the entire service, passenger and goods alike, in the County of Cornwall. They could handle the heavy goods work as competently as the 'Aberdares', and could run up to 70 mph, with passenger trains, in other words they were the ideal mixed traffic locomotive. Ultimately, several hundreds of them were built.

At the conclusion of Chapter 4 of this book reference was made to the first Gresley locomotive design, the 5 foot 8 inch superheater express goods 0-6-0 of the Great Northern Railway. This, as mentioned earlier, was developed in the 'Mogul' type, reference 3, in the table on page 175. These

engines, of which 10 were built, provided evidence of the increasing popularity of the Walschaerts valve gear, mounted outside. The boiler, though larger than that of the 0-6-0s from which they were developed, was on the small side by Great Northern standards, and the enginemen found this to their cost when they took over certain express goods duties which had previously been worked by the large-boilered 'Atlantics'. This was corrected, however, in the second batch of 'Moguls' built at Doncaster in 1914 (reference 6) which had considerably larger boilers for the same sized cylinders. These latter became the well-known 'K2' Class of the LNER, of which a large number were built.

In their early days these large-boilered 2-cylinder 'Moguls' were used for a great variety of work, including main line passenger trains, on the decelerated schedules of war time. They were also used on ambulance trains. That they proved very suitable for relatively fast running was due in no

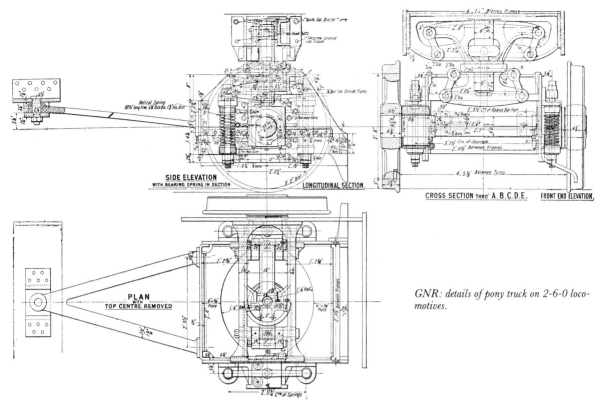

SIDE ELEVATION
WITH BEARING SPRING IN SECTION

LONGITUDINAL SECTION.

CROSS SECTION THRO' A.B.C.D.E.   FRONT END ELEVATION.

PLAN
WITH
TOP CENTRE REMOVED

GNR: details of pony truck on 2-6-0 loco-motives.

small measure to the design of the 'pony truck' carrying the leading wheels, shown in the accompanying drawing. The truck was pivoted by a radius bar to a cross-frame stay-plate behind the cylinders, and it carried a swing bolster connected to its frame by inclined links. A similar inverted swing bolster was carried by other inclined links from the main frame of the locomotive and engaged by means of a cup-shaped centre with the pony truck bolster. There were no side bearings between the locomotive and the pony truck and the links were so arranged that one pair inclined in an opposite direction to the other, and the tendency of either of the wheels to lift on a curve was thereby obviated. Riding on their footplates in more recent years I found they ran steadily at speeds up to 60 mph.

The Caledonian inside-cylinder 2-6-0s of 1912 were main line equivalents of the 5 foot superheater 0-6-0s used on the Clyde Coast trains, and which had a rather heavy overhanging weight at the front end. The 2-6-0s, of which there were only five, had exactly the same boiler and machinery but, with a pair of leading wheels, a rather better distribution of the weight. Like the 0-6-0s from which they were derived, they had the Schmidt superheater with

piston valves above the cylinders. They were the first 2-6-0s to run in Scotland, and worked on main line goods trains between Glasgow and Carlisle.

In later years, when the former Glasgow and South Western shed at Currock Road, just to the south of Carlisle, was closed and all LMS engines working into Scotland were accommodated at the former Caledonian shed at Kingmoor, the McIntosh 2-6-0s could often be seen alongside their G & SW counterparts (reference 7) which also had inside cylinders, and were derived from a some-what ponderous 0-6-0. But Peter Drummond's 2-6-0s were very fine engines indeed and without much doubt the best he ever built. They were just as economical on coal and water as the non-super-heated Drummonds which preceeded them were extravagant. In pre-grouping days, when the G & SW sheds were at Currock Road, most of the drivers and firemen were Cumbrians, but all of them as imbued with that intense loyalty to their railway as their northern colleagues in Ayrshire and on Clydeside.

The working of through freight trains was every bit as much of a prestige job on the railways of pre-grouping days as the most elite of the passenger turns; and this was no where more so than on the

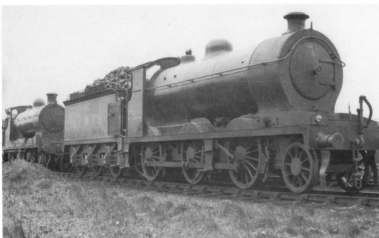

Above *Great Northern Railway: the first of the larger boilered 'Moguls' (forerunner of the numerous 'K2' Class of the LNER) introduced in 1914 by H.N. Gresley* (British Railways).

Left *Glasgow and South Western Railway: one of Peter Drummond's superheater 2-6-0s, at Carlisle in LMS days, standing just ahead of one of the Caledonian engines of the same type.*

Below *London Brighton & South Coast Railway: a Billinton 2-6-0 of 1913, for the fast Continental freight service via Newhaven* (British Railways).

London Brighton and South Coast Railway. A notable volume of goods traffic to and from the continent of Europe had always flowed through the port of Newhaven, to and from Dieppe, and William Stroudley had built a special variation of his famous 'Gladstone' Class 0-4-2s, with smaller coupled wheels for the so-called 'Grande Vitesse' express goods trains between London and Newhaven. In 1913 L. Billinton introduced a fine modern express goods engine of the design shown under reference 5, in the table on page 175. They were, neat, handsomely proportioned engines, and at first they were built rather sparingly. The first was completed at Brighton in September 1913, and the second followed in December. No more than two additional units had been put into traffic when war broke out in August 1914. Although in the initial emergency of the war, Southampton was the principal port of embarkation for the transport of the British Expeditionary Force, and its equipment, in order to meet the anticipated immensity of the land struggle, and munitions it would need to sustain it, port facilities were developed and greatly expanded at Newhaven and Littlehampton.

It was then that an unprecedented volume of freight traffic became centred upon the London Brighton and South Coast Railway and, to reinforce the four original 'Moguls' (and a fifth that had been built at Brighton in November 1914), a further five were built in the late autumn of 1916. The work done by these 10 'Moguls' was prodigious. Naturally the 'Moguls' could not do it all, for there were times when the Brighton railway was working more than 60 trains a day to the two ports. At Newhaven alone it was not unusual for 10,000 tons of special war freight to be handled in 24 hours. But the 'Moguls' played a major part. In their conventional way, with inside Stephenson link motion they were the epitome of an age in locomotive styling and lineaments that was soon to change for ever.

On most of the British railways there was little time in those war years to devote much, if any, attention to design of new locomotives, and the South Eastern and Chatham was vitally concerned in the transport of troops to Folkestone and Dover, the main ports through which reinforcements, leave and ambulance trains for the British armies in France and Flanders passed. But R.E.L. Maunsell, the recently appointed Chief Mechanical Engineer, was also appointed CME to the Railway Executive Committee. As such he had to provide, if not necessarily new locomotives, then certainly an ample supply of spares for the heterogeneous collection of rolling stock which eventually came together behind the battle line under the jurisdiction of the Railway Operating Division of the British Army, commanded so brilliantly by Lieutenant Colonel (as he became) Cecil Paget.

At first James Clayton, as Chief Locomotive Draughtsman of the SE & CR had his hands exceedingly full preparing drawings of parts of Belgian locomotives which had been saved from falling into the hands of the enemy during the invasion of that country, but for which no drawings were available; but after a while there was time to think about new designs for the SE & CR, and Maunsell secured authority to build two prototypes. One, in the increasing fashion of the day, was to be mixed traffic 'Mogul', and the other a 2-6-4 express tank engine, which it was hoped would provide for the Kent Coast express services, as distinct from the Continentals.

In the later stages of the war other influences came to impinge upon Clayton's precepts of design. Looking forward to the time when post-war reconstruction of the administrative set-up of the British railways must surely take place, the Association of Railway Locomotive Engineers (ARLE) that rather exclusive 'club' of which only the chief engineers, and their immediate deputies were members, was asked to consider the formulation of new standard designs for the whole country. The benefits of war-time co-ordination under the Railway Executive Committee were such that thoughts were turning, in Government circles at any rate, to some form of unification afterwards, and Clayton, as chief draughtsman to the REC, became involved in the preliminary discussions. Only four of the existing chief mechanical engineers took an active part in these proposals for new British standard designs, and these were Churchward, Hughes, Fowler of the Midland (who had succeeded Deeley after the latter's stormy exit in 1909) and H.N. Gresley. They were, on reflection, a curiously assorted quartet, and before recalling the only thing that eventuated, it is worth looking at their past records.

Churchward was of course the 'GOM' of the British locomotive world, not only the most senior in appointment to topmost status, but also with the glittering record of the new standard range of Great Western locomotives behind him. Hughes was the next senior, having been rather unexpectedly called upon to suceed Hoy as CME of the Lancashire and Yorkshire in 1904, when he was 39 years of age. Under him it was once said that the locomotive department at Horwich 'had gone all scientific', at any rate in its aspirations and in its public utterances, though as earlier chapters of this book have shown their record had not been particularly brilliant. Fowler, during the war seconded to the Ministry of Munitions and one of the most 'scientific' of Aspinall's pupils at Horwich, had transferred to the Midland in 1900; but though an exceedingly first class brain, his interests were principally in the metallurgy rather than the basic design of locomotives, and his Government service in that direction was rewarded by a KBE. Gresley, the youngest of the four, was the real 'go-getter' of the party: as dedicated a 'locomotive man' as Churchward, and bursting with energy and novel ideas. From his intimate contact with them all, and not least, of course, from his day-to-day association

with Maunsell, Clayton formed his own ideas about future design policy.

The prototype 'Mogul', No 810, which was completed at Ashford in 1917, was an interesting synthesis of different design in practices. In its use of a medium degree of superheat, taper boiler, and of long-lap long-travel valves, one could discern the influence of Churchward. However, to provide the accessibility demanded by Maunsell, no doubt with an eye upon what Urie had done on the London and South Western since he succeeded Dugald

Left *A very famous prototype, on the South Eastern and Chatham Railway—R.E.L. Maunsell's first 'Mogul', No 810, of 1917, forerunner of a large family of 2-6-0s on the Southern Railway (the late W.J. Reynolds).*

Below *A later example of the Brighton design of 'Mogul', fitted with top feed apparatus, seen here at Battersea sheds.*

Moguls: 1902-1918

Ref no	1	2	3	4	5	6	7	8
Date	1902*	1911	1912	1912	1013	1914	1915	1917
Railway	Great Western	Great Western	Great Northern	Caledonian	LBSC	Great Northern	G & SWR	SE & CR
Engineer	Dean/ Churchward	Churchward	Gresley	McIntosh	Billinton	Gresley	P. Drummond	Maunsell
Cylinder position	Inside	Outside	Outside	Inside	Outside	Outside	Inside	Outside
Cylinders Diameter (inches)	18	18 ½	20	19 ½	21	20	19 ½	19
Stroke (inches)	26	30	26	26	26	26	26	28
Coupled wheel diameter (feet/ inches)	4 7 ½	5 8	5 8	5 0	5 6	5 8	5 0	5 6
Heating surfaces (square feet) Tubes	1,689	1,228	981	1,071.3	1,156	1,523	1,344	1,390.6
Firebox	128.3	122.9	137	118.78	139	144	147	135
Superheater	—	215.8	302.8	266.92	279	403	211	203
Grate area (square feet)	20.56	20.56	24.5	20.6	24.8	24	26.2	25
Boiler pressure (lb per square inch)	200	200	170	160	170	170	180	200
Tractive effort (lb)	25,700	25,670	22,050	22,400	25,100	22,050	25,200	26,040

* 'Aberdare' Class as fitted with Churchward No 4 non-superheater boiler.

Drummond, the new engine had to have outside valve gear. Not since 1884, I believe, had a British locomotive been fitted with Stephenson's link motion outside, and then it was on an isolated Great Western 7 foot 8 inch 2-2-2, No 9. So SE & CR No 810 had Walschaerts; with its use the special Swindon setting of the gear could not be included, because the Walschaerts gave a constant lead, for all positions of cut-off. But the most unusual feature of the new engine lay in the arrangements for top feed. In my many contacts with Southern Railway men in later years the identity of the man who devised that extraordinary thing on the top of the boiler was never vouchsafed to me. On No 810, outwardly, it looked innocently enough like a dome, but inside it contained trays, as used on the Great Western but in the form of a descending spiral. At Ashford it became known as the 'helter-skelter lighthouse'!

This engine, and the companion 2-6-4 No 790, when introduced in 1917 caused a considerable stir in British Locomotive circles. Apparently the 'helter-skelter lighthouse' proved effective enough to be tried in 1919 on one of James Stirlings 'B'

Class 4-4-0s, to horrible aesthetic effect. Recalling how the veteran engineer speaking in 1906 at the Institution of Mechanical Engineers had chastised Churchward for spoiling the appearance of British locomotives, one feels that the old master must have veritably 'turned in his grave' when engine No 34, built by him in 1899, emerged from Ashford surmounted with a 'helter-skelter lighthouse' just ahead of the safety valve.

But, reverting to the Maunsell 'Moguls', immediately after the Armistice of November 1918, Winston Churchill, as Minister of Munitions, was anxious to maintain the flow of production in factories that would be affected by the sudden end to the demand for war production, and sought to achieve it by ordering large quantities of locomotives. On this suggestion being referred to the ARLE little progress was made, because the locomotive engineers were all sparring for their own designs. Eventually an order for 100 'Moguls' of the Maunsell design was given to Woolwich Arsenal but, as completion approached, none of the British railways, the SE & CR included, wanted them!

12. Picturesque survivals in the early 1920s

British locomotive history would not have been what is is, had it not been for the diversity of styles and traditions practised by the railway companies of the pre-grouping age. Passing into the eventful 1920s there were a remarkable number of survivals of the 19th century enterprise and genius in design that were not only lingering in what may be termed the 'backwoods' of the railway system of the country, but which were playing a continuing and sometimes vital part in main line train operation. One feels that in this chronicle of modern design development the part that these veterans were playing should not be forgotten. There were men in very high positions who did not forget, as will be told later; and so, for one chapter it is not merely a case of rolling back the curtain, but of seeking out and giving warm appraisal to engines of 1899 and much earlier that were still splendidly carrying on. Inevitably this chapter will have a high proportion of personal reminiscence.

In 1920 I spent part of the Easter holidays with an Uncle who then lived at Eastbourne; and armed with a Box-Brownie camera it was not long before I found my way to the station. To a teenager, of course, the occasional presence of Earle-Marsh's 'Atlantics' on the London expresses was a major attraction, but I was fascinated by the great variety of older engines which always seemed in and around the station.

It was only a year since the inimitable E.L. Ahrons had dealt with 19th century happenings on the 'Brighton' in his famous series of articles in *The Railway Magazine*. I have always thought that his stories of 'Brighton' shortcomings were among the wittiest he ever wrote, yet between the fun, such was his skill, that he conveyed a penetratingly accurate picture of the locomotive practice so ably engineered by William Stroudley. It was not surprising that the 'Brighton' of the 19th century had a greater proportion of devotees per locomotive than any other of the pre-grouping railways; and here, in 1920, was a teenager steeped in the grandeur of North Country railroading rapidly becoming an ardent 'Brighton' fan! It is worth recording also that it was mainly through the energies of 'Brighton' enthusiasts, both professional and amateur, that the Stephenson Locomotive Society* was formed, in 1909 and, with membership rapidly growing and lines of cleavage in interests becoming apparent, the more professional moved away to form the Institution of Locomotive Engineers in 1911.* The nucleus of the latter was almost entirely in Brighton Works, at the outset.

In 1920 the justly celebrated 0-4-2 express engines of the 'Gladstone' Class were still much in evidence. Then 25 out of the original 36 were in traffic, and although the majority were on fairly light duties the locomotive department had no hesitation in putting them on to main line expresses when necessary. I still have a much treasured, but quite indifferent, 'snap' of one of them on a local coast train of 6-wheeled coaches standing in Eastbourne station; but in that same year, when the late Cecil J. Allen made his then annual pilgrimage to the southern lines to collect data for his articles in *The Railway Magazine*, he sought out the 11.55 am from Victoria for a return trip to Eastbourne, and found to his surprise (and one senses not entirely to his liking!) that the engine was a 'Gladstone'. It had no light task, for the gross load of a very crowded train was no less than 270 tons. This would have been a very unusual load for a 'Gladstone' in its prime; but though to keep time was not going to mean getting over the road as rapidly as in Stroudley's own time, with the fastest of the Brighton expresses, the actual running in the early stages was such as to suggest that this veteran locomotive, then 30 years old, had been requisitioned at short notice to replace the engine actually booked for the job.

Allen, in his description, makes no reference to this; but the engine in question, No 180 and once named *Arundel*, was stationed at Battersea, and would not be likely to be put on to such a turn normally. The Eastbourne trains were usually worked by the Billinton 'B4' Class 4-4-0s which, with 19 inch cylinders and 180 lb pressure, were much more powerful than the 'Gladstones'.

Having said this much, the crew of engine No 180 made a plucky try. In Stroudley's time the fastest trains used to pass Three Bridges, 29.5 miles, in 39 to 41 min with loads of around 200 tons. On this 1920 occasion the 11.55 am from Victoria was due to stop there in 45 minutes, taking the more steeply graded new line, south of Coulsdon. Engine No 180 made rather heavy weather of the first 10.5 miles to East Croydon, taking 22 minutes and strongly suggesting that the engine was not fully prepared for hard express work; but she held her own from there onwards and would have been no more than 2 minutes late at Three Bridges, but for a

---

*At first known as the 'Stephenson Society'.

*At first known as the Junior Institute of Locomotive Engineers.

slowing for permanent way work near Gatwick. Onwards to Lewes the work was excellent, with a fine uphill acceleration to 35 mph at Balcombe Tunnel, and downhill speeds up to 66 mph before the severe slowing necessary over the junction for the Lewes line at Keymer. The 20¾ miles from Three Bridges to Lewes took 28¾ minutes, a very creditable start-to-stop average of 43 mph over this relatively short distance. In their prime the 'Gladstones' used to take the celebrated 'Stockbrokers Express', 5.1 pm from London Bridge non-stop to Brighton, up the long 1 in 264 gradient to Merstham tunnel at about 45 mph with a 200-ton load. To accelerate to 35 mph in 2½ miles from a standing start on the same gradient, with a 270-ton load in 1920, was no mean counterpart to those earlier feats.

When I knew them, however, it was not often that those elegant engines were called upon for such hard work. They steamed pleasantly along on the coast trains with short trains of 6-wheelers more suited to their advancing years. They were all in the chocolate brown livery at that time, and looked very smart, though I must admit that in still later years the survivors looked well in Southern green. The maximum speeds attained on that 1920 journey were if anything higher than those reached in their hey-day. Then 60 mph was rarely exceeded. It could well have been that the civil engineer, rather than locomotive capacity, was the controlling factor in this, as indeed it was on the neighbouring South Eastern Railway. Stroudley exercised a very firm control over the running of his engines, and from much contemporary data it seemed that the normal practice was to go fairly hard uphill, and then drift downhill on the merest breath of steam. And so, when our grandchildren gaze in some curiosity at No 214 *Gladstone*, in the National Railway Museum at York, it is just as well to have some factual reminders of what these engines did in their prime, and how they responded to calls for maximum effort when they were at least 30 years old.

Above *One of the much-loved Brighton 0-4-2s of the 'Gladstone' Class, No 177, formerly named* Southsea, *still going strong under the electrified wires in Southern Railway days* (the late C. Laundy).

Right *North Eastern Railway: one of the 'Tennant' 2-4-0s of 1885. The author travelled behind one of these from Leeds to Bridlington in 1919* (The Locomotive Publishing Company).

North Eastern Railway: a 'J' Class 4-2-2, in its original condition as a 2-cylinder compound. In 1920 engines of this class, rebuilt as simples, were still working express trains in the East Riding (The Locomotive Publishing Company).

Turning the wheel arrangement round from 0-4-2 to 2-4-0, I shall always cherish memories of North Eastern engines of both the Tennant and the Fletcher Classes that I travelled behind and photographed in 1919-23. For it was in that same year when I had enjoyed my fill of 'Gladstones' at Easter that I pointed the same juvenile camera at vintage North Eastern engines at Bridlington. The 'Tennants' were very handsome engines, and contributed to the very striking assemblies of engines often to be seen outside Bridlington running sheds. It might well have seemed that the shed staff used to pose them specially for photographs, and I have many times regretted the inadequacy of the apparatus I then owned, and the inexperience behind the subsequent processing that robbed me of so many attractive groups.

The 'J' Class 7 foot 7 inch 4-2-2s were still working in and out of Bridlington in 1919, and to see one of these beside an 'F' Class 4-4-0 was a picture of engine grace indeed. One of my best groupings, of which the 'snap' is unfortunately quite beyond any hope of reproduction, was however, worked up into a splendid painting by the late Jack Hill to make a colour plate in one of my earlier books*. In it one of the graceful 'F' Class 4-4-0s is alongside a 'Tennant', and one of the last Worsdell 0-6-0 goods engines to remain as a 2-cylinder compound. In 1919 the 'Tennants' were being used on expresses to and from Leeds, and on these trains they had not only to skip along the level stretches of the East Riding, as it used to be known, but also to negotiate the stiff climb over the wolds between Market Weighton and Driffield.

All 20 of the 'Tennants', dating from 1885, remained in passenger, indeed *express* passenger service until 1926, and the last of them survived until 1929. When I first went to Bridlington there

The Golden Age of Steam (A & C Black).

were none of the still-older 2-4-0s of the Fletcher '901' Class stationed there; but, remarkable to relate, those old warriors, with 7 foot coupled wheels, were then working the *entire* passenger service over that terribly graded line across the very crest of the Pennines from Darlington to Tebay and Penrith. It is true that most of the trains were not very heavy, but some engines of that class were then getting very close to their 50th birthday! Of course they had been fitted with boilers of a more recent design than the originals, but even so it is striking testimony to the design and workmanship put into their machinery that they lasted so long and so well. The last one to remain in service was No 367, and she was taken out of traffic in July 1925, aged 45 years.

One day in the early autumn of 1923 I had spent a long and gloriously fine day photographing the West Coast main line expresses on that beautiful stretch where it passes through the deep gorge of the River Lune between Low Gill and Tebay; and after the last of the down expresses had passed, making a dramatic high speed charge at the Shap Incline, I made my way back to Tebay station. Fortunately I had one of two exposures left on my last film, for there in the bay at the north end of the station heading the evening train to Darlington was the old 'Fletcher' No 367, newly painted in LNER colours, and perfectly positioned for a picture. All locomotive enthusiasts rejoice in the knowledge that examples of both of these famous North Eastern 2-4-0 classes, Tennant and Fletcher are preserved, and in the National collection.

Earlier in that same day it had been nothing out of the ordinary to see the morning Liverpool and Manchester Scotsman come storming up the valley piling on every ounce of speed for the charge on Shap, with one of the little 'Precedent' Class 2-4-0s double-heading one of the latest 'Claughtons'. The load was very heavy, and the two engines were really digging into it. When they took water at Tebay troughs, just at the foot of the incline, the speed must have nearly reached 70 mph. There were certainly no inhibitions about speed on the LNWR main line, and not long after I took the photograph of that train at Tebay I clocked another 'Precedent' and a 'Claughton' at 77 mph descending the very slight gradient from Whitmore towards Stafford. Those little 'Jumbos', as we called them, were then about 35 years old though, if the dates on their nameplates were to be believed, they were a great deal older. They were renewals of earlier engines of the 2-4-0 type, and took not only the same numbers and names, but the nameplates as well.

With the 'Jumbos' piloting, one sometimes saw combinations of names that were often rather inappropriate, or amusing. On that day when I photographed them at Tebay the engines, from the front, were *Countess* and *Lady Godiva*. The last mentioned was the regular train engine on the job for some weeks; but on an occasion, a few days earlier, the shades of that austere Quaker of Stockton and Darlington days *Henry Pease* would have been shocked when the little Jumbo bearing his name was coupled to *Lady Godiva*! Other combinations I recall were *Hector* and *Lucknow;*

Right *London and North Western Railway: one of the celebrated 6 foot 6 inch 'Jumbo' or 'Precedent' Class, No 787, Clarendon.*

Below *A 6 foot 'Jumbo' (Whitworth) Class, No 604, Narcissus, piloting a 'Claughton' with a very heavy load on the 1.30 pm Scotch Corridor train climbing Camden bank* (British Railways).

Duchess and *Plynlimmon* on the Irish Mail; *Miranda* and *Samson*—a pity about this one, because the LNWR had *Prospero* and *Caliban* as more fitting partners for a 'tempestuous' ride! There was a nice alliteration in *Vimiera* and *Vindictive*, behind which I travelled on the down Scotch 'Corridor' Express, but perhaps the most amusing in its suggestion of 'Combined Operations' over the centuries, was *Caractacus* and *Admiral Jellicoe*. How those little 'Jumbos' could fly, and what a picture they made coupled ahead of a 'Prince of Wales' or 'Claughton' 4-6-0.

I travelled for the last time behind one of them in 1931, and then it was actually solo, on a local express that ran non-stop from Northampton to Rugby. The engine was the *Talavera*, and at that time all North Western enthusiasts were agog with delight that another of the class, *Hardwicke*, was to be preserved. For 'she' was the most famous of them all, being one of the four engines, two North Western and two Caledonian, that made the amazing final run in the 1895 'Race to the North', when the 540 miles from Euston to Aberdeen were

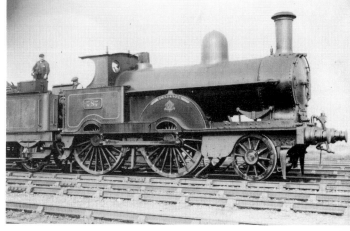

Above *The ex-LNWR 6 foot 6 inch 'Jumbo',* Talavera, *at Northampton in 1931 (just before the author travelled behind her) for the last time in ordinary service with one of these engines.*

Below *London & North Western Railway: the last Webb 3-cylinder compound passenger engine to remain in service, the 2-2-2-2, No 1505,* Richard Arkwright, *which was not scrapped until 1912. It was then stationed at Shrewsbury and, as shown here, worked stopping trains on the Joint LNW and GW line to Hereford. Note the superb condition in which this last survivor had been kept* (The Locomotive Publishing Company).

covered in 512 minutes. *Hardwicke*'s share was on the second 'leg' of the journey—141 miles from Crewe to Carlisle in 126 minutes—in 1895!

What could be called the 'St Martin's summer' of the 'Jumbos' was over by about 1926, when many new engines of LMS build were going into traffic and those great little engines were no longer needed as main line pilots in cases of heavy loading. How *Hardwicke* has arisen, phoenix-like, from her retirement and preservation to become a working engine once again must be told in a later chapter, and how in a certain emergency she was called upon to pilot no less a celebrity than the *Flying Scotsman*.

When the Midland Railway steamed into the grouping era with such confidence, and, be it whispered, with such arrogance, its huge stud of more than 3,000 locomotives was very largely an anachronism. A high proportion of its engines, if not downright obsolete, were certainly obsolescent. How this extraordinary state of affairs developed on a railway that, prior to 1914, was one of the busiest and most prosperous in the country, is discussed in the next chapter; but for those who loved engines for their own sake, amongst whom I certainly count myself, it meant that there were very many vintage designs in regular passenger service, and mostly in beautifully clean condition. Midland engines were never overworked. For five years, 1916-21, I lived within sight of two of the most picturesque of the northern lines and, of the four broad groupings of 19th century express engines, three were almost everyday sights on one or another of those two lines. The very beautiful 4-2-2 Johnson 'singles', known collectively as the 'spinners' did not normally come our way, or indeed anywhere north-east of the erstwhile Derby-Manchester main line; but of the others we certainly had our fill.

When it came to travelling behind the veteran 2-4-0s I had some typically Midland experiences. The first, and the only one involving a Kirtley, came on a raw winter's night in 1926, when I had waited at St Albans for the long overdue 6.37 pm non-stop to St Pancras. It came in eventually headed by No 53, a Kirtley veteran of the celebrated '800' Class, and a '2P' superheater 4-4-0. We did the 19.9 miles to St Pancras in 25¼ minutes and, checking up, I found the load had been 270 tons tare. The usual load was less than 200, but on this occasion the train had been augmented at Bedford. The driver had refused to take it, and demanded a pilot. So they had sat in Bedford station for over half an hour, while the old Kirtley was got ready. The driver of the '2P' explained most forcibly—but unconvincingly!—that to have taken such a load would have knocked the engine to pieces. But if he had taken her gently up the bank to Luton he would

LNWR: the much rebuilt Trevithick 8 foot 6 inch 2-2-2, Cornwall, *in 1919-20 reserved to run the Chief Mechanical Engineer's private saloon. It conveyed C. J. Bowen Cooke from Crewe to Euston on the morning of July 20 1920 on what proved to be his last journey over this line. He was travelling to Falmouth to convalesce after the illness which had stricken him earlier in the year, but he never returned, dying in Cornwall in October. The famous engine was returned to Crewe on July 20 as pilot to the War Memorial 'Claughton' engine, No 1914,* Patriot, *the last time the old 8 foot 6 inch 2-2-2 worked on a revenue earning train* (British Railways).

have lost but a tiny fraction of the time he actually did by waiting in Bedford station.

On another occasion, when I was travelling by the 3.30 pm from Leeds to St Pancras, the 'slick' provision of a pilot seemed part of the job. We had a not very onerous 242 tons tare, and another '2P' superheater to haul it. We kept time to Sheffield, 37.7 miles in 52 minutes, and then a Johnson 2-4-0 No 84, was waiting to couple ahead. There is certainly a stiff climb out of Sheffield, for just over 4 miles, at 1 in 100, and evidently, by the rules, our '2P' was overloaded with 242 tons. The pilot looked every inch a Johnson, though she was actually one of the Kirtley '890' Class, having inside frames to the coupled wheels, and subsequently very much rebuilt. At first I wondered if she was working home to Nottingham; but, having assisted us up the bank to Dore and Totley, and coasted downhill afterwards, she coupled off at Chesterfield. Her assistance was provided for no more than 4¼ miles, after which she had to work back 'light engine' to Sheffield.

Another curious case of piloting came to my notice just before Christmas in 1927, when I was travelling from Derby to Manchester, by the 2.25

pm express from St Pancras. With a load of 305 tons tare there was justification in giving one of the new 6 foot 9 inch compounds a pilot up to Peak Forest, and we had coupled ahead No 144, a 6 foot 2 inch 2-4-0 of the old '1070' Class that was designed specially for that hard road. With a very crowded train the two engines made good time until we came to Miller's Dale, where apparently there was a misunderstanding between the two drivers. The pilot man who was, of course, controlling the brakes, thought they were 'right-away' to Manchester, and made to pass Miller's Dale at full speed; and we should have done so had not the compound driver made an emergency application, and stopped us, but not before we had run about four coaches ahead of the platform! By detaching of the Buxton through carriages the load was then reduced to 221 tons, an easy proposition, one would think, for a compound to take up the remaining 4½ miles to Peak Forest, even though the gradient is 1 in 90. But no; both engines continued to the summit, to stop again for 3¼ minutes to put the pilot off. By the time we were under way again it was nearly 13 minutes from our start at Millers Dale. This was near the end of the year 1927, but signs of the new order had not then begun to penetrate the Midland fastnesses.

By that time, sadly, most of the beautiful single-wheelers had been scrapped. At Christmas 1927 only three out of the original 95 remained, and they were all to be withdrawn in the following year. One of these, No 673, was saved for preservation, and is a treasured member of the National collection today. Before their withdrawal one can be thankful that Midland piloting regulations were as strict as they were, and those lovely engines had so many opportunities of heading express trains. The post-

Top *Midland Railway: the preserved Johnson 7 foot 9 inch 4-2-2, No 118, more recently repainted in the style later adopted on the MR and numbered 673. It was in this later form that the engine took part in the Rainhill parade of May 1980* (British Railways).

Above *Midland Railway: a Johnson 4-2-2, No 644, piloting a Class '3' Belpaire 4-4-0 on a northbound express near Mill Hill* (the late C. Laundy).

Left *Midland Railway: one of the 'Princess of Wales' Class of 4-2-2s, No 689, on a southbound dining car express near Mill Hill* (The Locomotive Publishing Company).

war years were a period of reprieve for most of them because, during the most restricted train service of 1917 to 1919, many of them were stored out of traffic, only to be brought out to pilot *coal* trains between Toton, or Wellingborough, and Cricklewood. The latest and largest of them, the 'Princess of Wales' Class, engines 685 to 694, had the shortest lives of all. They had larger boilers that were not standard with any other Midland class and, when their boilers were worn out, there was no case for building any renewals.

I shall not forget my last sight of one of them. On a wintry day very early in 1922 we had been playing 'rugger' at Harpenden. After an exciting game on a snow-covered pitch, we arrived back at the station just as a down train was starting. In the gloom, silhouetted against the station lamps, was the unmistakeable outline of a 'Princess of Wales' getting away cleanly enough despite the state of the rails. It was too dark to see the number, but at that time only five of them remained, Nos 687, 688, 689 and 691 were withdrawn in March of that same year, and the last one, No 690 went in July, leaving none to enter LMS ownership.

Reverting to the engines of that much loved of pregrouping railways, the 'Brighton', the longevity of the Stroudley 0-6-0 and 0-4-2 tanks never ceased to amaze one. It was in 1924 in *The Railway Magazine* that one of their most devoted and scholarly admirers, the late J.N. Maskelyne of model engineering fame, wrote an article entitled 'The Jubilee of a Famous Locomotive Class'. The oldest of the 'D1' 0-4-2 tanks were then just over 50 years old; but they were to survive for very many years afterwards, in fact, 28 of them survived the *Second* World War.

In the days following the grouping there seemed no end to the usefulness of these splendid little engines. The Southern found them ideal for most branch line duties down in the West Country. I very nearly wrote 'all' instead of 'most'; but there was one case that beat them. As tank engine counterparts of the 'Gladstones', they were subject to the same facility of front coupled wheels, riding beautifully round curves; but there was one line down in the west that beat them—the Lyme Regis branch from Axminster. One of them was tried but the front-coupled wheels took most unkindly to the sharp reverse curves. The Southern had found that the ex-London and South Western 'M7' 0-4-4 tanks were unsuitable, and were using two of the Adams 4-4-2 tanks with radial trailing axle boxes and, after the disappointment with the 'D1', the Adams engines remained there for some years.

The neighbouring Seaton branch, in the early 1930s, was being worked by one of the oldest of the

'D1s', No B214, then rebuilt with a Marsh boiler. This was originally No 13 of the LB & SCR and named *Pimlico*. Present day enthusiasts, aware that the preserved *Gladstone*, in the National Railway Museum, carries the number 214 might wonder what a 'D1' tank was doing with it; but the 'Brighton' used to have a number changing habit that some times made it difficult to trace the original identity of engines, and the 'D1' at Seaton in 1931 was perhaps one of the most exceptional of all. In 1907, when she shed her original yellow livery she became 77, then 77A in 1909, and 347 in 1913 when her number was taken by one of the new 'I3' superheater 4-4-2 tanks. Then, in 1920, *Gladstone* was renumbered 618, for some reason, and the 'D1' that had started life as 13 got her number, subsequently becoming B214. Other 'D1s' also came to the West Country, and I saw one at Barnstaple as comparatively recently as 1945. At that time only the last nine of the 125 originally built by Stroudley were less than 60 years old, and the oldest of them all, the original No 18, *Stockwell* and then Southern Railway No 2215, was exactly 70 years old in 1945.

Another of them that I remember well was Southern Railway No 2259, stationed at Horsham in 1936. She also was an engine with a history though in this case it was one of name, rather than number changing. Out of the 125 engines of the class there were only three that were not named after stations or districts served. These ranged from positive 'slumming' in South London, with titles such as *Borough, Southwark, Walworth* and *Bermondsey* to the fragrant countryside of Sussex. Then, in browsing through the original list of names, one came across 259 *Telford*, 272 *Nevill**, and 294 *Rosebery*, respectively a great historical figure in civil engineering, a director of the LB & SCR, and a distinguished statesman. But from 1897, when Billinton's 'B2' Class of 4-4-0 express engines came out, and were named mostly after famous men, the foregoing three names were transferred, and fresh Sussex villages found for Nos 259, 272 and 294, which became *Barnham, Goring* and *Falmer*. The first of these merely had an additional 2 as prefix to her original number after the LB & SCR became part of the Southern Railway. When I used to see her around Horsham she was always very smart in the Southern (not malachite) green. She survived the Second World War, being 63 years old in 1945, but was not to last much longer.

No lesser monument to William Stroudley were those amazing little 'Terriers'. One would hardly think that a class of little 0-6-0 tank engines with cylinders no larger than 13 inches by 20 inches, with

*Lord Henry Nevill.

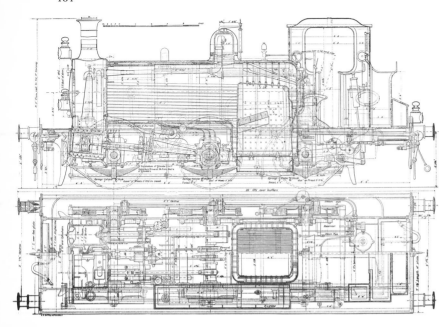

London Brighton & South Coast Railway:
the ever-memorable Stroudley 'Terrier'
0-6-0 tank engine.

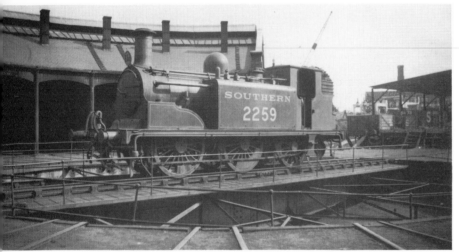

One of the ex-Brighton 0-4-2 'D' Class
tank engines at Horsham in Southern Railway days. This engine was originally built
in 1882 and named Telford, one of the
very few of the class not named after a
station on the line. This photograph was
taken 55 years later.

Ex-London and South Western Railway:
one of William Adams' 4-4-2 radial tank
engines of 1882 photographed 50 years
later at Axminster while working on the
Lyme Regis branch.

coupled wheels of 4 foot diameter, and an all-up weight of 24¼ tons, would rise to be one of the immortals of the locomotive world; yet so it has befallen. With their immaculately kept yellow paint standing out vividly against the rather drab back-cloth scenery of the South London line, and still more so in the depths leading down to the Thames Tunnel, they endeared themselves to the earliest of the enthusiasts. and to their drivers and firemen by their unfailing reliability and a capacity for work seeming far beyond their modest dimensions. When they were first introduced the traffic on those two lines was very light, and the permanent way likewise; and the extremely light construction of the engines was a necessity.

By the end of the 19th century, however, the morning and evening 'breadwinner' trains had grown to 10 or 12 close-coupled 4-wheelers, packed like so many sardine tins, and still the little 'Terriers' whisked them smartly around. The names were hardly exotic, and the first to be completed at Brighton, in October 1872, set the fashion for the class: *Wapping*! A wag once suggested that the first name was something of a leg-pull, because they were so far removed from being 'wopping' big engines! As the class was multiplied, up to an eventual total of 50 by September 1880, and the *Shadwell, Shoreditch, Blackwall* and *Rotherhithe* districts had been exhausted of names, the titles became more countryfied.

At the end of the Second World War there were still 13 of these engines in service, and we owe it to that thorough-going modernist, O.V.S. Bulleid, that one of them was preserved in 1947. The circumstances were felicitous beyond measure. It was appropriate that a locomotive man should be President of the Institution of Mechanical Engineers of its Centenary Year, recalling that the first President, in 1847, was George Stephenson; and in 1947 a visit was arranged to Brighton Works, where a pageant of locomotive development was staged. It was in 1920 that the engine No 682, formerly No 82, *Boxhill*, had been taken out of ordinary traffic and allocated to Brighton as the works pilot. When the large party of I Mech E members visiting the works in 1947 saw *Boxhill* restored to her original glory, it was not only that; but that another 'Terrier', taken out of traffic to replace her as works pilot, had also been restored to the original livery, and lettered 'Brighton Works'.

Perhaps my own most vivid memory of one of these grand little engines is of an occasion at Lewes, three years later, when I was on the station waiting for an express to London. The signals were pulled off for the down line from Brighton, and in a minute or so there came not a modern electric but a little

'Terrier' running light. She gave a shriek on the whistle as she ran through, and then as she headed in the direction of Newhaven the driver opened up. From that tall chimney the exhaust came as from a model, as a fusillade of popping corks, and the sight and sound took one back, as it were, into another century.

The two 4-4-2 Adams radial tanks that I saw in 1931 holding the fort on the Lyme Regis branch, continued on that job, believe it or not, for another 30 years. They were originally Nos 125 and 520 of the London and South Western Railway, built in 1884-5; and after a notable record of fast suburban service in the London area, while most of the original 50 were being scrapped in the mid-1920s, after a life of 40 years, these two were put into the care of Exmouth Junction shed for use on the Lyme Regis branch. They were then fairly thoroughly renewed. The boilers, of course, were not the originals, and they had new frames to the original design; but one of the most important adjustments made to them was to provide the leading bogies with extra side play, to accommodate the very sharp curves on the branch.

A third engine of the class had been sold out of service in 1917 but, 30 years later, it was still in good condition and the Southern Railway bought it back. The three engines together saw steam out on the Lyme Regis branch, all then approaching the great old age of 80 years. In British Railways stock they were numbered 30582 to 30584. The first and last of these (originally 125 and 520) had Drummond type boilers, with lock-up safety valves mounted on the dome; but No 30583 (old 488) was reboilered with an Adams type boiler and, apart from the chimney, which was of Drummond type instead of the original stove pipe, looked remarkably similar to the original of 1884. There may have been only three of them surviving after 1928, but they were tremendous little jobs. That they had 17½ inch by 24 inch cylinders, 5 foot 7 inch coupled wheels and carried a boiler pressure of 160 lb per square inch is almost incidental; it was the excellent basic design and care put into their maintenance that mattered.

Posed facing Turntable 'A' in the National Railway Museum at York is a 2-4-0, No 490, in the majestic Royal blue livery of the Great Eastern Railway. The citation tells that she was built at Stratford Works in 1894, and that she was withdrawn from active service in 1959—another sexagenarian locomotive. When James Holden was appointed to succeed T.W. Worsdell as Locomotive Superintendent, in 1885, there had been five locomotive superintendents in 20 years, each with very definite ideas on locomotive design, and the outcome was naturally to present the new incumbent with a considerable variety of styles: Sinclair, S.W. Johnson, William Adams, Massey Bromley and T.W. Worsdell.

Fortunately the demands for locomotive power, either in tractive effort or speed, were not severe; but, while the sheer variety of the scene was a delight to locomotive enthusiasts, it was not a situation to be commended for the efficient running of a locomotive department. Some engineers, faced with a similar diversity, have allowed the different designs gradually to wear themselves out on country branches or on secondary main line service, during which time the efforts of the headquarters drawing office was concentrated on new, and perhaps novel, express passenger designs. James Holden's record, between 1885 and 1907, looks like a pretty ruthless one of 'scrap and build', the scrapping not omitting some of his own, erstwhile very celebrated engines.

When James Holden retired at the end of 1907, and handed over to his son, S.D. Holden, what could be termed the standard locomotives of the line were comprised in no more than seven classes (only five wheel arrangements), which between them accounted for about 1,150 engines out of a total of some 1,300 for the whole line. One of his earlier designs that was to enjoy remarkable longevity was

the branch line and mixed traffic 2-4-0, of which No 490 in the National Railway Museum is an example. There were 100 of them, all built at Stratford between 1891 and 1902, and all of them passed into LNER ownership in 1923. They had a simple sturdy look about them, emphasised by the stovepipe chimney; and they proved ideal for East Anglia. In later years they had an interesting extension to their activities.

After the withdrawal of the ex-North Eastern 7 foot 2-4-0s, the working of the passenger service over the very severe Darlington-Tebay and Penrith line, over Stainmore summit, devolved upon the ex-NER 'C' Class 0-6-0s; but in 1936 six of the ex-Great Eastern 5 foot 8 inch 2-4-0s were fitted with side-window cabs for use on that wild route. They had a considerably higher tractive effort than the 'Tennants' for, although the cylinders were ½ inch less in diameter, the smaller coupled wheels of 5 foot 8 inches diameter, against 7 feet would make a big difference. In addition to these six engines on the Darlington-Tebay run, 12 others had survived to enter National ownership in 1948.

There is certainly no more remarkable an historic survival than the now-well-known 'Caley Single'— engine No 123, and dating from 1886. She presents the very unusual case of a locomotive becoming a far more familiar sight among railway enthusiasts in

Left *Ex-Great Eastern Railway 2-4-0 mixed traffic engine, 1891 design, in original condition at Norwich in 1927, apart from being in LNER colours* (P. Ransome Wallis).

Below *Caledonian Railway: the restored 4-2-2, No 123, with two restored CR coaches, leaving Perth for Edinburgh on a special in the 1950s* (W.J.V. Anderson).

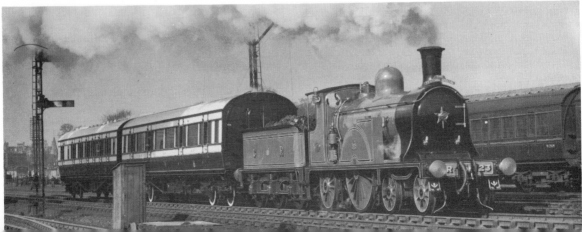

her rejuvenation, in the 1950s and 1960s, than ever she was in her prime. For she was an unusual engine from the very start, in that she was not built to a Caledonian Railway order. There was to be a great exhibition in Edinburgh in 1886, and the Glasgow firm of Neilson & Co, later to become one of the most important constituents of the North British Locomotive Company, built a beautiful engine of the 4-2-2 type to be the centre piece of their exhibit. Even then the firm had a very substantial export trade in locomotives, and the 4-2-2 was a worthy showpiece. Design-wise she could have been described as a single-wheeler version of Dugald Drummond's very successful 'Carbrook' Class 4-4-0 on the Caledonian; and there must have been some understanding as to her ultimate destination, because she bore a number plate inscribed Caledonian Railway and was painted in the standard dark blue livery.

Although the idea of a single-wheeler was completely outside the precepts of current motive-power thinking on the Caledonian at the time, No 123 quickly became a great favourite, and the story has often been told as to how she covered herself with glory in the first 'Race to the North', in 1888. Soon afterwards, however, in the drive towards larger boilers, successive batches of 'Dunalastairs' and then to 4-6-0s, she dropped out of the picture, being kept for the occasional, if prestigious, duty of hauling the directors' saloon. When grouping took place in 1923 she was subsequently painted in Midland red, with the number 14010 in characteristically huge numerals on her tender. Still her public appearances were no more than occasional, and in her first LMS guise she retained the original boiler, with Ramsbottom type safety valves on the dome. Fortunately she could take a boiler that was standard with the numerous small 0-6-0s of the former Caledonian Railway, and, in August 1927 when the original boiler was due for scrapping, she was fitted with a standard type. Though losing some of her original distinction by the loss of the 'moustachio' effect on the dome cover, she was repainted in red and, early in 1930, sent to Perth to work out her usefulness on local trains between there and Dundee—a level stretch of line very suitable for a single-wheeler.

It was then that she began to attract the interest of railway enthusiasts of every estate. They travelled north from England to see and photograph her; articles about her appeared in *The Locomotive* and *The Railway Magazine*, and the photographs that accompanied those articles showed her in red, with the LMS coat of arms on her cab sides. But, in the winter of 1930, after her first season of running between Perth and Dundee (four return trips with a

Great Northern Railway: a memory of the early 1900s—one of the last Stirling 8 foot bogie singles, No 1003, (withdrawn May 1915) working a northbound stopping passenger train through Hadley Woods. Apart from the preserved No 1, only No 1006 remained after the withdrawal of No 1003 (the late C. Laundy).

total daily mileage of 164) she went into St Rollox for a repaint and, to the horror of her admirers, emerged in unlined Black! Her five-figure number was painted in yellow on the cab sides, and she just had the initials LMS on her tender. In the late summer of 1932 when I was on my way to Portree I spent a week-end at Perth and on the Sunday walked out to Friarton sheds. There, to my delight, I found No 14010 sitting out in the yard, clear of all other engines and perfectly positioned for photography. By that time a campaign for her preservation, most vigorously waged by Norman Doran Macdonald, had succeeded; but more regular revenue-earning service was demanded from her, and it was not until April 1936, in *The Railway Magazine*, that other than Scottish enthusiasts were able to see her repainted in Caledonian colours and standing shivering in the snow outside St Rollox Works. There she remained inside, I hasten to add(!), during the Second World War. She was drawn out for me to see and photograph when I was doing the field work for my book *Scottish Railways* in 1948 but, at that time, her second 'life' lay far ahead. There is much to be written of this in the second volume of this book.

13. Grouping 1923: its first effects, in retrospect

Looking back 60 years later on such a cataclysm in business management as the Government-ordained grouping of the British railways in 1923, it is terribly easy to be wise after the event, and to pontificate upon what should or should not have been done. While in this book my concern is predominantly with locomotives, the treatment meted out to the locomotive departments of some of the old railway companies, devoid of all logic and engineering commonsense, was so much the result of intercompany rivalries and railway power-politics, that some understanding of what went on in these directions is necessary to even the sketchiest appreciation of what transpired in some of the main works, and in many of the running sheds. It was not everywhere so difficult. On the Great Western the amalgamation of the various Welsh railways had an almost negligible effect on general policy, and on the Southern, while all the more important posts in the locomotive department were awarded to men of the former South Eastern and Chatham Railway, the presence of a very strong hand at the helm, in the person of Sir Herbert Walker as General Manager, acted as a very effective damper to any internecine rivalries that might arise, in disagreements between the former South Western, Brighton and SE & C locomotive factions.

On the London and North Eastern Railway matters were not so clear cut. On the Board of the new company the former North Eastern Railway was very strongly represented with eight directors, plus one from the recently amalgamated Hull and Barnsley Railway. The Great Central, Great Eastern, Great Northern and North British had four each, and from these William Whitelaw, from the NBR, and Lord Faringdon, from the GCR, were chosen as Chairman and Deputy Chairman respectively. Transcending all other appointments, and announced before the end of 1922 were those of R.L. Wedgwood and R. Bell, as General Manager and Assistant General Manager, both from the North Eastern Railway. Bell in particular was to prove a mighty 'power behind the throne'.

Four locomotive engineers of commanding status were in office at the end of 1922: J.G. Robinson, Sir Vincent Raven, A.J. Hill and H.N. Gresley. Raven had already expressed a wish to retire, but was persuaded to remain for a year as Technical Adviser; and, largely on the recommendation of Lord Faringdon, Robinson was offered the post of Chief Mechanical Engineer. But he was then 65

years of age, and he explained to Whitelaw and Lord Faringdon that he could not hope to stay in office long enough to effect the co-ordination in practice between those of the five large pre-grouping companies that he would feel necessary.

At that time, however, it was by no means mandatory, or even expected, that senior officers would automatically retire at or around their 65th birthday and indeed C.B. Collett, on the Great Western, continued in office until he was over 70. In 1923, however, Robinson, although pressed to reconsider his decision not to accept the very tempting offer, stood firm, and recommended Gresley instead. As things turned out he outlasted Gresley by more than two years, living to the advanced age of 87. It is interesting to speculate upon how the course of British locomotive history might have been changed had he accepted, and reigned as Chief Mechanical Engineer of the London and North Eastern Railway for the first five or six years of its existence. Gresley, who at one time looked forward to being his chief assistant, never failed to show his gratitude for the recommendation that led to his appointment as Chief Mechanical Engineer, and on two occasions when locomotives of intermediate power were needed quickly, he specified Great Central standard designs. Furthermore, with W.G.P. Maclure, another Great Central man, appointed as Locomotive Running Superintendent of the Southern Area, Gresley was ready to accept the long-term usage of Great Central engines on certain prestige express passenger duties over the Great Northern main line.

The locomotive situation on all the major constituent companies of the LNER at the time of grouping was healthy enough, albeit widely dissimilar from each other, and for many years Gresley showed no inclination to impose his own ideas upon divisional establishments with the traditions and reputations of Cowlairs, Darlington, Gorton and Stratford. The disfiguring of Robinson's beautiful Great Central engines by the substitution of 'flower-pot' chimneys, and truncated dome covers for the gracefully curvaceous forms of the originals, can be seen as a crude attempt by some subordinate at Gorton to curry favour from the fountain-head at Doncaster. It was not at all to Gresley's liking. His own work on the Great Northern, referred to earlier in Chapters 7 and 11 of this book, had lain almost entirely in the realm of heavy freight and mixed traffic designs, until the

production of his first 'Pacifics', in 1922. But, before the building of these engines, of which there is much to be told later, he had been much involved in the development of his conjugated valve gear, for 3-cylinder locomotives in which the valve motion for the inside cylinder was derived from a link mechanism connected to the gears for the two outside cylinders.

This arrangement, which was the very cornerstone of the machinery on all but one of the large main line engines that Gresley built for the LNER in the ensuing 18 years, has never quite ceased to be a subject of controversy among locomotive engineers. Its origins, and some of the drawbacks initially experienced, were ventilated when Gresley read a paper on 'Three Cylinder Locomotives' at the summer meeting of the Institution of Mechanical Engineers, in 'Railway Centenary' year—1925. Sir Vincent Raven was then President and, as the builder of a large number of 3-cylinder locomotives himself, it can be well imagined that he was more than ordinarily interested. In all his engines he had used three sets of Stephenson's link motion, all between the frames, and he assured the meeting that if he went back to locomotive work he would continue to do the same.

The most telling criticism of the derived gear for the middle cylinder came from James Clayton, of the Southern, from experience with one engine of the 2-6-0 type that had been so fitted. It was a practical difficulty arising from the taking up of slack in the pin joints causing overrunning of the valve of the inside cylinder. This became serious when a locomotive was put into full gear when coasting and, to obviate the worst effects, drivers were instructed to put their engines into no more than 45 per cent cut-off when coasting. The evils of overrunning of the valve spindles due to slack in

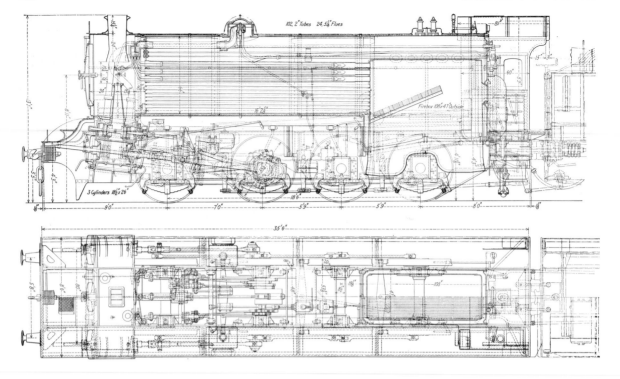

North Eastern Railway: Raven's 3-cylinder 0-8-0 mineral locomotive, Class 'T3', having three sets of Stephenson link motion.

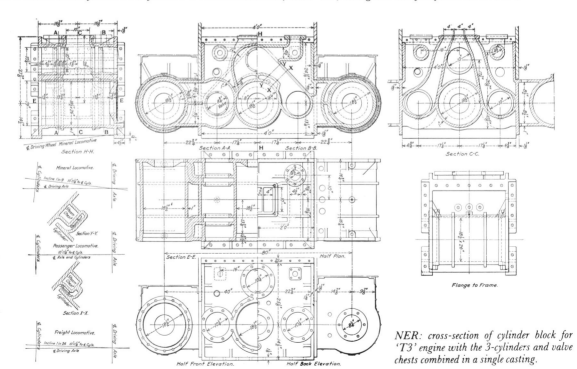

NER: cross-section of cylinder block for 'T3' engine with the 3-cylinders and valve chests combined in a single casting.

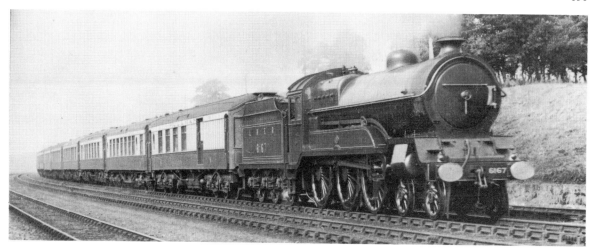

Ex-Great Central 4-cylinder 4-6-0, No 6167, (at one time named Lloyd George) on the up Harrogate Pullman express, non-stop Leeds to Kings Cross, seen here near Potters Bar (the late C. Laundy).

the pin joints were not finally overcome, until a former Great Western man, K.J. Cook, was appointed Chief Mechanical Engineer of the Eastern and North Eastern Region in British Railways days; then by introducing the optical system of lining up cylinders, the evils of over-running valve spindles were reduced to a minimal extent.

Prior to the grouping of the railways in 1922 and to his appointment as Chief Mechanical Engineer of the LNER, Gresley's first introduction of the derived valve gear for the middle cylinder had received a powerful 'shot-in-the-arm' from H. Holcroft. The I Mech E paper of 1925 and the discussion upon it does not give an entirely true account of the origins of that gear. Gresley's first 3-cylinder engine, the 2-8-0, No 461, built at Doncaster in 1918, had all three cylinders in line, and with the valve casing for the inside cylinder in a different transverse plane from that of the two outside ones, it required vertical levers in the derived valve motion, and made a rather compli-cated layout. The arrangement was very fully described in the technical press of the day, and was not very well received.

One of the critics was H. Holcroft of the SE & CR, by then away from Maunsell's staff at Ashford, and in charge of an Army depot at Purfleet. As a result of correspondence in the technical press Holcroft was invited to read a paper on 3-cylinder locomotives to the Institution of Locomotive Engineers, and this he did towards the end of 1918. It was then revealed that as long previously as 1909, when he was a draughtsman at Swindon, Holcroft had designed a much simpler version of the derived conjugated valve gear, which on Churchward's instructions had been patented. At that time, of course, the Great Western had entirely settled for

the 4-cylinder system for its large express locomotives and no further action was taken upon the 3-cylinder patent.

Gresley at once realised how much simpler Holcroft's layout was than that fitted to the 2-8-0 engine, No 461, and called him into consultation; this he could conveniently do while Holcroft was away from Ashford. As a result it was the modified form of the gear which was used on all future Great Northern and LNER locomotives having three cylinders, during Gresley's time. Those who knew the inside history, however, were upset in 1925 by the rather uncharitable attitude which Gresley showed in the discussion following his Centenary Year paper to the 'Mechanicals'. In opening the discussion, James Clayton, then Holcroft's close colleague on Maunsell's personal staff at Waterloo, very tactfully pointed out that Gresley was not correct in claiming originality from the valve gear, and referred to the 1909 patent. Unhappily Gresley's reply was neither tactful nor correct. He is reported thus: 'Mr Clayton drew attention to the valve gear. He did discover, after designing his arrangement, that Mr Holcroft had devised a valve-gear for 3-cylinder engines, but it had not the same arrangement of levers. Mr Holcroft had far more levers than he used'. This was not a very kind state-ment seeing that, in his three final designs for the Great Northern Railway (the large-boilered 'Mogul' No 1000, the later 2-8-0s, and finally the 'Pacifics'), the layout of the valve-gear was exactly as Holcroft had devised, rather than his own original version applied to engine No 461.

It would seem that Gresley was in a slightly festive mood at the time of that paper, determined to brush aside all criticism. The peroration of his reply to the discussion was typical: 'He thanked the President for his remarks. They all had their own opinions as to whether it was better to have two or three valve gears. He knew that Sir Vincent preferred the Stephenson gears and preferably three. It was obvious, being in Darlington, the home of Stephenson, that the Stephenson valve-gear must be used there'.

Only two 3-cylinder engines on the Southern Railway were fitted with the conjugated form of valve-gear for the inside cylinder. One was the 2-6-0 illustrated in Gresley's paper and claimed to have *his* arrangement of the derived motion; the second was one of a batch of 2-6-4 tank engine, named after 'Rivers' and built at Ashford in 1925. In Maunsell's time all subsequent 3-cylinder engines on the Southern Railway had three sets of Walschaerts valve gear. The subsequent development on the Southern is referred to in Chapter 17.

The post-grouping situation reached its heights of confusion and acrimony on the LMS. There, the assertion of dominant personalities at first over-whelmed all logic and engineering considerations, and fostered a sense of grievance, frustration and bitter resentment from the highest to the lowest

levels of the staff in the Locomotive Department. The unrest had begun a year before the grouping proper, with the amalgamation of the London and North Western Railway with the Lancashire and Yorkshire, and the subjugation of the locomotive administration of Crewe to that of Horwich. As things were then, this was unfortunately inevitable on the grounds of seniority alone; because the untimely death of C.J. Bowen Cooke in the autumn of 1920, and the appointment of his deputy, Captain H.P.M. Beames, to succeed him as Chief Mechanical Engineer, left the LNWR chief very much junior in years of senior status to George Hughes on the Lancashire and Yorkshire, who had been CME since 1904. It was apart from the point that the record of achievement at Horwich in the intervening years bore no comparison to that of Crewe. Unless Hughes was to retire and make way for a younger man, as Robinson had done on the LNER, his was undoubtedly the job of CME of the amalgamated company.

In the LNWR-LYR combination the trouble stemmed from the top. A year earlier, following the retirement of Sir Thomas Williams as General Manager of the North Western, the Board, cognisant of the pending amalgamation with the Lancashire and Yorkshire, had appointed the General Manager of the latter company, Arthur

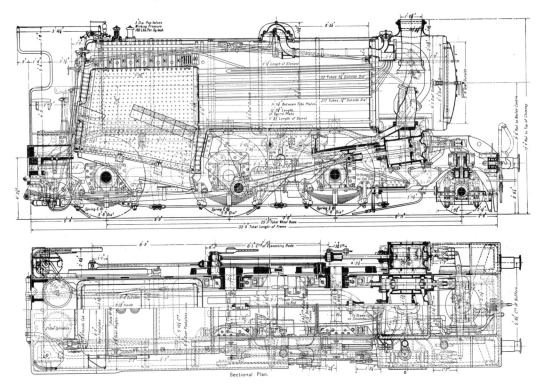

Sectional Plan.

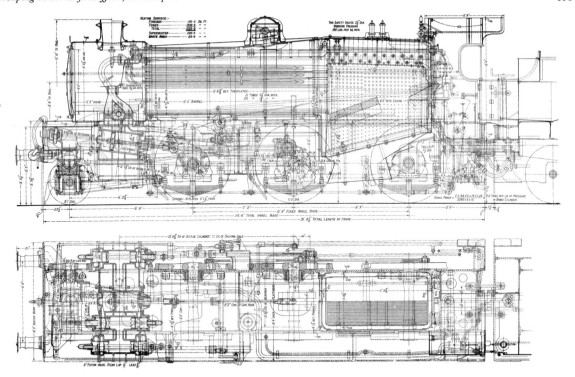

Left *Great Northern Railway: 3-cylinder mixed traffic 2-6-0 by H.N. Gresley, '1000' Class, forerunner of LNER Class 'K3'.*

Above *Southern Railway (SE & C Section): the 3-cylinder 2-6-0 mixed traffic locomotive, with 2:1 conjugated lever mechanism for actuating valves of the inside cylinder.*

Below *Southern (SE & C): 3-cylinder 2-6-0—sectional elevation, plan and end views of cylinders and valve motion.*

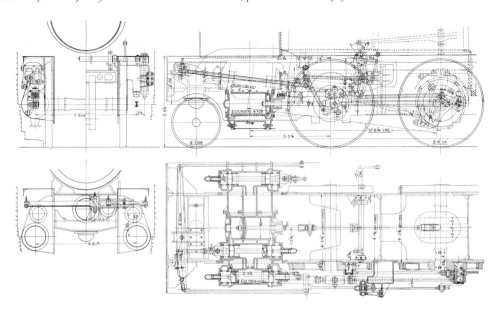

Above *The SE & CR 3-cylinder 2-6-0, No 822, fitted with the Holcroft arrangement of conjugated valve gear for actuating the valves of the inside cylinder* (the late W.J. Reynolds).

Below *Great Northern Railway: the second large boilered 3-cylinder 2-6-0, No 1001, with the Gresley conjugated gear for the inside-cylinder valves* (British Railways).

Bottom *Great Northern Railway: the first Gresley 'Pacific', No 1470,* Great Northern. *This photograph has been autographed by the designer* (British Railways).

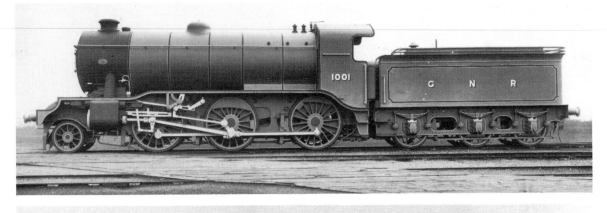

Watson, to succeed him while retaining his former post as well. But it was soon realised at Euston that the new man was not at all in the courtly tradition of North Western General Managers, every one of whom for 30 years past had been knighted, while in office. Watson, however, was no respecter of tradition, and there was soon every sign that he intended to assert the 'superiority' of the Lancashire and Yorkshire in every way, sometimes quite ruthlessly. George Hughes, on the other hand, was a charming, and almost retiring personality, and his take-over of Crewe and all its far flung out-stations was done in the spirit of a benevolent step-father. It is true that some of his staff, gone 'all scientific', undoubtedly wished to cash in on the new situation, but it was done in a thoroughly friendly way.

The ex-LYR men had good reasons for their aspirations. Barely two years had passed since, with the rebuilding of one of the big 4-cylinder 4-6-0s with superheater and Walschaerts valve gear, they had begun to repair the sadly tattered image of Horwich locomotives. By the end of 1921, 15 of the original 20 had been rebuilt, and eight more to the same design had been built new. Beside these 23 4-6-0s the LYR entered the year of amalgamation with six Aspinall 4-4-0s which had been rebuilt with superheaters, and the 40 ageing 'Atlantics', half of which were to be scrapped within 10 years. This was the sum total of the Horwich express passenger stud, discounting the numerous Aspinall non-super-heater unrebuilt 4-4-0s which dated back to the 1890s. Against the modest array Crewe had 245 superheater 4-6-0s of the 'Prince of Wales' Class; 130 4-cylinder 4-6-0 'Claughtons'; 104 non-super-heated 4-6-0s of the 'Experiment' Class and 220 powerful 4-4-0s, more than half of which were super-heated. Hughes and his men were very proud of the rebuilt and superheated 4-6-0s and lost no time in arranging for competitive dynamometer car trials, ostensibly to show how much better they were than the LNWR 'Claughtons'.

By the standards prevailing at the time the rebuilt 4-6-0s were reasonably good. Apart from the introduction of high degree superheating, the more important changes were the fitting of new cylinders, with vacuum relief ball valves, and substitution of piston valves with long travel, actuated by Walschaerts gear for the previous circular slide valves, with Joy's gear. They worked easily and, against the modest demands made upon them by the express train services of the Lancashire and Yorkshire Railway, they made some smart running.

No details of the competitive dynamometer car test running were made public, but the general impression conveyed in the railway press at the time was that they had proved superior to the LNWR

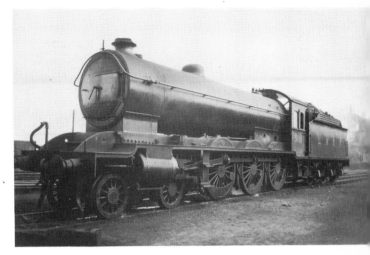

North Eastern Railway: Sir Vincent Raven's system of 3-cylinder propulsion on the 'S3' 4-6-0 express goods engine of 1920 which uses three separate sets of Stephenson link motion.

engines. Subsequent researches, made many years later, proved, however, that the reverse was the case. Reports of a dynamometer test run from Manchester to Blackpool and back, with a train load of 385 tons, showed a very heavy coal consumption in relation to the work done. The overall average speeds for the 48.8 miles, including one stop, were 40.7 mph outward and 41.6 mph on the return, and this needed 75, and 55 lb of coal per mile. Why there was such a difference between the two trips was not explained; even if one takes the average between the two it seems rather extravagant. But, seeing that the old non-superheated 4-6-0s could use anything up to 100 lb of coal per mile, with considerably lighter and slower trains, one can suppose that Horwich were pleased enough with the results of the rebuilding; and they obtained authorisation for construction of another 25 to be built between December 1922 and August 1923.

At the end of 1922 the enlarged London and North Western Railway became part of the LMS, and it was then that the real 'crunch' began, for Crewe in particular. At once the whole management structure of the railway was reorganised in the Midland style with the transfer of responsibility for locomotive running from the Chief Mechanical Engineer to the operating department. J.H. Follows, who had succeeded to the high office of General Superintendent of the Midland Railway, in 1919, had been one of Sir Cecil Paget's 'discoveries'; and faithfully and painstakingly he had absorbed the precepts of the 'master' and carried the

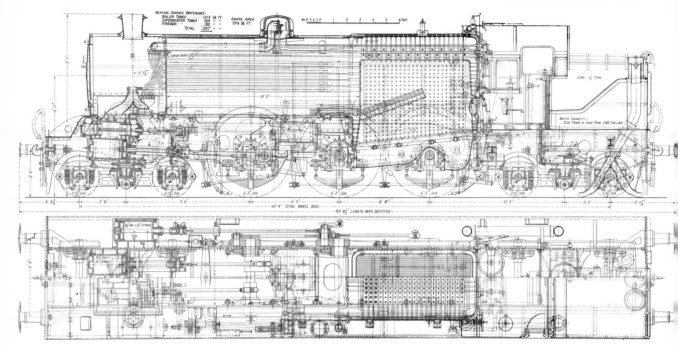

operating department through the long years of war while Paget himself was in command of the Railway Operating Division of the British Army. But Follows, while a very diligent executive officer, had neither the imagination nor the dynamism of Paget; and, when he was appointed Chief General Superintendent of the LMS in 1923, nothing more than a straightforward extension of Midland methods throughout the system could be expected, however inappropriate that might be for some of the far-outlying areas.

It should be appreciated that Sir Guy Granet, who was voted one of the two Deputy Chairmen of the LMS, was a mighty power in the land, and had virtually dictated the terms of amalgamation. If Follows in his new appointment felt confident of enjoying the solid backing of his former General Manager, it was perhaps even more so with the second key appointment that concerned locomotives, that of the Motive Power Superintendent, reporting to Follows. For this post J.E. Anderson, former Deputy Chief Mechanical Engineer of the Midland, was chosen. It was said of him that all engines other than Midland were beneath his notice. Portents for the future were not rosy. Neither were they so in the Chief Mechanical Engineer's department; for while Hughes, as expected, got the job, he had only three years to go, and, ill-concealed beneath the benign façade of Horwich, was the iron hand of the Derby faction

confident in the support they could expect at the highest level, with the tremendous personality of Sir Guy Granet so weighty an influence around the Board Table. And so Midland locomotive men quickly developed a terrific superiority complex. At this distance in time it seems inconceivable that this should have come about, so unjustifiable were the circumstances.

Consider first the simple statistics of the situation: the Midland had not produced a new passenger engine design since 1913—the small-powered Class '2' superheater 4-4-0, limited to a maximum load of 180 tons on the fastest trains south of Derby. Accountancy-wise they were classed as rebuilds but, apart from the frames, they were completely new engines. In the No 4 Class, limited to loads of 240 tons, there were the 45 3-cylinder compounds, only 23 of which were superheated, and the 10 non-compound 4-4-0s of the '999' Class, by that time all superheated and working north of Leeds. Between these upper and lower limits of passenger locomotive power there were the 80 Johnson 'Belpaire' 4-4-0s,

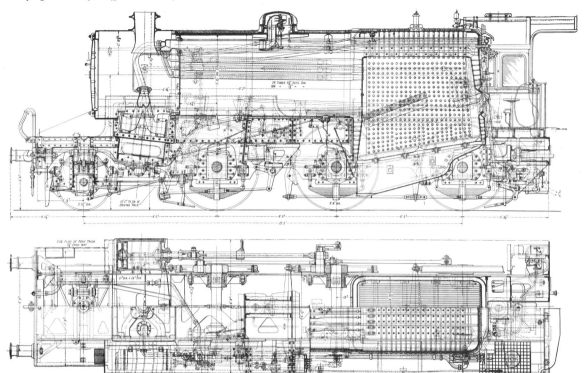

designated Class '3'. Many of these were still non-superheated. Although Sir Henry Fowler himself had written a learned paper before the Institution of Civil Engineers on the design and performance of those of his engines that were superheated, the record of the Midland passenger locomotive stud in actual work—ton-miles of revenue earning haulage per engine hour—must have been about the lowest of any major British railway in the year 1922.

Altogether contrasting was the situation on the London and North Western Railway, on which the superheater 4-6-0s of the 'Prince of Wales' Class, 245 in all, and the 4-4-0s of the 'George the Fifth' Class, then 130 strong by additions to the original

90 of many 'Precursors' superheated with piston valves, were expected to take loads of 400 tons, without a pilot; and 155 of the 'Prince of Wales' Class were new engines, of post-war build. In a still higher power class were the 4-cylinder 'Claughtons' of which, again, 70 out of the total of 130 were new. However, these engines might be regarded at Horwich, *vis-a-vis* their newly-rebuilt 4-6-0s of Hughes' design. It should not be forgotten that the

Lancashire and Yorkshire Railway: one of the first Hughes 4-cylinder 4-6-0s to be rebuilt and superheated was No 1522 in 1920 (British Railways).

highest horsepower record yet attained by a British locomotive stood to the credit of the 'Claughton' engine No 1159 *Ralph Brocklebank*, in the 1913 trials. While it could be agreed that something still more powerful than those 4-cylinder 4-6-0s, both LNWR and LYR, was needed for future traffic developments at the maximum end of the haulage scale, the 'Prince of Wales' Class (with its high route availability and capacity for substantial load haulage and fast running up to at least 75 mph) would have seemed an ideal general purpose engine for the whole group, seeing how short of competent locomotives in the medium power range both the Midland and the L & Y sections were in 1923.

While Hughes remained as Chief Mechanical Engineer, authorisation was given for construction of many more of the Horwich 4-cylinder 4-6-0s with the idea of substituting them for the 'Claughtons' on the northern section of the West Coast main line. But this did not fall in with the ideas of the Midland dominated operating department. Follows, whose methodical unimaginative mind did not, apparently, extend beyond the system of passenger train working evolved on the Midland, in the Paget era, felt there was no need to have any locomotives of greater capacity than the Midland No 4 group, and preliminary schemes were propounded for a complete reorganisation of the LNW section train services, to permit this to be done. Anderson, whose opinion of Crewe locomotives had always been abysmal, had decreed that the maximum load to be taken unpiloted was 360 tons, 'Prince of Wales', 'Claughton' and Horwich 4-6-0s alike. At one stroke he made inevitable an epidemic of double-heading which recalled the last days of the Webb regime. Anderson's first activities in his new appointment seemed to be confined to England, and there was perhaps a strong reason why he left Scotland alone at the start.

It was very unfortunate that the top level change in policy should have been exacerbated by the infusion of ex-Midland inspectors at lower levels,

After the LNW/LYR merger: a dynamometer car test run (Manchester to Blackpool) with a 15-coach train passing Irlam o' th' Height hauled by 'Claughton' Class, No 192, later named Bevere *(the late E. Mason).*

who attempted to inject the precepts of their own operating department into locomotive and traffic working on the West Coast main line. The result was widespread friction with the men. I shall not forget the bitter words of the driver of a 'Claughton' Class engine at Euston who had been provided with a pilot which he considered quite unnecessary, and a reflection on his skill as an engineman. 'If this goes on', he said, 'we'll all go "cacanny", and then we'll have the line blocked from end to end'.

I shall not forget, either, a journey when our through carriage on the late afternoon train from Barrow-in-Furness to Euston was attached as usual at Preston to the 10.5 am from Aberdeen. The load was 374 tons tare, and under the new order of things we should have been piloted throughout. But at Preston there was not even *one* 4-6-0 available. We were taken by a superheated 'Precursor', unassisted, with all the dash and competence of the old LNWR. Having reached Crewe, however, and changed engines we were double-headed all the rest of the way, one 'Claughton' and its pilot being succeeded by another pair at Rugby, and neither pair of enginemen making the slightest attempt to regain any of the few minutes of lateness with which we had left Crewe. On the second stage the pilot was a 'Prince of Wales' 4-6-0!

In Scotland at first the situation was virtually unchanged for the first year of grouping. On the East Coast side the North British 'Atlantics', by that time nearly all superheated, were touching their topmost form. On the main line from Edinburgh up to Aberdeen, with its many difficulties of gradient, curvature, and many permanent speed restrictions, the maximum tare load going north was 380 tons; but southbound, including the very difficult starts

from rest from station stops at Stonehaven, Montrose, and Dundee, not to mention the steeply graded approach to the Forth Bridge from the severe speed restriction through Inverkeithing, the maximum load for those very competent engines was 340 tons. On the North British line, generally, if an assistant engine was needed it was always inserted between the regular engine and the train, instead of leading as was almost always the case on the various railways incorporated in the LMS.

While the 'Atlantics' provided a very effective top-line power stud for the North British section, additional locomotives were required for the Edinburgh-Glasgow main line, and for secondary duties elsewhere, and the 4-4-0 group, headed by the superheated 'Scott' Class 4-4-0 were re-inforced, almost at once, by the arrival of the 15 Ivatt superheated 4-4-0s from the Great Northern, and in 1924 by the introduction of 24 new engines of the Great Central 'Director' Class, with suitably reduced-height boiler mountings. These latter engines were built by contract, 12 by Kitsons, of Leeds, and 12 by Armstrong, Whitworth & Co. The respective dimensions of these additional 4-4-0s, as compared to those of the superheated 'Scotts' are tabulated below.

The batches of Great Central type 4-4-0s, delivered in 1924 were at first unnamed, but from 1925 onwards they had names from characters and events in the Waverley novels. In view of the romantic interests of these names the complete list is appended. It is well known that William Whitelaw, Chairman of the LNER, took a strong interest in the naming of the Scottish orientated locomotives, and it is generally understood that he chose the titles for those introduced in 1924. While one cannot but admire the resounding titles of these two-dozen engines, I just wonder how a challenger for the title

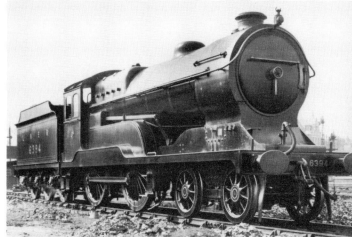

Top *LYR/LMS: one of the Hughes 4-cylinder 4-6-4 tank engines, only 10 of which were built in 1924* (Real Photographs).

Above *LNER grouping developments: the modified 'Director' Class 4-4-0 for use in Scotland, No 6394, subsequently named* Lord James of Douglas (P. Ransome-Wallis).

LNER (NB Section): Express passenger 4-4-0s

Class	GN 'D1'	'Scott'	'Improved Director'
Engineer	H.A. Ivatt	W.P. Reid	J.G. Robinson
Number in class	15	27	24
Cylinders			
Diameter (inches)	18½	20	20
Stroke (inches)	26	26	26
Coupled wheel diameter (feet inches)	6 8	6 6	6 9
Heating surfaces (square feet)			
Tubes	852	1,145.8	1,388
Firebox	120	139.7	155
Superheater	258	355.2	209
Grate area (square feet)	19	21.13	26.6
Boiler pressure (lb per square inch)	160	170	180
Tractive effort (lb)	14,550	19,050	19,644

North British Section: Superheater 4-4-0's

'Scott' Class		'G.C' Design	
363	Hal O' the Wynd	6378	Bailie MacWheeble
400	The Dougal Cratur	6379	Baron of Bradwardine
409	The Pirate	6380	Evan Dhu
410	Meg Dods	6381	Flora MacIvor
411	Dominie Sampson	6382	Colonel Gardiner
412	Laird of Monkbarns	6383	Jonathan Oldbuck
413	Caleb Balderstone	6384	Edie Ochiltree
414	Dugald Dalgetty	6385	Luckie Mucklebackit
415	Claverhouse	6386	Lord Glenallan
416	Ellangowan	6387	Lucy Ashton
417	Cuddie Headrigg	6388	Captain Craigengelt
418	Dumbiedykes	6389	Haystoun of Bucklaw
419	Talisman	6390	Hobbie Elliott
420	The Abbot	6391	Wizard of the Moor
421	Jingling Geordie	6392	Malcolm Graeme
422	Kenilworth	6393	The Fiery Cross
423	Quentin Durward	6394	Lord James of Douglas
424	Lady Rowena	6395	Ellen Douglas
425	Kettledrummle	6396	Maid of Lorn
426	Norna	6397	The Lady of the Lake
427	Lord Glenvarloch	6398	Laird of Balmawhapple
428	Adam Woodcock	6399	Allan-Bane
497	Peter Poundtext	6400	Roderick Dhu
498	Father Ambrose	6401	James Fitzjames
499	Wandering Willie		
500	Black Duncan		
501	Simon Glover		

of 'Mastermind', taking as his specialised subject the Waverley Novels, would be able to answer questions about some of these characters!

While the North British entered the grouping era in good form, especially as its Chairman became Chairman of the LNER and remained so for many years afterwards, the Caledonian did not; and neither for that matter did the Glasgow and South Western. It was in 1921 that Pickersgill brought out what was intended to be his masterpiece, the big 3-cylinder 4-6-0 which was to have the highest tractive effort of any existing British 4-6-0—28,000 lb. The Gresley-derived valve gear for the inside cylinder was carefully studied, and the criticism of it noted and, when the big No 956 was nearing completion, Pickersgill euphemistically described the inside valve gear as '. . . a wee contraption of my own'. It consisted of a group of floating levers actuated in the manner shown in the accompanying drawing; but in addition to having more pin joints than the Gresley arrangement, and thereby liable to over-running on the middle cylinder valve spindle when wear developed, the stresses imposed on the guide at the end of the outside slide bars caused the slide bars themselves to break. But one need not be unduly concerned with this unusual gear; for, while the four engines of the class were completed at St Rollox in June-August 1921, it had been removed from all of them within a year and separate Stephenson link motion fitted for the inside cylinder.

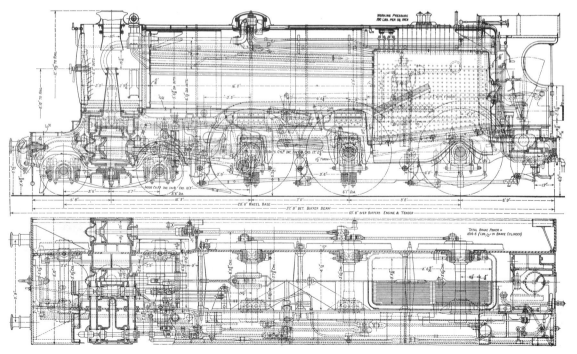

Below left *Caledonian (LMS): Pickersgill's 3-cylinder 4-6-0 of 1921—general arrangement.*

Below left *Caledonian (LMS): Pickersgill's 3-cylinder 4-6-0 of 1921—general arrangement.*

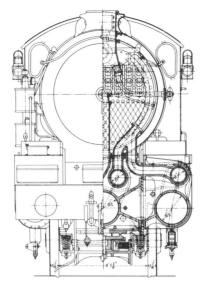

Right *Caledonian: 3-cylinder 4-6-0 cross sectional views.*

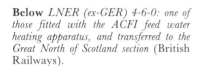

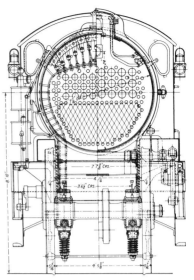

Below *LNER (ex-GER) 4-6-0: one of those fitted with the ACFI feed water heating apparatus, and transferred to the Great North of Scotland section* (British Railways).

Dimensionally they were very large engines, and very handsome ones too. With three cylinders of 18½ inches by 26 inches stroke, and coupled wheels 6 foot 1 inch in diameter there was ample tractive effort, on paper, and the boiler had an evaporative heating surface of 2,200 square feet. The 24-element superheater of the Robinson type, had, however, no more than 270 square feet of heating surface, about the same as that of a Great Western 'Star'; and the grate area was 28 square feet. When new they were naturally kept under very close observation and confined to 'star' drivers: 956 at Balornock (Glasgow); 957 and 958 at Kingmoor (Carlisle) and 959 at Perth. A variety of test runs was made with No 956, with the 'ace' driver of the Caledonian, James Grassie, but with generally indifferent results. A good deal of the blame was put upon the valve gear, for the general sluggishness of

the running. The late Cecil J. Allen had what he described as a very 'decorous' run on the 10.10 am Liverpool and Manchester express out of Glasgow, with a modest load for so large an engine of 315 tons; while, after Pickersgill's 'wee contraption' of a derived valve gear had been removed, the dissimilar gears for outside and inside cylinder were blamed.

Many years later, during his brief stay as Chief Mechanical Engineer of the LNER after the early death of Sir Nigel Gresley, Edward Thompson told me of the investigations he made into the derived valve gear before deciding on a complete re-arrangement of the front end of the 'Pacifics'. At one time he was thinking of putting Stephenson's link motion in for the inside cylinder, and mentioned his idea to Stanier, who was horror struck! 'Whatever you do, don't do that', came his instant reaction; and Stanier went on to say that he had four big

Caledonian engines like that: '. . . they were useless, and I had to scrap them'.

However, with the one detailed account of a return footplate journey on one of them, from Glasgow to Carlisle and back, I wonder if the valve gear really was the predominating cause of their failure. After his death some years ago, the travelling diaries of the late Lord Monkswell were bequeathed to me and, in one of them, there is an account of a run he made from Glasgow to Carlisle and back on No 956, driven by James Grassie, and with W. Barr in attendance on the footplate. With such a galaxy one might be very sure that the finest possible work was got out of the engine. But the round trip was the most dismal failure. On the outward journey, with a load of 415 tons, they lost 2½ minutes on the leisurely 1922 schedule of 138 minutes for the 102 miles from Glasgow to Carlisle, and the return was disastrous. With 325 tons to Carstairs, and 220 to Glasgow, the total time was

155 minutes inclusive of one stop, instead of the 140 minutes booked.

Lord Monkswell summed it up tersely: 'The work was poor throughout. The trouble was primarily that the engine would not steam'. Poor indeed, but why? The engine had then been in service for more than a year, and it seemed extraordinary that St Rollox, with its long reputation for large and successful boilers, should have come so badly adrift with what should have been their final, culminating masterpiece in design and construction. In actual running one can quite imagine that the dissimilar valve gears did not help towards a free running engine; but this did not explain why the pressure got down to 130, and even 125 lb per square inch on the heaviest climbs.

Nevertheless, when the Locomotive Publishing Company produced the LMS-sponsored, *Locomotive of the LMS, past and present*, in 1931, with eight colour plates by that most photographically accurate of

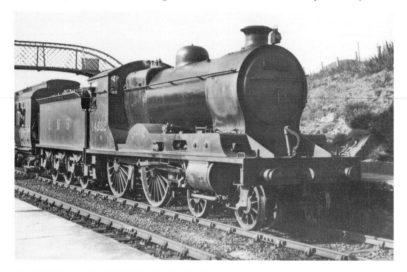

Left *LMS (ex-Highland): one of the two Cumming superheated 4-4-0s (Snaigow and Durn) built in 1917 for working the mail trains between Inverness and Wick* (P. Ransome-Wallis).

Below *Caledonian Railway: one of the impressive but sadly ineffective Pickersgill 3-cylinder 4-6-0s in LMS colours* (British Railways).

LMS (ex-Caledonian): Pickersgill's small non-superheated 4-6-0 for the Callander and Oban Line, photographed at Stirling in 1927 (P. Ransome-Wallis).

railway artists, M. Secretan, of the three non-standard locomotives chosen for illustration in this sumptuous manner, two were Caledonian, but at that time of course, in lined black. One of the two was 956, at that time numbered 14800. It seemed as though she was something of a prestige symbol, and described as 'express passenger', although for some time she and her three sisters had been relegated to goods workings. When I was at Kingmoor shed in March 1933, No 14801 (old 957) was outside, standing disconsolately with the forward cover of the left hand outside cylinder removed. She was scrapped a year later, but 14800 had been scrapped as early as August 1931.

Pickersgill's final design was a little outside cylinder 4-6-0 for the Oban Line, remarkably built to use saturated steam, and having a tractive effort no more than fractionally greater than the McIntosh '55' Class of 1902. The basic dimensions may be compared as in the table at right.

The Pickersgills were feeble things. They rode comfortably on the winding sections of line but, like the big '956' Class, they just could not produce enough steam for the job. I rode on the footplate of one of them piloting the heavy 5.15 pm express up

from Oban and, on all the heavy banks when she was taking no more than a third of the total load, the boiler pressure was around the '130' mark. It rose quickly enough when steam was shut off. These two Pickersgill 4-6-0 Classes, the '956' and the 'Obans', were a sad anti-climax to the proud saga of locomotive development on the Caledonian Railway.

4-6-0s for the Oban Line

Engineer	McIntosh	Pickersgill
Year built	1902-5	1922
Works	St Rollox	NB Loco Co
Cylinders		
Diameter (inches)	19	19½
Stroke (inches)	26	26
Valve gear	Stephenson	Walschaerts
Coupled wheel diameter (feet/inches)	5 0	5 6
Heating surfaces (square feet)		
Tubes	1,800	1,707
Firebox	105	116
Grate area (square feet)	20.63	21.9
Boiler pressure (lb per square inch)	175	185
Tractive effort (lb)	23,269	23,310

14. Interchange trials: 1923-6

It was only natural with grouping of the railways that intense partisanship for one or another of the old railways and their locomotives should develop immediately, not only among amateur enthusiasts but in the ranks of the professionals, from the highest to the lowest levels. In pre-grouping days the railways had worked in relatively watertight compartments, and while locomotive subjects were discussed at meetings of the Institution of both Civil and Mechanical Engineers, the divergencies of view sometimes revealed were couched in such gentlemanly and diplomatic phraseology as to avoid any suggestion of a real confrontation. It was the same in the railway and engineering press. Commendation was uniform for all, very often a little over-optimistic as to the potentialities of this or that new design. In the 'British Locomotive Practice and Performance' articles in *The Railway Magazine*, Cecil J. Allen, despite obvious and extreme temptation at times, maintained a notably unbiased view of current events—at any rate until the fateful year of 1923.

When, however, the great combinations represented by the LMS and LNER systems were set up, and each had dynamometer cars of modern design, all the interested parties, railway staffs and enthusiasts alike, were agog to know how the pre-grouping designs of comparable tractive power compared with one another for overall efficiency, and general usefulness, though the objects in view on the two great groups were rather different. On the LNER, Gresley, as one of the youngest of the chief mechanical engineers, sought confirmation of the practice he had been developing on the Great Northern Railway, to justify it as a future standard

LNER: the Gresley 'Pacific', No 4472, which, when unnamed and numbered 1472, ran in competition with NER No 2400. Here it is seen as the Flying Scotsman, *specially painted for exhibition at Wembley in 1924* (British Railways).

for the whole LNER; and the fact that his former counterpart on the North Eastern Railway had, late in 1922, built a 'Pacific' engine of comparable size and tractive effort to his own, but with an entirely different arrangement of the machinery, suggested that comparative trials should be carried out without delay. His neat and accessible layout of the valve gear, avoiding the need for a third set between the frames, had not escaped criticism. Sir Vincent Raven's 'Pacifics' had three sets of Stephensons link motion, all between the frames.

The trials were carried out in June and July 1923 between Doncaster and Kings Cross, with the heaviest of the West Riding trains at that time, the 10.51 am up, and the 5.40 pm, loading generally to around 500 tons behind the tender. In assessing the subjoined table of results it must be pointed that the Great Northern engine had the original setting of the valve gear, with relatively short travel, and that the North Eastern engine had the conventional Gateshead/Darlington setting of the Stephenson link motion, with about 4¼ inches travel in full gear, with a lead of about an ⅛ of an inch. It would have been very interesting to see a 'return match' played between the two Pacific designs, with the 'Gresley' fitted with the gear later adopted as standard and giving such economical working, and the 'Raven' having the link motion modified as was that fitted to the Great Eastern 4-6-0s when equipped with the larger boiler of the B12/2 type. This provided long valve travel, and negative lead in full gear as on the Great Western 2-cylinder 4-6-0s. It will be seen that the overall results of the trials favoured the Great Northern engine, if no more than slightly though the only detailed logs I have seen* showed that the North Eastern engine made the harder running.

*See *LNER Steam* by O.S. Nock.

LNER: 'Atlantic' trials—a standard Great Northern superheater engine in pre-grouping livery.

LNER: the same type, but with shortened chimney, boiler, mountings and cab, for running competitively over the North British section to Edinburgh (British Railways).

LNER 'Pacific' trials: June/July 1923
Average results of all tests

Engine no	1472*	2400
Section	**GN**	**NE**
Average speed (mph)	53.7	53.0
Actual 1,000 ton miles (train only)	73.11	76.5
Average drawbar (horsepower)	663	673
Superheat temperature (degrees F)	547	574
Boiler pressure (lb per square inch)	164	197
Steam chest pressure (lb per square inch)	118	106
Cut-off (per cent)	40	40
Coal (lb/mile) (inclusive)	52.6	58.7
(lb/mile) (exclusive of lighting up)	48.6	54.5
(lb/dhp hour)	3.94	4.29
Water (gallons per mile)	38.3	40.4
(lb/dhp hour)	31.0	31.7
Evaporation (lb of water per lb of coal)	7.47	7.7

*Later 4472 *Flying Scotsman.*

LNER 'Pacifics': 1923

Section	**GN**	**NE**
Cylinders		
Diameter (inches)	20	19
Stroke (inches)	26	26
Piston valves diameter (inches)	8	8 ¾
Coupled wheel diameter (feet/inches)	6 8	6 8
Boiler proportions		
Small tubes		
Number	168	119
Outside diameter (inches)	2 ¼	2 ¼
Distance between tubeplates (feet)	19	21
Superheater flues		
Number	32	24
Outside diameter (inches)	5 ¼	5 ¼
Heating surfaces (square feet)		
Small tubes	1,880	1,472
Flues	835	692.7
Firebox	215	200
Superheater	525	509.9
Grate area (square feet)	41.25	41.5
Boiler pressure (lb per square inch)	180	200
Tractive effort (lb)	29,835	29,918

In the autumn of 1923 some interesting trials were run between Newcastle and Edinburgh with 'Atlantic' engines of the three East Coast constituents. The only disadvantage of these was that the Ivatt 32-element superheater type of the Great Northern had to be modified to clear the Scottish loading gauge. Engine No 1447, the chosen representation, had her chimney and dome cover shortened. Whether or not some adjustment to the position of the blast pipe was made I do not know; for, although the chimney was tapered internally, the shortened version might have resulted in the exhaust cone from the blast pipe not *quite* filling the chimney, and resulting in some lessening of the draught so essential to free steaming. Although one of the most resolute and adaptable Kings Cross drivers of the day went north with her, none other than Albert Pibworth, who was to do so well on another Interchange Trials, two years later, the Great Northern 'Atlantic' turned in the poorest performance of the three between Newcastle and Edinburgh. One can speculate upon how different the results might have been if the test route had been between Doncaster and Kings Cross.

These 'Atlantic' trials in 1923 are very important in dispelling some very wrong impressions that may have been created in more recent times, by a Scottish writer who should have known better, as to the performance and general efficiency of the North British 'Atlantics'. A driver himself, with an easy and attractive style of writing, he was inclined to besmirch his consistent plaudits of the Gresley engines by occasional denigration of all others, and the North British 'Atlantics' came in for no small share of this. Unfortunately, because of his work on the footplate, readers in the 1950s would tend to regard his views as authentic, instead of being a matter of personal preference; and it was unfortunately not until these effusions had been published that in another quest altogether I gained access to

the official reports of the 1923 trials, as contained in the records of the Darlington dynamometer car runs. The truth is evident from the statistics tabulated below; but by the way of a supplement I can say that from personal experience on the footplate, mainly with Dundee men in the mid-1930s, I found the North British 'Atlantics' hard working and willing engines, very comfortable to ride, and the reverse of extravagant in coal consumption in heavy express work. The North Eastern 3-cylinder 'Atlantics' of the 'Z' Class I never rode; but all who had anything to do with them praised them to the skies!

LNER 'Atlantic' engines
The 1923 dynamometer car tests: Newcastle-Edinburgh

Railway	GNR	NER	NMB
Engine no	1447	733	878*
Average load (tons tare)			
Service trains	307	311	345
Special trains	406	406	406
Average speed (mph)†			
Service trains	49.3	49.0	48.8
Special trains	46.0	47.2	47.5
Average drawbar (horsepower)			
Service trains	393	391	529
Special trains	527	529	525
Average steam chest pressure (lb per square inch)			
Special trains	97	132	138
Average cut-off per cent			
Special trains	40	42	38
Coal (per dhp hour)			
Service trains	5.08	4.45	4.12
Special trains	4.42	3.63	4.15
Average superheat temperature (degrees)	624	577	520
Evaporation (lb of water per lb of coal)	7.2	8.6	8.2

*Named *Hazeldean*.
†Inclusive of various checks on most runs.

LNER: one of standard Great Northern 'Atlantics' experimentally fitted with a booster engine which drove the pair of trailing wheels under the cab (British Railways).

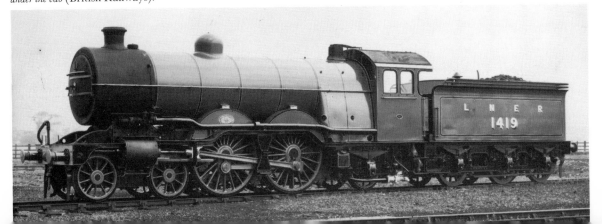

The curiosity among the above results is how the crew of the North Eastern 'Z' managed to bring the basic coal consumption down from 4.45 to 3.63 lb per drawbar horsepower hour, between the service and special train test runs. When another engine of the class, No 729, was put through a week of trial running a year later, in competition with a 2-cylinder 'V1' Class 'Atlantic' having exactly the same boiler, with loads made up daily to 365 tons tare, and making average speeds of 45.7 mph, the coal consumption over the five days averaged 4.6 lb per drawbar horsepower hour, so that one can regard the 3.63 lb in the one round trip in 1823 as something of a freak result. One feels that 4.63 would be nearer the mark. In passing I may add that the 2-cylinder 'V1' engine, No 701, working the same trains at comparable average speed, had an average coal consumption of 6.03 lb per drawbar horsepower hour. There were no movements of 'Atlantic' engines away from their originating areas as a result of these runs.

On the LMS; the process of establishing the Deeley-Fowler superheater compound as the premier passenger locomotive of the line (in readiness for the projected reorganisation of the whole timetable on Midland principles) took place in four stages, all accompanied by full-dress dynamometer car trials. These four stages were:

1 Carlisle-Leeds and back: Class '4' engines: Compound: '999' 4-4-0: LNWR 'Prince of Wales' 4-6-0.

2 Carlisle-Leeds and back: Compounds: LNWR 'Claughton' Caledonian Pickersgill 4-4-0 (Class 3).

3 Carlisle-Leeds and back: Experimental changes to 6 foot 9 inch standard compounds.

4 Carlisle-Preston and back: Compound: 'Prince of Wales': 'Claughton': L & Y 4-6-0.

Referring particularly to groups 1 and 2, made in December 1923/January 1924 and November/December 1924 respectively, four different compound engines were involved, two of the

North Eastern Railway: a Class 'V1' engine, No 697, attached to the Darlington dynamometer car (British Railways).

standard Midland Railway 7 foot superheater type, and two of the new short-chimneyed LMS series, with 6 foot 9 inch wheels, and larger cylinders. Of the 7 foot engines the performance of No 1008 in Group 1 was as good as that of No 1023 in Group 2 was bad. In the official report no explanation was given for the complete failure of the latter engine to keep anywhere near to schedule time; and the basic coal consumption recorded, while generally in line with average compound performance relates to what was virtually a train with a much lower running speed.

The Midland '999' Class, although running over her regular route, was outclassed, and dropped out of further consideration while, in the first group of trials, the LNWR 'Prince of Wales' Class 4-6-0, while making an excellent return so far as time-keeping was concerned, was up against an outstanding compound in No 1008. The average coal consumption of the LNWR engine on five return trips from Carlisle to Leeds and back was 4.6 lb per drawbar horsepower hour, whereas No 1008 used, on an average, no more than 4.0 lb. This was the kind of data that the Midland faction needed to secure authorisation for constructing many more compounds, and it was with some of the earliest of these latter that the second group of trials took place, in the winter of 1924.

Three compound engines were involved this time, the unfortunate 1023 which did totally inferior work throughout, and two new engines, Nos 1065 and 1066. Largely as the result of the remarkable work of engine No 1008 in the first group of trials, Derby had been encouraged to increase the tractive effort of the new compounds authorised, by increasing the cylinder diameters to 19¾ inches high pressure and 21¾ inches low pressure. At the same time the coupled wheel diameter was reduced to 6 feet 9 inches. The latter remained standard for all compounds built by the LMS.

In the second group of trials, carried out between Carlisle and Leeds in November and December 1924, the first two engines of the short-chimneyed series, Nos 1065 and 1066, did some very fine work;

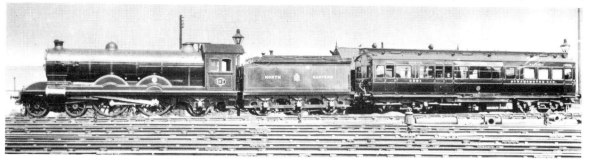

the latter engine in particular made the fastest time (with a 350-ton load) ever recorded in these trials between Settle Junction and Blea Moor. But the pundits of Derby were disturbed to find that both this engine and No 1065 were doing their consistently fine work on a considerably higher coal consumption than that of No 1008, a year earlier, while the abject failure of No 1023—by all official reckonings a sister engine of No 1008—added to the feelings of concern. Six tests with engines 1065 and 1066 gave an average coal consumption of 4.46 lb per dhp hour, not much less than the 4.6 lb of the LNWR 'Prince of Wales' and 11½ per cent higher than that of No 1008.

The rivals of the compounds in the second group of trials had no influence on immediate LMS policy. The Caledonian Pickersgill 4-4-0, tried at the express wish of W. Barr, was manifestly unequal to the job, and lost time with 300-ton trains and even that on a very heavy coal consumption. The 'Claughton' was not in the best of condition, and although finding no difficulty in running even the heaviest of the test trains to time, did so on a coal consumption greater than that of the competing compounds. But concern at Derby over compound performance in the most severe conditions led to experimental changes being made to two engines, Nos 1060 and 1065, and a further set of trials was run in February 1925. The former had the blast pipe orifice reduced from 4¾ to 4½ inches, and a 'petticoat' fitted to the underside of the chimney to ensure that the reduced cone of exhaust steam exactly fitted the chimney. Engine 1065 had the cylinders lined up to the original size of the pure-Midland compounds, namely 19 inches high pressure, and 21 inches low pressure. As might be expected, No 1060, with the reduced blastpipe orifice, steamed very freely; but the opinion expressed in the test report was that No 1065 had given a better all-round performance, on a reduced coal consumption compared to her work in the

North Eastern Railway: a Class 'Z' 3-cylinder 'Atlantic', No 709, fitted with indicator shelters for dynamometer car testing (T.B. Parley).

previous November. Her average was now 4.18 lb per dhp hour against 4.71 lb of No 1060. As a result the arrangements on No 1065 were adopted as standard on all compounds subsequently built for the LMS.

The group 4 tests were engineered by Horwich. There is no doubt that the paper presented to the World Power Conference of 1924 by C.B. Collett, Chief Mechanical Engineer of the Great Western Railway, in which he quoted a coal consumption of 2.83 lb per dhp hour, on behalf of engine No 4074, *Caldicot Castle*, had shaken Horwich to its foundations. They had been pleased enough that the rebuilding and superheating of the 4-cylinder 4-6-0s had brought the basic coal consumption down from something over 7 to 5 lb per dhp hour; but 2.83—it was staggering! (I found later, when I had an opportunity of studying the Swindon records, that the '2.83' was the best of three return trips from Swindon to Plymouth and back; but the differences between the three were really no more than marginal.)

Anyway, Horwich set to work to produce a layout of long-lap, long-travel valves for the Hughes 4-cylinder 4-6-0s, and the first engine so equipped was in some ways the centrepiece of attraction in the series of trials run between Carlisle and Preston in the spring of 1925. This was a quadripartite affair in which Class '4' and Class '5' engines were involved, the results therefrom I analysed very fully in *The Railway Magazine* for May 1963. These tests were perhaps the most important of any conducted in the early days of the LMS. All four engines involved were in comparably good condition, and all were enthusiastically driven and fired, so that one can say they were representative of the best performance of the engines concerned.

The two Class '4' engines, the North Western 'Prince' No 90, *Kestrel*, and the Midland compound No 1065, were tested with 300-ton trains, while the Class '5s', 'Claughton' No 30, *Thalaba*, and the Horwich 4-6-0, took trains of 400 tons; and all four made runs with 350-ton trains. Southbound from Carlisle the schedule allowed 114 minutes for the 90.1 miles to Preston, but returning north the allowance was only 103 minutes—one minute faster than that of the pre-war 2 pm 'Corridor' from Euston, and generally regarded as a standard of comparison for this section of the West Coast route. The enginemen were given a free hand as to how they handled their engines, except for a strict instruction that the uphill point-to-point timings must be kept. There was to be no 'coal-dodging', by going easily uphill, and regaining time by high speed afterwards, and the voluminous details of the running contained in the official report make it clear that this instruction was obeyed. The compound ran true to the excellent form she had shown on the Midland line in February while, on the Hughes 4-6-0, the fitting of long-lap, long-travel valves failed to bring her basic coal consumption below that of the 'Claughton', or indeed below 5 lb per dhp hour.

LMSR Carlisle-Preston trials: May 1925

Coal consumption

Railway (pre-group)	LNWR	LMS (Midland)	LYR	LNWR
Engine no (name)	90 *Kestrel*	1065	10460	30 *Thalaba*
300-ton trains				
lb/mile	40.1	38.1	—	—
lb/dhp hour	5.1	4.29	—	—
350-ton trains				
lb/mile	48.3	43.4	51.3	42.4
lb/dhp hour	5.05	4.25	5.07	4.78
400-ton trains				
lb/mile	—	—	58.1	52.7
lb/dhp hour	—	—	5.13	4.75

One point that will immediately be noted from the summary results tabulated herewith was that the coal consumption of the 'Claughton', in working the 350 ton train, was the lowest of all the competitors, in pounds per train mile. That of the Midland compound was higher, because of a somewhat exhuberant climb of the Grayrigg bank, gaining time and using more coal than would otherwise have been necessary to fulfil the test conditions. Related to the actual work done, in drawbar horse-power hours, her consumption was the lowest. It should be added that these tests were completed,

Above *LNER/North British: The 'Queen of 'Scots' Pullman express arriving in Edinburgh from Glasgow hauled by ex-NBR 'Atlantic' engine, No 9877, Liddesdale.*

Below *Midland Railway: one of the '999' Class '4' superheated 4-4-0s competing in the Leeds-Carlisle trials of 1923* (British Railways).

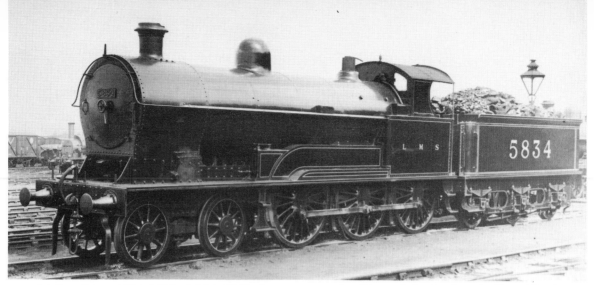

LNW/LMS: a 'Prince of Wales' Class 4-6-0 in LMS colours. Engine No 388 of this class ran in the 1923/4 trials (British Railways).

and the report issued from Horwich just before Hughes' retirement. The results from the ex-LYR 4-cylinder 4-6-0, despite the alteration to the valve-gear, was a continuing disappointment to Horwich, and henceforth that works became subjugated to Derby. By that time there were 55 of the 4-6-0s in service. The last 20 were originally ordered as 4-6-4 tanks, as an addition to the 10 engines of the 11110-9 Class, and the frames were already cut; but the need for large express tank engines was not pressing, and they were completed as 4-6-0s.

The 1925 trials between Carlisle and Preston were made with special trains. No report was made public at the time and, apart from a five-line paragraph in *The Locomotive* of May 15, noting the commencement of the work 10 days earlier, no further references were made in any journal of the railway press. It was not surprising, because at that time the British railway world, and all its non-professional followers, were agog with interest in the results of the recent interchange trials between a Gresley 'Pacific' of the LNER and one of the latest Great Western 4-cylinder 4-6-0s of the 'Castle' Class. The seeds of this widely publicised, and often misrepresented, confrontation were seen at the British Empire Exhibition at Wembley in 1924, when engines 4073, *Caerphilly Castle*, and the Gresley 'Pacific' No 4472, specially named *Flying Scotsman*, stood back to back on adjacent stands.

The 'Castle' was of course no more than a development of the very successful 'Star' Class of Churchward's design, and was in the first place something of a compromise. It was the heaviest engine that the civil engineer would then permit over the West of England main line. The larger boiler, with the evaporative heating surface increased from 1,841.38 to 2,018.07 square feet, brought the maximum axle load from 18.6 to 19.7 tons, and the increase in cylinder diameter from 15 to 16 inches pushed the nominal tractive effort up from 27,800 to 31,625 lb, making the 'Castle' nominally the most powerful passenger engine in Great Britain. The publicists of Paddington did not fail to emphasise this in their display at Wembley in 1924.

How this mild 'challenge' to the abilities of the much larger engine on the adjoining stand became blown up into the Interchange Trials that eventuated in the following spring will never be entirely clear; but one thing is certain, the 'challenge' to the 'Castle', if such it ever was, did not originate with Gresley, or any of his staff. It was engineered at considerably higher level, even than that of chief mechanical engineers. At the time Gresley was by no means satisfied with his 'Pacifics', and experiments had already begun at Doncaster with changes in the valve gear. He was, from all accounts, a rather unwilling participant in the whole idea of an interchange trial. Horwich was not the only locomotive centre that had been shaken by the paper C.B. Collett presented to the World Power Conference of 1924; and although the Gresley 'Pacifics', from the trials of 1923 referred to earlier in this chapter, seemed a good deal better than the Hughes 4-6-0s, there was a big difference between 4 lb per dhp hour registered in the Kings Cross-Doncaster tests against the NER engine, and the 2.83 lb claimed by Collett. The work actually commenced at Doncaster before the time of the 1925 interchange trials, had the object of redressing the adverse balance.

The running of the competing engines during the week April 27-May 2 was more fully documented.

so far as times and speeds were concerned, than any similar event before or since, and a mass of data was published in *The Railway Magazine* of July and August 1925, by Cecil J. Allen. But, even before this first article appeared, the fires of acrimony had been well and truly stoked. Even at that early date Allen had made his mark as a broadcaster in some of the modest programmes put over the air in the early days of the BBC, and, shortly after the trials were ended, he gave a reasoned commentary which apparently was not to the liking of Paddington. When it became known that he was an employee of the LNER, the rivals felt that it was up to them to issue their views of the results, and this they did in somewhat equivocal style in the *Great Western Railway Magazine* for June, including details of the coal consumption, which were not intended to be made public. The fat was now truly in the fire! Gresley was furious, and although *The Locomotive* in its issue of June 15 tried to smooth things over in its peroration to a brief comment on the results, the locomotive department of GWR found itself outside the comity of the profession for many years afterwards. The article in question concluded: 'Each locomotive is built for its own special service, conditions and road, and the recent friendly exchange of engines, although interesting and providing healthy competition, is of little value from a technical standpoint'.

One could not, of course, disregard the sporting aspect of an event which attracted a tremendous amount of popular interest, and intense partisanship on the Great Western side; and, as a contest in train running, the Great Western undoubtedly won. The result did not, however, have the startling influence on future LNER locomotive practice that some of their most perfervid supporters imagined. Gresley was well enough aware that, so far as overall economy in working was concerned, his 'Pacific' engines were not in the top flight, although they seemed better than most of the engines for which he had assumed responsibility at the time of grouping. The 'Pacifics' were amply adequate for any service requirements on the East Coast main line at that time, and experiments with the valve gear could be taken with the deliberation desirable in dealing with that part of the engine machinery. Discussion continued into the autumn in the columns of *The Railway Magazine*, and Cecil J. Allen himself wound up a particularly controversial phase of it with the apposite words: 'Publicity, indeed, seems to have gained more than science in the locomotive exchange of 1925'.

After all the excitement generated by the GW

Great Western Railway: the 'Castle' Class 4-6-0 of 1923 figured prominently in several interchange trials.

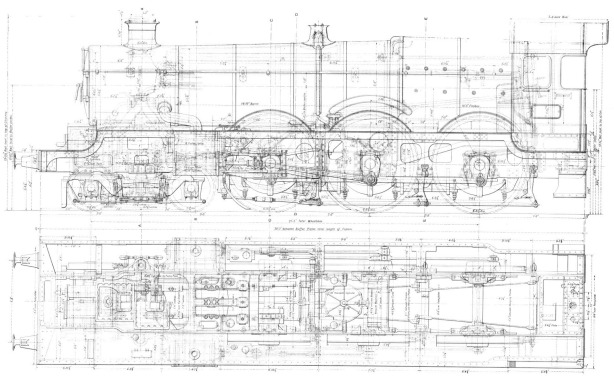

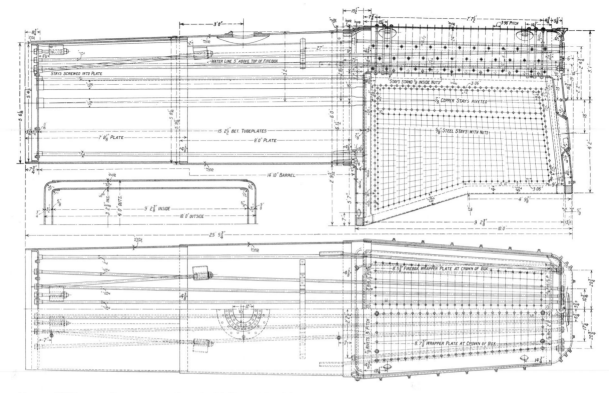

Above GWR: *general arrangement of standard boiler on 'Castle' Class locomotives.*

Right Caledonian Railway: *a Pickersgill 4-4-0, of which No 124 of this class made a return trial trip from Carlisle to Leeds and back in 1924* (British Railways).

Below *Sectional views of the 'Castle' boiler showing the changing cross-sections from front to rear.*

Below right LMS/LNW: *'Claughtons' were involved in various trials in the 1920s, seen here is No 5938 (LNW 2097 built in 1917) at Willesden shed.*

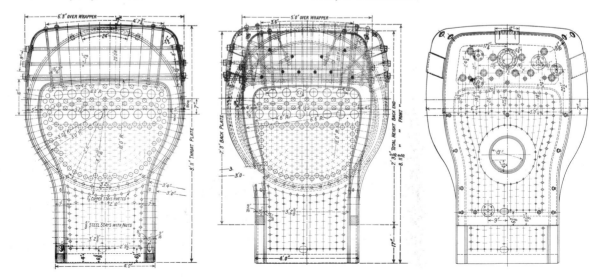

versus LNER exchange, the centre of technical development reverted for a time to the LMS. There, following Fowler's appointment as Chief Mechanical Engineer, in succession to Hughes, the headquarters of the department was moved from Horwich to Derby; and, in view of the results of the Carlisle-Preston trials of May 1925, it was felt that a super-Midland compound with the 4-6-0 wheel arrangement would be a better proposition than either the 'Claughton' or the Horwich 4-6-0 for the heavier West Coast main line duties. In the autumn of 1925 the design of a 3-cylinder compound 4-6-0 on purely Midland lines was worked out in some detail in the Derby drawing office. The important difference from the compound 4-4-0s was that it was to have piston instead of slide valves for the low pressure cylinders, and that the valve gear was to be Walschaerts.

In the meantime one of Sir Henry's pupils, E.L. Diamond, had been preparing a paper for the graduate's section of the Institution of Mechanical Engineers that was to prove a positively monumental effort. He, with others of the young men of Derby had been one of the dynamometer car crew on the Carlisle-Leeds trials of March 1925, when the two compounds, Nos 1060 and 1065, were in competition. Those trials were more elaborate than the earlier ones in that the engines were indicated, and that one could make an assessment of what was happening in the cylinders as well as measuring the end product, as it were, in the work done in hauling the train. Diamond's paper, which was presented to the Institution early in 1926 was entitled: 'An Investigation into the Cylinder Losses in a Compound Locomotive'. By a meticulous examination of all the indicator cards taken on tests, and

construction of the 'combined' indicator diagrams showing the work done in the high and low pressure cylinders in correct juxtaposition, he was able to evaluate the losses occurring at different speeds and in different conditions of working.

The Midland compounds were generally considered to be locomotives of high efficiency, and yet the total losses due to restricted passage given to the steam at admission and exhaust, admittedly through two stages of expansion, rose to no less than 67.6 per cent at 68 mph, of which not more than about 15 per cent was necessary for production of draught. Put in other words, an amount of power equal to half that being used in hauling the train was being wasted in throttling losses. This was a somewhat staggering revelation, and to no one more so

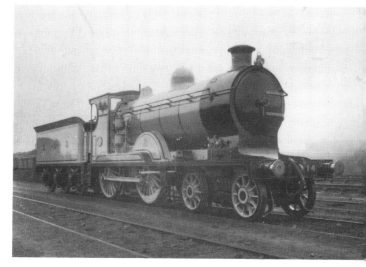

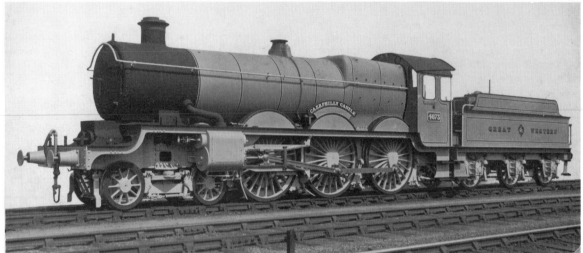

Opposite page, top to bottom

LMS: one of the Hughes 4-cylinder 4-6-0s (LYR design) in the LMS style of painting (British Railways).

Great Western Railway: an official photograph of the first 'Castle' Class 4-6-0 in the summer of 1923 (British Railways).

GWR: the second 'Castle', No 4074, Caldicot Castle, with a dynamometer car and train of empty coaches ready for the Swindon-Plymouth test runs of March 1924. This engine also represented the GWR in the Interchange Trials of 1925 against the LNER on the Cornish Riviera Express (British Railways).

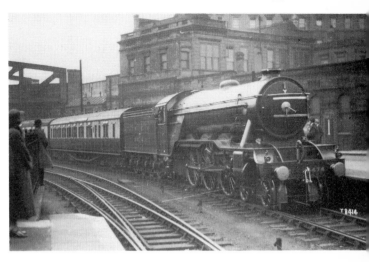

Right *LNER: Gresley 'Pacific' No 4474, then unnamed, entering Paddington, on time, with the up Cornish Riviera Express during the 1925 Interchange Trials* (Real Photographs).

than Sir Henry Fowler himself, who was in the audience. He took the manuscript of the paper back to Derby with him, and promptly scrapped the design of the valve gear of the new 2-6-4 tank engines then on the drawing boards. He also laid aside the plans for a 3-cylinder compound 4-6-0, and began work instead on a 4-cylinder compound 'Pacific', on the lines of the Bréville type recently introduced on the Northern Railway of France. Details of the cylinder losses measured on these locomotives were communicated by Monsieur Bréville himself in the written discussion on Diamond's paper.

The year, nevertheless, was 1926, and train working on the LMS and everywhere else was disrupted, first by the 'General Strike', and then by the prolonged coal strike. To save fuel, the strict piloting regulations on the West Coast main line of the LMS were waived, and the ex-LNWR locomotives, particularly 'Claughtons', took very heavy loads without assistance, and on schedules little or nothing decelerated from normal times. The success with which they did so, and the readiness of the footplate staff to drive and fire the engines appropriately hard impressed the Superintendent of Motive Power, not to the extent of relaxing his natural antipathy to anything except Midland engines, but to oppose his former chief's plans for the 4-cylinder compound 'Pacific', which he considered quite unnecessary. The fact that a larger-boilered 'Claughton' was being planned in the Crewe drawing office encouraged him in this view.

However, the construction of two compound 'Pacifics' had already been authorised and the frames had been cut. Swift action was necessary; the weighty influence of the operating department prevailed with the high management and Fowler was

instructed to stop work on the 'Pacific'. Plans for the enlarged 'Claughton' went quietly ahead, but significantly enough for Cecil J. Allen to mention this development in *The Railway Magazine* in November 1926. To have written thus he would need to have been in possession of the information by the latter end of September.

In the meantime events had been moving in the very highest echelons of the LMS. By that time Sir Guy Granet had succeeded Lord Lawrence as Chairman, and there is evidence to show that he was growing increasingly concerned about the interdepartmental rivalries which seemed to be bedevilling progress, particularly in the locomotive departments. While appreciating the loyalty of the former Midland men to the precepts of operation originally propounded, and brilliantly executed by Sir Cecil Paget, he began to form the opinion that a blend of North Western and Midland practice would be more appropriate to the prevailing conditions in the later 1920s. It is known that Granet was a close personal friend of Sir Felix Pole, General Manager of the GWR and it is unlikely that at some time he did not confide his misgivings, particularly on the vexed question of motive power. It is also equally likely that Pole, always anxious to publicise the merits of his own company, suggested, 'Why not try one of ours?'. Whether this was the precise sequence of events cannot be said for certain; but in fact arrangements were made for a 'Castle' Class 4-6-0 to be loaned to the LMS, and Fowler was instructed to subject it to dynamometer car trials between Euston and Carlisle.

Actually the trials were carried out in two stages, the first was two weeks between Euston and Crewe, making the runs on a double-home basis, and then, after a week's pause, the second stage was on the

Sequel to many LMS trials: the Midland compound standardised. No 1137 was one of a batch of 25 built by the North British Locomotive Company in 1925 (North British Locomotive Company).

Crewe-Carlisle section. It was only during the second week of running on the 1.10 pm from Crewe to Carlisle, and on the 12.20 pm up, that the Horwich dynamometer car was actually used. On the southern section of the line, against non-stop schedules of 175 minutes in each direction for the 158.1 miles, the 'Castle' made net times of 167 minutes with 470 tons, and 166½ minutes with 505 tons, with time generally well in hand on all occasions; but in the north things did not go quite so smoothly. The maximum load taken unassisted over Shap was 430 tons, and in bad weather difficulty was experienced when strong side winds blew the sand clear of the rails. The Great Western Railway had always used gravity, instead of steam sanding,

and this feature was not effective in the Westmorland fell country in November. Otherwise, however, the engine had no difficulty in maintaining overall time, although the basic coal consumption in lb per drawbar horsepower was far above the 2.83 that had 'set the heather on fire' in 1924. Between Crewe and Carlisle in 1926 it was 3.8 lb, only a little below the best compound figures between Preston and Carlisle.

The last of the dynamometer car trials with *Launceston Castle* were not completed until November 20, and Fowler was then instructed to get 50 engines of comparable power ready for the summer traffic of 1927—*50!* How the 'Royal Scot' 4-6-0s were designed, constructed, and the first of them got into traffic by July of the following year, was an epic in itself, though a sequel rather than a constituent part of the interchange trials of the 1923-6 period. Some of the test runs made by *Launceston Castle* on the LMS were detailed in *The Railway Magazine* for March 1927.

15. The Gresley 3-cylinder designs

At the time of the Railway Centenary celebrations in 1925 the presentation of Gresley's paper on 'Three-Cylinder Locomotives', at the summer meeting of the Institution of Mechanical Engineers in Newcastle-on-Tyne, drew attention to the origins of the derived valve gear for the piston valve of the inside cylinder, by which the need for a separate third set of motion was obviated. James Clayton, of the Southern Railway, had referred to H. Holcroft's patent of 1909, and it was this form of derived gear, rather than the one designed at Doncaster and fitted to the first Gresley 3-cylinder engine, the 2-8-0, No 461, that was adopted as the future standard on the Great Northern, and later on the LNER. The first engine to be so equipped was the very much enlarged version of the mixed traffic 'Moguls', No 1000, built at Doncaster in 1920. Although extremely massive, by current standards, it was a very handsome and elegantly proportioned locomotive, and while the preceeding Great Northern 'Moguls' of the '1640' or 'K2' Class had been finished in freight engine grey the '1000' Class, of which there were 10, were painted in the handsome and traditional 'passenger' green.

In 1920 one can recall that they attracted more attention from the unusually large diameter of their boilers than from the valve gear. There was good reason for this interest, because it was the first time a British locomotive had been fitted with a parallel boiler having an outside diameter as great as 6 feet. The barrel was relatively short, 12 feet, and ideally proportioned for free steaming. This was necessary for the total heating surface, including the 32-element superheater, 2,308 square feet was not unduly large for a locomotive with a tractive effort of 30,031 lb. Although originally designated 'fast goods' the 10 engines of the class were extensively used on express passenger trains during the period of restricted service following the coal strike of 1921, and train loads up to 600 tons were taken on the schedules then in force. These engines had a very efficient firebox, deep and narrow sloping towards the front. The length was 8 feet $2\frac{1}{8}$ inches inside, with a grate area of 28 square feet. The original 10 engines had the traditional Great Northern style of cab; but when in later years the design was made into an LNER standard, and many more were built, a larger side-windowed cab of North Eastern type was fitted. The basic dimensions were, cylinders $18\frac{1}{2}$ inches by 26 inches; coupled wheel diameter of 5 feet 8 inches, and boiler pressure 180 lb per square inch.

The piston valves, 8 inches in diameter, were large in relation to the cylinder diameter and this, with good port openings, made a very free-running locomotive. In passenger service, speeds of 75 mph were regularly attained. The free running was also assisted by the high degree of superheat attained which, by the fluidity of the hot dry steam, contributed to the freedom with which it flowed through ports and passages. The 10 engines Nos 1000-1009 were fitted with pyrometer gauges in the cab, so the driver could see the actual temperature of the steam entering the steam chests. Some foot-plate observations made by the Technical Editor of *The Railway Magazine*, when witnessing the working of an express passenger train of 605 tons, in 1921, showed that first on engine No 1006 and then on No 1007, the superheat varied between 650 and 700 degrees F. With this very heavy train, the first engine made a net running time of $97\frac{1}{2}$ minutes for the $79\frac{1}{2}$ miles from Doncaster to Peterborough, including the slowing down and acceleration from three intermediate stops. Engine No 1007, covered the 63.7 miles from Peterborough start to passing Potters Bar in 75 minutes; but a deviation to slow line afterwards, with running under caution signals, caused the last 12.7 miles into Kings Cross to take 20 minutes.

Great Northern Railway: the first 3-cylinder 'Mogul' No 1000 (then painted green) on the Scotch express goods (vacuum fitted) (F.E. Mackay).

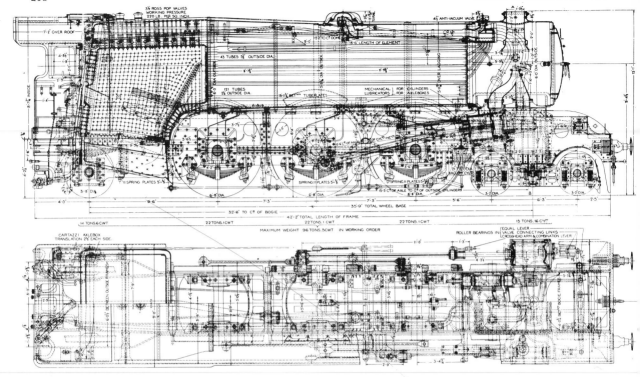

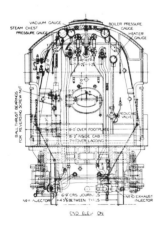

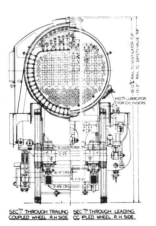

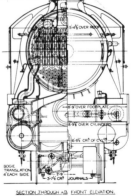

LNER: the Gresley non-streamlined 'Pacific' as finalised in the 'A3'—the general arrangement.

The modified arrangement of the derived valve gear for the inside cylinder was next applied to a batch of 2-8-0 heavy freight engines. They had the same cylinder dimensions and boiler pressure as the '1000' Class 'Moguls', and a tractive effort of 36,470 lb. One of these engines was the subject of an interesting comparison with an earlier 2-cylinder 2-8-0 of the type referred to in Chapter 7 of this book, and described in Gresley's paper to the 'Mechanicals' in 1925. Each engine made two return trips from Peterborough to Clarence Yard, Hornsey, outward with coal trains loaded to a tonnage of around 1300, and returning on the following day with a corresponding load of empties, weighing around 420 tons. Weather conditions favoured the 2-cylinder engine, though at the relatively slow speeds maintained strong winds and rain that were encountered by the 3-cylinder engine would not have made any appreciable difference. In any case the coal consumption per drawbar horse-power hour was consistently lower by the three-cylinder engine. The four successive trips by the two engines gave the following values of lb per dhp hour: 2-cylinder—5.26, 5.36, 5.23, 4.92; 3-cylinder, 4.99, 4.75, 4.58, 4.71. These figures were enough to establish the 3-cylinder '02' as the standard heavy freight and mineral engine of the line.

At the same time Gresley was always prepared to go one better, and prepare against possibly heavier freight haulage requirements, and in the Centenary year of 1925, when the stud of 'Pacific' engines had been augmented by the 40 'general service' engines, with boiler mountings of reduced height, built in 1924, and numbered 2543 to 2582, the two experimental 2-8-2 freight engines, Class 'P1', were built at Doncaster. These engines, No 2393 and 2394, had the same boilers, cylinders and motion as the 'Pacifics', but with 5 foot 2 inch coupled wheels the tractive effort was 38,500 lb. These engines were fitted with boosters on the rear trailing axle, and when this was in operation the tractive effort was increased by 8,500 lb. They worked loaded coal trains of 1,600 tons between Peterborough and Clarence Yard. It was a great sight to see and hear them in full blast, with the booster in action, climbing the long 1 in 200 gradient from Hitchin to Stevenage.

Gresley's final contribution to Centenary Year was the Garratt. This great engine, like Fowler's 4-cylinder 0-10-0 on the Midland, was designed purely for banking, on the 2½-mile Worsborough incline between Wath and Penistone. The west-bound coal trains were made up to a gross load of about 1,000 tons, and from Wath yard hauled by two ex-GCR 2-8-0s (LNER Class 04). From Wombwell there was usually one 2-8-0 in front, and another banking in rear until the train came to Wentworth. There a stop was made and the Garratt buffered up in rear to assist up the 2½ miles of 1 in 40 to West Silkstone Junction. The Garratt was the equivalent of two '02' 2-8-0s, and had a tractive effort of 72,940 lb. The machinery was exactly the same as that of the '02', and to supply the six cylinders, a huge boiler of typical Garratt proportions was provided: short length, very large diameter, and a grate area of 56.4 square feet. In her strenuous career she managed about 18 banking trips every 24 hours. She was, of course, built by Beyer, Peacock & Co, though using standard

Right *Great Northern Railway: the kind of working the 'Pacifics' eliminated—the 'Flying Scotsman' leaving Kings Cross with a superheater 0-6-2 tank, No 1727, piloting an Ivatt 'Atlantic'.*

Below *Great Northern Railway: heavy load test run (610 tons) with the second Gresley 'Pacific', No 1471, in 1922, passing New Southgate* (Real Photographs).

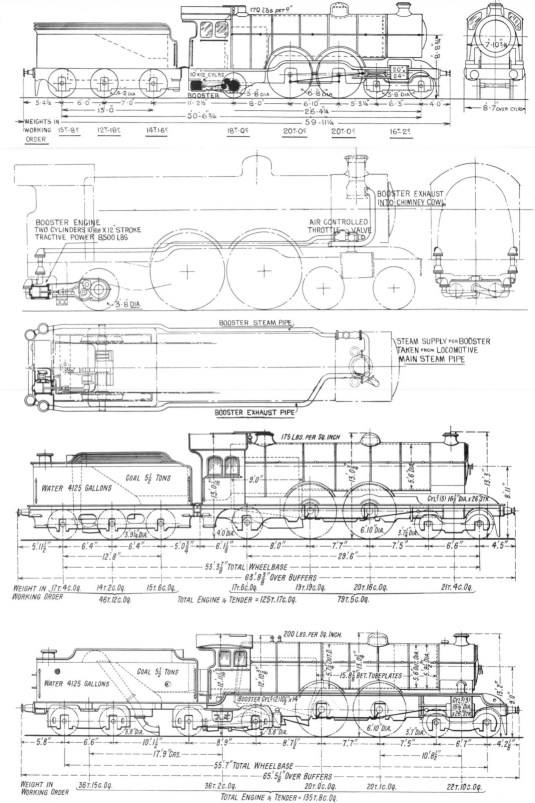

Left *LNER: two drawings of Gresley's experiments with boosters showing the dimensioned diagram of the large boilered GNR Atlantic No 1419, as so equipped, and details of the application.*

Below left *LNER: the North Eastern application of the booster—a Class 'Z' before and after modification.*

Right *LNER: diagrammatic layout of booster and connections.*

Below right *Tabulated details of engines as equipped.*

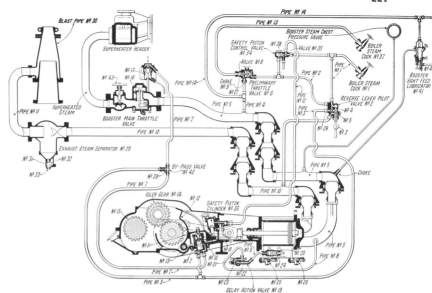

Doncaster parts for all the machinery. She, again, was a tremendously impressive engine to see in action.

Returning now to the 'Pacifics', Gresley had sometimes to tread warily with the various main works, particularly in matters with which his assistant, O.V.S. Bulleid, was dealing. Bulleid was never exactly the soul of tact, and there were times when friction was generated, and so Gresley did not press Wintour over the modified valve gear that he was developing at Doncaster. No acceleration of main line train services was contemplated in the immediate future, and generally the 'Pacifics' were coping well with current demands, even in cases of exceptional loading. In the summer and autumn of 1926, when large tonnages of foreign coal had to be imported to offset the effects of the prolonged strike in our own coalfields, following the collapse of the General Strike in May, there were cases of bad steaming; but this was common enough on all the British railways at that time. By that same autumn, however, Wintour had the first 'Pacific' fitted up with the modified valve gear, No 4477 *Gay Crusader*. Some indicator trials were run between Doncaster and Kings Cross, and the results seemed promising.

Because of Gresley's apparently lukewarm attitude to the project the drawing office at Doncaster determined that there should be a minimum of alteration to existing parts. New piston valves with $1\frac{5}{8}$ inches lap (instead of $1\frac{1}{2}$ inches) were fitted, but the maximum valve travel was increased by no more than $\frac{3}{8}$ inch to bring it up to a maximum of $4\frac{15}{16}$ inches and no more than a few slight changes to the links were necessary. *Gay Crusader* proved a free running engine, but Bert

	N.E. Section—Atlantics.			G.N. Section—Atlantic Class C.1.	
	As Originally Built.	As Rebuilt.	Booster.	Engine.	Booster.
Grate area	27	30	—	13	—
Tractive effort at 85 per cent. B.P.	19,300 lb.	22,012 lb.	5,000 lb.	17,340 lb.	8,500 lb.
Weight in working order—					
Engine	79 tons 5 cwt.	—	—	74 tons 2 cwt.	—
Tender	46 tons 12 cwt.	—	—	45 tons 2 cwt.	—
Engine and tender	125 tons 17 cwt.	135 tons 8 cwt.	—	117 tons 4 cwt.	--
Tender—					
Water capacity	4,125 gals.	4,125 gals.	—	3,500 gals.	—
Coal capacity	$5\frac{1}{2}$ tons	$5\frac{1}{2}$ tons	—	$6\frac{1}{2}$ tons	—

Spencer, Gresley's personal assistant for locomotives, who had accompanied the first trials, felt that better results could be obtained from a more complete redesign of the valve gear, to give good port openings for both inlet and exhaust in 15 per cent cut-off. Back in London he schemed out a new layout, but at first Gresley showed little interest. At that time both he and Bulleid were very much involved with the design of the 'hush-hush' high pressure compound 4-6-4. At length, however, entirely in response to Spencer's persistence, he agreed to have a 'Pacific' fitted up with the revised valve gear.

The engine chosen for alteration was naturally one based at Doncaster, so that she would be conveniently on hand for the trials which would ensue. The vital statistics of the new gear were $5\frac{3}{4}$ inches travel in full gear, $1\frac{5}{8}$ inches steam lap, lead $\frac{1}{8}$

LNER: the second heavy freight 2-8-2, No 2394, with experimental use of a 62-element 'E' type superheater (British Railways).

inches, exhaust lap 'line and line'. The new gear had larger exhaust openings in 25 per cent cut-off, and good valve events when pulled up as short as 15 per cent. Spencer was convinced it was essential to be able to work freely at this short cut-off in order to equal the thermal efficiencies regularly achieved on Great Western locomotives. The engine thus altered was No 2555, *Centenary*, and, after she had been 'worked in', trials were run between Doncaster and Kings Cross with her matched against a standard engine No 2559, *The Tetrarch*. The result was a triumph of No 2555, because on the round trip, southbound on the 10.51 am and back on the 4 pm, the coal consumption averaged about 40 lb per mile, against something over 50 lb for No 2559. With a sense of triumph Spencer laid the results before Gresley, but to his chagrin the 'great man' appeared to show little interest, and put them on one side. It seemed they had been shelved. Weeks passed, and then one day Gresley called Spencer into his office and said: 'I'm very pleased with that engine. Have the whole lot altered'. Without saying a word to any of his staff he had sought out the workings of No 2555, made a footplate trip on her, and formed his own conclusions.

The change came at a very opportune moment, because having seen the effects of working with higher steam pressure on the Great Western 'Castles', Gresley had determined upon a trial of higher pressures on one or two of the 'Pacifics', quite experimentally. A new boiler was designed for a pressure of 220 lb per square inch. While this was very near to the 225 lb per square inch of Swindon,

in other respects there was no resemblance. Not only was the evaporative heating surface much larger, but the 220 lb 'Pacific' boiler was equipped with a 43-element Robinson superheater, having a heating surface of 703 square feet, against the 262 square feet of the 'Castle'. Comparative dimensions of the 180 and 220 lb 'Pacific' boilers were as follows:

LNER Pacific boilers

	180	220
Pressure (lb per square inch)	180	220
Heating surfaces (square inch)		
Tubes	2,715	2,477
Firebox	215	215
Superheater	525	703
Total	3,455	3,398

The first engine to have the 220 lb boiler, Doncaster based as before, was No 4480, *Enterprise* and, as the original 20 inch cylinders were retained, the tractive effort was increased from 29,835 to 36,465 lb; but although providing greatly enhanced performance, No 4480 was rather too powerful for the duties then required, and had to be run with a partly closed regulator. The Gresley 'Pacifics' since the alteration to the valve gear were the most consistent, in driving technique, of all British locomotives, even including the 4-cylinder 4-6-0s of the Great Western. In my own extensive footplate experience of them it was only once, and then with an engine badly out of condition, that a driver used anything but a fully opened regulator and the shortest cut-off that would do the job. This technique could not be used on No 4480, and on the second engine to be rebuilt at Doncaster with a 220 lb boiler No 2544, *Lemberg*, the cylinders were lined up to 18¼ inch diameter, to make the tractive effort approximately equal to that of the standard engines with 180 lb

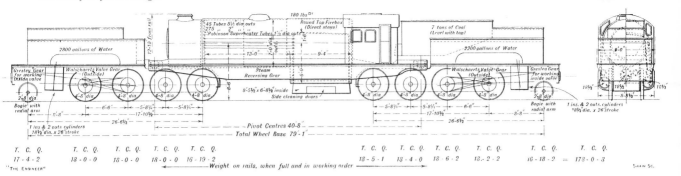

LNER: the Garratt bank engine—dimension and weight diagram.

boilers. Also in 1927 three further 'Pacifics' attached to the North Eastern Area, Nos 2573, 2578, and 2580, received 220 lb boilers, while retaining 20 inch cylinders, it being considered that the higher tractive effort would be an advantage in dealing with the heavier gradients of the East Coast main line north of Berwick-on-Tweed.

Early in 1928 the 18¼ inch engine, No 2544, was subjected to a week of dynamometer car testing between Doncaster and Kings Cross in competition with a standard 180 lb engine, that had been fitted with the modified valve gear. The usual trains were worked, namely the 10.51 am up, and the 4 pm down, and both engines, expertly and enthusiastically driven and fired, turned in an excellent performance. The average results from the fortnight of running slightly favoured the 180 lb engine No 4473, *Solario*, which had an average coal consumption of 3.08 lb per drawbar horsepower hour against 3.12 lb from *Lemberg*; but both showed an astonishing improvement over the figures returned by engine No 4472 in the comparative trials against the North Eastern 'Pacific' in 1923, when, as related in Chapter 14 of this book, the

corresponding figure was 3.94 lb. In quoting the figures for the 1928 trials, however, emphasis must be laid on the variations likely to occur from day to day in tests made on service trains, subject to all the incidental occurrences and delays of ordinary traffic conditions, even when the coal consumption is related to the actual work done on the drawbar between the tender and the dynamometer car. On *Solario*'s six return trips from Doncaster to Kings Cross and back, the coal per dhp hour varied between a maximum of 3.44 and a minimum of 2.89 lb while, in the following week with *Lemberg*, the variations were between 3.27 and 2.92 lb.

These tests took place at a time when an unusual amount of data relating to dynamometer car runs on British railways was being published, and inevitably perhaps the performance of one class of locomotive was being compared with others with a meticulous regard for 'decimal points' that the nature of the tests certainly did not justify. The fact that coal consumptions were not being related merely to the train miles run, leaving inferences to be drawn when the speeds made and the loads

LNER: the 6-cylinder Beyer-Garratt 2-8-0 + 0-8-2 locomotive for use on the Worsborough Incline, near Penistone (Beyer, Peacock & Company).

hauled were taken into account, but were equated to the actual work done on the drawbar of the dynamometer car, seemed to establish a much more reliable basis of comparison—until, that is, one finds that the same engine and crew, on the same round of duty in virtually identical weather conditions, returned consumptions of 3.44 and 2.89 lb per dhp hour on successive days!

Until the road testing of locomotives by dynamometer cars on service trains was superseded by the 'controlled road' system of testing, developed at Swindon in the years following the Second World War (to be described in Volume 2 of this work), the more detailed minutiae of test results must necessarily be regarded in the general light of averages covering a week or more of trial running. The overriding importance of the LNER 'Pacific' trials of February 1928 lay in the demonstration of how careful attention to the valve gear can result in a well-nigh spectacular improvement in the overall efficiency of a locomotive, with a reduction in the basic coal consumption of some 20 per cent. No comparable advance had been made since the introduction of high degree superheating which, as related in an earlier chapter, produced a 25 per cent reduction in express locomotives of the London and North Western Railway.

The LNER tests of February 1928 did not in themselves establish the superiority of the 220 lb boilers, and for the next seven years the 180 and 220 lb engines were used indiscriminately on all the principal express trains. One important point to be noted in the high pressure engines is that the heavier boiler resulted in a maximum axle load of 22 tons (66 tons total adhesion) compared to the 20 tons maximum of the 180 lb engines. That the civil engineer was able to accept this heavier axle loading was due to the findings of the Bridge Stress Committee set up in 1923 by the Department of Scientific and Industrial Research, on which committee the Universities, the Ministry of Transport, the railways, and the consulting engineers to the Indian railways were represented. It is indeed necessary to pause in this account of the Gresley 3-cylinder locomotives to give some account of the work of the Bridge Stress Committee, because its work and the principles it established had no small influence upon the development of later locomotive designs on the LNER, both in Gresley's lifetime and afterwards.

Before leaving the 'Pacifics', however, and the greatly improved performance of those that were fitted with Spencer's arrangement of the valve gear, reference must be made to the inauguration of one of the most spectacular train services the world has ever seen, before or since: the Kings Cross-Edinburgh non-stops, first introduced in the summer of 1928. The upsurge of Anglo-Scottish tourist traffic in the height of the summer had suggested, in 1927, the running of the 9.50 am

LNER post-grouping development of the 3-cylinder 'Mogul' Class 'K3', engine No 134, one of a batch built at Darlington Works in 1925 with a side-windowed cab (The Locomotive Publishing Company).

LNER 'K3' Mogul with a later tender design, one of a batch built by Armstrong Whitworth and Company in 1931 (British Railways).

'relief' to the down 'Flying Scotsman' non-stop to Newcastle, and subsequent market-research showed that in an average summer season there would be enough through traffic to justify a train catering exclusively for passengers travelling from London to Edinburgh, and points north thereof. It was then that the idea of running the 'Flying Scotsman' itself non-stop between Kings Cross and Edinburgh developed.

The greatly improved performance of the 'Pacifics' made this a thoroughly practical proposition from the locomotive point of view, but not for the enginemen; to meet the manning question Gresley devised his celebrated corridor tender, through which one crew could relieve the other at the half-way point of the journey, about 10 miles north of York. No acceleration of the end-to-end time was made, and with the then-standard allowance of 8¼ hours, the average speed over the 392.7 miles was no more than 47.6 mph. But the run, the longest ever regularly made non-stop, *anywhere in the world*, brought immense prestige and publicity to the LNER, and was well worth the care taken to run the train punctually throughout the summer service. For the record, four 'Pacifics' were originally fitted with corridor tenders. The two Kings Cross engines, 4472, *Flying Scotsman*, and 4476, *Royal Lancer*, both retained their original 180 lb boilers, while the two working from Haymarket shed, Edinburgh, were both ones that had been provided with 220 lb boilers, namely 2573, *Harvester*, and 2580, *Shotover*.

Gresley 3-cylinder locomotives

Class (LNER)	'K3'	'O2'	'A1'	'P1'	Garratt*	A3†
Type	2-6-0	2-8-0	4-6-2	2-8-2	2-8-0 + 0-8-2	4-6-2
Cylinders						
Diameter (inches)	18½	18½	20	20	18½	20
Stroke (inches)	26	26	26	26	26	26
Coupled wheel diameter (feet/inches)	5 8	4 8	6 8	5 2	4 8	6 8
Heating surfaces (square feet)						
Tubes	1,719	1,868.5	2,715	2,715	2,644	2,477
Firebox	182	163.5	215	215	224	215
Superheater	407	430.5	525	525	646	703
Grate area (square feet)	28.0	27.5	41.25	41.25	56.4	41.25
Boiler pressure (lb per square inch)	180	180	180	180	180	220
Tractive effort (lb)	30.031	36,470	29,835	38,500	72,930	36,465

*Six-cylinder. †Engines 4480, 2573, 2578 and 2580 only.

Above *LNER: a Gresley experiment with poppet valve gear on a very successful Great Eastern design—one of 10 Class 'B12' 4-6-0s built in 1928 by Beyer, Peacock & Company, with Lentz valve gear* (Beyer, Peacock & Company).

Left *LNER: one of the 1923 batch of A1' 'Pacifics', as fitted with long-lap, long travel valve gear—No 4477,* Gay Crusader.

Left *LNER: a famous Kings Cross 'A1' No 2561,* Minoru, *on the up afternoon* Scotsman *ready to leave Newcastle* (the late W.B. Greenfield).

16. The bridge stress committee and locomotive design

While it is axiomatic that locomotives should not be built to a greater weight than the track and the underline bridges can safely carry, the inter-relation of bridge and locomotive design had not reached critical proportions in Great Britain until the increasing use of heavy corridor stock on express trains timed at start-to-stop average speeds of 50 to 55 mph demanded the building of much larger locomotives than hitherto. Mechanical engineers then found themselves constrained by the limits of maximum axle loading laid down by their civil engineering colleagues, and in the case of certain very large engine designs the routes over which they could operate was very much restricted. On the principal main lines of this country the generally accepted maximum loading was 20 tons per axle; but even where this norm was not exceeded there were some routes, notably that of the shortened West of England main line of the Great Western, where the concentrated weight of Churchward's 'Pacific' engine, *The Great Bear*, could not be accepted. Following 19.9 tons on the leading bogie the weights were 20, 20, and 20 tons, with 17.4 tons on the trailing truck under the firebox.

There was, however, another fact that was to be shown to have an even greater significance than dead weight in the ultimate effect a locomotive had upon the track when running at high speed. With the construction of larger and more powerful locomotives, which until the early 1900s had been most generally of the 2-cylinder type, increasing attention

had necessarily to be given to the balancing of the revolving and reciprocating parts, in order to produce a smooth riding engine; and this was usually done, as evident from many photographs, by casting large balancing weights into the driving wheels. In the early 1900s what was not generally appreciated, in Great Britain at any rate, was the seriousness of the effect of these balancing weights *on the track*; for they induced a 'dynamic augment' to the dead weight on some of the coupled wheels axles, a hammer blow effect, which at high speeds was the most devastating of all loads, a pulsating one of relatively high frequency. On the London and North Western 'George the Fifth' Class 4-4-0, for example, whereas the maximum dead weight on the driving axle was 19.15 tons the hammer blow at maximum speed was no less than 14.1 tons; and this meant that the load applied to the rails was varying between 33.25 and 5.05 tons!

In Chapter 10 I referred briefly to the difficulties put in the way of the LNWR Chief Mechanical Engineer, C.J. Bowen Cooke, at the time the design of the 'Claughton' Class 4-6-0s was in hand at Crewe. The principle on which the drawing office was then working had an historic background that was not generally accepted in British railway circles

London & North Western Railway: a notable example of the 'Claughton' Class which, by arrangement of the machinery, had no hammer blow. The war memorial engine, No 1914, Patriot.

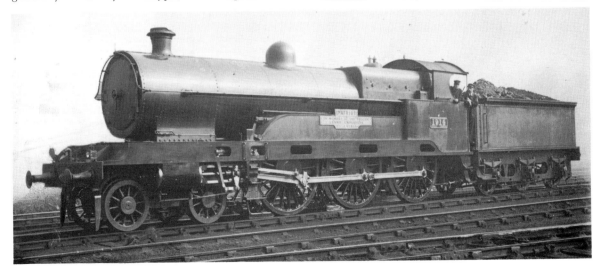

until the proceedings of the 1923 Bridge Stress Committee had been under way for some little time. Bowen Cooke, like his contemporary on the Great Western, G.J. Churchward, was far more internationally minded than the great majority of his fellow locomotive superintendents; and while Churchward's interests had become directed towards current practice in the USA and France, Bowen Cooke, from his 'finishing school' days at Neuwied in the Rhineland, had retained a keen interest in German developments. Compound locomotives were then very much to the fore in Europe, but while Alfred de Glehn, for whose work Churchward had such an admiration, was building 4-cylinder engines with the drive divided between 2-coupled axles, the German firm of Maffei built some 4-cylinder compound 4-6-0s for the Bavarian railways in which all four cylinders drove on to the leading coupled axle. By this arrangement, hammer blow was completely eliminated.

In 1909 Bowen Cooke, with his ear very much to the ground, as it were, regarding continental locomotive happenings, and as the architect of so much 'interchange' running at home, became interested in the outcome of a locomotive exchange in Holland. The State Railway needed more powerful engines than its existing 4-4-0s and 4-4-2s, and arrangements had been made to borrow one of the very beautiful 4-6-0s of the North Brabant German Railway, which had been built by Beyer, Peacock & Co. These engines, though powerful on a tractive effort basis had relatively small boilers and a correspondingly light axle load of only 14½ tons. The State Railway wanted larger boilers for its contemplated 4-6-0s, and the civil engineer advised his locomotive colleague that he was prepared to accept an axle load of 16 tons if the unbalanced centrifugal forces induced by the balance weights could be eliminated. So, the 4-cylinder engine layout was chosen, with all four cylinders driving on to the leading pair of coupled wheels. The new Dutch engines were also built by Beyer, Peacock & Co and, working on the same principle, Bowen Cooke considered that if the 'George the Fifth' Class 4-4-0, with its heavy hammer blow, could be accepted, his new 4-cylinder 4-6-0 could have a maximum axle load of at least 21 and possibly 22 tons. But the civil engineer, E.F.C. Trench, was deaf to all such argument and insisted on no axle load greater than 20 tons.

When the Bridge Stress Committee was set up, in 1923, it seemed by its membership that it was to be almost entirely a 'party' for the civil engineers. Apart from eminent scientists like Professor W.E. Dalby, Professor C.E. Inglis, Mr R.V. Southwell, and the Chairman himself, Sir Alfred Ewing, each of the four 'group' railways was represented by a leading civil engineer, and in retrospect it might seem ironical that E.F.C. Trench, then the most senior of all the railway civil engineers, represented the LMS. In view of the ultimate findings of the Committee one wonders if he ever had pangs of conscience for his attitude to Bowen Cooke in 1911! Sir Henry Fowler was the only locomotive engineer to be a member of the Committee, but although he had an illustrious scientific record, he had not, by the year 1923, been called upon to design any express passenger locomotive likely to trouble the bridge engineers. Incidentally, however, his little Class 2 superheater 4-4-0 of the Midland Railway had a healthy 11.8 tons of hammer blow to add to its maximum axle load of 17.5 tons! It being realised from an early stage in the investigation that the unbalanced revolving masses in the driving wheels of locomotives were the chief agents in producing bridge vibration, the railway companies were asked

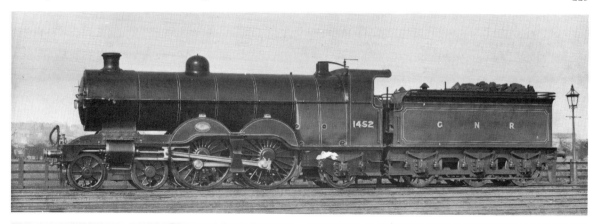

Left *LNWR: a 'Precursor' superheated with piston valves, and assimilated to the 'George the Fifth' Class, No 2062, Sunbeam. These engines had a very heavy hammer blow effect* (British Railways).

This page *East Coast 'Atlantics', differed in their effects on the track: a) Great Northern—30.4 tons at 86 mph* (British Railways); *b) North Eastern—23 tons at 88 mph and c) North British—31.6 tons at 87 mph.*

to provide for testing purposes engines having large hammer blows. It was revealed that the variation in rail pressure produced by unbalanced revolving masses was in certain classes of engine so great that, with increase in speed, it might reach a magnitude above the static load, in which case the wheel would actually lift clear of the rail!

The balancing of engines was an aspect of railway mechanical engineering in which Professor Dalby, my old teacher at Imperial College, was acknowledged as the greatest expert of the day, and his contribution to this aspect of the work of the Committee was vital. It is interesting to record that, because of its propensity to cause severe vibration in bridges, one of the Robinson 'Atlantics' of the former Great Central Railway was used on nearly every bridge tested. As was to be expected, locomotives with three or four cylinders were generally found to have a less severe effect than their 2-cylinder counterparts. In the published report of the Committee, particulars of hammer blow for various types of locomotive were classified uniformly at speeds corresponding to 6 revolutions per second of the driving wheels and, to take three 'Atlantics' of the LNER as an example, the results were:

Former railway	GNR	NER	NBR
Class	'251'	'Z'	'868'
Max axle load (tons)	20	19.95	20
Speed at 6 rps (mph)	86	88	87
Max combined load at 6 rps	30.4	23.1	31.6

The superiority of the 3-cylinder 'Z' in this comparison is very obvious.

It did not, however, necessarily follow that because a locomotive had more than two cylinders it was inherently a better balanced machine. The investigations of the Committee brought to light the anomalous case of the Great Western 4-cylinder

4-6-0s, hitherto considered to be among the most advanced designs of any British locomotives at that time. In these engines, as running at the time the investigation started, a considerable portion of the *reciprocating* parts was balanced separately for the inside and outside cylinders, in the leading and middle pair of coupled wheels respectively. Although the balance applied to the leading axle was opposed to that in the middle one, and the total engine hammer blow was relatively small, the hammer blow from each of the individual axles actually exceeded that of the 2-cylinder 'Saint' Class, which was not more than 7 tons on any axle. The effect of the 4-cylinder 'Star' on the track was therefore worse than that of the 'Saint'. During the course of the Committee's work, the method of balancing was revised at Swindon, and the maximum hammer blow from any axle was reduced to 2.9 tons.

Another revelation that came out of the Committee's work concerned the ex-Highland Railway 'River' Class 4-6-0s, which, as related in Chapter 9, were banned from the moment of their arrival from the builders. Again, as in the case of the LNWR 'Claughton', it was dead weight alone that provided any criterion for the stand taken by the civil engineer, and the new engines were certainly considerably heavier than any of their predecessors. Their designer, F.G. Smith, was a first rate technologist, albeit a very poor diplomat, and the 'River' Class engines were very skilfully balanced. At the time these engines were built conventional practice was to balance two thirds of the reciprocating masses by weights cast into the

Midland Railway: the rebuilt and superheated Class '2P' 4-4-0, exemplified here by the Royal Engine, No 502, also had a hammer blow of 11.8 tons to add to the dead weight on its driving axles (British Railways).

Top *Highland Railway: a 'Castle' Class 4-6-0 by Peter Drummond with a maximum combined load on track of 21.2 tons (the late W.J. Reynolds).*

Above *Highland Railway: 'River' Class 4-6-0 by F.G. Smith, a much heavier engine basically but, by skilful balancing, had a maximum combined load of only 21.4 tons, yet it was banned.*

driving wheels, at the same time as the whole of the revolving masses were balanced; but in the 'River' Class Smith, knowing that the hardest work the engines would be called upon to perform would be a relatively slow speed, considered that the balance for the reciprocating parts could be very much less than the conventional. Furthermore, by careful division of the balancing effect between the leading and middle coupled axles, he was able to effect a very marked reduction in the total engine hammer blow. The comparative figures for the 'Castle', 'River' and 'Clan' Classes—the last mentioned accepted by the civil engineer who had banned the 'River'—are revealing, thus:

Highland Railway 4-6-0s

	'Castle'	'River'	'Clan'
Max axle load (tons)	15.15	17.75	15.33
Hammer blow at 6 rps (tons)			
Whole engine	16.3	1.7	15.3
Axle	6.2	4.2	7.1
Max combined load (tons)	21.2	21.4	22.4

This analysis of the balancing characteristics of Highland 4-6-0s was taken advantage of, even before the Report of the Bridge Stress Committee was issued, on February 1 1929; for, in time to take an important share in the heavy summer traffic over the Highland line, the six engines of the 'River' Class were transferred in 1928 from express freight workings on the Caledonian section to the job for which they were originally designed, and they rendered excellent service in express passenger train haulage between Perth and Inverness. At the time there were some explanations, not official, that certain bridges had been strengthened to permit this; but the details set out in the foregoing table make the true reason obvious. In the previous year the man, Alexander Newlands, who as Engineer-in-Chief of the Highland Railway, had banned them in the first place, had been appointed to succeed Trench as Chief Civil Engineer of the LMS, but I cannot say if he had any hand in the closing stages of the work of the Bridge Stress Committee. Trench himself, who was only 60 when he retired, remained for a time as Consulting Engineer to the LMS.

The Bridge Stress Committee performed an immense service to the British railways as a whole for the way in which it brought together the civil and the locomotive engineers. It is true that there was only one locomotive man on the Committee itself, but its work fostered a much closer appreciation of the problems each department had to face, especially at a time when traffic requirements were demanding the introduction of heavier and more powerful locomotives. One result of immediate importance, was that the previous limit for maximum axle load of 20 tons, was increased to 22 tons, a relaxation that was put to advantage on the LNER in the introduction of 'Pacific' engines with 220 lb boilers.

17. In the steps of a master: GWR and Southern

When George Jackson Churchward retired at the end of 1921 he had become something of a legend on the Great Western Railway—at Swindon, 'The Old Man'—not that he was all that old in years, because he was not yet 65 years of age when he retired. It is fairly certain that the Board would have been only too glad for him to continue for another five years at least, as did his successor; but Churchward felt that his work in locomotive engineering was done, and he had already been much irked by developments in personnel in the post-war world, and realised that he would no longer be able to 'rule the roost' as of old. He left behind traditions that were to carry the Great Western locomotive departments through two more decades with little or no deviation from the principles that he had established in the preceding 20 years.

It did not prove to be a very enterprising period so far as new locomotive design was concerned. The new Chief Mechanical Engineer, C.B. Collett, was primarily a workshop man, and his main interests proved to lie in the improving of constructional techniques, and the incorporation in existing designs of details likely to reduce the maintenance costs of locomotives. At the time of his appointment G.H. Burrows was Chief Locomotive Draughtsman, but he was near the retiring age, and he was soon succeeded by F.W. Hawksworth. Stanier, as Principal Assistant to the CME, was second in command. The driving force, so far as new express passenger locomotive design was concerned, seemed to be not at Swindon at all, but at Padding-

ton in the person of the General Manager, the dynamic Sir Felix Pole. It was the upsurge of holiday traffic to the West of England, resulting in many express trains loading to over 500 tons, that had prompted the design of a super-Star 4-6-0 in 1923, the ever-famous 'Castle'. Its tractive effort of 31,625 lb took it comfortably above that of the Gresley 'Pacific'. Pole was satisified in having the most powerful passenger engine in the country. There was, however, a profound shock in store for him towards the end of 1924 when it was learned at Paddington that Collett had scrapped *The Great Bear*.

From the engineering point of view it was a perfectly logical step. The great engine needed a new boiler. Because of route restriction her sphere of activity was very limited, and she was much under utilised, so the frames were cut back to turn her into a 4-6-0, and she was fitted with a 'Castle' type boiler. But Pole was very annoyed that such a step should have been taken without his being consulted. Although it had been surpassed in tractive effort, the engine was regarded as a prestige symbol at Paddington. Churchward also was very upset, even though he of all men realised the limitations on use of the engine. In answering the severe cross-examination to which Pole subjected him, Collett explained the route restriction to which *The Great Bear* was limited, which had precluded its use on the West of England main line, via Castle Cary. Then, with all the excitement of the Interchange Trials of 1925, and the labour troubles of 1926, the episode of *The Great Bear* slipped into the

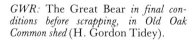
GWR: The Great Bear *in final conditions before scrapping, in Old Oak Common shed* (H. Gordon Tidey).

background until suddenly, late in 1926, the Southern Railway produced 'the most powerful passenger engine in Great Britain', the 4-cylinder 4-6-0, *Lord Nelson*, with a tractive effort of 33,500 lb. At once Collett was instructed to produce something big enough to put the GWR once again substantially in the lead, and again Pole was astonished to learn that it could not be done!

It was explained to him that the 'Castle' had been designed up to the very limit the civil engineer would accept. This, however, was to ignore a proposal that had been put up to him in that same year by Stanier and Hawksworth. The former had the idea of a compound 'Castle' conceived on the best French precepts. It was to have 17 inch diameter high pressure cylinders and 25 inch low pressure ones, and the starting tractive effort would have been 35,700 lb. It would have required some adjustment of the 'Castle' wheelbase, with the bogie centre moved forward by 1 foot 10 inches; but Hawksworth, with his usual designing skill, had contrived a handsome exterior appearance for the proposed engine. The design had progressed far enough for Stanier to suggest it was time to show it to Collett. It was Hawksworth who told me the outcome: 'We went in to see him', he said, 'and in about five minutes we were out again'! And that was that, so far as the compound 'Castle' was concerned.

So far as a more powerful engine for the West of England line went, the Chief Civil Engineer, J.C. Lloyd, was next called into consultation and asked why it had not been possible to use *The Great Bear* on this route, and it then transpired that for the last 22 years all new bridges had been designed for a maximum axle load of 22 tons, yet neither the General Manager nor the Chief Mechanical Engineer had been advised of this. The chief officers of the old railways did indeed work in watertight

compartments! (He also reported that in 1926 only four bridges on that route remained that were not up to the 22-ton standard.) In view of the findings of the Bridge Stress Committee he was asked if he could accept 22½ tons for 4-cylinder engines, and to this he agreed. The race was then on. Pole instructed him to have the four bridges strengthened to take the 22½ tons load in time for the summer traffic of 1927, while Collett was authorised to get a new 4-cylinder 4-6-0 of maximum power ready by the same time. Such was the origin of the 'King' Class of locomotives, purely 'enlarged Churchward' in every respect except the leading bogie.

That the nominal tractive effort was over 40,000 lb —40,300 to be exact—was also due to the urging of Sir Felix Pole; but there are two versions of the late-hour changes in the design that achieved this. K.J. Cook in his book, *Swindon Steam*, states that 6 foot 6 inch driving wheels were decided upon at an early stage and, with 16 inch diameter cylinders it gave a tractive effort of 39,200 lb. It was just possible to get the extra Pole wished for by boring out the cylinders to 16¼ inches. The other version is that Collett was anxious to use the standard 6 foot 8½ inch coupled wheels, and avoid the capital expense of making new patterns. With 6 foot 8½ inch wheels and 16¼ inch cylinders, the tractive effort came out at 39,100 lb. Reducing the wheel diameter to 6 feet 6 inches put the tractive effort up to 40,300 lb. However the various features of design came to be determined, the capital cost of introducing the new engines, in patterns, tools and special machinery, was high. It was felt afterwards that a good deal of this could have been avoided if insistence on topping the 40,000 lb mark had not been made.

The only non-Churchward feature of the design was the leading bogie, with its unique arrangement of outside bearings for the leading pair of wheels

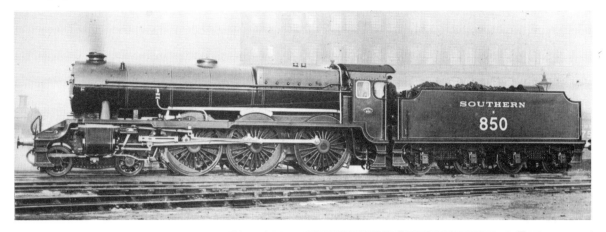

Below left *GWR: engine No 111, with frames shortened and fitted with a 'Castle' Class boiler which was renamed* Viscount Churchill, *retaining the original 8-wheeled tender* (British Railways).

Above *Southern Railway: the new 'most powerful express locomotive' in 1926 was Maunsell's 4-cylinder 4-6-0, No 850,* Lord Nelson *(the late W.J. Reynolds).*

Right *The Great Western reply: the* King George V, *equipped with the Westinghouse brake, ready for the American tour of 1927 (the late W.J. Reynolds).*

and inside for the rearward pair. It was perhaps to be expected that some teething troubles would occur with this bogie; but it was fortunate beyond measure that the alarming derailment of the bogie of engine No 6003 near Midgham, on August 10 1927, while working the Cornish Riviera Express, was not fraught with any serious consequences, other than loss of sleep by some senior officers at Swindon! The trouble lay in the suspension springing of the bogie and when, after some experimental changes, the trouble was rectified the 'Kings' became among the steadiest and most comfortable riding engines in Great Britain. As traction units they performed fully in the Churchward tradition, and brought further fame to Swindon as a locomotive centre.

The visit to the USA of the first engine, No 6000, *King George V*, in the late summer and autumn of 1927 created immense interest in British locomotive practice generally at the Centenary celebration of

the Baltimore and Ohio Railroad and by the performance on a dynamometer test run to Philadelphia. On test runs made from Swindon in maximum load haulage the economy of the engines was shown to be as good as that of the 'Castles', with a coal consumption per drawbar horsepower hour of a little under 3 lb. With the introduction of the 'Kings', and the cause of the Midgham 'incident' diagnosed and eradicated, no further development in express passenger power was considered necessary, and none in fact was made for another 18 years.

At the same time it must be observed that the design of the 'Kings' was entirely traditional, not only in its basic proportioning, but also in the details of the front-end, at a time when steam locomotive practice was entering upon a period of striking evolution. The streamline age was just dawning, and although the 'Kings' dealt admirably with the heaviest of the tasks imposed upon them by the traffic department, the same could also have been said of the 'Atbara' and 'City' Class 4-4-0s, 24 years earlier; and yet they were merely the prelude to one of the most remarkable developments in British locomotive history. The 'Kings', as introduced in 1927, looked like the culmination point of that development, beyond which no further advance was to be discerned, at any rate while Collett was in command at Swindon. It was shown later that locomotives designed in the later 1930s, having an equal or slightly *lower* nominal tractive effort, were capable of developing and sustaining far higher indicated and drawbar horsepower than the 'Kings', not only by use of a higher degree of superheat, but because of notable refinements in design of the front-end.

From 1927 to 1940 all other new locomotive classes produced at Swindon were generally derivatives of the basic Churchward 2-cylinder design. The exceptions were a taper-boilered modern version of the highly successful Dean goods 0-6-0, which in its superheated form was continuing to render outstandingly good service, and certain small, though very useful, tank engine designs, all with domed boilers. The three tank engine designs (none were superheated) were as follows:

GWR modern 6-wheeled tank engines

Class	'4800'	'5400'	'5700'
Year introduced	1932	1931	1929
Type	0-4-2	0-6-0	0-6-0
Tank position	Side	Pannier	Pannier
Cylinders			
Diameter (inches)	16	16½	17½
Stroke (inches)	24	24	24
Coupled wheel diameter (feet/inches)	5 2	5 2	4 7½
Heating surfaces (square feet)			
Tubes	869.8	1,004.2	1,075.7
Firebox	83.2	81.8	102.3
Grate area (square feet)	12.8	16.76	15.3
Boiler pressure (lb per square inch)	165	165	200
Tractive effort (lb)	13,900	14,780	22,515

The '5700' Class of pannier tank was an extremely successful and numerous design, ultimately totalling more than 750 locomotives. All three classes were very lively and willing little engines in their particular ranges of loading.

Two new classes of large 2-cylinder 4-6-0 were derived directly from the Churchward 'Saint' Class varying only in the size of the coupled wheels. These were the 'Hall', with 6 foot wheels, and the

'Grange' with 5 foot 8 inch wheels. With the same boiler, cylinders, and the standard Swindon arrangement of the Stephenson link motion, the respective tractive efforts were 27,275 and 28,875 lb. Both had the 'Collett' type of cab, and the more conveniently accommodated screw reversing gear, but were otherwise essentially of standard Churchward design. The 'Manor' Class of 1938 was a lightweight version designed particularly for the former Cambrian Railways line, with a maximum axle load of 15.85 tons and a considerably smaller boiler. This latter was not an existing standard, but was introduced specially for this class. It did not prove very successful, and certainly could not sustain the requirements of a front-end having a nominal tractive effort of no less than 27,340 lb, based on cylinder volume, wheel diameter and boiler pressure alone. It was not until after the Second World War that the class was taken in hand. A series of tests were made on the stationary plant at Swindon and, with adjustments to the draughting, the 'Manors' were turned into satisfactory motive power units.

The new tank engines introduced during the Collett regime were even more direct derivatives from the standard Churchward range. It had been found that the 4-4-2 tanks of the '22XX' Class, having 6 foot 8½ inch coupled wheels, were not ideal for the increasingly heavy suburban trains in the London and Birmingham areas, and that a 6-coupled tank engine with 5 foot 8 inch coupled wheels would be more suitable. The existing standard engines of the '3150' Class, however, with the No 4 boiler, had a maximum axle load of 19¼ tons, and an engine with a considerably higher route availability was produced by using the No 2 boiler, as had been fitted on the '22XX' 4-4-2 tanks. So, were introduced the '5100' Class, in 1929. The boiler pressure was 200 lb per square inch. There were two sub-varieties of this class: 70 engines had boilers with 225 lb pressure but which were otherwise similar, and 10 with coupled wheels 5 feet 6 inches diameter. The three varieties of the '5100' Class were thus:

Running numbers	5100-5199 4100-4139	6100-6169	8100-8109
Coupled wheel diameter (feet/inches)	5 8	5 8	5 6
Boiler pressure (lb per square inch)	200	225	225
Tractive effort (lb)	24,300	27,340	28,165

In 1934, with the gradual withdrawal of the 2-6-0

Right *GWR: engine No 6002,* King William IV, *on the up Cornish Riviera Express near Reading in August 1927* (M.W. Earley).

Right *The* King George V *in the USA with 'Britannia' (Miss Lillian Schuler, daughter of one of the directors of the Baltimore & Ohio RR) on the running plate* (British Railways).

Below *The* King George II *at Swindon, December 1929, fitted for full-dress dynamometer car tests* (British Railways).

'Aberdare' Class of inside-cylinder heavy mineral engines, the need was felt for a main line coal traffic engine for shorter hauls than those undertaken by the standard 2-8-0 tender engines of the '2800' Class. The situation was met by fitting a number of the '4200' Class 2-8-0 tank engines with larger coal and water capacity, and extending them to the 2-8-2 type. When first introduced, in 1910, the '4200' Class had 18½ inch diameter cylinders; but subsequent additions to the class in the '5200' series had 19 inch diameter cylinders. Comparative dimensions of these latter, and the new 2-8-2 development were as subjoined. The boilers and machinery of both types were the same, with a tractive effort of 33,170 lb.

GWR coal traffic tank engines

Class	4200, 5200	7200
Type	2-8-0	2-8-2
Coal capacity (tons)	3	6
Water capacity (gallons)	1,800	2,500
Total weight in working order (tons)	82.1	92.6

The '7200' Class worked through coal trains from South Wales to Salisbury, for the Southern Railway, and on such comparatively long and heavy hauls, via the Severn Tunnel, Bath and Westbury, their ample coal and water capacity suited them admirably for the work.

Turning now from the Great Western to the Southern Railway, it was during the critical years between the end of the First World War and the grouping, when the Association of Railway Locomotive Engineers was endeavouring to evolve new British Standard designs, that James Clayton came into close association with Churchward. In 1919 he had been promoted from Chief Locomotive Draughtsman of the SE & CR to Personal Assistant of the CME, and this association was to lead to an almost fervent admiration for Great Western practice when he came to recognise the genius that seemed to lie behind it. Certainly in most respects Churchward's standard locomotives were among the most thoroughly designed of any running in Great Britain in 1919-21, with a great amount of thought and experimenting lying behind the introduction of most of the detail features. At the same time Churchward could be regarded above all as a master co-ordinator, rather than a master originator of design. Many of the most important features of his engines came from ideas put forward by members of his staff.

No one at Swindon sat more admiringly at the feet of the master than James Clayton and, long before they were adopted by the LMS or the LNER, he was using long-lap, long-travel valves on the South Eastern and Chatham Railway, on the prototype 2-6-0 and 2-6-4 tank, and most effectively of all on the 'D1' and 'E1' superheater rebuilds of the Wainwright 4-4-0 express engines. These splendid little engines had a maximum valve travel of no less than 6½ inches and a steam lap of 1⅝ inches. Their rebuilding had been a stringent exercise in weight conservation. When the Continental boat train services were restored after the war it was decided to work them all from Victoria, instead of from Charing Cross as previously, and that meant use of

GWR: one of the numerous 'Hall' Class 4-6-0s, as finished in full passenger engine colours, No 5930, Hannington Hall (British Railways).

the Chatham route as far out as the Chislehurst junctions. The powerful 'L' Class superheater 4-4-0s of 1914 could not be used because of weight restriction, and the superheating of the Wainwright engines had to be carried out with no increase in maximum axle-load. The rebuilds proved remarkably successful engines, and worked the Continental boat trains with loads up to 300 tons.

Their working confirmed Clayton's assessment of the Churchward practice in valve gear design, though he did not go to the ultimate extent of providing the Stephenson link motion with negative lead in full gear. The 'D1' and 'E1' rebuilds had ⅛ inch, positive lead. After grouping, with Maunsell appointed as Chief Mechanical Engineer of the Southern, and Clayton as his personal assistant, the traffic department almost at once asked for a locomotive that would haul 500-ton trains at start-to-stop average speeds of 55 mph, particularly having in mind the holiday services on the South-Western section of the line. Such an advance over existing haulage requirements was clearly going to require the most careful study and planning before any detailed design could be undertaken. Instructions to go ahead were given as early as October 1923, and at once two questions arose: should the new engine be a 4-6-0 or a 'Pacific', and should it have three cylinders or four. Clayton with his enthusiasm for Great Western practice thought that an engine of 'Castle' proportions would do the job, but Maunsell was not so sure, while Clayton's junior partner, H. Holcroft, also a headquarters assistant to Maunsell, put forward a proposal for cranks at 135 degrees, giving eight exhausts per revolution, a very soft blast, and more even turning moment.

To put the 135 degrees proposal to the test, one of the 6 foot 4-cylinder Drummond 4-6-0s of the 'G14' Class, No 449, was rebuilt with the crank axle altered, and at the same time superheated. The

GWR: prototype for the 'Hall' Class; engine No 2925, Saint Martin, *rebuilt in 1925, with 6 foot diameter instead of 6 foot 8½ inch coupled wheels and a modernised cab* (British Railways).

engine was then put back into the ordinary link working mainly between Salisbury and Exeter. The wheel arrangement of the new '500-ton, 55 mph' was settled after Clayton had made some footplate trips in October 1924. He rode a 'Castle' non-stop from Paddington to Plymouth when the 'Cornish Riviera Express' was at its maximum loading, 530 tons as far as Westbury and, 10 days later, went down from Kings Cross to Grantham on a Gresley 'Pacific' working the 'Flying Scotsman'. His verdict was unhesitatingly in favour of the 'Castle' and this, coupled with the successful running of the rebuilt Drummond 4-6-0, No 449, settled the basis of the new Southern locomotive as a 4-cylinder 4-6-0 of 'Castle' capacity, but with cranks at 135 degrees. It was then November 1924, and at the most optimistic forecast it would be 12 months before the detail drawings, patterns and tooling for an entirely new engine would be available and, allowing for all contingencies, the first units would not be steamed before midsummer 1926, at the earliest. The traffic department wanted more engines for the summer service of 1925, and so the quickest way to meet their needs was to build to existing designs.

Unfortunately no existing design was entirely satisfactory, and early in 1924 the running department had laid before Maunsell the troubles they were having with the latest and largest of the existing 4-6-0s, the Urie 'N15' Class. In response, a comprehensive series of tests was begun on engine No 742, working between Waterloo and Salisbury. There was a collateral exercise at the same time. Even before grouping an order had been given to Eastleigh works to rebuild the 6 foot Drummond 4-6-0s of the 'G14' Class as 2-cylinder engines, in the Urie style. But no action had been taken by the beginning of 1924 and, after consultation with the running department, Maunsell obtained authority to replace, rather than rebuild, the 'G14' Class, which would allow the original engines to remain in traffic for the summer of 1924 when there was expected to be a shortage of 4-6-0s. In the meantime the replacement engines could be built at Eastleigh. These latter were to be improved 'N15s', though taking the Drummond tenders off the 'G14s'. Clayton would have liked to have gone the whole Churchward way, and given the improved 'N15s' 18½ inch by 30 inch cylinders, and 225 lb pressure; but this would have involved new patterns for cylinders and wheels, and he had to be content with retaining the original 28 inches stroke, with 20½ inches diameter, and 200 lb pressure, instead of 180.

In the meantime the tests with the Urie 'N15', No 742, were revealing what rather poor tools those engines were. In hard continuous steaming it was not possible to maintain more than 140 lb per square inch and, when the firing was relaxed a little on a level and easier stretch, the pressure dropped to 100 lb per square inch. The first step to try and improve matters was to increase the area of the steam and exhaust ports, to provide freer flow of steam; but the improvement was no more than marginal. The next step gave an excellent opportunity to try out the modified blastpipe and chimney Clayton had designed for the improved 'N15s' that were to replace the 'G14s'. It worked like a charm, and transformed the performance of the engine. Heavily loaded on a test run from Waterloo to Salisbury, the modified 742 steamed continuously at 170 to 180 lb per square inch all the way, and 16 sets of indicator cards showed indicated horsepower values varying between 1,000 and

1,200. Instructions were given to get all the Urie 'N15s' altered as quickly as possible, and work began at Eastleigh on building the 'G14' replacements. These differed from the 'N15s', not only in the cylinder dimensions and boiler pressure, but in having long-lap, long-travel valves: $1\frac{5}{8}$ inches and $6\frac{9}{16}$ inches, against 1 inch and $5\frac{1}{8}$ inches. The Urie 'N15s' had always been free running engines and, once they had been redraughted, they became excellent motive power units. Indeed, the first time the late Cecil J. Allen clocked a maximum speed of 90 mph anywhere on the Southern Railway was with one of these engines.

In the autumn of 1924, while the construction of the 'G14' replacements was going ahead at Eastleigh, consultations about the traffic requirements for the following summer, particularly in respect of the Continental services, showed that more large engines would be urgently needed. There was no possibility of getting any of the projected '500-ton, 55 mph' giants into traffic, and so an order for another 30 of the improved 'N15' was passed to the North British Locomotive Company. These would be the same as the 'G14' replacements being built at Eastleigh, but with the Urie double-bogie tender, instead of the Drummond type with inside bearings. But, despite the essentially sound mechanical engineering policy that was becoming evident from Maunsell's careful handling of the situation, the Southern Railway generally was at the mercy of a bitterly hostile and sustained press campaign, not lessened by the waspish attitude shown to it by Sir

GWR: the powerful development of the pre-war standard 2-6-2 tank, using the No 2 boiler, and 225 lb per square inch pressure— engine No 6110 (British Railways).

GWR: the 5 foot 8 inch mixed traffic 4-6-0 Class, No 6800, Arlington Grange (British Railways).

Herbert Walker himself. By the autumn of 1924, however, it was evidently judged to be time to grasp the nettle; and it was done in the most effective way imaginable by the appointment of John Blumenfeld Elliot, then Assistant Editor of the *Evening Standard*, as personal assistant to Sir Herbert Walker, taking charge of advertising and publicity.

Up to that time, while the Great Western could do nothing wrong in the eyes of the popular press the Southern could do nothing right. One of Elliot's first suggestions was that the new 4-6-0s, then being built at both Eastleigh and Glasgow, should be named. The Southern served the North Cornwall districts associated with the legends of King Arthur and the Knights of the Round Table; but when the suggestion was first made Sir Herbert Walker said, 'You'd better see Mr Maunsell; we've not had named engines before'. So Elliot went, cap in hand, as it were, to the CME who heard him out in silence; and then with a touch of his native Irish wit, said: 'Tell Sir Herbert I have no objection, but I warn you, it won't make any difference to the working of the engines!' And so, the improved 'N15s' became the 'King Arthur' Class, in three varieties:

a) the Eastleigh 'Arthurs', replacing the 'G14' Class with Drummond style cabs and Drummond tenders.

b) the 'Scotch Arthurs', built by the North British Loco Co, with Maunsell cabs and Urie tenders.

c) the 'Urie Arthurs', the original 'N15' Class with improved draughting, 22 inch by 28 inch cylinders and the original valve gear.

As first constituted the 'King Arthur' Class was 60 strong, with running numbers as follows: (a) 448 to 457, (b) 763 to 792, (c) 736 to 755. To these were added a further 14 in 1926-7, built at Eastleigh, and having 6-wheeled instead of bogie tenders to suit the smaller turntables of the Brighton line.

With the exception of engine No 454, *Queen*

Guinevere, varieties (a) and (b) were all named after Knights of the Round Table, while variety (c), which had been built by the London and South Western Railway, had names added of other personalities and places connected with the legend. Inevitably perhaps, when a systematised code of naming is introduced, there were some inconsistencies, as with two of the Urie 'Arthurs', which were named after the same lady; because *Elaine* (engine 747) *was* the *Maid of Astolat*. There was nearly a *faux-pas* over engine No 767, which was originally listed to become *Sir Mordred*, the traitor. Fortunately this was pointed out before the engine left Glasgow, and it came south as *Sir Valence*. The engines that were replacements of the 'G14' Class were mostly used on the West of England main line, while the Urie engines remained at their existing sheds. The 'Scotchmen' (as the 763-792 batch were always known on the Southern) were allocated 763-772 to Stewarts Lane, for the 'Continentals'; 773-782 to Nine Elms, and 783-792 to Bournemouth.

Having launched the 'King Arthurs' into traffic, attention became concentrated on the new 4-cylinder 4-6-0 and, because of its many new features, only a single prototype was at first constructed. Although Clayton's predilection for Great Western practice was shown in the shaping of the firebox, in other respects there were marked differences. The four cylinders were nearly in line and, as the drive was divided between the leading and the middle pair of coupled wheels, there was a great difference in the length of the connecting rods. The outside ones were 11 feet long, and the inside only 6 feet 11 inches. There were four separate sets of Walschaerts valve gear, providing a maximum travel of 6½ inches with 1½ inches lap. The cranks were set at 135 degrees giving eight exhausts per revolution. Very great care was taken in design to keep the weight down and, whereas the 'King Arthur' had a weight of 81 tons, for an engine with a tractive effort of 25,320 lb, the new 4-cylinder 4-6-0 weighed only 83½ tons for a tractive effort of 33,500 lb.

The new engine, No 850, and named *Lord Nelson*, was completed at Eastleigh in August 1926 and, as the 'most powerful passenger engine' in the British Isles, fairly 'set the heather on fire' in Great Western circles. The time was not propitious for demonstrating whether the new engine fulfilled the severe target performance of start-to-stop average speeds of 55 mph with loads of 500 tons. With the coal strike in progress, and reliance having to be placed on imported fuel, maximum performance was not to be expected, and in that same autumn I had runs with 'King Arthurs' when there was difficulty in keeping the boiler pressure much above 100 lb per square inch—let alone 200!

On a Sunday in April 1927 conditions were favourable for an all-out run and a load of 16 coaches 521 tons tare was taken from Waterloo to Exeter. The schedule laid down was for a start-to-stop average speed of 55.5 mph over the 83.2 miles to Salisbury and, if it had not been for incidental delays on the journey, this target speed would have been maintained. Very hard running was involved on the continuation from Salisbury to Sidmouth

Junction—75.8 miles in 87¼ minutes. The engine was indicated and many readings between 1,300 and 1,500 indicated horsepower were obtained. The engine steamed well, but the coal consumption seemed to be on the high side compared to 'Castle' performance on the Great Western. With 66.5 lb per train mile, this worked out at 2.68 lb per IHP hour, with best quality Welsh coal. The corresponding 'Castle' figure in 1924 had been 2.1 lb. No dynamometer car was used, so that no figures in relation to the drawbar horsepower were obtained.

When a further 15 engines of the 'Lord Nelson' Class had been constructed, in 1928-9, and they were in regular service on both the Eastern and Western sections, I cannot say that my general experience of them, on the basis of many runs, was very favourable. Often they seemed to be short of steam, and not generally so reliable as the 'King Arthurs'. I did have two runs of first-rate quality—one indeed, exceptional. The first was on the Atlantic Coast Express, when a 450-ton train was worked from Waterloo to Salisbury at an average speed of 59 mph from start to stop. For 45 miles, on gradually rising gradients, an average speed of 60 mph was maintained, with an indicated horsepower of 1,150.

The second run was on the outward bound Night Ferry train, with the heavy French built sleeping

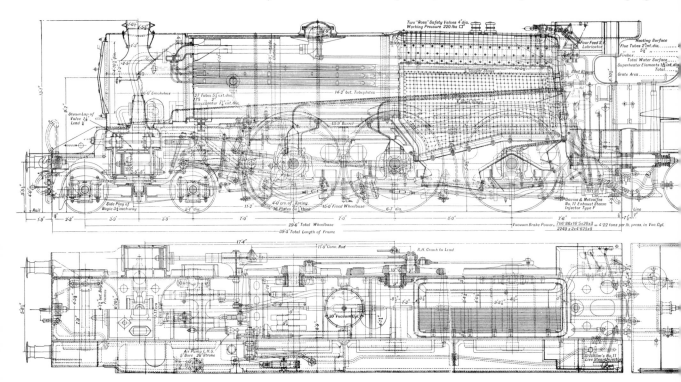

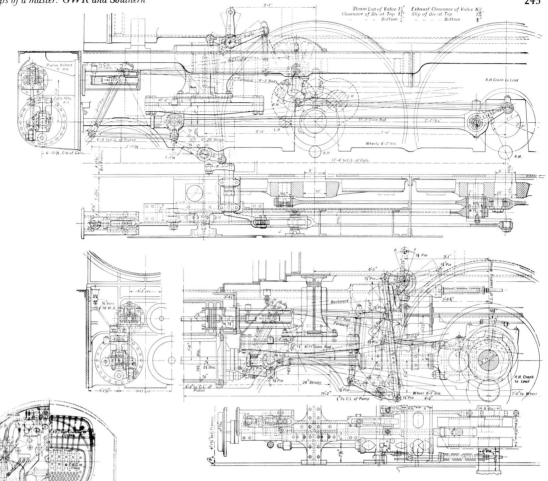

Far left *Southern Railway: the* Lord Nelson, *4-cylinder 4-6-0, with cranks at 135 degrees.*

Left *Southern Railway: the* Lord Nelson, *cross-sections, showing the cab and firebox and the front end.*

Top *The* Lord Nelson: *detail showing the outside cylinder and motion.*

Above *The* Lord Nelson: *detail showing one of the inside cylinders and motion.*

cars, about 440 tons all told; and, after initial delays, a very hard effort was put forth to regain lost time, and an average speed of 67 mph maintained over the 23.5 miles from Staplehurst to Sandling Junction, against rising gradients averaging about 1 in 500. The calculated drawbar horsepower was 1,165, suggesting at least 1,500 indicated power, and fully equal to the 'all-out' test run of April 1927. For the record, the two engines concerned in these experiences of mine were No 856, *Lord St Vincent*, and 854, *Howard of Effingham.*

Before leaving the express passenger 4-6-0s of the Southern it must be mentioned that the 'King Arthur' Class, both east and west of Salisbury, were turning in some remarkable performances in the 1930s, and summary details of some of these are given in the tables below.

From these tables it is evident that even the original Urie type, with the improved draughting, could almost run up to the '500-ton, 55 mph' requirement, as exemplified by the run of *Etarre*, while, even on the hilly road west of Salisbury, the 'King Arthurs' proper (both Eastleigh and Scottish built) could substantially exceed a 55 mph start to stop average with loads of 450 tons. The modified Urie series fully maintained their early reputation for high speed running, and more than once I clocked maximum speeds of up to 88 mph with them.

Dimensional details of derivatives of some of Clayton's earlier designs are tabulated, and beyond adding that all did good work, no further comment is needed. I must pass on to what was undoubtedly the phenomenon of the Maunsell era on the Southern, the 3-cylinder 4-4-0s of the 'Schools' Class. Its success was the more remarkable in that

the design was a synthesis of existing parts, assembled very largely as a compromise. It originated in a request from the traffic department for an express passenger locomotive of intermediate capacity, to work trains of 400 tons at an average speed of 55 mph, but to work on routes when structural restrictions precluded the use of 'King Arthurs'. The CME's department found an answer readily to hand in three quarters of a 'Nelson', using the same cylinders, wheels and motion, but with three cylinders instead of four. Good dynamic balance of the reciprocating parts enabled the civil engineer to accept a maximum axle load of 21 tons, though the original proposal, using the 'Nelson' flanging plates for the boiler and firebox, would have made the engine still heavier. The basic proportions, cylinders 16½ inches by 26 inches, coupled wheels of 6 foot 7 inch diameter, and boiler pressure 220 lb per square inch, gave the new engines the highest tractive effort of any British 4-4-0, namely 25,130 lb, almost equal to the 25,320 lb of a 'King Arthur'.

Historic rivals, on the basis of past performance, to the claim of the most powerful ever of British 4-4-0, were the LNWR 'George the Fifth', with 20,050 lb tractive effort, and a very brilliant pre-war record; the Midland compound, 22,649 lb and the Gresley 3-cylinder 'D49' with 21,556 lb. Connoisseurs of locomotive performance eagerly sought out the workings of the new engines to try and discern to what extent such impressive dimensional promise was fulfilled in day to day performance on the road. As it turned out those obervers had some little time to wait. The first 20 engines of the class were allocated to the South Eastern section, and worked on the steeply graded

King Arthur Class runs, Salisbury-Waterloo: 83.8 miles

Engine no	777	456	776	751
Engine name	**Sir Lamiel**	**Sir Galahad**	**Sir Galagars**	**Etarre**
Variety of design (origin)	NB Loco	Eastleigh	NB Loco	Urie modified
Load (tons gross) behind tender	345	450	450	490
Net average speed, allowing for time lost by checks	68.9	57.4	62.2	54.8

Salisbury-Exeter: 88.0 miles

Engine no	744	779	453	768
Engine name	**Maid of Astolat**	**Sir Colgrevance**	**King Arthur**	**Sir Balin**
Variety of design (origin)	Urie modified	NB Loco	Eastleigh	NB Loco
Load (tons gross) behind tender	380	415	450	455
Net average speed, allowing for time lost by checks	55.8	60.4	57.5	58.7

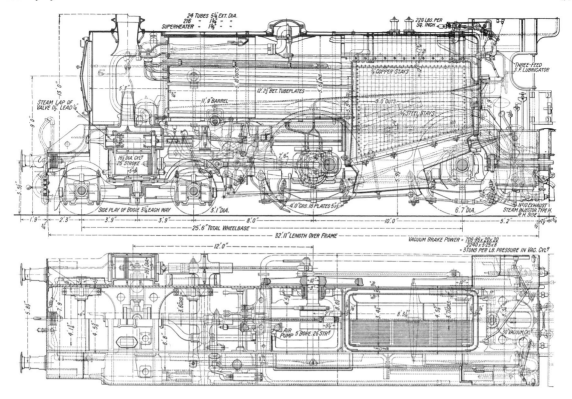

Above *Southern Railway: sectional elevation and plan of the 'Schools' Class 3-cylinder 4-4-0.*

Below *SR 'Schools' Class 3-cylinder 4-4-0—half-end elevation and half cross-sectional views.*

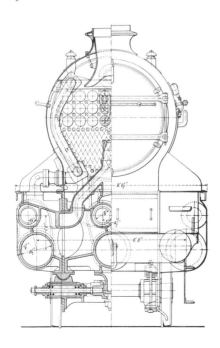

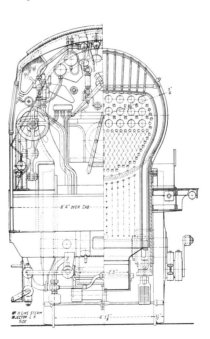

Hastings line in addition to the fast services between Charing Cross and Ramsgate, via Folkestone. They took loads up to 11 bogie coaches, 360 tons tare, on trains that required a start-to-stop run of 76 minutes over the 69.2 miles between Waterloo Junction and Folkestone Central, and generally kept very good time. I was travelling frequently over this route at the time; but, while I logged a number of excellent performances, there was nothing that would have been beyond the capacity of a 'George the Fifth' in its prime.

It was following the electrification of the Portsmouth District Line in 1936, and the transfer of the 924-933 batch of 'Schools' Class engines from Fratton to Bournemouth shed, that the reputation of the class touched its heights. It was the more remarkable because the Bournemouth men were, by long tradition, not among the hardest runners of ex-LSWR drivers. They handled their engines on a light rein, and took pride in low coal consumption and freedom from incidental casualties. The 'Schools' Class engines responded readily enough to this kind of treatment, to such an extent, indeed, that I sometimes wondered if the Bournemouth crews fully realised how hard they *were* going! The designed output, with a full opened regulator and 25 per cent cut-off was 1,270 indicated horsepower at 60 mph and the accompanying details of six runs with heavy trains, over the 43 miles from Hampton Court Junction to Litchfield signal box, suggest that on every occasion the performance must have been fully up to maximum predicted output. See the table at the top of page 247.

The results relate to a section with an average rising gradient of 1 in 675, a distance of 43 miles out of the Waterloo-Southampton run of 79.3 miles, booked in 87 ½ minutes; and in all these conditions of loading, for which large 4-6-0s, or 'Pacifics' would be provided on other railways, these 4-4-0s of no more than 67 tons total weight kept good time.

I have always felt that it was a pity no fully detailed analysis of the performance of the 'Schools' Class engines was not made on one or other of the stationary testing plants in British Railways days. Then, of course, it would have been no more than an academic study, because the day of the 4-4-0 was past. Had it been done, however, one can be sure that our knowledge of the steam locomotive would be the richer in consequence. The basic dimensions of these engines, alongside those of the 'Lord Nelson' Class, were as follows:

The later Maunsell express locomotives

Class	'Schools'	'Lord Nelson'
Type	4-4-0	4-6-0
Cylinders (number of)	3	4
Diameter (inches)	16 ½	16 ½
Stroke (inches)	26	26
Piston valve diameter (inches)	8	8
Max travel (inches)	6 ½	6 ½
Steam lap (inches)	1 ½	1 ½
Heating surfaces (square feet)		
Tubes	1,604	1,795
Firebox	162	194
Superheater	283	376
Grate area (square feet)	28.3	33
Boiler pressure (lb per square inch)	220	220
Tractive effort (lb)	25,130	33,500

'Schools' Class: Hampton Court Junction–Litchfield signal box

Engine no	**931**	**925**	**926**	**932**	**926**	**927**
Engine name	**Kings Wimbledon**	**Cheltenham**	**Repton**	**Blundells**	**Repton**	**Clifton**
Load (tons gross) behind tender	480	485	490	510	525	525
Average speed (mph)	57.1	58.3	53.7	58.6	54.8	55.8
Average estimated drawbar horsepower	985	1040	895	1095	1000	1034

Southern Railway: standard types

Class	**N**	**U**	**U1**	**W**	**Z**	**S15**
Year introduced	**1917***	**1928**	**1931**	**1931**	**1929**	**1927**
Type	2-6-0	2-6-0	2-6-0	2-6-4T	0-8-0T	4-6-0
Cylinders (number of)	2	2	3	3	3	2
Diameter (inches)	19	19	16	16½	16	20½
Stroke (inches)	28	28	28	28	28	28
Coupled wheel diameter (feet/inches)	5 6	6 0	6 0	5 6	4 8	5 7
Heating surfaces (square feet)						
Tubes	1,384	1,384	1,384	1,384	1,173	1,716
Firebox	135	135	135	135	106	162
Superheater	285	285	285	285	—	337
Grate area (square feet)	25.0	25.0	25.0	25.0	18.64	28.0
Boiler pressure (lb per square inch)	200	200	200	200	180	200
Tractive effort (lb)	26,040	23,866	25,387	29,452	29,376	29,860

* Introduced by SE & CR.

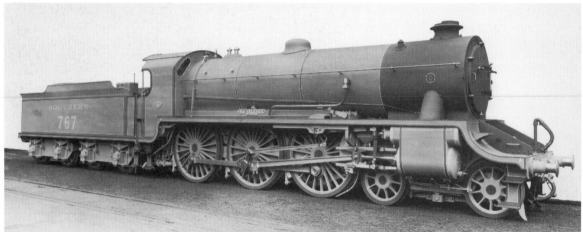

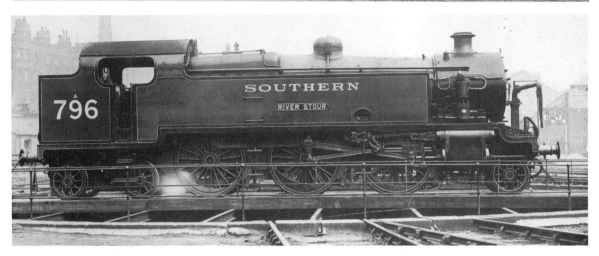

Opposite page top to bottom

Southern Railway: an experiment prior to use of cranks at 135 degrees on the Lord Nelson, *a 'G14' Drummond 4-cylinder 4-6-0 rebuilt and superheated (the late W.J. Reynolds).*

Southern Railway: the 'Scotch Arthur' which was nearly named after a traitor to the Round Table! Engine No 767, Sir Valence, *as originally built (North British Locomotive Company).*

Southern: one of the ill-fated 'River' Class 2-6-4 tank engines, No A796, River Stour, *fitted with the Westinghouse brake, and on the turntable at Victoria (Brighton side). These engines were converted into 2-6-0 tender engines after the Sevenoaks disaster (the late W.J. Reynolds).*

Right *Southern Railway: one of the 'Brighton Arthurs' with 6-wheeled tender, No 796,* Sir Dodinas le Savage, *on the* Southern Belle *(the late C. Laundy).*

Right *Southern Railway: a 'Lord Nelson' in the boat train link at Dover, No 852,* Sir Walter Raleigh, *with 6-wheeled tender (the late W.J. Reynolds).*

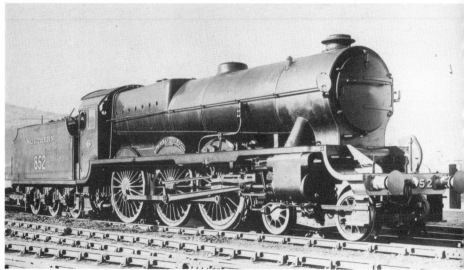

Above *Southern Railways: one of the 3-cylinder Class 'U1' Moguls of 1931, No 1905. These engines had three separate sets of Walschaerts valve gear (the late W.J. Reynolds).*

Below *Southern Railway: after the electrification of the Brighton line the former 4-6-4 tank engines were converted into 4-6-0s, and given distinguished names. This is engine No 2332, Stroudley, at Waterloo (C.R.L. Coles).*

Opposite page, top to bottom

Southern Railway: Class 'S15' fast goods 4-6-0, No 833 (a goods version of the 'King Arthur') (the late W.J. Reynolds).

Southern Railway: one of the earliest of the 'Schools' Class 3-cylinder 4-4-0s, No 902, Wellington, at Charing Cross (the late W.J. Reynolds).

Southern Railway: a 'Schools' Class 4-4-0 in later standard condition, No 934, St Lawrence (British Railways).

Bibliography

Technical papers

Institution of Mechanical Engineers

1880 A New Reversing and Expansive Valve gear, David Joy

1902 Application of Cylindrical Steam Distributing valves to Locomotives, Walter M. Smith

1906 Large Locomotive Boilers, George J. Churchward

1907 Presidential Address, T. Hurry Riches

1907 Road Trials of three Express passenger locomotives on the GNR in 1906, Henry A. Ivatt

1910 Compounding and Superheating in Horwich Locomotives, George Hughes

1925 Three-Cylinder Locomotives, H.N. Gresley

1931 High-Pressure Locomotives, H.N. Gresley

1936 Presidential Address, Sir Nigel Gresley

1941 Presidential Address, Sir W.A. Stanier

Institution of Civil Engineers

1914 Superheating Steam in Locomotives, Henry Fowler

Institution of Locomotive Engineers

1946 Modern Locomotive History (LMS), E.S. Cox

1946 Ten years Experience with the LMS 4-6-2 non-condensing turbine loco No 6202, R.C. Bond

1947 The Development of LNER Locomotive Design 1923-41, B. Spencer

1950 The late G.J. Churchward's Locomotive Development on the GWR, K.J. Cook

Journals

Engineering, The Engineer, The Locomotive, The Railway Engineer, The Railway Gazette, The Railway Magazine

Books

Aspinall Era, The, H.A.V. Bulleid, Ian Allan, 1967.

British Locomotives, C.J. Bowen Cooke, Whittaker, 1899.

British Steam Railway Locomotive
    Vol 1 1825-1925, E.L. Ahrons, Ian Allan, 1960.
    Vol 2, 1925-1965, O.S. Nock, Ian Allan, 1966.

Development of British Locomotive Design, E.L. Ahrons, Locomotive Publishing Co, 1914.

Lectures on the Locomotive, Dugald Drummond, Locomotive Publishing Co, 1921.

Lifetime with Locomotives, R.C. Bond, Goose & Son, 1975.

Locomotive Compounding and Superheating, J.F. Gairns, Griffin, 1907.

Outline of Great Western Locomotive Practice, 1837-1947, H. Holcroft, Ian Allan, 1957.

Steam Locomotive Design, Phillipson, Locomotive Publishing Co, 1936.

Swindon Steam, 1921-51, K.J. Cook, Ian Allan, 1974.

Index

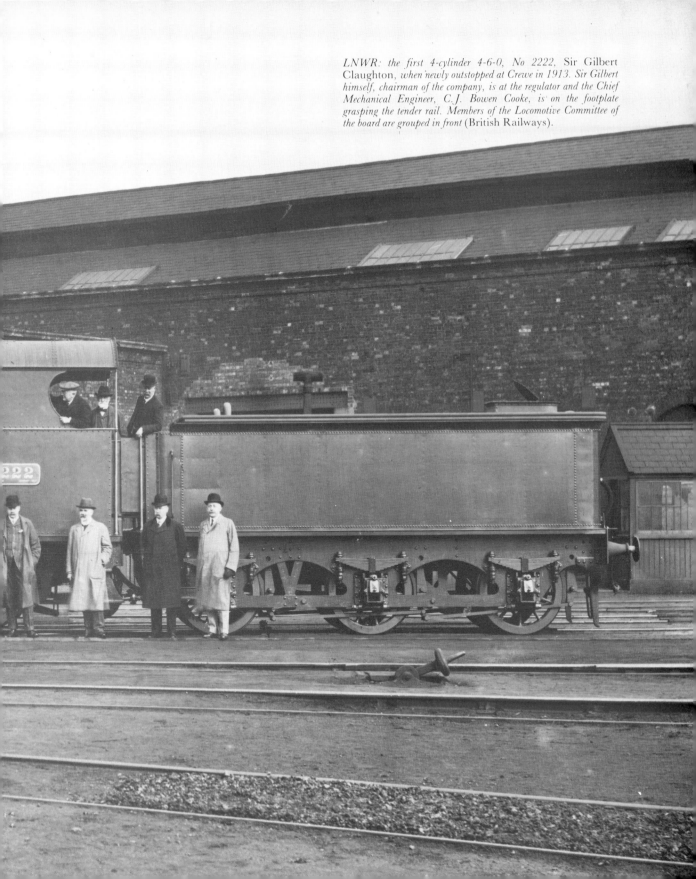

LNWR: the first 4-cylinder 4-6-0, No 2222, Sir Gilbert Claughton, when newly outstopped at Crewe in 1913. Sir Gilbert himself, chairman of the company, is at the regulator and the Chief Mechanical Engineer, C.J. Bowen Cooke, is on the footplate grasping the tender rail. Members of the Locomotive Committee of the board are grouped in front (British Railways).